D0162801

THE AMERICAN FARMER AND THE NEW DEAL

OTHER BOOKS BY THEODORE SALOUTOS

Agricultural Discontent in the Middle West, 1900–1939
(*with John D. Hicks*)

They Remember America: The Story of the Repatriated Greek Immigrants

Farmer Movements in the South, 1865–1933

The Greeks in the United States

Populism: Reaction or Reform

THE HENRY A. WALLACE SERIES
ON AGRICULTURAL HISTORY AND RURAL STUDIES

THEODORE SALOUTOS

The American Farmer and the New Deal

THE IOWA STATE UNIVERSITY PRESS ● AMES

338.1
S17am

IN MEMORY OF

JOHN D. HICKS (1890–1972)

© 1982 The Iowa State University Press. All rights reserved
Composed and printed by The Iowa State University Press, Ames, Iowa 50010

No part of this book may be reproduced in any form, by photostat, microfilm, xerography, or any other means, or incorporated into any information retrieval system, electronic or mechanical, without the written permission of the copyright owner.

First edition, 1982

Library of Congress Cataloging in Publication Data

Saloutos, Theodore.
    The American farmer and the New Deal.

    Bibliography: p.
    Includes index.
    1. Agriculture and state—United States. 2. Agriculture—Economic aspects—United States. 3. Farmers—United States. 4. United States—Economic policy—1933–1945. I. Title.
HD1761.S2   1982   338.1′873   81-12396
ISBN 0-8138-1076-0   AACR2

CONTENTS

UNIVERSITY LIBRARIES
CARNEGIE-MELLON UNIVERSITY
PITTSBURGH, PENNSYLVANIA 15213

EDITOR'S INTRODUCTION

THE HENRY A. WALLACE SERIES on Agricultural History and Rural Studies is designed to enlarge publishing opportunities in agricultual history and thereby to expand public understanding of the development of agriculture and rural society. The Series will be composed of volumes that explore the many aspects of agriculture and rural life within historical perspectives. It will evolve as the field evolves. The press and the editor will solicit and welcome the submission of manuscripts that illustrate, in good and fresh ways, that evolution. Our interests are broad. They do not stop with Iowa and U.S. agriculture but extend to all other parts of the world. They encompass the social, intellectual, scientific, and technological aspects of the subject as well as the economic and political. The emphasis of the series is on the scholarly monograph, but historically significant memoirs of people involved in and with agriculture and rural life and major sources for research in the field will also be included.

Most appropriately, this Iowa-based Series is dedicated to a highly significant agriculturist who began in Iowa, developed a large, well-informed interest in its rural life, and expanded the scope of his interests beyond the state to the nation and the world. An Iowa native and son of an agricultural scientist, journalist, and secretary of agriculture, Henry A. Wallace was a 1910 graduate of Iowa State College, a frequent participant in its scientific activities, editor of *Wallaces' Farmer* from 1921 to 1933, founder in 1926 of the Hi-Bred Corn Company (now Pioneer Hi-Bred International, Inc.), secretary of agriculture from 1933 to 1940, and vice president of the United States from 1941 to 1945. In the agricultural phases of his wide-ranging career, he was both a person of large importance in the development of America's agriculture and the leading policymaker during the most creative period in the history of American farm policy.

Wallace figures prominently in this volume, the first in the Series. I am pleased that the Series begins with this book by a most distinguished agricultural historian—and a historian who contributed to other historical fields as well. Theodore Saloutos made major contributions to agricultural history, both in the publication of his work and in his training of graduate students. His last book is an ambitious one that reaches to farmers as well as prices and policies, officials and agencies. It focuses on a development—the New Deal for agriculture—that has attracted the attention of many scholars and become an area of vigorous scholarly debate. The book takes a stand, and the Saloutos interpretation commands respect, for no other scholar has attempted to see so much of the New Deal for agriculture and to work out an interpretation that takes into account all of its many facets, policies, and programs and the many pressures that played upon it.

Richard S. Kirkendall

FOREWORD

WHEN THEODORE SALOUTOS DIED, suddenly, on November 15, 1980, he had worked on about two-thirds of the copy-edited typescript that became this book. Professor Richard Lowitt of Iowa State University volunteered to get the work to the galley proof stage and I offered to read the galleys. All of us who have worked on the final stages are acutely conscious that, if Ted Saloutos were still with us, certain last minute queries might have been answered in another way and that some decisions that we made might have been reversed. Above all we are aware that he was not here to make the kinds of final changes that almost inevitably occur as an author reads the galleys for the first time. All of us have tried to produce the kind of volume that he would have wanted. But what needs to be emphasized is that Ted did read the edited typescript and that subsequent changes have largely involved such matters as editorial consistency and not matters of substance or interpretation.

The American Farmer and the New Deal is, in essence, the third volume of a trilogy that Saloutos wrote about modern American agricultural policy. The three volumes, which span his professional career, are all characterized by thorough research in primary sources and by rigorous, hardheaded analysis. A lifelong urbanite who neither romanticized nor denigrated the American farmer, Saloutos was always careful to differentiate between the desirable and the practical.

His first volume, *Agricultural Discontent in the Middle West, 1900–1939* (Madison: University of Wisconsin Press, 1951), was an outgrowth of his doctoral dissertation, "Farmer Movements since 1902," completed at Madison eleven years earlier. The published work, to which his mentor John D. Hicks contributed three chapters, was, as Hicks generously used to say, "Ted's book," although the work of student and mentor was a subtly blended whole.

The second volume, *Farmer Movements in the South, 1865–1933* (Berkeley and Los Angeles: University of California Press, 1960), was originally envisaged as paralleling the first in temporal scope. But, as Saloutos wrote in his preface:

"The more I probed into the history of the Southern movement, the more convinced I became that both dates [1900 and 1939] were unsatisfactory. The endless references to the pre- and post-Civil War years, the Negroes, the sharecropping, and the crop-lien system left me no choice but to begin with the Reconstruction period. The terminal period of 1933 was prompted by the fact that the philosophic ties between the South and the farm policy makers had been clearly delineated by this time; and also by a realization that the South, after the First World War, had a less complicated history of organized unrest—hence a less diversified farmer movement than the Middle West." (p. v.)

In the conclusion of this work he made the argument, all too often ignored by students of the New Deal, that, in terms of agricultural policy at least, there was much more continuity between the thought of Populists and New Dealers than between that of Progressives and New Dealers.

The third and final volume can speak for itself. If Saloutos had seen the book through the press I am sure that he would have gratefully acknowledged the devoted labor of Judith Gildner and her staff at Iowa State University Press. She, and my friend Richard Lowitt, have been of great assistance to me.

Ted Saloutos was my teacher, and, more important, my friend. For nearly a quarter of a century he was there when he was needed. In reading certain parts of the galleys, especially the many analytical summings-up which were his forte, I could imagine his voice reading the measured phrases. It has been a privilege to help bring his final work into print.

Roger Daniels

Cincinnati
Thanksgiving, 1981

PREFACE

MY INTEREST IN AGRICULTURAL HISTORY, of which *The American Farmer and the New Deal* is merely one phase, goes back to the days of the New Deal at the University of Wisconsin when John D. Hicks, my mentor, suggested a minor farmers' organization as a possible topic for my Master's thesis. Being an eager city boy without any knowledge of agriculture, I accepted my mentor's suggestion with some skepticism and curiosity, researched the subject for a while, and came away fascinated with what I discovered. This opened up a brand new world to me that eventually blossomed forth into a much broader study subsequently published under joint authorship with Hicks, *Agricultural Discontent in the Middle West, 1900–1939*. In addition I published numerous articles dealing with various phases of agricultural unrest, a study titled *Farmer Movements in the South, 1865–1933*, and now this study, *The American Farmer and the New Deal*.

My interest in agricultural history was quickened, as well as sustained, by the constant encouragement I received from John Hicks. Without his encouragement and support I probably would never have ventured in this direction. I have been everlastingly grateful to him for enriching my intellectual life, and am dedicating this volume to his memory as a small token of appreciation for his help and understanding.

A major problem faced by any scholar working with a subject of the magnitude and complexity of the present volume is how to deal with the vast quantities of materials in the government archives—the endless government reports, bulletins, memos, and statistical data—the personal correspondence in historical societies and university libraries, the scholarly studies—some more specialized than others but scholarly studies nevertheless—and the numerous articles written for popular consumption, memoirs, newspaper accounts, and various other sources. Selectivity of materials and topics to be treated become a major problem.

From the beginning I decided to concentrate on developing a broad picture of the American farmer and the New Deal. Therefore I chose to deemphasize, but not ignore, topics of a more conventional nature and to work for an overall view of the agricultural scene. I also wanted in-depth studies, region by region, commodity by commodity, and agency by agency, of the various farm groups adversely affected by the Great Depression.

An effort has been made to deal with the human aspects of New Deal programs, aspects often ignored by specialists who concern themselves mostly with commodities, prices, and farm income as though such statistics were unrelated to human beings. However, this is not as easily accomplished as might be imagined. Few farmers left diaries of their New Deal experiences; thus materials needed to bring out the human aspects have not been readily available. Relying on oral tapes also may not be as trustworthy a source as sometimes is supposed, especially when the information has been gathered by persons untrained for the assignment and insufficiently knowledgeable in the field to ask the right kinds of questions.

A word of gratitude must be expressed to those many who helped make this study possible. I am especially indebted to members of the staff of the National Archives, notably Helen Finneran. I also wish to thank members of the staffs of the National Agricultural Library in Washington, D.C.; the Historical Section of the USDA, especially Dr. Wayne D. Rasmussen and Dr. Gladys Baker; the Library of Congress; the Oral History Records Office at Columbia University, New York; the Sterling Memorial Library, Yale University; the Wisconsin State Historical Society, the Archives of the University of Wisconsin, the Library of the Wisconsin College of Agriculture, and the Wisconsin State Legislative Reference Library, all in Madison, Wisconsin; the Kansas State Historical Society, Topeka, Kansas; the Giannini Library, University of California, Berkeley; and the Library of the University of California, Los Angeles. I likewise am grateful to D. Clayton Brown for preparing a lengthy draft on rural electrification on which the much shorter chapter in my text is based, and to the members of the staffs of the Sam Rayburn Library, Bonham, Texas; the TVA Library, Knoxville, Tennessee; and the Library of the University of North Carolina, Chapel Hill, which placed the needed materials at Brown's disposal.

I learned a great deal from graduate students of mine who wrote doctoral dissertations on agricultural subjects under my direction, especially D. Clayton Brown, Harry McDean, David Ganger, Bernard Klass, Jackie Sherman, Lawrence J. Jelinek, Robert Pritchard, and Francis Schruben.

Nor can I say too much in behalf of the staff of the Central Stenographic Bureau at UCLA for the excellent service and goodwill extended me over the years, especially to Ellen Cole, to the Research Committee of the Academic Senate of UCLA for its support, and to the John Simon Guggenheim Foundation for its assistance during my sabbatical year.

My acknowledgements would be incomplete if I failed to mention the patience and indulgence of my wife Florence who endured while I labored in the vineyard. To her I extend my everlasting thanks and appreciation.

Theodore Saloutos

INTRODUCTION

SCHOLARS OF THIS ERA HAVE TENDED TO FOCUS on some of the more dramatic aspects of the New Deal in agriculture: the farm strikes; relations among the sharecroppers, tenants, and farm laborers; and the dust storms and the droughts, areas in which much good work has been done. But equally important are those other phases discussed in *The American Farmer and the New Deal*. Much needs to be told for instance about the never-ending internal problems of the New Dealers in agriculture; the various individuals, groups, and agencies, private and governmental, who advanced ideas and programs to alleviate the plight of the farmers during the 1920s and early 1930s before the New Deal assumed office; the personalities brought together to work in the Agricultural Adjustment Administration (AAA) and other agencies, and the circumstances under which they entered the administration; the internal rivalry and the inter- and intradepartmental feuding; and the political aspirations of some of the more ambitious members.

As a student of general farmers' organizations, I quickly detected a gradual withering of influence of these organizations beginning as early as the Federal Farm Board years in the late 1920s. The superagencies such as the Farm Board and the AAA, with ample funds at their disposal, acquired a political clout that the government rarely possessed in the earlier periods of economic crisis. This political leverage diminished the power of the general farmers' organizations, which found themselves relegated to a secondary role in influencing the farmers, Congress, and the agencies.

A logical starting point for this present study is World War I because of the effects that the war had on farmers and the spate of proposals generated during this period to ameliorate their plight. Almost one-fifth of the text, as a consequence, is devoted to the difficult twelve years preceding the New Deal when serious thinking about farmer programs and policies occurred. Thoughts and plans spawned during these years were put into action in one form or another after the New Deal began. Examining the pre–New Deal proposals helps provide better insight into how much of the thinking on agriculture was new and how much was not, and places the New Deal in historical perspective.

Differences prevail among scholars as to whether the farmers were in a perpetual state of depression throughout the 1920s. Because I believe the farmers were in deep economic difficulties, even though they might have experienced brief periods of relief, *The American Farmer and the New Deal* emphasizes the nature of these difficulties, the means employed to try to resolve them, and the obstacles encountered. I have avoided endless discussions of the legislative debates on the floor of Congress and the testimony taken in committee hearings on legislation affecting agriculture because these arguments had been voiced repeatedly by advocates and foes of the various proposals before they reached the floor of Congress. An effort obviously has been made to maintain a balanced perspective on the role of the various pressure groups during these years.

Critics of the New Deal would have a more realistic picture of what the administration was up against if they had a better insight into the various impediments, frustrations, and infighting that occurred in shaping up the programs—the differences, personal, philosophic, sectional, as they bore specifically on the programs and general policy. This is brought out, at least in part, in the sections devoted to the tenants and sharecroppers, rural poverty, rural electrification, the Blacks, the personalities, politics, and clashing sectional interests.

The farm programs under the New Deal beginning with the political campaign of 1936, especially in the latter stages, began to take on a political coloration that surpassed anything identified with the farm programs in the earlier years. This politicization occurred because of the consuming desire of Wallace's admirers, coworkers, well-wishers, and others within his inner circle to advance his candidacy for the presidency in 1940 in the event Roosevelt chose not to run for a third term. Wallace's growing concern with nonagricultural matters such as the "packing of the Supreme Court" in 1937, his growing sensitivity to criticism from congressmen, senators, and farmers over the unwillingness of certain program administrators to bend to the wishes of the politically motivated, his diminishing concern with agriculture as his sole and exclusive responsibility, and the growing influence of his trusted subordinates in this area bespeaks in part a man maturing in political ambitions and practice. The behavior of those close to Wallace furnishes eloquent testimony to the growing importance of political considerations, as do the observations of Chester C. Davis, Howard R. Tolley, John B. Hutson, Samuel B. Bledsoe, and newspapermen familiar with the politics of the USDA and the period.

One can be highly critical of the New Dealers for not doing more for the sharecroppers and small farmers who needed help the most. However, the New Deal inherited an agricultural situation that had been generations in the making, one unlikely to be undone in a year or a decade by administrative decree. The decision makers might have had a variety of wands to wave and they waved them, but they were not magic wands. The problems facing the various sectors of the American farm economy to a great degree were institutionalized, and overcoming them in a democratic society required a unanimity of purpose among a majority that was difficult to obtain and retain over the needed time. The sharp differences over programs, the dependence for appropriations on Congress, which in turn was sensitive to public pressures, an explosive racial situation, the threat of totalitarianism from abroad, the impending war in Europe and the Far East, and the sectional rivalries all combined to make a very difficult situation almost impossible for the administration and the farmers.

Critics of the New Deal, especially those to the left of center, maintained that the changes that needed to be made—changes which were never elaborated upon—could have been inaugurated by the New Dealers but for their unwillingness to do so because of their alignment with the conservative forces. Despite their plight, the tenants, sharecroppers, small farmers, and farm laborers resorted to little if any violence, in part because of the options open to them. Even the invalidation of the first AAA, which by all accounts was popular with the farmers, did not elicit much of a reaction.

One thing is relatively clear. Politicians gave a great deal of lip service to the preservation of the family farm. Despite endless political rhetoric the disappearance of the traditional small farm continued in large measure because there was relatively little that was done by those capable of preventing it from happening. The old-fashioned small family farmer was not as readily adaptable to capitalistic methods of production as was the more efficient producer, the farmer with the latest machinery, equipment, talent, supplies, capital, and labor at his disposal who produced in larger volume and had a better understanding of the market and its demands. Some administration spokesmen were willing to concede that the USDA had not given as much thought to the small farmer at the lower end of the economic ladder as it had to the farmer who was likely to make a go of it.

The outlook for assistance to the low-income farmers in other words was bleak from the outset, not merely because of an explosive racial situation, but also because of a growing conviction on the part of many influential citizens, politicians, and scholars that there were too many farmers on the land. They further believed that the best interests of society would be served if those far down the economic ladder were persuaded or forced to abandon the land and migrate to the cities. This was an appealing argument in a period of mounting international tensions and the opening up of job opportunities in the cities—defense-related industries and plants and other areas in an expanding wartime economy. This explains at least in part the unwillingness of many to support an elaborate program to keep the tenants and sharecroppers on the land. Nor can one overlook the opposition of farmers and others who made it on their own without the help of the government. Many low-income farmers had no choice but to leave the land; others who might have remained on the land a little longer heeded the advice and migrated to the cities. Still, poverty persisted in the post–World War II decades in both the rural and urban areas, and many of those who abandoned the land for the cities found themselves caught up in a situation that was as bad if not worse than the one they left behind.

ACRONYMS USED FREQUENTLY IN
THE AMERICAN FARMER AND THE NEW DEAL

AAA   = Agricultural Adjustment Act (or Administration)
ACCA   = American Cotton Cooperative Association
AFBF   = American Farm Bureau Federation
AFEA   = American Farm Economics Association
ALGCU = Association of Land Grant Colleges and Universities
BAE   = Bureau of Agricultural Economics, Department of Agriculture
BPI   = Bureau of Plant Inspection, Department of Agriculture
CCC   = Civilian Conservation Corps
CIO   = Congress of Industrial Organizations
CREA   = Committee on the Relation of Electricity to Agriculture
CWA   = Civil Works Administration
EHFA   = Electric Home and Farm Authority
FCA   = Farm Credit Administration
FCIC   = Federal Crop Insurance Corporation
FERA   = Federal Emergency Relief Administration
FERC   = Federal Emergency Relief Committee
FSA   = Farm Security Administration
FSRC   = Federal Surplus Relief Corporation
IWW   = Industrial Workers of the World
MVC   = Mississippi Valley Committee
NAACP = National Association for the Advancement of Colored People
NCMPF = National Cooperative Milk Producers' Federation
NCRSP = National Committee on Rural Social Planning
NELA   = National Electric Light Association
NFU   = National Farmers' Union
NRA   = National Recovery Act (or Administration)
NYA   = National Youth Administration
PWA   = Public Works Administration
RA   = Resettlement Administration
REA   = Rural Electrification Administration
RFC   = Reconstruction Finance Corporation

SCDAA = Soil Conservation and Domestic Allotment Act
SCS   = Soil Conservation Service
SES   = Soil Erosion Service
STFU = Southern Tenant Farmers' Union
TVA   = Tennessee Valley Authority
USDA = United States Department of Agriculture
WPA   = Works Projects Administration (later Works Progress Administration)

THE AMERICAN FARMER AND THE NEW DEAL

CHAPTER ONE

Farm Crisis: 1918–1933

THE PRE–WORLD WAR I YEARS HAVE BEEN VIEWED BY MANY as "the golden age of American agriculture," at least when compared with the 1920s, but the more knowledgeable, aware of the prewar maladjustments, have not been surprised by the effects that the war had on agriculture. Wartime prosperity was followed by cycles of panic, recovery, expansion, and a short-term boom. The initial shock of war in 1914, for instance, brought an overnight collapse in the foreign sales of wheat and cotton, especially cotton. Then the farmers recovered to discover they were unable to keep up with the demands of the Allies for food, fiber, materials, shipping, and credit—all of which were provided by the United States. With the soaring demand for goods and services came soaring prices.[1]

Once the United States formally declared war in April 1917, the demands for food and fibers soared to even higher levels. Farmers were admonished: "If You Can't Fight, Farm: Food Will Win the War!" and "Plow to the Fence for National Defense." Forty million new, unbroken acres of land were turned to the plow, and thirty millon of these acres were in the Great Plains states which later became a center of acute distress.[2]

Expansion in farm production came more from readjustments in the use of the land than from massive increases in the acreages put under the plow, and these readjustments unfortunately were accompanied by bad farming practices. Land that should have remained in livestock production or fallow was converted to grain production. Excessive grazing by animals and the planting of wheat and corn yielded surpluses that glutted the market, removed the natural protection of the soil, and helped prepare the way for the dust storms of the 1930s.[3]

Cotton growers in the South, on the other hand, suffered from the temporary loss of their European markets as early as the summer and fall of 1914. The resulting depression in the cotton fields helped accelerate the exodus of black labor, as did the newspaper ads in northern newspapers that flooded the cotton fields with promises of jobs that paid two, three, and four times as much as those in the South. The appeal to emigrate north became even greater after the warring European nations halted the emigration of their own males of military age who otherwise would have provided for the manpower needs of an expanding northern industrial economy. One effect of these developments was to help dislocate the southern economy which depended heavily on the prosperity of cotton growing.[4]

Agriculture was affected by the war in still another way. The stabilizing influences of the Underwood Tariff of 1913, a moderate tariff, were nullified by the outbreak of war, which was disadvantageous to the farmers. Past wars had provided industries the equivalent of full protection and World War I was no exception. It encouraged the growth of industries that wanted to retain the benefits of wartime protection in times of peace; heightened nationalistic tensions that were to hurt U.S. peacetime markets, and forced the farmers to pay higher prices for the goods and services they bought.[5]

Conversion of the United States from a debtor to a creditor nation— making it the banker of the world—although unnoticed at the time, worked to the disadvantage of farmers who had been dependent on the foreign market. Before the war, when the United States owed three billion dollars to foreign creditors, some of these obligations were paid with American securities and some with farm products. But from 1915 to 1918 when exports of food and munitions rose sharply, large quantities of foreign securities began flowing into the United States. Once the Allies became heavy debtors to the United States, they exchanged places in the payment of principal and interest. After the war, the United States continued to make loans to its former allies and they continued to buy America's products. Once the loans stopped, these countries ceased buying from the United States, especially the products of the farm, and the economic woes of the farmers multiplied.[6]

The abnormal demand for American products continued for about a year and a half after the Armistice. Russia's collapse in 1917 removed it from the marketplace as a large supplier of grains, while in central and eastern Europe the breakup of large landed estates delayed the return of these nations to their prewar levels of production. Furthermore, transportation problems that interrupted the flow of goods from competitor nations, such as Australia and Argentina, and the inflationary practices of some of the vanquished nations forced European countries to continue to rely on the United States for their needs a little while longer. Loans and short-term credits from the United States enabled them to obtain needed goods, which in turn helped sustain the U.S. export market. When the debtors sought new, or an extension of old, loans, the requests were granted time and time again, until the loans ceased or were reduced to a mere trickle. This artificial boom also was helped along after the United States government "and various charitable agencies . . . entered the markets of the United States to purchase food supplies for various relief undertakings abroad, and the farmers . . . gave trainloads of grain outright for export to the stricken areas of Europe."

Unfortunately, the favorable position of the United States in the early postwar months raised the hopes of the farmers for a permanent prosperity and encouraged them to keep the production of grains, hogs, cattle, and other products at high levels. American farmers expected to have a substantial foreign market for many years; they were unaware that in becoming a creditor nation—and the foremost lender in the world—the government adopted an economic policy designed to keep foreign products out of U.S. markets. This caused the affected countries to retaliate by keeping U.S. products, including those of the farm, out of their markets. In expanding production to meet what they perceived as an expanding market, farmers continued to ignore farm and soil practices that were a part of good farming before the war.[7]

The price decline of 1920, and the short-lived depression that followed, affected all sectors of the farm economy; income dropped sharply while mortgage indebtedness, interest payments, taxes, and labor costs remained high. Bankruptcies skyrocketed, farm values fell, and the purchasing power of the farmers in terms of prewar levels declined.[8] What made this depression different from earlier ones was that it occurred after the United States and the major nations of Europe had stopped fighting the bloodiest and costliest war on record, when the country's rural population for the first time had fallen behind that of the cities, and shortly before the United States embarked on a policy of economic nationalism.

Authorities, investigating committees, organization leaders, and others might have differed over the causes, length, and severity of the farm depression, but two things remained clear. The hardest hit were the small farmers who had overexpanded their operations and found it difficult to readjust themselves to the smaller markets of a peacetime society. Industry made a relatively quick comeback from the general recession of 1921–1922; agriculture, which—its most fanatical advocates insisted—had to get back on its feet before the rest of the economy could prosper, languished.

Part of the cause for the crisis was in the nature of the agricultural industries and the inability of many farmers to make quick adjustments to the sudden changes. Most farms were small and inefficient. Agriculture had become a business; survival, let alone success, hinged upon the ability of the farmers to obtain maximum efficiency at a minimum cost, which meant some control over their production. Advances in scientific and technological knowledge did not simplify matters. Before the war only a smattering of such knowledge had filtered down to the rank and file farmer; after the war it came down in quantities. Besides calling for the use of new and efficient farm machinery, the new knowledge included application of the latest findings of the county agents, who worked closely with the county farm bureaus. Adult education, boys' and girls' clubs, and the agricultural high schools, which taught scientific farming to a rising generation of young farmers at the beginning of their working careers instead of at the end, all presaged change. The gap between the practices of farming and the frontiers of knowledge, in other words, was widening.[9]

Edwin G. Nourse, a distinguished agricultural economist, noted how the advances in hog production, for instance, added to the total output and aggravated the surplus problem. Under the old system of slow growth and wasteful fattening in filthy pig sties, the losses from cholera and other diseases were heavy, in periods of epidemics, devastating; but they kept production down. By the mid-1920s, however, because of advances in scientific breeding, feeding, and the prevention of diseases, these losses were drastically reduced, if not eliminated. Larger litters were the result, often in the fall and spring, as well as greater returns. Henry A. Wallace estimated that scientific advances enabled Corn Belt farmers to produce a hundred pounds of pork on at least one bushel of corn less than they had needed to produce the same amount of pork twenty years earlier. This meant an increase in efficiency of nearly 10 percent.

Comparable progress was made in other areas of production. Scientific seed selection and cultivation made it possible for corn to be grown in Minnesota and South Dakota. Use of the silo enhanced the potential of some of the best farmlands by making possible the preservation of a crop that had not completely matured, and thus helped the dairy industry break one production record after another. Poultry growers who once dreamed of hens that would lay 150 eggs a year discovered that through "trap nesting and line breeding" birds could lay 200 eggs a year. Similar advances were made in the development of pure strains of cereals selected for disease resistance or moisture requirements.[10]

Of even greater significance were the technological changes. Unlike the late nineteenth century when the changes were based on low-priced land, cheap transportation, and horse-drawn implements, the changes after World War I came from the growing use of mechanical power and equipment. The horse as a provider of animal power began to decline about 1918. Innovations, meanwhile, seemed to come in ten-year intervals. The stationary engine came into use between 1890 and 1900; electricity, the gas tractor, the motor truck, and the automobile between 1900 and 1910; and all other forms during the 1920s. By 1930 the horsepower derived from the automobile exceeded the horsepower derived from all other sources on the farm, but the automobile was more of an aid to the farmer in his business than a source of power on the farm.[11]

Use of mechanical power was welcomed by those who wanted to free themselves from expensive and unreliable transient labor and regularize their farm operations. The man-hours required to produce some crops were reduced by as much as 50 percent from 1900 to 1930; the greatest reductions came in the Great Plains states where the land was nearly level, and the fields large and regular.[12]

The reductions in human labor varied from crop to crop. In wheat it was most noticeable in harvesting and threshing; and in corn, in the cultivation and harvesting stages. What labor reductions were realized in cotton before this had come through the introduction of improved equipment and methods of tillage and the opening up of new land where large-scale equipment could be used. However, the variety of soils on which cotton was grown, the climatic conditions, and cotton's physical characteristics seemed to defy the designers and inventors who sought to develop a successful picker. As late as 1933 machinery for chopping, hoeing, and picking cotton had not been perfected. The almost 10.5 million employed in agriculture in 1930 represented only 21.5 percent of all workers in the United States. While the ratio of farm to nonfarm workers had been declining over the years, the harvested acreage and the yields had been increasing.

The general picture fails, however, to provide an accurate view of what had been happening in states where the acreage under cultivation had expanded substantially. In the Great Plains, topography, soil, and climate were suitable for the use of large-scale machinery. The per acre requirements were small; hence, the average farm worker could care for more than 100 acres: in North Dakota, 161; South Dakota, 138; Nebraska, 111; and Kansas, 107.[13]

Mechanization also released additional land previously used for the feeding of work animals; fewer animals were needed for horsepower, and between fifteen and twenty-five million more acres became available to raise food for human consumption from 1918 to 1930. Farmers who previously depended on their farms for most of their needs now were compelled to find more income to obtain the machinery, equipment, fuel, and petroleum products that could not be grown on the farm.[14]

Improvements in transportation also stimulated the productive capabilities of the farmers. The surface roads built across the country during the 1920s made it possible for the farmer's automobile and truck to penetrate interior points that hitherto had been inaccessible, thereby encouraging the intensive farming of wheat and other crops in the Great Plains, and fluid-milk production in and near metropolitan areas. Living conditions in the rural areas also had improved to the point where the more efficient farmers tilled lands at greater distances from the city, but still were close enough to the city to take advantage of the social opportunities it provided.[15]

Unfortunately, the farmers' capacity to produce food increased at a pace faster than the food could be consumed at a profit to the growers. For instance the annual average per capita consumption of wheat had declined from 224 pounds during 1897 to 1902 to 176 during 1922 to 1927. The decline in corn consumption was even more precipitous—from 120 pounds to 46. Rising living standards meant a preference for foods other than wheat. Southern blacks and whites who made great use of corn now began to show a preference for wheat flour and other products. Barley pursued a similar descending pattern. Before prohibition it had been used to a considerable extent for beer, salt extracts, and cereal beverages. But after prohibition the average annual per capita consumption, which had been seventeen pounds from 1897 to 1920, dropped to an insignificant two pounds over the years 1923 to 1927. The per capita use of grain, in short, had decreased by more than 20 percent in the years from 1922 to 1927; corn over 60 percent; rye flour 60 percent; and barley products nearly 90 percent.

Even cotton, which held a dominant position on the world and domestic markets, was challenged by synthetic fibers. The principal competitor in the 1920s was rayon; and the nations showing the largest production of rayon fibers, unfortunately, were the very ones that had been the largest consumers of American cotton.[16]

The future for livestock was equally discouraging. The average annual per capita consumption of beef and veal had been sixty-seven and three pounds, respectively, from 1897 to 1901, but declined before it returned to the same level in the first half of the 1920s; and it showed few prospects of improving in the latter half of the decade. The outlook for mutton and lamb was even gloomier, but was encouraging for pork and lard. The 9 percent increase in the use of pork and lard, which were major parts of the American diet from 1922 to 1926, went a long way in erasing the deficit in income from declining grain consumption. The remainder of the deficit was offset by the greater use of milk, which in 1929 was around 1,000 pounds per person, an increase of 12 percent over 1900. The most significant postwar gains occurred in the consumption of vegetables and sugar.

The per capita consumption of beef, veal, and eggs in 1929 remained the same as it had been in 1900; but the combined uses of mutton, lamb, and chickens declined. Americans used 10 percent more pork and 12 percent more milk. If this downward or stationary trend in the use of red meats and poultry continued into the 1930s, obviously a smaller amount of land would be required for crops than for animals which yielded food with the equivalent caloric contents.[17]

Other reasons for the changing preferences for food, besides the rising standard of living, were the changes in the price of food, the food conservation programs of World War I days, the Prohibition Law, the wide publicity given to vitamin values in food, and the recognition of the relation of foods to health.[18]

When people had been hungry in the past, the coming of prosperity normally meant an increased consumption of the necessities of life, but this was not true after 1918. The prosperity of the war and postwar years enabled many, if not most, with purchasing power to consume all the food they needed; but the size of the human stomach did not expand with the expansion of purchasing power. So instead of spending more money for gastronomic pleasures, the Americans spent it on a wide variety of goods ranging from automobiles to xylophones.[19]

During the war Americans, as part of the crusade to defeat the enemy and protect their health, conserved flour, meat, butter, and sugar, which could be shipped to the Allies easily, and substituted fresh fruits and vegetables in their daily diets. The introduction of "wheatless" and "meatless" days, the elimination of waste, and the more liberal use of foods rich in proteins, such as corn, barley, oats, rye, and even rice, meant the saving of more wheat and meat for the Allies. Such campaigns boosted the demands for fruits and vegetables at the expense of wheat and meat. The public also was advised to eat a variety of foods to protect its health, even though the scientists of the 1920s had little accurate information on the vitamin contents of foods and how much of a particular vitamin an individual needed. The producers of livestock and wheat did not realize that eating habits acquired during the war were going to carry over into the postwar period.[20]

Cooperative marketing associations contributed to enlarging the market for fruits and vegetables. In the 1920s, such cooperatives as the California Fruit Growers' Exchange, the Wisconsin Cheese Producers' Association, the Dairymen's League Cooperative Association, and others capitalized on the vitamin value of their products and spent large sums of money advertising them. Brand names such as Sun Maid raisins, Sunkist oranges, Land O'Lakes butter, and Eatmore cranberries became popular. The spread of restaurant chains and cafeterias which, unlike the older restaurants, included more fruits and vegetables in their menus also encouraged the change in food habits.[21]

The market for farm products was further adversely affected by the decline in the birthrate. The largest increase in population in any single decade occurred during the 1920s when slightly more than seventeen million people were added to the population rolls, but the annual rate was downward despite this. Each successive year (except for the immediate postwar years when the trend was upward) brought a smaller gain in population than the previous one, until the gain dropped to a low of 875,000 in 1931. Except for 1918 when the influenza epidemic broke out and wartime restrictions were in effect, this number was well below the gain of any single year since 1910 and almost every year since 1870. Warren S. Thompson and P. K. Whelpton, two of the leading population authorities of the day, projected that at that birthrate the population of the United States would show only modest gains over the next fifty years: 132,500,000 and 134,000,000 in 1940; 140,500,000 and 145,000,000 in 1950; and 145,000,000 and 170,000,000 in 1980. These projections proved wrong, but in an age of bumper crops and slumping prices, they were discouraging to food growers.[22]

Immigration restriction likewise took its toll in the loss of potential consumers. In previous years large numbers of immigrants worked in the cities and were customers for the products of the farm. Prior to the quota laws of the 1920s, emigrants, except for those originating in Asia, were relatively free to enter the country; in fact from 1900 to 1914 the entries never fell below 800,000 a year. After the restrictions went into effect, the numbers dropped from 805,000 in 1921 to about 23,000 in 1933.[23]

The newly gained creditor position of the United States, as indicated, had an injurious effect on the U.S. export market. As a debtor nation before the war, the United States sold from $250 to $300 million worth of farm products annually to satisfy principal and interest payments; but in 1922, Sir George Paish estimated the United States had to buy almost one billion dollars worth of goods and services abroad annually to enable European debtors to pay the principal and interest they owed.[24]

The significance of the foreign market to the prosperity of the domestic economy was hotly debated. Many who favored a high tariff argued the loss of a market that absorbed less than 10 percent of our production and amounted to about $5 billion could be overcome easily by an expansion of our domestic trade. Authorities on international trade, however, maintained that the 10 percent of U.S. production that went into the export market had an important effect on the price of cotton, tobacco, wheat, lard, and the purchase of nonagricultural products such as automobiles, copper, petroleum, and machinery produced at home. Production of these commodities had grown in response to a large foreign and domestic demand, and it would be difficult to compensate for the decline in foreign demand by expanding sales at home. American wheat exports, for instance, totaled less than 18 percent of production, but the price of wheat in the home market was affected by the world price; the same was true of cotton and tobacco. The erosion of the foreign market alone could make the difference between sixteen- and six-cent cotton and seventy- and fifty-cent wheat. Lower prices for wheat, cotton, and tobacco simply meant less purchasing power for consumers in the home markets. One thing became clear: U.S. prospects of selling abroad were contingent upon the purchasing power of foreign buyers.[25]

Great Britain was a case in point. As late as 1931 Britain headed the list of America's customers for lard, tobacco, and wheat, even though its share was smaller than in earlier decades. Great Britain took from the United States larger quantities of tobacco and lard than before, and held its own in wheat; but its imports of cotton were considerably less than they had been before the war, and it alternated with Germany as the chief importer of the American staple. Britain's imports of wheat, lard, and tobacco hinged upon its international income, while the volume of its cotton imports depended on its cotton product exports and manufactures.[26]

Britain held a precarious position in international trade that affected her ability to pay. Her imports in 1929, for instance, exceeded her exports. Then the big question was how long the United States could count on her as an important buyer. Finally, in 1931, owing to the cumulative effects of the depression, Britain found it difficult to continue making investments abroad while paying for imports. Short-term creditors had lost their confidence in Britain, started withdrawing funds from British banks, and helped push it off the gold standard. British imports from the United States, as a consequence, fell from $748.1 million in 1930 to $471.1 million in 1931 and $293.6 million in 1932.[27]

The Americans also had to worry about Germany, their second largest purchaser of farm products. Germany, like Britain, imported substantial quantities of food and fiber for home use and cotton to process and export as a finished product. Germany's ability to buy, however, depended on the reparation payments it had to make. By means of immense borrowings and a small income from international services, Germany had been able to meet her debt payments from 1925 to 1930, and import from abroad. When the end to Germany's foreign borrowing came in the summer of 1931, it came in the disastrous fashion many predicted. Germany responded by imposing protective tariffs and milling regulations as a means of keeping foreign products out of its markets and paid subsidies to its farmers as a means of encouraging them to increase food production at home.[28]

Italy had a textile industry that also depended on American cotton and had to compete with Britain and Germany for the patronage of their neighbors. Because Italy had a large foreign debt and had to have more exports than imports, its agricultural program was geared to improving its balance of payments position by reducing imports. The methods employed by Italy and Germany to resolve their balance of payment problems cut heavily into their demand for farm products and aggravated the problems of the American producers.[29]

A bright spot in the foreign market was in the Far East. Japan had dislodged the great industrial nations of Europe as the purveyors of cotton. China, which once had been a negligible factor in the tobacco trade, imported more tobacco from the United States by the early 1930s than France, Germany, and the Netherlands combined, and ranked second among foreign purchasers of American tobacco. Wheat occupied a comparable position because of an expanding trade with the Orient, South and Central American countries, and other areas.[30]

Devices other than the traditional tariffs were employed by European countries to keep out American products. Variations in the use of the quota system limited the quantity of imports and the proportion of each miller's grindings that could contain foreign wheat. International cartels parceled out trade territories among their members and imposed their own controls. Some central and eastern European countries placed controls on foreign exchange as a means of regulating imports, while the purchase, sale, import, and/or export of products became subject to government license or monopoly. Bounties also were employed to encourage home production and discourage imports. The most complete control of imports was exercised by the Soviet Union.[31]

Although the relative importance of agriculture as a source of income had been declining steadily through the years, the seriousness of this decline was felt especially after the drop in farm prices in 1920, when the farmers' share of the national income had fallen precipitously to 12.6 percent in 1921 from the 25 percent it had been in 1918–1919, and to 10.4 percent in 1929. Gross income fell from almost $17 billion in 1919 to less than $12 billion in 1929 and to about $5.3 billion in 1932. In 1932 farmers got 60 percent less for their output than they received for a similar crop in 1929.[32]

Certain states suffered from the depression more than others. In the eight adjoining states in the South, farmers had incomes ranging from $200 to $400 per capita in 1929. The agricultural states running north and south from North Dakota to Texas, including Iowa, New Mexico, and Louisiana, fell into this income range, as did Virginia, West Virginia, and Florida. Minnesota, Wisconsin, Indiana, Ohio, and Missouri fell into the $600 to $800 range; and Illinois, if it were not for metropolitan Chicago, whose higher income was included in the general average, would have found itself in this income range. South Carolina found itself at the bottom of the scale with a per capita income of $261 while Mississippi, Arkansas, North Carolina, Alabama, Georgia, and Tennessee had slightly higher incomes.[33]

Indebtedness was a crushing burden in a period of declining incomes. The total outstanding farm debt was almost $8.5 billion in 1920; it reached an all-time high of $10.7 billion in 1923, fell slightly to $9.8 billion in 1929, and to $9.1 billion in 1932. These debts were owed to federal land banks, life insurance companies, commercial and savings banks, and other agencies and individuals. Credit for eligible borrowers was available from mortgage and insurance companies, and later from banks at official rates that ranged from 8 to 12 percent, and often higher. The small, hard-pressed farmers, the tenants and sharecroppers in particular, usually found themselves at the mercy of their creditors.[34]

An index of retail prices compiled by the USDA in the early 1920s shows how far behind the farmers had fallen in purchasing power. Their buying power, using 100 for the base period 1910 to 1914, fell from 102 in

1919 to 89 in 1928. A closer study of the figures shows that the purchasing power of the farmers had improved from 1921 to 1925; a minor slump occurred in 1926 and 1927, but evidence of recovery was recorded in 1928. In the fall of 1929, Secretary of Agriculture Arthur Hyde said that conditions in agriculture had improved to the point where the farmers could look ahead to better times. Events were to prove him a poor prophet.[35]

The farmers' tax burden was heavy. Rural America spent generously for improved schools, roads, and other social services before and immediately after the war, and taxes almost doubled between 1917 and 1930. Hence, the farmers needed more bushels of wheat or corn, more bales of cotton, and more quarts of milk to pay a dollar's worth of taxes. Estimates in 1930 and 1931 showed that between one-third and two-fifths of the net income of farmers was absorbed by taxes. Farm taxes consumed two-fifths and city taxes one-fifth of the farmers' rent from his land in Indiana. Pennsylvania farmers spent 13 percent more for taxes; 52 percent of the net income of Michigan farmers between 1919 and 1925 went for taxes.[36]

Problems also were created by the variations and irregularities in the assessments of local tax officials who had little, if any, training in the assessment of property. Assessments on small property tended to represent a higher proportion of the full value than assessments on large property holdings. Likewise, the poorer the land the higher the ratio of the assessed to the true value. Supporting government services in a poor county cost more per family than in a rich one.

Rural government was costing more money, too. School enrollments in the 1920s were much higher, and the children remained in school for longer periods of time. Better qualified teachers were being demanded, and public services such as schools, roads, and government cost more in areas in which the density of population was low.

The inability to pay high taxes inevitably resulted in the loss of many farms. About 109 of every 1,000 farms were sold for taxes in Montana between 1925 and 1931, 86 in North Dakota, 66 in South Dakota, 68 in Idaho, 70 in Virginia, 68 in West Virginia, 23 in Missouri, and 17 in Kansas. In the northern Wisconsin counties nearly one-third of the land in one county was sold at a tax sale, more than 30 percent in three other counties, and 20 percent in still another twelve counties.[37]

Meanwhile an urban fixation had gripped the minds of many rural Americans who looked to the city for the ultimate in good living. Urban values had been replacing rural values, and urban enterprises had outbid rural enterprises for manpower and finances. Hundreds of thousands of young people knew that the city offered them better schools, churches, houses, more recreation and social contacts, and higher financial rewards.

Those who remained in the country rarely reached the point of weighing the advantages and disadvantages of farm living or of entering into new enterprises, and made no comparable demands. Instead they remained on the farm where they farmed in the traditional manner, accepted lower standards of living without protest, and made no effort to put small-scale farming on a scientific basis. In the opinion of many, the move from the farm to the city was leaving behind a "decadent civilization" in the rural districts, and the cities were robbing the rural areas of their best minds and most useful citizens.[38]

In essence these were the major problems that hounded the farm policy-makers: too many small inefficient producers who lacked the capital, equipment, and talent needed to farm in a society subject to sudden changes; too great a disparity between what the farmers paid and received; inequities in the tax structure; crushing indebtedness; faulty land policies; changing food habits; a declining birthrate; immigration restrictions; shrinking markets; and poor farm morale. From an export standpoint the United States suffered because of its shift from a debtor to a creditor nation, and an unwillingness to assume a leadership role commensurate with its newly found position in world economic affairs. The rise in tariffs, the drift toward self-sufficiency, deteriorating world economic conditions, and the heightening of national suspicions promised to make conditions worse before they became better. The agricultural problem then was not one problem, but a whole series of interrelated problems that varied from farm to farm, crop to crop, and region to region.

The Quest for a Farm Policy Begins

JOHN D. BLACK, perhaps the most influential farm economist of his generation, told a learned audience in 1930 that he spoke with some embarrassment on the subject of agricultural policy because it was only within the previous eight or ten years that anything approaching a farm policy had begun to shape up in the United States. From the standpoint of the immediate needs of an action program, Black probably was right; from the vantage point of an historian, he was wrong. Suggestions for what could have been called a farm policy had emerged from within the United States Department of Agriculture (USDA), as well as without, even before the Bureau of Agricultural Economics (BAE) was organized in 1922.[1]

Government assistance to farmers had been confined largely to the exploitation of U.S. agricultural resources before the United States entered the war in 1917, such as giving encouragement to education, research, and the extension service; developing foreign markets; placing tariffs on farm products; and providing limited amounts of credit and assistance for marketing. If the United States had anything resembling a farm policy before the war it consisted of the cultivation of more land, increasing crop yields, making livestock and its products healthier, marketing economically, and promoting better and more cultivated lives.[2]

No serious plans for postwar adjustments were developed during the war years. When farmers urged David F. Houston, secretary of agriculture, to help provide them with information on the cost of producing crops, Houston replied: "The farmer is not entitled to any information on the cost of production. His business is to produce." After the Armistice no one was in a position of authority to advise the farmers: "Reduce acreages to a normal basis." The farmers kept on producing as though the market were insatiable.[3]

Leadership in shaping a much-needed farm policy could have come from the Association of Land Grant Colleges and Universities (ALGCU); members of the newly formed American Farm Economics Association (AFEA); the general farmer organizations, such as the Grange, the National Farmers' Union (NFU), and the American Farm Bureau Federation (AFBF); senators and representatives from the agricultural states; the USDA and its multiple agencies; and business and community leaders dependent on agriculture. None of these agencies, groups, or individuals working singly or in concert were equal to the task.

Leaders in agricultural education plodded along in their usual ways. Cautious, conservative, and unwilling to offend the taxpayers by adopting any aggressive courses of action, they confined themselves to seeking research funds for their universities and colleges. The annual meetings of the ALGCU in 1920 were cluttered with professional papers that ignored the crisis in farm prices and the problems facing farmers. The few alert to the needs of the day pleaded helplessness and a lack of authority and the necessary intellectual equipment to cope with these problems, and limited budgets.[4]

A committee of the AFEA in 1920 showed greater concern with gathering more reliable information that could be passed on to the individual farmers than in proposing a general overall policy that would help them make postwar adjustments.[5] Such priorities reflected more of a commitment to farm management practices than an ability to view agriculture in its relation to a changing economy. Agricultural fundamentalism, or the belief that the prosperity of the nation was primarily dependent on the prosperity of the farmer, was still alive; and most farm thinkers had difficulty thinking beyond the individual farm.

Marketing reforms had been urged by the Grangers, the Farmers' Alliance, the Farmers' Union, and the American Society of Equity, which on previous occasions tried to prod the agricultural colleges into action. But it was only in the immediate prewar and postwar years that the colleges began to stress the importance of marketing in their course offerings. The experiences of the U.S. Food Administration in regulating the distribution of food during the war helped create a favorable climate for marketing reform. Many believed those phases of the Food Administration's work that advanced the general good, such as the marketing of perishables, the elimination of unnecessary middlemen, and insuring the public of fair and stable milk prices, should be retained as specific principles or regulations. The accomplishments of the Food Administration were praised by Edwin G. Nourse, and by Lewis C. Gray, one of the nation's foremost land economists of the day.[6]

Many agreed with Professor George F. Warren, the leading farm management expert of his generation, that keeping "a fair proportion of the intelligent and able citizens of the nation . . . on the farm" was one of the great needs of agriculture. E. T. Meredith, the interim secretary of agriculture, said much the same thing in a more emphatic way when he remarked: "Neither force nor exhortation will keep people in the rural districts if they are . . . deprived of . . . modern social, educational, and other opportunities. . . ." Both Warren and Meredith had good reason for their concern; the federal census in 1920 showed that the urban population had surpassed the rural. To the more pessimistic this was the point of no return for the farmers. Warren, however, was more optimistic; he believed that postwar America was receptive to new ideas and that the farmers had better take advantage of what could be their last opportunity.[7]

Officials in the USDA before Henry Cantwell Wallace became secretary of agriculture opposed government action to hasten economic adjustments. This view was best reflected by David F. Houston who, before resigning as secretary of agriculture to accept a more congenial position as secretary of the treasury, radiated optimism over the future of agriculture and saw no need for government action, even though he warned of the dangers of rising land values, speculation, and other risks facing the farmers. Houston was viewed with suspicion, if not outright hostility by the farmers; his tenure as secretary was too brief for him to become a factor in the postwar debates.[8]

Things, however, began to happen in 1921. A committee of farm economists saw the need to assemble data on the marketing and use of farm crops, and other basic information, before suggesting action to bring about changes for the better in farming. About the same time Henry C. Taylor, who in 1922 became the chief of the newly created BAE, hoped some kind of mechanism would be devised that could prevent farm prices from dropping more rapidly than those of the goods and services the farmers bought, and keep prices at a proper ratio whether they went up or down. To Taylor the problems of farm organization, land tenure, farm finance, country life, and drafting a farm policy merited the attention of the best minds in the country. Scholars had to join hands with activists, and the AFEA had to take a bold stand on such issues. Cold scientific studies that could not be put to use were sterile and unproductive.[9]

Wallace, an Iowa Republican with influence in agricultural circles and a welcome relief from Houston, had been a severe critic of Herbert Hoover's handling of the Food Administration and treatment of farmers during the war. Wallace was credited with having helped write the Republican plank on agriculture in 1920. And he had the misfortune of sitting in the same cabinet with Herbert C. Hoover, who had been named secretary of commerce and had a farm relief plan of his own which influential Republicans were going to take seriously.[10]

Among Wallace's first actions as secretary of agriculture was to merge five units within the USDA that concerned themselves with economic issues into the BAE. He appointed fellow Iowan Henry C. Taylor, an activist and pioneer agricultural economist, its first chief. Taylor, before coming to Washington in 1919 to become chief of the Office of Farm Management and Farm Economics, had been chairman of the Department of Agricultural Economics in the University of Wisconsin where he helped establish perhaps the foremost department of its kind in the country and trained farm economists who assumed positions of influence in the USDA and the large agricultural colleges of the nation.[11]

The importance of the BAE as a research and educational agency cannot be overemphasized. It attracted as full- or part-time employees some of the foremost thinkers in agriculture and began exploring hitherto neglected fields. The BAE helped establish a graduate school of studies in the USDA in which courses often were taught by leaders in their respective fields, set standards that ranked ahead of most, if not all, federal departments with cabinet rank in the federal service, and promised to launch a series of studies touching every phase of production and prices.[12]

Ties between the farm economists and the USDA had become so close by 1922 that the AFEA took an official stand against transferring the marketing activities of the USDA to the Department of Commerce. The arguments of the AFEA against this transfer were logical and persuasive. Through the years the USDA had developed close ties at considerable expense with the agricultural colleges, experiment stations, state departments of agriculture, and state departments of markets. Eventually, transference of these activities to the Department of Commerce brought these relations to an end and forced the latter agency to spend large sums of the taxpayers' money to reestablish relationships that probably could never be fully restored.[13]

Of even greater importance in policymaking matters were the general farmer organizations whose proposals congressmen and senators could ill afford to ignore, especially in a period when pressures from the farmers were at a peak level. Most influential of the farmer organizations was the newly formed American Farm Bureau Federation whose strength was concentrated in the Middle West and which had one of the most powerful agricultural lobbies in history. Well financed and appealing to the middle-income farmers, the AFBF in the early years commanded the support of some of the most powerful business, financial, political, and educational interests of the country. The local base of the AFBF was rooted in the county agents who sought to make better producers of the farmers. The contributing role played by the Extension Service, of which the county agents were a part, in bringing the AFBF into existence infuriated the Grange and the Farmers' Union, which resented use of the taxpayers' money to finance a rival organization.

AFBF leaders realized they had to take immediate steps to try to solve the marketing, if not the major, problems of the farmers. For a time they welcomed Aaron Sapiro, a high-priced attorney and fiery salesman of cooperative marketing and the ironclad contract; and they enthusiastically supported cooperative marketing associations and formed committees to hasten their formation. The high point was reached with the election of Oscar E. Bradfute as national president in 1923. Bradfute said:

> Service through cooperative marketing—that is the program for next year. Cooperative marketing is trumps. All the departments, all the officials, and all the officials of the American Farm Bureau Federation will be expected to play the trump card.[14]

Farm Bureau leaders soon discovered that trying to resolve the marketing problem involved more than recognizing its existence, appointing committees, and organizing marketing associations. Rival groups resented the efforts of the AFBF to become the umbrella organization and preempt areas which they believed were rightfully theirs. Some naturally feared the loss of their identity, and there were differences over what the national marketing programs should be. Some wanted arbitrary price fixing based on "cost of production plus a reasonable profit," while the majority favored cooperative marketing.[15]

Cooperative marketing and purchasing associations had a precarious position in interstate commerce and could be adjudged combinations in restraint of trade under the Sherman Antitrust Act. The Grange was among the general farmer organizations that pressed for federal legislation that would assure farmers collective bargaining rights and short-term financing to insure the orderly shipment of their products. Passage of the Capper–Volstead Act in 1922 brought an end to the question of illegality posed by the Sherman Antitrust Act for farmers to sell their products through cooperatives. A National Market Act, a sort of precursor of the Agricultural Marketing Act of 1929, was urged. The earlier enthusiasm of the Grange for cooperative marketing soon took a precautionary tone. The farmers had gone wild on the subject of cooperatives; too many cooperatives were being organized on a large scale by men who were unfamiliar with them. Many suffered from poor management and were doomed to fail. Finally in 1924 the Grange conceded that cooperative marketing was not the answer to the agricultural depression.[16]

The more militant and less influential National Farmers' Union, which appealed to the low-income farmers, was divided, if not handicapped, in its efforts, by two schools of thought that had developed within its ranks. One emphasized cooperative marketing, purchasing associations, and legislation to protect the cooperatives. The other, although cognizant of the value of cooperatives, maintained the gravity of the agricultural situation was such that it demanded something more—such as guaranteeing the farmers their "cost of production plus a reasonable profit."[17]

The "farm bloc," a coalition of Republicans and Democrats, came into existence in 1921 after the Republicans failed to provide a satisfactory agricultural program in the special session of Congress called by President Harding. The credo of the farm bloc was that the prosperity of the nation was contingent on the prosperity of the farmers and that it was urgent to elevate farming to a status of equality with industry through use of the machinery of the federal government in the same fashion this machinery had been used to aid industry, finance, and commerce. The farm bloc claimed credit for legislation to regulate the packers, the trading in futures acts, extension of the life of the War Finance Corporation, and the strengthening of the federal farm loan system. The life of the farm bloc was prolonged by the tenor of President Harding's call for an agricultural conference in 1922 which suggested the farm depression would be of short duration.[18]

Legislative enactments or proposals that indicated the direction farm policy was taking during the 1920s included the Capper–Volstead Act of 1922 and the Agricultural Credits Act of 1923. The latter set up two fundamentally different systems of farm credit: one was the government owned, operated, and controlled Federal Intermediate Credit Banks that proved to be of help to farmers in securing short-term credit; the other was the National Agricultural Credit Corporations, private agencies that received governmental support. Still other legislative proposals sought ways of stabilizing the dollar and providing crop insurance, cheaper electricity, and fertilizers. Farmers also were admonished to cut their overhead costs, diversify, and adjust production to demand, and organize to protect their interests.

A key idea of these years, embodied in the McNary–Haugen plan, proposed the building of an effective tariff wall around the products of the farm as a means of providing the producers with a fair exchange of parity value for their efforts in terms of the goods and services they bought. This proposal was a compound of economic nationalism and agricultural fundamentalism, and was consistent in some respects with the thinking that was shaping farm policies in the nations of the western world.

Advocates of the McNary-Haugen plan believed that the tariff, which had been responsible for the profitableness of certain manufactures and industries, could also be made to work for the benefit of the farmers if an effective tariff barrier, instead of a nominal one, was placed around the products of American agriculture. The effectiveness of a tariff, according to one of its proponents, was to be measured by the ability of the domestic farm producers to determine the price of their products behind a tariff wall.

Unless the producers could do this they would have to content themselves with depressed prices for their products as they had in the past. The men primarily responsible for getting this campaign off to a fast start were George N. Peek and Hugh S. Johnson. The two men had lost their farm machinery business in the depression and pleaded in behalf of the farmer in a pamphlet they wrote in 1922, *Equality for Agriculture*. Peek and Johnson maintained that agriculture, like industry, had to have "a fair exchange value" for its products if it was to survive.

The notion of equality, or parity, for the farmers had been publicized in 1903, if not earlier, by James A. Everitt, an Indianapolis seed salesman and publisher who urged farmers to seek prices equal to those enjoyed by the best regulated manufacturing or commercial enterprises. In 1919 E. G. Nourse observed that "American agriculture stood in just the same subservient position to American industrialism that the colonies occupied toward England a century and a quarter earlier." But it was the farm depression of the early 1920s, sagging prices, high costs, diminishing returns, and crushing indebtedness that helped persuade farmers they were being sacrificed for industry and commerce.[19]

Fuel was added to this argument when Secretary Wallace reminded President Harding that the drop in farm prices had not been accompanied by a corresponding drop in the costs to farmers. Wallace was doubtful that more liberal credit for the farmers would narrow the disparity. Better prices for the crops they sold and lower prices for commodities they bought were needed more than cheaper credit and the opportunity to go further into debt. In August and September of 1922, according to Wallace, farm products purchased only about two-thirds as much as in 1913.[20]

The battle lines between those who favored equality for the farmers and those who were against cooperative marketing were drawn early in the life of the AFBF. At first that organization refused to endorse the McNary–Haugen plan, but later became a staunch supporter of it. Many members believed that cooperative marketing was the answer to their needs. Cotton growers, who initially had not been hit as hard by the depression as the wheat and corn-belt farmers and who exported nearly half their annual crop, believed the McNary–Haugen plan would hurt their foreign market; dairy farmers in the East and the special crop producers in the Far West thought the plan was ill suited to their needs.[21]

A similar division surfaced in the USDA after the death of President Harding. Wallace had hoped to win over Harding and the businessmen of the nation to the McNary–Haugen plan. Calvin Coolidge knew little about the states west of the Alleghenies, cared even less, and thought the farm depression was unimportant politically; thus Wallace, an advocate of the McNary–Haugen plan, found himself hemmed in by Coolidge, who farmers felt was insensitive to their needs, and Herbert Hoover, an advocate of high protective tariffs for industry and cooperative marketing for the farmers.[22]

Evidence of the widening rift within the USDA came into fuller view in the fall of 1923 when Coolidge sent Eugene Meyer, Jr., and Frank Mondell of the War Finance Corporation into the agricultural regions of the Northwest and Far West to emphasize the virtues of cooperative marketing. Wallace looked upon this as a deliberate attempt to circumvent his authority as secretary. The Meyer–Mondell report recommended cooperative marketing as a way out for the farmers, but also acknowledged the existence of sentiment for a government agency that bought and sold surplus wheat as a means of keeping up farm prices.[23]

Wallace, hoping to counteract the work of the Meyer–Mondell mission, sent Henry C. Taylor, his BAE chief, into the wheat producing states to obtain firsthand information on the plight of the farmers and the steps to be taken to relieve them. Taylor's plans to visit Oklahoma and Kansas, however, were canceled after Coolidge asked Wallace to summon Taylor back to Washington to report his findings. Apparently William Jardine, president of Kansas State College of Agriculture at the time, who became secretary of agriculture after the death of Wallace, had wired Coolidge not to send Taylor to Kansas. Taylor started back for Washington within twenty-four hours after being advised to return and prepared a report which he later said had not been seen by anyone.[24]

Wallace believed that cooperative marketing with all its virtues was incapable of eliminating the unfavorable price ratios and low purchasing power which beset farmers. The proposal to merge the existing cooperatives into larger ones capable of controlling the flow of wheat into the market and reduce marketing costs was sound; but even if accomplished, the fundamental disparities would still prevail. Congress had to establish a government agency with power to buy and export wheat and other surplus products. The government by doing this also could atone for its mistake of the war years when it arbitrarily denied profits to wheat farmers that rightfully were theirs. Losses by such an agency could be recouped through an assessment on the wheat growers who benefited from the plan and also through the treasury.[25]

Basic to the McNary–Haugen argument was the theory that the principal culprit behind the farmers' difficulties was the protective tariff on industrial and manufactured products that boosted costs to the farmers and depressed the prices they received. In an era of protectionism such as the 1920s, the McNary–Haugenites believed it would be much easier to put a protective umbrella over certain basic farm commodities as the manufacturers and industrialists had done for their products than try to lower or remove the tariff from all goods and services the farmers bought. Whether the McNary–Haugenites were right or wrong in what they believed is beside the point; they believed in what they were arguing and pressed to put their beliefs into law. They further believed that if they segregated the portion of the crop consumed at home from the portion consumed abroad, what they called the "exportable surplus," the price of the domestically consumed portion could be forced to rise and provide the farmer with a measure of prosperity that thus far had been denied him.[26]

Ratio prices, which were complicated to the "ordinary mind" but simple to the statistician, were to be determined by a mathematical formula and have the same relation to the prewar averages that the prevailing prices had. Since the price of the portion sold on the export market was to be lower than the price of the portion sold on the domestic market, the difference in the price recouped on the portion sold abroad would be the farmer's equivalent of the protective tariff or the "equalization fee."[27]

The Republican response to the McNary–Haugen advocates was to give more credit and encouragement to cooperatives. The Agricultural Credit Act had been passed in 1923. Less than three weeks after the first McNary–Haugen bill was introduced in February 1924, Coolidge called another agricultural conference. On March 7 the tariff on wheat was increased from thirty-two to forty-two cents a bushel, and in April Hoover helped frame the Capper–Williams bill which provided for a farm board to be administered and assisted by the advising commodity groups.[28]

The elevation of William Jardine to the cabinet as secretary of agriculture is believed to have been urged by Commerce Secretary Hoover after he, himself, declined the post. One of Jardine's first moves was to force out Henry C. Taylor, the chief of the BAE. Charles J. Brand, who played a big role in drafting the first McNary–Haugen bill, and others, also left the department. Jardine felt he had good reason to be optimistic about the future of agriculture. Conditions in the farm belt had taken a definite turn for the better in 1924 and continued into 1925. Although the farmers had not achieved parity with other groups by 1925, their position on the whole was better than it had been in any year since 1920. Jardine viewed agriculture as a business that had to maintain a favorable balance between production and distribution. To his way of thinking, cooperative marketing was one means of achieving this balance. Since each farm product had a special problem of its own, it was advisable for the farmers to organize around commodities as wheat growers, cotton growers, cattle growers, and hog producers, and keep the number of associations handling the same product within reason. If hundreds of small cooperative associations handled the same product there would be price cutting, confusion, gluts, and losses.[29]

Another farm relief proposal to attract attention was the export debenture plan, which was reminiscent of the export bounty plan of the 1890s. The Grange endorsed it in 1926 and even made it a major part of its program to restore agricultural prosperity to the nation. The philosophy of the export debenture plan, like that of the McNary–Haugen plan, was based on the premise that the major cause of the farmers' problems was the low purchasing power generated by sale of the products of the farm. Simpler in design than the McNary–Haugen plan, the export debenture plan offered a premium or bounty on the export of commodities in question. However, it never mustered the enthusiasm or support of the McNary–Haugen plan.[30]

Among the most outspoken academic farm economists to take a bold stand on farm policy in the mid-1920s was John D. Black, a professor of agricultural economics at the University of Minnesota. Black, with a Ph.D. from Wisconsin, had been a student of Taylor before he went to Washington, and of Benjamin H. Hibbard. Black gained a reputation as a developer of new techniques and a superior teacher of graduate students. He frequently was called to Washington as a consulting economist where, because of his abrasive ways, he came to be known as "the insulting economist."[31]

Black, in a hard-hitting statement in 1925, said the objective of a farm policy should be "to put agriculture on a basis of equality with industry" by subsidizing agriculture and country life, at least for the present. Raising farm incomes would enable farmers to enjoy a higher standard of living and help reverse the flow of people from the rural to the urban areas. Conceivably such a turn of events could persuade more of the efficient and enterprising people, who otherwise might leave the farm, to remain. The final aim of such a policy was to provide rural society with most of the educational and cultural opportunities provided by the city.[32]

Meanwhile, business groups and leaders in agricultural education joined in the quest for a farm policy. The reports of the National Industrial Conference Board, a research organization founded in 1911 to aid management, the Business Men's Commission on Agriculture, set up jointly by the National Industrial Conference Board and the U.S. Chamber of Commerce, and the Association of Land Grant Colleges and Universities reflected the prevailing differences of opinion over the causes of the depression, the means by which the depression was going to be solved, and a late realization that some of the responsibility for solving this perplexing problem rested with the industrial, financial, and commercial leaders of the nation. The National Industrial Conference Board report, *The Agricultural Problem in the United States,* was widely publicized and exerted considerable influence in the business community. Few informed people in the United States questioned that agriculture represented about a fifth of the country's national wealth, contributed about a sixth of its national income, and was a determining factor in its national welfare. But whether agriculture formed "the basis of our national prosperity," was more vital to national security, more important as a reservoir from which to draw future citizens, or faced problems more complicated than those faced by other sectors of the economy, as the conference board stated, was highly questionable.[33]

Joseph Stancliffe Davis, director of the Food Research Institute at

Stanford University, liked the general overall view and general tone of the report, but found its analysis and interpretation of economic history inaccurate and unsafe as a guide in considering remedial measures.[34] He agreed that agriculture was important to the national welfare but said the report exaggerated the importance of agriculture as "the basis of our industrial prosperity." The bases for such prosperity were the contributing elements of the American economy of which agriculture was but one, Davis argued. When the nation was young, the role of agriculture was predominant, commerce an important second, and industry a poor third. In the course of time the order was reversed: industry made the most rapid strides, commerce came next, and agriculture last. Those in industry and commerce found themselves in a better position to take advantage of advances in technology, organization, and finance. In the continuous processes of adjustment and readjustment, agriculture just simply lagged behind.

The decline of the needed crop acreage per capita, the changes in the diet of the American people that reduced the total consumption of food, the substitution of the automobile for the horse, and America's increased efficency as a producer were not necessarily unwholesome changes even though they helped reduce the relative importance of agriculture. If the products of large-scale industries were exported in larger quantities, it was because new areas of agricultural production developed abroad, reducing the need for U.S. farm products. Davis also found that using the dollar as a yardstick of success in farming exaggerated the disparity because the farmer's dollar went further than that of the city worker and businessman: farmers produced a large share of what they consumed and their requirements were fewer. Those who wanted more dollars, and had the option, simply left farming. If the financial rewards from farming had corresponded to those in other occupations, the drift into agriculture would have been enormous.[35]

Black agreed with much that Davis said, but still could not accept his criticisms of the conference board report. Davis, in Black's opinion, came closer than he intended in creating the impression that farm people were as well off as city people. Black concurred, however, that the conference board report was not a very sound guide for an agricultural program, but that it contained a lot of sound analysis. If nothing else, Black said, it "made more business men think seriously about the problems of agriculture than anything else published on the subject." Black believed that the "real per capita income of the farm people fell badly behind from 1870 to about 1895, improved from then until 1919," and then dropped with a resounding crash in 1920 and 1921.[36]

More significant than the conference board report was that of the Business Men's Commission on Agriculture, *The Conditions of Agriculture in the United States and Measures for Its Improvement,* which Davis characterized as "the most comprehensive, best balanced and most significant" of all the reports published. The commission stressed that solution of the agricultural problem depended on the generous and intelligent cooperation of private initiative and state and federal agencies, the building of the machinery, and methods by which accumulated knowledge and experience could be placed in operation, and this required time. The commission likewise advised that protective tariffs be subjected to careful reconsideration with the view of equalizing their effects. It was recommended that the McNary–Haugen and export debenture plans and their radical features of protectionism be shunned. But certain features of the program proposed by the Coolidge administration "merited attention," such as the buying and selling of farm products (with the advice of a Federal Farm Board) "for the purpose of stabilizing prices." Still other recommendations included reducing the costs of marketing and production, conserving natural resources, lowering farm taxes, improving credit facilities, readjusting railroad rates, extending the waterway system, coordinating research efforts by federal, state, and other agencies, and increasing agricultural appropriations.[37]

The Association of Land Grant Colleges and Universities had taken a position of noninvolvement. A study of agricultural conditions finally was undertaken by a special committee of the ALGCU but only after high government officials, including some congressmen, kept asking whether or not it was one of the chief functions of the land grant colleges to assist farmers when they were in difficulties. A member of the association's executive committee conceded: "This problem as everyone knows, comes exceedingly near to the field of politics." The special committee assigned to do the study, comprised of deans of colleges of agriculture, directors of experiment stations, and members of the USDA, reiterated in fewer and somewhat more ambiguous words what others had said before: "equalization with reference to . . . taxation, tariff, and freight rates . . . a sound land policy . . . further improvements of credit facilities," and legislation to bring relief well before the occurrence of the emergency.[38]

Despite the findings and recommendations of the various investigating groups and the outpourings of writings on the agricultural problem, the debates on farm relief focused on only three topics. They were the McNary–Haugen plan, the drive for which was headed by the Corn Belt Committee; the export debenture plan, endorsed by some farmer, civic, commercial, and booster organizations, as well as some senators and representatives; and the policy of the Coolidge administration which asked for protective tariffs, encouragement to large-scale cooperative marketing associations, and a federal farm board.

William Jardine disagreed with those who claimed that industry got everything from the tariff while agriculture got nothing. He cited spring wheat (especially in the years of short crops), flax, sugar, wool, butter, and certain kinds of livestock as examples of farm commodities that benefited from tariffs. He also denied that everything the farmers bought had a tariff on it.

Farm implements, machinery, harnesses, boots and shoes made chiefly of leather, cattle and horses for breeding purposes, fertilizer materials, rough lumber, gasoline, binder twine, repair parts, and other articles were on the free list; the duty on furniture was nominal and ineffective. He likewise held that the increases in population, the relative decline in the number of farmers and farm acreage per capita, and increased efficiency helped make the tariff on farm products more effective. It was advisable to modify the tariff where it was discriminatory, but inadvisable to effect a rapid shift from protection to free trade. Jardine, however, turned out to be a poor prophet in predicting that the home market would eventually absorb more of agriculture's production until within a short time there would be a greater need for an effective tariff on farm products than on manufactures.[39]

The Republicans, despite the attacks from the farm belt and farmers' unyielding position on the tariff, could point with a sense of accomplishment to the encouragement they had given the cooperatives. Congress enacted the Capper–Volstead Act in 1922, the "Magna Carta of Cooperative Marketing." The same year Congress passed the Grain Futures Act to protect cooperatives from discrimination by boards of trade and chambers of commerce. A comparable act was passed in 1927 that helped prevent discrimination against the large cooperatives, especially in grain, that paid patronage dividends. The Purnell Act of 1925 made more funds available for marketing research and the Division of Cooperative Marketing created in the BAE in 1926 was designed to provide cooperatives with more intelligent bases for pricing their products and more efficient marketing units.[40]

Advocates of the McNary–Haugen plan, however, were unconvinced about the benefits that cooperatives would bring to farmers and stepped up their campaign for an effective tariff on agriculture. Their lobby was formidable and ranks among the most powerful in history. Apart from the congressmen and senators from the farm states, the lobby included the American Council of Agriculture, the Corn Belt Committee, the Grain Committee of the Farm Organizations, the Executive Committee of Twenty-Two of the North Central States Agricultural Conference, and the representatives of the cotton states who wanted to form an alliance between the Middle West and the South. The prospects of a 16-million-bale crop in 1926 that would add to the stocks of the past year and a government warning that the cotton acreage should be curtailed by at least 30 percent in 1927 played right into the hands of the McNary–Haugen advocates. Administration leaders fearing a rapprochement between the Middle West and South approved a proposal to withdraw 4 million bales of the 1926 crop from the market.[41]

Revised McNary–Haugen bills containing more favorable provisions for cotton cooperatives came before Congress in 1927 and 1928 and passed both houses but were vetoed by Coolidge. Embittered farmers and leaders were convinced the Republican party was the party of effective industrial tariffs, ineffective agricultural tariffs, and low food prices. Industrial leaders, they reasoned, were intolerant of any attempts to tamper with the protective tariff system as it related to industrial products.[42]

As the presidential election of 1928 neared and the clamor for relief mounted, Jardine seemed to have undergone a change of heart. He said:

> The surplus problem is of vital importance . . . to the Nation as a whole . . . and the solution of it is in some measure a governmental responsibility. . . . As an initial step it should suffice to create a Federal Farm Board with adequate authority to finance the handling of surpluses through central stabilization corporations, for which purpose a revolving fund should be provided . . .

"This," wrote Arthur P. Chew some years later, "was a concession to McNary–Haugenism forced on by events. It brought him within a hairbreadth of Henry C. Wallace's position."[43]

Despite the threats of the organized farm groups, the Republican ticket of Herbert C. Hoover and Charles Curtis scored a sweeping victory in 1928. Race, religion, Prohibition, and urban prosperity, not the farm depression, were the decisive factors in the election. Hoover, however, claimed he had a mandate to grant relief to the farmers of the kind he prescribed in his campaign. Hoover's plan included: creation of an agency capable of transferring the agricultural question from the realm of politics into economics; a Federal Farm Board to organize the marketing system of the farmers; investigation of every field of economic betterment; guidance to the farmers in production; elimination of marginal lands from cultivation and their diversion to other uses; the development of industrial by-products and any other means by which farmers could be aided.[44]

The Agricultural Marketing Act of 1929, which was Hoover's answer to the farm depression, had a twofold purpose: to aid, strengthen, and extend the scope of producer owned and controlled cooperatives; and to establish stabilization corporations that would help steady prices. A Federal Farm Board and a revolving fund of $500 million, a huge outlay for the times, was to aid these efforts. Opinion at first was sharply divided over the merits of the act and the details of the law, but in general the farmer organizations which preferred the McNary–Haugen plan and minimized the benefits of cooperative marketing began to rally behind the Federal Farm Board, especially after it began releasing money to cooperatives. For a time, at least, the debates on farm relief came to a halt and a period of action began.

The Federal Farm Board was inspired in part by the government's wartime experience with boards and in part by the faith Hoover had in the trade associations he had been identified with and in boards dominated by specialists. Congress, in establishing the board, had no intention of having it supercede the USDA or of creating an agency with overlapping duties. The board, if anything, was expected to coordinate its activities with those of other federal agencies and supplement the work of the USDA. Secretary of Agriculture Arthur M. Hyde explained that the farm board would become an action agency, while the USDA would retain its role as an educational and research body.[45] Alexander Legge, former president of the International Harvester Corporation, vice chairman of the War Industries Board and advisor to Hoover when he was secretary of commerce, accepted the chairmanship of the farm board. He explained that he did so because the federal government for the first time recognized the critical position agriculture was in and he wanted to do his part in helping to resolve it.

When the Federal Farm Board undertook its task, the Division of Cooperative Marketing had about 12,000 or more farmer cooperatives on its register. The vast majority were small and their business confined to one or two communities. The board concluded that the cooperatives would realize greater economies if they merged into regional and national associations. Cooperative sales agencies, as a consequence, were set up on a national scale in grain, cotton, livestock, wool and mohair, and pecans. Regional associations handled dairy products and some varieties of fruits. The Grain and Cotton Stabilization corporations were designed to regulate surpluses and influence prices.[46]

Hostility to the Federal Farm Board was formidable, but was not the only cause of its major difficulties. Fears of commission firms uneasy over how they would fare in the face of new competition were overcome by the appointment of recognized cooperative leaders and successful businessmen to the board and to management of the associations. Many Southerners, however, felt slighted when Hoover failed to appoint a Southerner to his cabinet or to the farm board; others looked upon the selection of Legge, the former president of the International Harvester Corporation, with suspicion. Business opponents charged it was unfair to use government funds to help cooperatives compete with established agencies.[47]

Legge expressed his feelings about business opposition when he told members of the United States Chamber of Commerce:

> I do not recall in years gone by of hearing you businessmen making any such complaint against this government aid that was extended to the manufacturing industry, to transportation and to finance. And these all played their part in adding to the disadvantages of the farmers as did also the preferential treatment of labor through immigration restriction and other measures.
> Is there any reason why those who have prospered and grown apace through governmental aid and assistance to various industries should object to the farmer getting his![48]

The problems the Federal Farm Board faced were insurmountable. Apart from the opposition of the private marketing agencies and the feuding among rival organizations and the larger cooperative associations, it had to contend with the worst depression on record. Prices sagged and then plunged to ruinous levels. Loans to producers, stabilization operations, and pleas to the farmers to reduce their acreages proved futile. As individuals, farmers felt they could not afford to reduce their acreage, and neither the board nor the cooperatives had sanctions with which to force farmers to reduce their production.[49]

Making a fair appraisal of the farm board's operations is difficult. Certainly, the administration overestimated the capabilities of the farm board or else underestimated the seriousness of the agricultural depression. As a body the board functioned in a rather peculiar way. Mordecai Ezekiel, a former farm board employee, said individual members of the board were given responsibilities for individual commodities, then went ahead and developed a policy of their own, and later reported to the board. "So that, even though you had a Board dealing with things, it didn't have a really coherent philosophy or organization." Large sums spent in setting up national cooperatives for existing local cooperatives made for a sort of mushroom growth that proved counterproductive. Experience bore out that cooperatives had to grow slowly, with genuine farmer support behind them. Cooperatives imposed by government action from above would collapse as soon as federal support was withdrawn. Estimated losses of the farm board as of March 31, 1933 were $184 million, but they would have been smaller if the board had been credited with the full market value of the wheat Congress ordered donated to the Red Cross. Farm board members who were hard pressed to defend their actions replied that all farmers, not merely those belonging to cooperatives, benefited from the stabilization operations. They maintained that world prices of wheat probably were higher in 1929–1930 because of the stabilization operations and the keeping of American sales off the world market. Cash income of the wheat producers was increased by at least $100 million from August 1929 to June 1931 and about $160 million by June 1932. A grain operator appearing before a senate committee estimated the gains to the wheat growers from 1929 to 1931 were more than $200 million.[50]

The Cotton Stabilization Corporation and the American Cotton Cooperative Association (ACCA), the central marketing agency, were jointly responsible for the cotton stabilization program. Unfortunately, the use of cotton dropped substantially below production during this period and brought further declines in the price. Over a three-year period the farm board withheld 3.5 million bales, and the total of 10 million bales that had accumulated was clearly beyond the board's ability to carry. It was difficult to avoid losses brought on from the knowledge of large stockpiles in the warehouses and the carrying charges. The board could hardly be blamed for failing to foresee the depression which most others also had failed to foresee, but it could be blamed for making the loans too high. As one expert noted, "Ninety percent loans are always hazardous, and at the beginning of the price decline they can hardly be other than fatal . . . most of the commodity advances were supplemental to primary loans from the banks. . . . They involved risks which banks would not assume even in more normal times than these."[51]

Maintaining prices over a long period of time was impossible if the supplies were abundant and the demand low. It was necessary to control production, which was impossible without the cooperation of the farmers and within the framework of the existing organizations and legislation.[52] The cooperatives made progress along these lines in a few areas of specialized production, but the problem awaited a solution in key areas such as wheat and cotton production.[53]

American farm policymakers were alert to matters of agricultural policy in foreign countries, but the degree to which they were influenced by foreign developments is unknown. John D. Black, for instance, gave ample evidence of his awareness of such matters in his *Agricultural Reform in the United States,* as did Charles L. Stewart, while the USDA had been collecting information on the subject for a number of years.[54]

Economic planning was another widely discussed subject during the late 1920s and early 1930s. In 1923 the Division of Land Economics in the BAE had urged a systematic selection of land for crops, pasture, and forests; and expressed concern over the misdirection of agricultural expansion and the need for a coordinated approach to these problems. A few local studies were made to determine the character of the problem in these areas and formulate methods of investigation.[55]

The position of the USDA on land use began to crystallize. By 1926, if not sooner, the need for the federal and state governments to revert some of the farmlands to forest uses and classify the land was recognized. The importance of farm woodlots and land surveys, the dangers of timber shortages, the potential of the upper Great Lakes states for the growing of timber, and the need for forest research work were emphasized in 1927. By 1929 and 1930 a more comprehensive study of land use had been made and the role of the government defined. An overexpanded agriculture could be aided by curtailing production, holding expansion in check, and withdrawing marginal lands from cultivation. Public ownership of the forests could help protect watersheds, prevent soil erosion, conserve timber, grow forest crops, provide recreational needs, preserve scenic resources, encourage use of forest land, help convert marginal lands to timberland, stabilize agriculture, and control floods.[56]

Another phase in the quest for a farm policy was the informal conference called by the farm board in the spring of 1931 whose purpose was to enable the members of the conference to inquire about the policy of the board, clear up misunderstandings that were current, and possibly devise ways by which the board could profit from what economists had to offer. Another conference on farm policy at the University of Chicago in September of that year had been nurtured by the earlier conference of the farm board. After the Chicago conference a group of farm economists met and drafted a series of resolutions revolving around land policy and research. They called for a repeal of the Homestead Act "in all its expressions"; retention by the federal government of all federal lands until a land policy adequate to the needs of the nation was adopted; and withholding of federal funds for additional reclamation, power, and water projects until such time as the USDA and other federal agencies deemed such projects essential to the needs of the country.[57]

Secretary Arthur M. Hyde conceded that the federal government and the public had to devote more attention to the most economical and efficient uses of the land. Hyde, in collaboration with the ALGCU, called a national conference on land use in Chicago in November 1931 where a series of resolutions expressing the principles of a new land policy were adopted, and two national committees were appointed to develop such a policy.[58]

Land use planning and economic readjustment often were linked to the curtailment of production. Sentiment for curtailment of production had gained momentum after the farm depression worsened and the efforts of the farm board collapsed. Cotton and tobacco growers saw the need for reducing their output, and some voluntary but abortive efforts were made to curtail it. Wheat farmers on occasion followed in the footsteps of the cotton and tobacco growers, and the USDA kept close watch over the efforts of foreign governments to curtail production and influence prices.[59] A forthright advocate of curtailed production was Henry A. Wallace, the future secretary of agriculture, who as early as 1922 told members of the American Farm Economics Association:

> Farmers have just as much right to organize to control their output as union labor had to organize for the purpose of shortening hours and increasing wages. They have just as much right to cease production wholly or in part as union labor has to strike. It is no more wrong for farmers to reduce production when prices are below cost of production than it is for the United States Steel Corporation to cut pig iron production in half when prices are rapidly falling.[60]

During the 1920s the USDA and large numbers of farm economists insisted more land was being farmed than could be cultivated at a profit, and it was advisable not to develop new farm areas until population growth caught up with food supply. Representatives of the Department of Interior held that much land not under cultivation was actually better suited for farming than some of the land that was. They urged preparation of the unused better land for future use.[61]

The cotton growers, whose difficulties were more acute than those of the tobacco producers, were more insistent on reducing their acreage in periods of low prices. But once higher prices returned, this agitation died down and was not to be resumed until the next steep decline in cotton prices. Demands to reduce the acreage mounted as the depression of 1929–1930 worsened. The Federal Farm Board urged acreage curtailment on a voluntary basis, and the American Cotton Cooperative Association, the national marketing agency of the cotton growers, urged the cotton producers to heed this advice. Legislatures in Louisiana, Oklahoma, South Carolina, and other states in the South committed themselves to curtailment; and for a time Huey Long and "Alfalfa Bill" Murray, former governor of Oklahoma, outdid themselves in exhorting the farmers of their states to hold down their acreages. The American Farm Bureau Federation urged the farmers to adopt a "streamlined policy" of producing for a price and abandon the "horse-and-buggy policy" of producing for abundance. Industry kept prices up during the depression by curtailing production, while agriculture, which did not, suffered serious economic reverses.[62]

Ideas espoused during these searching years included adjusting production to demand by land-use adjustments, withdrawing submarginal lands from cultivation, curtailing production, long-range planning, more farm credit, parity for agriculture, and tariff and marketing reform. The Coolidge and Hoover administrations, with the exception of marketing reform, more credit, and the lip service given to land-use adjustments, rejected the concept of equality for the farmers, tariff reform, and acreage curtailment, except on a voluntary basis. Cost of production and a guaranteed price for the farmers also were ruled out. Men active in proposing ideas for a farm policy during the late 1920s and early 1930s, such as Milburn L. Wilson, Lewis C. Gray, Howard R. Tolley, John D. Black, Albert G. Black, Mordecai Ezekiel, and others carried their suggestions with them later into the New Deal as members of the administration. Two significant elements of the farm population overlooked, however, were the tenants, including the sharecroppers, and the small landowning farmers—black and white. The proposals sought to assist the better-placed farmers, expecting that improvements in the economic position of the better-placed elements in society would filter down to aid the less fortunate members of rural society.

CHAPTER THREE

Reviving, Modernizing, and Selling an Idea: The AAA Becomes Law

As THE PRESIDENTIAL ELECTION OF 1932 NEARED, it was clear the Federal Farm Board had failed to unclog the markets, raise farm prices, and bring relief. An alternative plan, the voluntary domestic allotment plan, which was a more modernized version of an old idea, emerged as the prime topic of relief. Popularized by Milburn L. Wilson, the plan was based on the premise that agriculture found itself in a subordinate position in contemporary society, was hampered by trade restrictions, and had to adjust its production to demand. Production on the farm had to be planned and controlled, as it was planned and controlled in all rational and profitable enterprises. This simple logic appealed to farmers, farm economists, business executives, industrialists, and financiers, who pooled their energies to help convert this idea into the law of the land.

The demand for order in production and distribution and a fair price for the farmer had been voiced often but in more elementary form by leaders of the Grange, Farmers' Alliance, Farmers' Union, the American Society of Equity, and cooperative spokesmen. A plan of the *Northwestern Farmer* in 1894, although a far cry from what Wilson suggested in the early 1930s, differed from contemporary proposals in that it sought to limit production by using the acreage of a particular crop in estimating the needs of the coming year, adjusting production accordingly, and establishing a fair price. The Farmers' Educational and Cooperative Union and the American Society of Equity, founded in 1902, both advocated acreage reduction as a means of controlling production; and some southern state legislatures sought to curb the production of cotton before the United States entered World War I.[1]

The allotment idea, as it came to be known, was lost amid a welter of relief proposals over the next thirty years, but it was revived by William J. Spillman after the war when he saw the farmers overwhelmed by surpluses and low prices. Spillman's version was presented in preliminary form by Harry M. Owen in the journal, *Farmstead, Stock and Home* in 1926, and in final form by Spillman himself in his book *Balancing the Farm Output* in 1927. Owen, although one of the most enthusiastic supporters, was too much of a realist to expect much support for the Spillman plan at the time. The inclination of the McNary–Haugen advocates at that time was to accuse those with alternative plans of relief of being "per se and prima facie traitors to farmers." There also were divisions in the ranks of the crop restrictionists. Some were inclined to limit the application of the Spillman plan to wheat and cotton; Spillman himself wanted it applied to all farm products, crops and livestock, feed and cash crops, regardless of the export and import markets.[2]

John D. Black probably was most instrumental in injecting Spillman's ideas into the farm policy discussions of the late 1920s after he obtained a grant from the Laura Spelman Foundation for his study, *Agricultural Reform in the United States*. Black began writing the first part of his book about the first of January 1929 with the idea of influencing the incoming Hoover administration, and collaborators began working on the second part about November first. The "transferable rights" version of the domestic allotment plan is what attracted the attention of economist Beardsley Ruml. The domestic allotment plan with the "transferable rights" feature proposed by Black consisted of a rather involved formula that sought to pay the producer a free-trade price and the tariff duty—in the case of wheat, forty-two cents a bushel—for that portion of the crop that was consumed in the United States, and the same price without the tariff duty for that part that was exported. Allotments were to be made by the United States Department of Agriculture and the United States Department of Commerce, or by a committee appointed by the two departments. Ruml was attracted to the feature that enabled the individual producer to sell the domestic part of the crop he was allotted if he chose to do so.[3]

Black also solicited the views of Oscar Stine, Mordecai Ezekiel, Howard R. Tolley, and Eric Englund in the USDA, Henry C. Taylor, the former head of the BAE and Black's mentor at the University of Wisconsin, and Chester C. Davis, a highly successful farm lobbyist closely identified with the McNary–Haugen movement. Ruml sent copies of Black's "transferable rights" version to Julius Barnes, the grain exporter and ally of Hoover, who found it objectionable on conventional grounds, and to Edwin G. Nourse, who praised its workmanship, thought it an improvement over the others, but did not think plans of this kind should be adopted. Eric Englund objected to the direct slap Black was taking "against the recent administration.'' For reasons of bureau policy, Englund declined to take ''a hand in the preparation or revision of this chapter.'' Ruml told Black that the book was going to be a very useful document but believed it important ''that we continue to maintain a strictly 'academic' attitude. . . . It would be very unfortunate for the opinion to be current that we have a 'plan' for which we are agitating. . . .'' Ruml also asked ''that any personal reference be eliminated, if this is possible.''[4] Given his way, Black probably would have pushed what he called ''the Ruml plan'' harder. This was one reason he sought the advice of Chester Davis who Henry Taylor said ''could tell you where to go for funds to put a large number of your books in the hands of Congressmen.''[5]

Davis, a former newspaperman, also had a good understanding of what the lay mind could grasp. On one occasion he advised Black: ''I am afraid that . . . these . . . chapters are going to be a little hard for the every day business citizen (Congressmen for example) to follow.'' Or, ''In the words of an old Texas friend of mine, you have 'hung the fodder pretty high' for the members of Congress, farm groups, press, etc., to reach.'' He suggested that Black bring his conclusions and recommendations together ''in the blunt language of the street, even though this will mean sacrificing some of the refinement, qualifications, and reservations . . . necessary in a strictly economic discussion.'' By applying his conclusions to the discussions of the day, Black could avoid the sin of oversimplification committed by popular writers, and help others besides economists.[6]

Davis also wished Black's book had been published sooner because of the difficulties in securing substantial changes in a legislative program once it was set and had administration backing. Likewise realizing there was slight hope of getting congressmen to read the materials in their entirety, Davis believed it wise to select the chapters of the greatest immediate importance, especially those on stabilization corporations and the probable effects of the carry-over programs, debentures, and the transferable rights plan, and have the publishers send advance galley proofs to a small select group of congressmen before publication.

Davis realized it was advisable for each member of Congress to have a copy of *Agricultural Reform*. He knew, however, that he could not be of any financial help to Black because he had dropped all ties with the farmer organizations when he entered the political campaign of 1928 in behalf of the McNary-Haugen plan. Ruml was a possible source of help, and he, Davis, probably could arrange for the distribution of the book by some responsible farm group. Davis, however, cautioned Black to ''look for the results to show much later than the present session of Congress.''[7]

Meanwhile, Milburn L. Wilson was tireless in his efforts to promote his plan. He corresponded with farmers, grain merchants, representatives of commerce, industry, finance, agricultural extension workers, administrators in the USDA and the colleges of agriculture, newspapermen, Republicans, Democrats, farm board officials, and anyone who could further the cause. He held private conversations, attended conferences, spoke before farmer, business, and educational groups, and in fact talked with almost anyone willing to listen. In the first phase of his crusade he sought to arouse the public interest and win converts; in the second, to incorporate the principles of the domestic allotment plan into legislation that would compete with the McNary–Haugen and export debenture plans in winning attention.

Wilson wrote James Stone, the chairman of the Federal Farm Board, of the influential support the domestic allotment plan was mustering, especially in the Northwest, a critical area; of the forthcoming meeting in Chicago on April 19; and of the willingness of members of his group to appear before the farm board to explain what they were trying to do.[8] Wilson thought the farm board members would welcome an opportunity to go over the tentative legislation that he and his associates had worked out before it was whipped into final form and introduced in Congress. He further was convinced that the equalization fee of the AFBF and the export debenture plan of the Grange had little chance of being passed by Congress, even though the leaders of these organizations would not admit this in public. The role suggested for the farm board at this stage was that of determining the acreage that the farmers or states would have to reduce before they could qualify for payments under the plan, and also of arranging the contracts between the farmers and the states.

Wilson added that the initiative to place the plan in operation would have to come from the growers of a particular product. As few as 10 percent of the producers of this commodity could sign a petition with the farm board, which then would enter into agreements with the states and set up committees to conduct a referendum. Each farmer would fill out a ballot giving his name, a legal description of his land, and the acreage and production of various crops during the past five years. A majority vote of 70 percent was proposed before the plan would go into effect.[9]

The April 19 conference in Chicago had been called by W. L. Stockton, vice-president of the Montana Farm Bureau Federation, who, like many other farmers, had shifted his allegiance from the McNary–Haugen to the domestic allotment plan. Wilson conducted much of his correspondence over Stockton's name in behalf of domestic allotment. Among those invited to the conference were Henry A. Wallace, the future secretary of agriculture; Frank Lowden, former governor of Illinois, McNary–Haugen proponent, and still a presidential hopeful; Henry I. Harriman, president of the U.S. Chamber of Commerce; Louis S. Clarke, president of the Nebraska Mortgage Bankers' Association; Burton Peek, president of John Deere Company and brother of George N. Peek; A. R. Rogers of the Prudential Life Insurance Company; Beardsley Ruml; representatives of the Grange,

Farmers' Union, and the AFBF; and agricultural economists from North and South Dakota, Iowa, and the University of Chicago. The object was to discuss and shape up an allotment bill and (possibly) a proposal for regional readjustment.[10]

The Wilson group, as a means of winning the goodwill of the farm board and the general farmer organizations, claimed that the domestic allotment plan would furnish all they had been striving for and more, including stabilization of prices and benefits to the markets without cost to the federal treasury. This plan differed from that of the farmer organizations in that it would mandate the farm board to put the plan in operation on any commodity that received a majority vote of the percentage of the farmers specified by the law. Changes could be made in the law once the general philosophy and some of the more important details of the plan had been worked out.[11]

When it became obvious that none of the bills introduced in Congress seeking a price for the commodities "equal as nearly as possible to the cost of production were likely to pass," Representative Henry T. Rainey of Illinois sponsored a bill asking for "the emergency application of a domestic allotment plan to wheat, cotton, and hogs," but nothing came of this either. Then on July 7 Congressman Clifford R. Hope of Kansas and on July 11 Senator Peter Norbeck of South Dakota introduced bills, much like the Rainey bill, that were largely the work of M. L. Wilson, John D. Black, and Mordecai Ezekiel. New features of the bills included referenda, the fulfillment of certain conditions before the plan could be applied to any commodity, and limits beyond which the tariff adjustment advantage could not be raised. Most bills, including those by Hope and Norbeck, came in the form of amendments to the Agricultural Marketing Act of 1929. The Hope–Norbeck bills designated the farm board the central agency for administering the plan because it was more expedient to use the existing federal machinery than to create a new agency or to appoint separate commissioners to administer the plan.[12]

The Republican platform in 1932 went about as far as one could expect it to go in behalf of the domestic allotment plan. According to M. L. Wilson, the efforts of C. C. Teague, a Federal Farm Board member from California, and Arthur M. Hyde, the secretary of agriculture, were responsible for the platform addressing the issue of parity: "We will support any plan which will help to balance production against demand and thereby raise agricultural prices, provided it is economically sound."[13] The key to the control of production, according to the Republicans, lay in the cooperation of the farmers in the planning of production, a tariff to hold the home market for the farmers, and control of the acreage under cultivation.[14]

The platform of the Democratic party was equally ambiguous. It stated in part:

Extension and development of the farm cooperative movement and effective control of crop surpluses so that our farmers may have the full
benefit of the domestic market.

The enactment of every constitutional measure that will aid the
farmers to receive for their basic farm commodities prices in excess of
cost.[15]

After Governor Franklin D. Roosevelt was nominated for president by
the Democrats in 1932, Rexford G. Tugwell, one of his closest advisers,
urged him to invite Wilson and Wallace to come to Albany to discuss farm
issues. In his reminiscences Tugwell recalls having said something like the
following to Roosevelt:

You've got this Topeka speech to make and this . . . ought to be written by M. L. Wilson because he comes from out there . . . he knows
how to talk to farmers, he knows how to put it up to them, and I want
you to be clear that you have committed yourself to something. You're
not going the Cornell way.

M. L. [went to Albany and] took the Governor into camp [in fact
everybody into camp including Wallace]. He had an extremely keen
mind and . . . wanted to talk about . . . the relationship of agriculture
to our whole economy. . . . So we became immediately not only
friends but congenial thinkers . . . M. L. and I began to say, "There is
our man for Secretary of Agriculture, we must arrange it somehow."[16]

In mid-August, Roosevelt's advisers asked Wilson to prepare a memorandum that might be used as the basis of a speech, and that Raymond
Moley and Wallace go over it before sending it in. Moley received the
manuscript from Wilson on August 23 and a letter telling of his discussions
with Wallace, the contents of the preferred statement, and the positions
taken. The emphasis on "Equality for Agriculture" was aimed at the
farmers who had been exposed to this argument over the past eight years
and might be influenced to switch their votes to the Democratic candidates.
Wallace believed the Topeka speech should show that Hoover was leaving
the farmers in "a rat hole" without any possible avenue of escape. Wilson
gave particular attention to the wording of the section on domestic allotment, because he believed this was the portion of the speech the farmers
would be listening to most carefully.[17]

Once Moley received the Wilson memo and the supplementary statement by Wallace, he began correlating it with the suggestions of others.
Henry A. Morgenthau, Jr., and his assistant Herbert E. Gaston prepared
material on the planned use of land, oppressive taxation, and the burden of
farm debts. Moley considered Hugh Johnson's statement excellent. When
the draft of the Topeka speech containing materials provided by Wilson,
Wallace, Hugh Johnson, Morgenthau, and Gaston was completed, it was

passed around to others for criticism. Tugwell, Adolph A. Berle, Jr., a bright young lawyer who had done some distinguished work on corporate finance, and Clifford V. Gregory, editor of the *Prairie Farmer,* added their suggestions. The Topeka speech, said Moley, "was the direct product of more than 25 people."[18] At Topeka, Roosevelt declared the Republicans failed to understand the farm problem, stressed the six points Wilson outlined, but did not mention the domestic allotment plan by name.

> I want now to state what seem to be the specifications upon which most of the reasonable leaders of agriculture have agreed, and to express my wholehearted accord with these specifications.
>
> First: The plan must provide for the producer of staple surplus commodities, such as wheat, cotton, corn (in the form of hogs) and tobacco, a tariff benefit over world prices which is equivalent to the benefit given by the tariff to industrial products. This differential benefit must be so applied that the increase in farm income, purchasing and debt-paying power will not stimulate further production.
>
> Second: The plan must finance itself. Agriculture has at no time sought and does not now seek any such access to the public treasury as was provided by the futile and costly attempts at price stabilization by the Federal farm board. It seeks only equality of opportunity with tariff-protected industry.
>
> Third: It must not make use of any mechanism which would cause our European customers to retaliate on the grounds of dumping. It must be based upon making the tariff effective and direct in its operation.
>
> Fourth: It must make use of existing agencies and so far as possible be decentralized in its Administration so that the chief responsibility for its operation will rest with locality rather than with newly created bureaucratic machinery in Washington.
>
> Fifth: It must operate as nearly as possible on a cooperative basis and its effects must be to enhance and strengthen the cooperative movement. It should, moreover, be constituted so that it can be withdrawn whenever the emergency has passed and normal foreign markets have been reestablished.
>
> Sixth: The plan must be, insofar as possible, voluntary. I like the idea that the plan should not be put into operation unless it has the support of a reasonable majority of the producers of the exportable commodity to which it is to apply. It must be so organized that the benefits will go to the man who participates.[19]

Wilson was delighted with the Topeka speech: "We made a ten pin strike . . . at Topeka," he wrote an acquaintance, ". . . and the six points are just as I submitted them to the committee with scarcely any change in phraseology." To Mordecai Ezekiel he wrote, "Our strategy . . . was that the Governor should set forth the elements of the Allotment Plan but . . . not mention it by name so that the opposition cannot shoot at it very hard." Wilson also believed that if the Topeka speech had been delayed any longer, the Republican Central Committee in Chicago probably would have come out openly with its domestic allotment plan. (In fact the Republicans employed Colonel Ralph M. Ainsworth, an agricultural propagandist, who said the Republicans should endorse the plan, explaining how it fulfilled the plank in the Republican platform and was workable, legal, and not bureaucratic.)[20]

Wilson wrote to Black,

[Tugwell] has just been fine and is certainly entitled to very great commendation from us. . . . This would never have happened had it not been for Tugwell . . . the Governor is going to stand pat with us on the Voluntary Domestic Allotment Plan. He doesn't know entirely what it is all about, but he has committed himself [and] I do not see how he can backwater.[21]

Moley called the Topeka speech

A first-rate document. . . . More than any other single speech . . . it captured the votes of the Middle Western farmers . . . outlined the Domestic Allotment Plan without mentioning its name—outlined it so delicately that the urban voters, editors, and newspapermen accepted its broad propositions as generalities too vague to require examination. It won the Midwest without waking up the dogs of the East.[22]

The general farmer organizations, however, still posed a big problem. Their support was needed, but they had budged very little on their position. Worse still, some of their representatives were spreading stories that the domestic allotment plan had been inspired by the U.S. Chamber of Commerce, the large insurance companies, and other agencies the farmers distrusted. Some state farm bureau presidents resented having anyone but themselves identified with farm relief programs on the theory that such matters should be left in the hands of the farmers and their legitimate leaders. Ed O'Neal, president of the AFBF, became more guarded in his comments, especially after it became obvious that the western states were likely to vote for Roosevelt.

Some who were sympathetic with the domestic allotment plan became apprehensive, claiming that the plan was too complicated and had to be simplified. Wilson, on the other hand, feared that when the bill came before the agricultural committees, congressmen would have "a thousand and one ideas and that they were in danger of getting some kind of monstrosity out of it"; because of this Wilson was inclined not to allow much compromise on the bill.

There also were differences over the stress on tariff equality and the place of hogs in the program. Henry Harriman, for instance, wanted greater stress placed on production control and was unsure of the drive to make the tariff effective on agricultural products. Wilson held that farmers had been educated to believe an effective tariff was necessary before moving into production control. Wilson, Harriman, and others also talked about trying out the plan first on cotton and wheat—if it worked with them, then include hogs. But the hog farmers did not like this. Wilson also argued that in presenting the plan to the public, emphasis should be placed on the prevailing conditions in Europe, i.e., the tariff barriers, import quotas, and the other unhealthy political and economic conditions that were clogging up the channels of foreign trade.[23]

By late October, if not sooner, the farmer organizations were giving more consideration to the domestic allotment plan, even though they had not been won over. Wilson felt that much depended on "how stiff-necked F. D. R." would be on his six points. If he stood firm, the prospects were that the organizations would come across; if he did not, something less desirable would be passed, minus the production control and allotment features.[24]

The election of Roosevelt in November simply heightened the expectations of Wilson and his associates. Along with the victory at the polls came sympathetic words from influential businessmen, financial leaders, and newspaper columnists. Mark Sullivan, noting that business leaders favored the idea, suggested that the domestic allotment plan might prove just the "white rabbit" to start a real swing to prosperity. Walter Lippmann believed the basic principles behind the plan were reasonable. "There is no use in pretending that this is not the most daring economic experiment ever seriously proposed in the United States. But what other remedy is proposed for the plight of agriculture that might be submitted for this one?"[25]

Unfortunately the general farmer organizations, much to the disgust of the incoming administration, remained divided; but a meeting was called at the Hotel Harrington in Washington on December 12 and 13 with the hope of reaching an agreement before Roosevelt took office. Behind closed doors they conferred with Henry Morgenthau, Jr., publisher of the *American Agriculturalist,* and at the time Roosevelt's close advisor on agricultural matters, until the various farm organizations agreed to support the domestic allotment plan.[26]

Late in January 1933 Ed O'Neal testified before the Senate Agricultural Committee that on October 28, 1932, the national farmer organizations had agreed tentatively to accept "this allotment plan." On December 13 a meeting representing roughly half of the organized farmers in the United States adopted four principles. They wanted restoration of the prewar purchasing power of the farmers to permit a fair exchange for the goods of the farm and factory; adjustment of production to actual demand; application of the fair exchange concept to those basic commodities that influenced the prices of other products on which the tariff had been ineffective; and making these plans self-financing and independent on any large new governmental agencies.[27]

While administration leaders, farmer politicians, and others envisioned a farm policy broader than mere acreage control—and one that would include land use reforms and rational farming practices in a rapidly changing world—others were talking about controlled inflation, and reducing the gold content of the dollar. In fact, a farm bloc of about 150 congressmen sought to force through the short session of Congress a four-point legislative program that included expansion of the currency, lowering of the gold content of the dollar, an end to farm mortgage foreclosures, and equality for agriculture and labor. The bloc members argued that what appeared to be sectional or selfish objectives were in reality national objectives.[28]

Passage of effective legislation before March 4 when the new administration took office was a remote possibility, but developments in Washington soon suggested what was likely to happen in Congress. On January 23, 1933, by a vote of 203 to 150 the House passed the Jones bill whose most radical provision was for production control. The Jones bill, as reported from the committee, covered only cotton, wheat, tobacco, and hogs in the belief that the prices of these commodities had a controlling effect on the prices of others. The dairy organizations, claiming they had been discriminated against, succeeded in including butterfat as a basic commodity; then the rice and peanut growers lined up enough votes to have their products covered. Senator Ellison D. Smith of South Carolina, after visiting Roosevelt in New York, said that while the president-elect approved of the allotment plan in principle, he believed at first it should be confined to wheat.[29]

Late in January 1933 Ed O'Neal told a senate committee he supported the allotment plan and warned that "unless something is done for the farmers, we will have a revolution in the countryside in less than 12 months." John A. Simpson, the embittered president of the National Farmers' Union, predicted "one of the biggest and finest crops of little revolutions, I ever saw all over the country right now." O'Neal's remedy "was inflation through the reduction of the gold contents of the dollar and the enactment of the allotment bill to bring back faith and confidence in the countryside." To Simpson this was "a pittance of a remedy." The farmer had to have his cost of production. Simpson maintained that "all acreage reduction legislation will prove a failure."[30]

The Jones bill, reported from the Senate Committee on Agriculture on February 20, limited its application of the plan to wheat and cotton, and omitted the acreage reduction and other features in the House bill. The Senate argued that while the measure was sound in principle it was chiefly experimental and for that reason should be simple in its initial form. If experience warranted it, the measure could be enlarged and extended later. But the Senate amended the bill to the point where it was unacceptable to the farm groups that sponsored it in the House, and final passage seemed unlikely.[31]

By late 1932 and early 1933 the domestic allotment plan and other proposals directly or indirectly related no longer were confined to correspondence among advocates and others who viewed them as preferable to the McNary–Haugen plan. Domestic allotment was becoming the heart of New Deal farm thinking.

Filling the secretary of agriculture vacancy was of special importance at this stage. George N. Peek yearned for the appointment, and Henry A. Wallace at one point considered him qualified for the job. Southerners wanted someone who would do something for cotton and were hoping that Cully A. Cobb, the editor of the *Southern Ruralist,* would become the new secretary; in fact as late as two weeks before inauguration day, *Kiplinger's Farm Letter* stated flatly that Cobb would become the secretary of agriculture. John A. Simpson also had his supporters. Henry Morgenthau, Jr., wanted the post, much to the amusement of Roosevelt and members of his inner circle, according to Tugwell. The names of Clifford V. Gregory, editor of the *Prairie Farmer,* Rexford G. Tugwell, and M. L. Wilson were likewise bandied about. The rumor of Tugwell becoming secretary, according to Russell Lord, ". . . received little credence, because Tugwell was . . . a city fellow . . . a New York City Columbia Highbrow, and Tugwell stated frankly that . . . the very thought of going to Washington, himself, seemed repulsive." Wilson, on the other hand, "was generally estimated to be too retiring of nature and obscure." When Wilson heard his name mentioned, he said, "This is impossible first of all from the political angle and next, I do not have the qualifications nor the finances for such a position.[32]

The question of who was to be appointed secretary, according to Russell Lord, was settled when Wallace and Tugwell visited Roosevelt at Warm Springs, Georgia the first week of December 1932, but no direct offer or acceptance was made at the time. Wallace said he got the official letter asking him to become secretary of agriculture on February 12, Lincoln's birthday, just as he was preparing to drive through a blizzard to make a speech.[33]

Wallace was invited into the official family of the president-elect because he was a doer, a man who had ideas, and his philosophy was one Roosevelt believed in—not just because he was a loyal Democrat. When Wallace heard he was mentioned as the secretary of agriculture, he said, "I desire as little publicity as possible regarding my chances for this office for I certainly am not seeking it."[34]

Those who knew and understood Wallace knew his becoming secretary meant "a new deal" in more than one way. County agents and agricultural extension workers were unhappy with him for writing in *Wallace's Farmer* that they were putting too much emphasis on production. None of the "sacred cows" or traditional practices of the USDA were safe with him as its head. "A government which spends public money in research to make the farmer's products worth less is highly negligent unless it also assists him in his readjustment and marketing problems.'' Wallace believed in research, but he believed ''in this other thing, too.''[35]

Events began to move swiftly. Ezekiel in fact had been sitting in on the committee hearings while still employed by the farm board and before Wallace assumed his new position. When Wallace became secretary he invited the heads of the major farmer organizations to come to Washington and make recommendations on the necessary legislation. They agreed to come. In fact, ''They met on the train on the way from Chicago to Washington,'' said Tugwell, ''and when they arrived they presented us with a memorandum which asked us to do what we already had done.'' A meeting was held in the USDA where the provisions of the proposed legislation were explained, and the farm leaders approved it. Then the group was taken to the White House where Wallace and Tugwell explained that the farm leaders wanted immediate action.[36]

Since Congress was willing to delegate broad powers to the president, little difficulty was expected in getting legislation passed. The idea soon emerged of passing an omnibus bill which carried the authorization to do any of the things that had been suggested for farm relief, leaving the decision of what to do up to the president and the secretary.

Several persons had a hand in framing the new farm bill. Ezekiel was a prime force. According to Tugwell, Frederick P. Lee, a Washington lawyer who was employed by the AFBF, Jerome Frank, who came to Washington at the suggestion of Felix Frankfurter, and Tugwell, himself, worked on the bill. ''The actual writing of the bill was done in my office,'' said Tugwell, ''by Lee, and Ezekiel and myself. We hammered it out through a great many hours.'' But Ezekiel mentions only one other person in his reminiscences besides himself as having had a direct hand in writing the bill— Frederick P. Lee, ''a very nice fellow and a very good lawyer.'' In drafting the legislation Ezekiel said that Lee wanted to know ''what the court thinks'' and not what comments there were about the court. So he read court decisions and drafted the bill. The financial portion of the bill dealing with the processing tax caused considerable difficulty. The aim was to have the processing tax shoulder the financial burden of the program, and to escape the charge of class legislation and any possibility of having the measure declared unconstitutional.[37]

Tentative drafts of the proposed allotment bill were sent to the men who had a hand in shaping it as well as influential persons who were genuinely interested in it. All were cautioned to keep this information confidential inasmuch as Wallace had not made any public announcements and wanted to release the plans by degrees that seemed most effective.[38]

About the same time, Wallace drafted a memo to Nils Olsen, a former brain truster of his father, who had become the conservative chief of the BAE. Olsen was asked to set up committees on hogs and corn, wheat, cotton, tobacco, and rice to compile what statistical material might be needed to administer the plan when the bill became law. Wallace realized his department was getting ready sooner than necessary, but he wanted the administrative force in Washington and the field selected and organized.[39]

Roosevelt sent a message to Congress on March 16, twelve days after he took office, asking for speedy action:

> To increase the purchasing power of our farmers and the consumption of articles manufactured in our industrial communities . . . to relieve the pressure of mortgages . . . [and] increase the asset value of farm loans. . . . I tell you with equal frankness that an unprecedented condition calls for the trial of new means to rescue agriculture.

He urged quick action "for the simple reason that the spring crops will soon be planted and if we wait for another month or six weeks the effects on the price of this year's crops will be wholly lost."[40]

Wallace kept close watch on developments after the bill was introduced. He wrote Representative Marvin Jones, chairman of the House Committee on Agriculture and Forestry, with whom the USDA worked closely to watch for any action that might harm the bill: "An apparently harmless amendment might in fact severely hamper or restrict work which might be done under a given section."[41]

Numerous petitions, resolutions, and memorials expressing warm approval of the president's actions and specific proposals for legislation followed in the wake of the president's speech. One of the most popular was the Frazier bill advocated by the National Farmers' Union, which was most active in the wheat states of the upper Mississippi valley. The Frazier bill, if enacted into law, would have refinanced distressed farmers at the rate of 1½ percent interest and ½ percent payment on the principal per year. Concurrent resolutions asking for swift action on this bill came from the legislatures of Kansas, Iowa, Montana, North Dakota, Minnesota, Wisconsin, Illinois, Michigan, and other states.[42]

Another series of petitions asked the secretary of agriculture "to save the hog market and prices from ruin" by forcing the packers to buy their supplies through the established open competitive market. An end to the direct buying of hogs by the packers from the farmers, which weakened competition, was called for. Packers purchasing directly from the producers manipulated their purchases in such a manner that the good hogs entered their plants without the benefit of competitive bidding, while only "the culls and throw-outs" were put on "the price-fixing open competitive markets." Undesirable hogs also established the market price which made it possible for the packers to go directly to the country again on the following day and buy hogs at the established price.[43]

The future of the cooperatives under the New Deal naturally concerned those who a few years back looked upon the cooperatives as the great hope of the American farmer. One eastern association, for instance, expressed warm appreciation for the work of the farm board, asked for the retention of the Agricultural Marketing Act of 1929, opposed the consolidation of the board with any other agency, and urged its retention as an independent unit.[44]

Nor was this all. A California cotton grower wired Senator William G. McAdoo that the cotton producers of his state had reduced their acreage voluntarily since 1929 by 60 percent and asked that the reduction be based on the production of the past five years as a means of protecting those who had been attempting to help stabilize supply and demand on a voluntary basis. The General Assembly of Nevada memorialized Congress to provide a moratorium of at least two years on the payment of grazing fees by livestock producers on government ranges, and the Colorado legislature passed concurrent resolutions likewise asking for a partial waiver of grazing fees on government forest reserves. The Minnesota legislature asked for a reduction in fees on the terminal markets of the state. Delaware cautioned against budget slashes that could easily result in the destruction of the school of agriculture in the state, and the halting of research, experiment stations, and extension workers in agriculture.[45]

The expected passage of the domestic allotment bill also created much concern among the state directors of the Extension Service. Among them was B. H. Crocheron, the director of the Extension Service, College of Agriculture, University of California, who inquired about the role of the county agents in the forthcoming national farm program. C. W. Warburton, the director of the Extension Service in Washington, D.C., replied about a month before Roosevelt's inauguration that the county agents' role would depend to a great extent on the new secretary of agriculture. Warburton, however, made his position clear. "When the bill finally takes form and a new Secretary is appointed, my efforts will certainly be directed toward maintaining the Extension Service as an educational agency, keeping it out of regulatory activities such as would be involved in carrying out provisions of the bill embodying the domestic allotment plan."[46]

The Extension Service already was harassed by budgetary problems. It also had earned the hostility of business and professional groups that accused the county agents of having invaded the field of private enterprise. Among the loudest critics were the veterinarians who besieged Congress with complaints. Warburton admitted his agency already had complaints from the states of Washington, Texas, Arkansas, and North Carolina, and some veterinarians appeared before a House committee in the summer of 1932 to complain about the treatment of livestock by county agents. Thus extension leaders dreaded the prospects of having their agency play an important part in the New Deal.[47]

Almost two months elapsed between the time Roosevelt asked Congress to act on March 16, the introduction of the administration bill, and the passage of the legislation. After "a good deal of tinkering" the administration measure embodying many of the features in the Jones bill became law on May 12, 1933 as the Agricultural Adjustment Act (AAA).[48]

The general objectives of the AAA were to overcome the disparities in the purchasing power of farm products that by February 1933 had dropped to about 50 percent of what it had been before the war. The federal government hoped to accomplish this in part by eliminating the surpluses in wheat, cotton, tobacco, rice, hogs and hog products, and milk, thus bringing the supplies of these products into line with the demand at a price that would bring the farmers a purchasing power commensurate with that of the 1909–1914 period. Benefits, however, were to be confined only to the producers of these seven basic commodities who cooperated with the government in trying to balance production with demand. Confinement of payments to such producers was based on the theory that these crops were in worse economic condition than others, that the United States had a surplus of nearly all of them, and that the changes in the prices of these commodities usually influenced changes in the prices of the other commodities. Farmers were free to produce as much as they chose, but if they did so they could not expect benefit payments from the federal government. The government further could become an arbiter and partner in marketing agreements with associations of producers, processors, and distributors; such agreements could be applied to all farm products and negotiated with producers, processors, and others engaged in foreign and interstate commerce.[49]

Acceptance of the domestic allotment plan meant acceptance of the principle that the farmers who produced an exportable surplus had to be protected by the tariff. Since the United States was committed to a high tariff, and foreign nations resorted to almost every conceivable form of restriction, the American farmer had to be protected for at least that portion of his product used at home. The American farmers, in other words, had to meet fire with fire. Farmers had been victimized by economic nationalism in the past and had to protect themselves by adopting a nationalistic plan of their own. The AAA was expected to equalize "the social costs of adjusting the agricultural plant of the United States" to a worldwide situation.[50]

The AAA became a part of the USDA instead of a separate agency independent of the department as George N. Peek and others wanted. It also had its own legal department to handle the large amount of legal work anticipated. The personnel and funds of the AAA were to be kept separate from the USDA. The AAA was to operate as an integral part of the department to avoid the rash of errors committed by the farm board, which functioned as a separate entity outside the USDA. There had to be some consistency between what the AAA and the rest of the department was doing in formulating programs and implementing them.[51]

The field force of the AAA could be administered in one of two ways. One was to have the departments of agriculture in the various states administer the program and the field personnel; and the other was to have the Extension Service, which had agents in almost every county of the United States, undertake it. "When Chester Davis and I heard about this," said Wilson, "we hit the ceiling. . . . Our conviction was that it would be a very great mistake and that it would be much better to ask the colleges and Extension Service to render this service, and the commissioners of agriculture to cooperate and assist, thus not shutting them out." Wilson and Davis reasoned that since there was a county agent in every county, the organization and educational phases of the program would get into action much better and sooner if the Extension Service took over. Thus the Extension Service, a federal-state-county superstructure with farmer contacts in every township and county in the nation, undertook the massive job, provided the field force and space for the administration, and nursed the AAA along in the initial stages. Most states cooperated, but there were states in which the cooperation was lukewarm or indifferent, and one or two states in which there was outright hostility.[52]

Staffing the AAA

STAFFING THE AAA POSED PROBLEMS, as did the establishment of the subadministrative agencies needed to carry out the purposes of the law. Expectations ran high. Much more was expected from the AAA than had been of the expiring Federal Farm Board, and those chosen to pilot its course had to move swiftly and effectively, and work without a backlog of experience to guide them. They had to labor with persons of diverse backgrounds and views, work for the integration of the AAA programs with the broader principles of the New Deal, reconcile themselves to personal and ideological clashes and the struggle for power that was bound to develop. What is more, they had to condition themselves to the harassment of politicians and disgruntled officeseekers and to endless attacks by the press. They had to continually defend the AAA programs in the face of rival schools of thought. Failure to deliver tangible benefits within a reasonable time could mean to the AAA a fate similar to that of the Federal Farm Board and the Hoover administration.

The selection of Henry Wallace as secretary of agriculture was viewed as a fortunate one by many. Wallace was a man with a wide range of interests and associations and the ability to express himself in the written and spoken word. It is doubtful if the USDA at any time since its formation had had a head who was as well known in agricultural circles as Wallace. He had an excellent reputation as a corn breeder, and he knew a great deal about statistics and mathematics. He also was a humanist free from tradition and orthodox practices, receptive to new ideas and challenges. He expressed great concern for his fellow men, the whites more so than the blacks, and the landowning farmers more than the tenants and sharecroppers. Certainly the programs initiated under his administration were aimed to protect the interests of the better-placed members of rural society than the others. Wallace had a much broader grasp of the social and economic problems of agriculture than any of his predecessors, and he understood the relationship of these problems to the broader issues of American society. He was in contact with the leading farm thinkers of the day and expressed a willingness to try new methods and experiments to bring about the desired results.[1]

For precisely these same reasons many of the commercial and financial leaders of the nation were apprehensive about what Wallace would do. He had hardly been in office two weeks when someone wrote M. L. Wilson,

> There was distrust of Mr. Wallace, but that has turned into real fear now. Our report from Washington last Saturday was to the effect that Mr. Wallace frankly "wants to experiment" and will do so, whomever is hurt, until he finds something that seems to work . . . it is hard for these men with properties to sit still and see what they think is a virtual confiscation of their property under the process of experimentation.[2]

Wallace was quick in developing a personal understanding and working relationship with most research bureaus in the department. Some of the prominent men in the department knew his father and both they and he sought to capitalize on this. When Henry came to Washington, Warner W. Stockberger and Wilson A. Jump were two of the first men he called on. The personnel of the research bureaus at the same time knew of the interests of the new secretary and made a point of speaking with him about new ideas and new techniques. And many liked Wallace as a person.[3]

Others viewed Wallace in a less charitable light. They criticized him for his strange assortment of interests: mysticism, science, politics, cultism, corn and hogs, poetry, religion, and other matters. This was a most unusual array of interests for a secretary of agriculture from the State of Iowa. The more caustic, such as Paul W. Ward, a staff man of the *Baltimore Sun,* stressed "the tripartite personality" of the secretary: "Wallace the politician, Wallace the scientist, and Wallace the Christian mystic." Such mystical qualities, wrote Ward, would have endeared him to Isadora Duncan, Gandhi, Krishnamurti, and Bernarr Macfadden, while his wide ranging interests in astrology, numerology, poetry, and vegetarianism were attributed to the loneliness he experienced as a child among the corn and hogs in Iowa. Ward characterized his religiousness as a curious blend: "Though he comes of Scotch-Irish Presbyterian stock, his faith at times seems to be an amalgam of Buddhism, Judaism, Zoroastrianism, Mohammedanism, and Eddyism. His sincerity awes all beholders."[4]

Russell Lord, a friend of Wallace, sought to respond with some "undistorted facts." Wallace, he said, was interested in astronomy and mathematics and the relationship of these two disciplines to planetary movements and their possible bearing on longtime weather forecasting, but he had never taken an interest in or seriously studied astrology or numerology. He did, however, consort with poets; he was a friend of A.E. (pseudonymn of George William Russell) and of Robert Frost; and he once spent an amusing evening in his own apartment with a number of others listening to an obscure poet known as "The Alabama Wildcat" but this never blossomed into a close friendship. As for the rumor that he corresponded with an Indian medicine man, this was not only false but it opened the way for the wide circulation of a series of forged letters during the campaign of 1940.[5]

Of Wallace's religious proclivities there was little doubt. M. L. Wilson and others who knew him well were hardly surprised when, in the early weeks of his administration, he offered a compilation of "Regular and Insurgent Prophets" as a guide to an informal discussion of the topics of the times. Members of his staff greeted this with the cry of "religious economics," to which Wallace replied, "Well, economic morality, if you like it better that way." Many of his aides were frightened, and he in turn amused, when he accepted the invitation of the Chicago Theological Seminary to deliver the Alden–Tuthill Lecture in 1934, the result of which was a book that he was never to hear the end of: *Statesmanship and Religion.* He had no thought of writing such a book when he accepted this and other invitations to speak. According to Lord,

> His thought was simply to talk religion—"One God, One World," as he put it, conversationally—may, indeed must, be brought into economics and government, without departure from the traditional separation of church and state. While the book made him endless trouble, providing marvelous material for distortion by piecemeal quotations torn from context, *Statesmanship and Religion,* if read as a whole, remains the most unstudied, revelatory and meaningful of Wallace's published works. . . .[6]

Wallace was generally viewed as an agricultural fundamentalist, and he gave strong support to measures aimed to bolster the economic well-being of the farmers, but he could also veer in the direction of the so-called "urban-liberals." The latter group was well represented, at first, in the office of the general counsel of the AAA, headed by Jerome Frank, and in the office of the consumers' counsel, headed by Dr. Frederic C. Howe. Rexford G. Tugwell, who more or less was the intellectual leader of this group in the early months and years, commanded the respect of both the president and Henry Wallace.[7]

The political side of Wallace, although always present, at first was reflected in his willingness to cooperate with southern political leaders in not tampering with the social structure of the South and in catering primarily to the needs and demands of the more substantial landowners and cotton growers. Doing violence to the accepted norm was ruled out as a means of winning the cooperation and support of southern senators and congressmen, a number of whom were members of strategic Senate and House committees.

This political side of Wallace came out much stronger after the presidential campaign of 1936, when his attention began to shift noticeably in directions other than agricultural matters, and when friends of his began telling him that he was the logical man to succeed Roosevelt in 1940. The appointment of a Georgian, Harry Brown, as assistant secretary of agriculture in 1937 was in large measure a political response to the idea of making the AAA a dirt-farmer-operated agency. Even more reflective of this tendency was the appointment of such men as Rudolph M. "Spike" Evans to the post of AAA administrator and Grover Hill to a lesser assignment.[8]

One of the most crucial appointments was the first administrator of the AAA. The position was first offered to Bernard Baruch, former head of the War Industries Board during World War I, a nonfarming industrialist who advocated relief for the agriculturalists during the 1920s. Baruch said he refused the post after considering it for several days because he believed it was unworkable, but he recommended his friend George N. Peek, who, he said, was reluctant to accept.[9]

The selection of George Nelson Peek as administrator of the AAA came as no surprise to those who knew farm politics. Peek was closely identified with the McNary–Haugen campaigns that dominated the political debates on farm relief during the mid-1920s, was recognized as a prime force in the farmers' crusade for tariff equality, and was highly respected by the major farmer organizations as a trusted friend of agriculture. He also possessed good industrial and financial ties, according to Mordecai Ezekiel, and Wallace had to "have a bridge over which the thing could get started and Peek was the best person he had handy to put the thing into action." Ed O'Neal, who rarely underestimated his own personal influence, or that of the American Farm Bureau Federation he headed, boasted:

> George Peek was the boy we recommended for the Triple-A. . . . [The] fight he made for our cause with the Republicans when they were in power was wonderful. That is really the fundamental reason why Wallace made him administrator, because we backed him. The Farm Bureau people of the Midwest backed him.[10]

An aggressive, stubborn, and outspoken man, Peek had positive views of what was right and wrong and he never hesitated to voice them. For a time he had hopes of becoming secretary of agriculture, and influential friends of his in agriculture and the business world spoke in his behalf. Later Peek reflected that he was offered the job of administrator of the AAA by the president in April 1933 but he deferred acceptance until he had gained a complete understanding of policy. Peek's decision to accept came after a White House meeting on the evening of May 3, which was attended by a number of Cabinet members, including Wallace, Tugwell, Moley, Morgenthau, Peek, and a large number of other government officials. "It was not a particularly quiet or harmonious meeting for everyone sensed that if the farm bill went wrong the Administration would be sunk."[11]

Peek objected to an elaborate administrative chart that had been devised by someone within the administration. The chart provided for reporting the entire administration of the AAA through the secretary of agriculture to the president. Peek stipulated that if he accepted the assignment, he had to "have direct access to the President with the Secretary." Peek presented an alternative administrative chart drawn up by Baruch and Hugh Johnson based on their experiences with the War Industries Board. Both the Wallace and the Peek plans provoked argument. The secretary's plan met with the most favor. When the meeting broke up, Roosevelt asked Wallace and Peek to remain behind, and, according to Peek, the president transformed the chart verbally to conform with what he, Peek, had submitted. Since the organization was revised to meet his objections, Peek saw no further reason for his not becoming administrator.[12]

Peek employed the tactics of a battering ram, knowing neither when to commence nor where to go. He was conscious of his abilities and rank and wanted no one to overlook them. He boastfully wrote,

> I entered the Administration on my own terms. I did not want a job or political preferment of any kind. My own salary as administrator of the Agricultural Adjustment Act I turned over to private counsel whom I retained to advise me independently of the A.A.A. counsel—in whom I had no confidence. . . . Through all my life I have been steadfastly against the promotion of planned scarcity. On this point Secretary Wallace and I disagreed sharply while the bill (AAA) was in the making.

Howard Tolley probably was right in characterizing Peek as "a man who liked to order things done."[13]

On May 12, the day the AAA became law, the administrator of the AAA dispatched a letter to Secretary Wallace asking for "a clear understanding and agreement of the broad principles of policy that shall prevail." He advised the secretary that conferences should be held with industries, trades, and agricultural groups before policy details were worked out. He also reminded Wallace that the job of the administrator was such that the authority conferred on him should be as complete as the statute permitted. In short, Peek was asking Wallace to transfer to him the power conferred by the legislature on the secretary, with the understanding that he would serve in the place of the secretary and that there would be continuous collaboration between the two. In case of differences, the president's decision would prevail.

Nor was this all. In the matter of recruiting personnel and building up the staff Peek wanted all appointments to be subject to the approval of the administrator and based on the ability of applicants to perform specific jobs. Preferential treatment was not to be allowed. Peek likewise emphasized the importance of reopening the foreign market to American farm products. "The great purpose" of the AAA in his mind was to increase the net farm income by raising farm prices and using any other means authorized by the law.[14]

Wallace replied to Peek on the very same day he received his letter. The secretary's letter, although restrained, indicated that there were going to be differences of opinion between the two men and that he, Wallace, was not about to divest himself of his responsibilities as secretary of agriculture. He agreed on the need for an understanding of the principles under which the AAA was to be administered, the procedures to be pursued, and on the wisdom of holding conferences with the groups concerned. He likewise made clear "that we ought to undertake acreage reduction in both cotton and corn but the extent to which this ought to go should depend upon the outcome of our various conferences." On the question of foreign trade Wallace reminded Peek that "my views are well known to you. It is my feeling that aside from cotton, we ought not to depend on a foreign market for any considerable outlet of agricultural commodities for some time in the future and that, with this in view, we ought to act for the moment as if we were a self-contained agricultural economy."

Wallace saw no reason why there should not be free and continuous collaboration between him and Peek. But Wallace hastened to add that the AAA placed final responsibility on him and through him to the president. In policy matters they could carry their differences to the president rather than risk serious differences between themselves. Wallace had no desire to hamper Peek as the administrator but he wanted him to understand that "since I am the Secretary of Agriculture, the weight of responsibility and decision must rest largely in my shoulders." Decisions about major appointments were to be made collaboratively. "I should not think of forcing anyone on you to whom you had an objection. At the same time, I should expect that in important decisions you would also consult me when acting."[15]

Charles J. Brand was appointed coadminstrator of the AAA. Brand, a former employee of the USDA and the first chief of the Bureau of Markets, had been the principal architect of the original McNary–Haugen bill and more recently the executive secretary-treasurer of the National Fertilizer Association. He became coadminstrator at the insistence of Wallace and Peek. An able man but inflexible, determined, and domineering, Brand, like Peek, lacked a broad comprehension of the major social, economic, and political issues of the day, and the relationship of the AAA to them.

However, he was viewed as an authority on marketing. Brand did not figure very conspicuously in public matters and held office until October 1933 when he became executive director of the fertilizer code under the AAA.[16]

A major appointment and key figure, and for a time the man second in importance in the USDA, was Rexford G. Tugwell. A prime adviser to Roosevelt in the campaign of 1932 and in the initial stages of the New Deal, Tugwell was a man to reckon with. He was one of the most articulate of the nonagricultural advisers in a department steeped in the agricultural tradition. His was a most unusual appointment in a most unusual period. To say that Tugwell was looked upon with a jaundiced eye in many quarters of the agricultural fraternity is to put it mildly. Often unfairly he became a convenient target for critics of the New Deal policies.

In a department filled with agricultural fundamentalists, Tugwell could not claim the important credential of having graduated from a land-grant college. Still, he was given a position of agricultural power, first as an adviser to the president on agricultural matters, then as assistant secretary, and finally as under-secretary of agriculture before heading the Resettlement Administration. Tugwell also had been one of the three members of the committee—Wallace and M. L. Wilson were the other two—charged with reorganizing the USDA along lines of national planning.[17]

Although it was administratively part of the USDA, the AAA had its own personnel, its own budget, its own legal staff, and its own information service. Mordecai Ezekiel had strongly recommended that the new agency be made a part of the department to avoid the kind of embarrassing situations that had occurred under the Agricultural Marketing Act, when the Federal Farm Board and its agencies formulated independent policies and courses of action. Peek might not have been satisfied with the arrangement, but he liked the idea of heading an agency that in a way was separate within the department.[18]

Once the major appointments had been made, the process of hiring capable and compatible people began. Many people indicated they wanted to work for the AAA. Peek recalled:

> They swarmed in on us for jobs. In two weeks from the time I took office I was told we had about 25,000 applications, some from deserving Democrats and some from Republicans who felt they were more deserving than the Democrats because they had voted Democratic . . . it seems, looking backward, that every applicant must have turned up in person. We paid no attention at all to party lines and Mr. Farley did not interfere with us. Secretary Wallace, Charles J. Brand, . . . and I would not have stood for politics in putting together the service. I do not know to this day how the force was divided politically.[19]

The principle appointments caused no problem. Chester C. Davis, an experienced old-timer in farm activities, an intimate associate of many influential farm leaders, and a close friend of Peek, was made chief of production. Oscar Johnston, the manager at a high salary of a big British-owned plantation in Mississippi, was designated chief of finance. General William I. Westervelt, an executive of Sears, Roebuck and Company, who knew processing and marketing from every angle, was acquainted with government operations, and had had experience here and abroad, became chief of processing and marketing. These men had very substantial upper-middle- or upper-class ties, with strong roots in the commercial, financial, and agricultural communities.[20]

From a policy standpoint the most important of the three men was Davis, who before the year ended was to become the head of the AAA. Davis was a man of considerable experience in areas that helped a public administrator. A native of Iowa and a graduate of Grinnell College in Iowa, Davis had been a newspaper reporter and editor in Redfield, South Dakota, and in the Montana towns of Miles City and Bozeman. Later Davis became the editor of the *Montana Farmer*.[21] In 1921 he left the publishing business to help reorganize the Montana Commission of Agriculture and Labor and to serve as its commissioner until 1925. For a brief period he was the director of marketing for the Illinois Agricultural Association, the state arm of the American Farm Bureau Federation, for which he did some lobbying. He became identified with Peek's theories on agricultural relief, and the two fought for the McNary–Haugen plan. Disillusioned with the Republican nomination of Herbert C. Hoover in 1928, Davis switched to Al Smith and became the "chief thumper for the Brown Derby among the dirt farmers." After the Hoover landslide, Peek, Davis, Frank Lowden, and a number of others "cooled their enthusiasm" by starting the National Cornstalk Process, Inc. to make wallboard out of cornstalks on the basis of processes developed at Iowa State College.[22]

As the depression wore on, Davis abandoned his earlier faith in the McNary–Haugen idea and shifted over to the domestic allotment plan which he believed was better equipped to meet the needs of the farmers. He had the confidence of Wallace, Peek, Wilson, Tolley, and many others in and out of the administration. Davis, a realist, knew how to work with people and make decisions; he was a discerning person who knew what he wanted and could compromise when the occasion demanded. Psychologically and temperamentally he was well equipped for the nerve-wracking pace he was going to pursue.[23]

The AAA had placed Alfred Stedman, a talented newspaperman with good credentials in farm circles and politics, in charge of publicity. As a representative of the *Saint Paul Pioneer Press,* Stedman had been sympathetic with the McNary–Haugen bills and kept abreast of happenings in farm relief. In Washington he came to know all the newspapermen, and important journalists such as Turner Catledge and Felix Belair of the *New York Times*. Stedman proved to be an expert in public relations and in news conferences. "He had a reporter's instinct of nosing around all the time, but not antagonizing anybody. And he was very good in getting people to talk, very good in concealing his sources, or keeping the confidence of people with whom he talked." Stedman also got along well with Wallace, Peek, Davis, and Howard R. Tolley.[24]

Among the others to occupy high positions in the AAA was the well known and highly respected M. L. Wilson, a prime mover behind the drive to make the domestic allotment plan a part of the law, who became chief of the wheat section before going over to the U.S. Department of the Interior for a brief stint as head of the Subsistence Homestead Project. Cully A. Cobb, a southern newspaperman with an extensive background in agricultural activities, headed the cotton section. Professor Albert G. Black, former head of the agricultural economics department at Iowa State College, became chief of the corn-hog section; and Guy C. Shepard, who had been with the Cudahy Packing Company, took charge of the processing end of the same section. Professor Clyde L. King of the University of Pennsylvania headed the dairy section; John B. Hutson, the tobacco section; and Jesse W. Tapp, who in later years was to attain fame in financial circles as chairman of the board of the Bank of America, became chief of the special crops section.[25]

None of these appointments even remotely suggested that the leadership of the AAA had designs on undermining the capitalist system and eliminating profits. As General William I. Westervelt, the chief of processing and marketing, said, "The Agricultural Adjustment Act exists primarily to raise the incomes of the farmers. By its success or failure in accomplishing this objective, it will stand or fall."[26] The key appointments were men with commercial, administrative, and academic backgrounds who believed in the capitalist system.

The backgrounds, philosophies, and associations of the personnel in the offices of General Counsel Jerome Frank and Consumers' Counsel Frederic C. Howe brought these offices into conflict with the administrators of the AAA—first with Peek, and then with Chester Davis. Jerome Frank was a brilliant lawyer and conversationalist whom Peek contemptuously viewed as a collectivist. Peek had little faith in Frank and used his own salary as administrator to hire a private counsel to advise him independently of the AAA counsel.[27]

Frank was born in 1889 in New York, the son of a lawyer who soon moved his family to Chicago where young Frank grew up. In 1909 he received his Ph.B. degree from the University of Chicago and then went on to the University of Chicago Law School where he was judged to be "one of the two brightest students of the pre-war generation." He was graduated in

1912 with Phi Beta Kappa honors and the degree of Doctor of Jurisprudence. That same year he was admitted to the Illinois bar and practiced as a corporation specialist for a law firm of which he was a partner. Frank showed a reformist spirit early. In Chicago he was a member of Mayor William E. Dever's "kitchen cabinet." He helped negotiate the traction settlement for the City of Chicago, and he also did corporate reorganization work for the First National Bank in Chicago where he displayed unusual concern for the small security holder. Among the companies Frank had had a hand in competently liquidating was that of George Peek's Moline Plow Works. In the process he acquired "a reputation for hard work, absent-mindedness and a habit of writing novels that never reached a publisher's office."[28]

In 1929 Frank joined a New York law firm as a partner. One of its members was quoted as saying: "It's worth $50,000 a year to us to have Jerry around just to hear him talk." He had met Felix Frankfurter and now that he was in New York he was to see him oftener; and he came to know other legal luminaries such as Benjamin Cardozo and Morris Cohen. In 1930 Frank had his first book published, *Law and the Modern Mind,* which had been written on trains in his spare time. It dealt with the psychology of individual judges in interpreting what were supposed to have been the "unchangeable rules of law." In the 1920s few judges and lawyers believed that the insights of Sigmund Freud could be applied to the judicial process, and Frank's book attempted to show the utility of Freud. There followed articles in law journals, lectures at the New School for Social Research, and an appointment as a research associate in the Yale Law School in 1932.[29]

Frank was recommended to the administration by Felix Frankfurter, a friend and admirer of the president, as a "lawyer who watches the breadlines more closely than the price-quotations." Against the opposition of James Farley in May 1933, Wallace made Frank general counsel of the AAA, which he held in conjunction with that of general counsel of the Federal Surplus Relief Corporation. Contrary to popular impressions, Rexford Tugwell was not the person who first suggested Frank. "None of them were people I had known before," said Tugwell, "including Frank. I hadn't known him before—never heard of him." However, the two held ideas in common and became closely associated.[30]

Frank in turn was responsible for bringing into the AAA persons such as Lee Pressman and Alger Hiss, who had known each other as members of the Harvard Law Review. Later Nathan Witt, born Wittkowsky, joined the department. It appears that he had been recommended to the authorities by an old school friend of his, Charles Krivitsky, who had joined the consumers' counsel staff late in 1933 and who in 1935 changed his name to Kramer. John Abt, another lawyer and graduate of the University of Chicago, joined the AAA in 1933.

Alger Hiss, a native of Baltimore, gained greater prominence after he left the AAA. He was born on November 11, 1904. A political science major at Johns Hopkins University where he graduated in 1926 as a member of Phi Beta Kappa, Hiss entered the Harvard Law School. There he attracted the attention of Felix Frankfurter. Frankfurter was so impressed with Hiss that he recommended him for the much coveted post as secretary to Supreme Court Justice Oliver Wendell Holmes. After practicing law in Boston and New York, Hiss accepted a position first as an assistant and then assistant general counsel of the AAA where his duties brought him into close contact with the Senate Agriculture Committee. Two senators on the latter committee were also members of the committee headed by Senator Gerald P. Nye investigating the munitions traffic. At their request, Hiss on July 30, 1934 became legal assistant to the Nye committee. He lent his services at first and continued to be paid by the AAA until 1935, at which time he resigned from the department and went on the committee's payroll.[31]

Lee Pressman, who, according to Gardner Jackson of the office of consumers' counsel, had "an abnormal domination on the personal level over Jerome Frank," also "had a very pronounced focus on the dispossessed of our country in agriculture, and elsewhere, but agriculture primarily." Jackson said,

> Pressman grabbed on to me as a useful companion. . . . Our first get-together was on the lowly agricultural workers which he espoused to beat hell. He worked like a Trojan, particularly in the sugar thing, then out in the onion fields in Ohio . . . we were together a great deal. On almost all the milk hearings I went to Lee Pressman was the representative of the legal division.[32]

Years later Pressman admitted before a house committee that he had joined a Communist group in 1934 but that he had given up all active participation the following year. He had been asked to join by Harold Ware and named three others in the department—Witt, Kramer, and Abt—as members of this same group. He said that Alger Hiss was not a member of this group.[33]

The position of consumers' counsel, whose task it was to protect the consumers from exhorbitant price increases, went to Frederic C. Howe, "a lawyer, public servant, reformer" and peripatetic scholar. A native of Meadville, Pennsylvania and the son of a local furniture manufacturer, Howe was born on November 21, 1867 and reared in a narrow Methodist society. He was educated at Allegheny College, graduating in 1889, and Johns Hopkins, receiving his Ph.D. in 1892. He also studied law abroad at the University of Halle, and in the United States. After preparing himself for the legal profession, he settled in 1894 in Cleveland and joined the law firm of Harry and James Garfield, the sons of the former president. However, Howe's Methodist-Quaker background prevented him from taking the legal profession too seriously; and he performed public services, social settlement work, the secretaryship of the municipal association, and a city councilmanship (1901–1903). He was greatly influenced by the reform mayor of Cleveland, Tom L. Johnson, and was converted to the single-tax views of Henry George.

Before coming to the AAA in 1933, Howe served in the Ohio State Senate and on the Cleveland Tax Commission; he authored books on taxation and municipal reforms in the United States and abroad; he headed the People's Institute, a cultural project in New York City; he served as Commissioner of Immigration for the Port of New York from 1914 to 1919; he espoused the Plumb Plan which called for the public ownership and management of railroads; he helped the Brotherhood of Locomotive Engineers form a cooperative bank in Cleveland; he advocated the building of a cooperative society; he became the research assistant of Senator Robert La Follette in the presidential campaign of 1924; and he directed "The School of Opinion" on Nantucket Island. Roosevelt's election in 1932 helped bring Howe back into public life where his views coincided to a great extent with those of Tugwell, Frank, and even Henry A. Wallace.[34]

Another member of the Howe group was Gardner Jackson, the son of wealthy parents, who was given to fighting the battles of the underdog. His father was William S. Jackson, the builder of the Denver and Rio Grande Railroad and at one time the largest landowner in Colorado and New Mexico. Young Jackson graduated from Harvard in 1921 and, while a reporter for the *Boston Globe,* he became interested in the case of Nicola Sacco and Bartolomeo Vanzetti, the two immigrant Italian anarchists charged the previous year with murdering a payroll guard during a holdup in South Braintree, Massachusetts. Convinced that the two men were being tried primarily for their political beliefs, Jackson resigned from the newspaper to join in their defense. Jackson joined other causes as well, such as the defense of Tom Mooney in California, the bonus army of the early depression years, the defense of interracial harmony, and protection of tenants and sharecroppers in the South.[35]

The office of the consumers' counsel was headed by Howe and staffed by men such as Jackson and Donald Blaisdell, an able economist who had written a Ph.D. dissertation at Columbia on the Federal Trade Commission. These men took seriously their assignment to protect the interests of the consumers, and they enjoyed close rapport with Jerome Frank and his legal staff. This formidable alignment first rankled George Peek and then Chester Davis. "Fred Howe was an economist and . . . quite a different person than I had visualized," said Mordecai Ezekiel. "He made it a sort of propaganda, agitating things, quite different from what I had in mind—he and Donald Blaisdell and Gardner Jackson. It developed into a sort of crusading group, but, in some respects operating to make sure that the process didn't impinge on the consumer too much."[36]

In every large department such as the USDA—which at the time was becoming the largest agency, if it was not already *the* largest, in the government—groupings of one kind or another are bound to emerge. In the 1930s these groupings were the result of personal relationships that had developed over the years or were the result of similar ideological beliefs. In the beginning, personal loyalties probably were more important in forging and holding groups together than ideological beliefs.

One of the groups was headed by Henry A. Wallace, who, because of his position as secretary of agriculture, his personal qualities, and his beliefs, attracted followers. Members of the Wallace group included M. L. Wilson, who believed in the AAA program and worked hard to make it the law; Howard R. Tolley, who years later admitted: "I belonged to that group if I belonged to any"; Albert G. Black, a student of John D. Black at Minnesota and a Wallace man "from the start to finish"; and Chester C. Davis, a former farm journalist, a McNary-Haugen battle horse, a superb farm lobbyist, the first production chief of the AAA and then its administrator.

Still other members of the Wallace group were Mordecai Ezekiel, an old employee of the department, an economist of the Federal Farm Board, one of the architects of the AAA law, and of late the economic adviser to the secretary; Louis H. Bean, the Russian-born economist with a graduate degree from Harvard, able and academic in manner, on whom Wallace relied for mathematical and economic advice; Paul Appleby, the executive secretary of Wallace, the son of a Congregational minister, a graduate of Grinnell College, and former editor and publisher of farm journals in Montana, Iowa, and Virginia; and C. "Beanie" (for Benham) Baldwin, the son of a Radford, Virginia flour miller, a former student at Virginia Polytechnic Institute and holder of an administrative position with the Norfolk and Western Railroad, a bankrupt electrical supplies businessman, and a close friend of Appleby, who had secured for him the job on Wallace's staff.[37]

Several things stand out about this group. Five of them—Wallace, Wilson, Black, Davis, and Paul Appleby—had strong ties with Iowa. The first three—Wallace, Wilson, and Black—had been identified with Iowa State College as students or faculty members, and the last two—Davis and Appleby—were graduates of Grinnell College. Apart from their Iowa backgrounds they were known to each other personally or professionally as a result of their many years of identification with agriculture as journalists, educators, practical farmers, or employees of the Department of Agriculture. Tolley, Ezekiel, and Bean had been employees of the USDA for many

JOHN D. BLACK. Professor of Economics at Harvard, 1927–1956. A distinguished agricultural economist. *USDA Photograph*

PAUL APPLEBY. Assistant to the Secretary of Agriculture, 1933–1940. Under Secretary of Agriculture, 1940–1944. *Franklin D. Roosevelt Library*

R. M. "SPIKE" EVANS. Special Assistant to the Secretary of Agriculture, 1936–1938. Administrator of the AAA, 1938–1942. *Franklin D. Roosevelt Library*

MORDECAI EZEKIEL. Economic Adviser to the Secretary of Agriculture, 1933–1944. *Franklin D. Roosevelt Library*

GARDNER JACKSON. Staff of the Consumers' Council, AAA, 1933–1935. Representative of the Southern Tenant Farmers' Union in Washington, D.C., 1935–1940. *Franklin D. Roosevelt Library*

HENRY MORGENTHAU, JR. Governor of the Farm Credit Administration, 1933. Secretary of the Treasury, 1934–1945. *Franklin D. Roosevelt Library*

EDWIN G. NOURSE. Director of the Institute of Economics of the Brookings Institution, 1929–1942

GEORGE W. PEEK. Administrator of the AAA, May–December 1933. Special Advisor to the President on Foreign Trade and President of the Export-Import Bank, December 1933–December 1935. *USDA Photograph*

HOWARD R. TOLLEY. Head of the Program Planning Division, AAA, 1933–1935. Administrator of the AAA, 1936–1938. Chief of the Bureau of Agricultural Economics, 1938–1946.

REXFORD G. TUGWELL. Assistant Secretary of Agriculture, 1933–1934. Under Secretary of Agriculture, 1934–1936. Administrator of the U.S. Resettlement Administration, 1935–1936. *Franklin D. Roosevelt Library*

CLAUDE R. WICKARD. Assistant Chief and Chief of the Corn and Hogs Section, AAA, 1933–1936. Assistant Director and Director of the North Central Division, AAA, 1937–1940. Under Secretary of Agriculture, February–August 1940. Secretary of Agriculture, 1940–1945. *Franklin D. Roosevelt Library*

HENRY A. WALLACE. Secretary of Agriculture, 1933–1940. *Franklin D. Roosevelt Library*

M. L. WILSON. Chief of the Wheat Production Section, AAA, May–September 1933. Director of the Division of Subsistence Homesteads, Department of the Interior, September 1933–June 1934. Assistant Secretary of Agriculture, 1934–1937. Under Secretary of Agriculture, 1937–1940. Director of Extension Service, 1940–1953. *Franklin D. Roosevelt Library*

years—Tolley since 1916, Ezekiel since 1919, and Bean since 1923. If anything held them together it was their personal friendships that had been built up through the years and their efforts to better the social and economic lot of the farmer. Although the label "agrarian" conveniently describes the members of this group, on occasion Wallace, Tolley, and others could stray away from the agrarian mold.

Agricultural fundamentalism, the credo with which the followers of Wallace were rightfully or wrongfully associated, was a carry-over from the days when the majority of the nation's population was rural and worked on farms. Henry A. Wallace, though basically an agricultural fundamentalist, was perhaps not as zealous as his father and grandfather. They believed, as did the overwhelming majority of the farmers, that a healthy and prosperous agriculture generated action, income, and wealth for farmers and nonfarmers alike; a nonprosperous agriculture meant debt and a decline in the purchasing power of the farmers, likewise an inability on the part of industry to sell its products, and consequently layoffs and depression. Someone, said Tolley, compiled statistics to show that the national income was seven times the agricultural income of the United States and that if the farm income was kept high the national income would customarily be seven times higher.[38]

Coupled with this was another attitude. Many and perhaps most, but not necessarily all, agriculturalists who had been trained in land-grant colleges had been inclined "to look with jaundiced eye upon anyone of other training and experience who [was] thrust by circumstance into a position of agricultural power." This might have been a defense mechanism and a retaliation against the general contempt visited upon agricultural students and professors in the early days of the land-grant college movement. "The agricultural profession," wrote Russell Lord, "has formed, in less active measure, its own standards, its own defense and pride."[39] Certainly, if others deeply rooted in the agrarian tradition reflected this land-grant college attitude, Henry A. Wallace exhibited little or none of it.

A second but a shorter-lived group was that headed by George Peek. Peek had been identified with Bernard Baruch and Hugh Johnson back in World War I days as a member of the War Industries Board, and he never forgot those associations and experiences. Given his way he probably would have depended greatly on the advice of Baruch, Frank Lowden, and Johnson, but he never had the free hand he craved. Chester C. Davis, who became a very strong supporter of Wallace, was to a very considerable extent Peek's disciple as well as his successor in the AAA. Other ostensible followers of Peek were Frederick P. Lee, who played a big role in drafting the first AAA, Glenn McHugh, General William I. Westervelt, Charles J. Brand, Adlai Stevenson, and others. Peek was business oriented, antireformist, a hard and fast believer in the protective tariff and the need for reopening the foreign market for farm products as quickly as possible. He insisted that the marketing agreement (instead of the acreage control) feature was the most important part of the AAA. Coupled with these beliefs was an aggressive manner that displayed nothing but contempt for those who were critical of wasteful competition and excessive profits and placed their faith in a planned economy and a farmer-labor coalition.[40]

A third group comprised followers of Rexford Tugwell and Jerome Frank, both of whom were bright and antiagricultural fundamentalists, more urban than rural in orientation, and known as "urban liberals" for the want of a more accurate label. Consumers' Counsel Frederic C. Howe, Gardner Jackson, Alger Hiss, Lee Pressman, and Francis J. Shea were in this group. Frank, according to Tugwell, "brought in Pressman and Hiss, Shea, and the whole bunch. . . . They were mostly young lawyers that he'd known in New York." Tugwell brought in people that were largely from Columbia University. These included Donald Blaisdell, redheaded Fred Bartlett, and Gardner C. Means, who with Adolf A. Berle, Jr., had co-authored *The Modern Corporation and Private Property*.[41]

Sometimes these people worked on committees in the Department of Agriculture where, M. L. Wilson said,

> They didn't mix too well. The people who were on the Departmental committees . . . had a great deal of experience in these fields and knew a great deal about the actual situation at the local level, whereas the people that Rex [Tugwell] brought in were mostly people . . . who had not had either administrative experience nor much concrete knowl-edge—down-to-earth knowledge of things they were dealing with.

Jerome Frank's ideas were catalyzed after a conference with Tugwell. Some years later Gardner Jackson recalled, "I think that the Tugwell–Frank combination is where the real decisive affirmation of ideas and steps to be taken was made."[42]

The Tugwell–Frank group believed that the time was ripe for social and economic changes. They were critical and unsympathetic with marketing agreements on the theory that they were primarily for the benefit of the businessmen, the processors, and the distributors. However, the AAA people, those handling the individual commodities, saw marketing agreements in a more encouraging light. The AAA tried to negotiate an agreement

> which began with the producers, and had visible and tangible results in it for the producer. They were taking care of other things so that the processor and marketer got their cut, but they didn't get the entire cut. The legal question that Jerome Frank was . . . raising was that we must see the books, and essentially we must fix profits and fix the terms of competition.[43]

Personalities played a part in the growing rivalry. Tugwell, a handsome, well-tailored man with a good mind, had a way of irritating farm people. He was impatient with getting reforms through. He assumed that because his father was in the cannery business near Buffalo and he himself had worked in a canning factory and had relations with the fruit growers there, and because he taught "a kind of course in agricultural economics" at Columbia University, he knew a great deal about agriculture and what was wrong with it. But the truth of the matter was that Tugwell had few close associations with farmers in the South and the Middle West where the maladjustments were the greatest, or, for that matter, with those who had been working to better the lot of these people. To many of them he was a stranger in power. Tugwell also was irritated "by the stupidity of the other side." He tended to be cynical, unwittingly making cutting remarks. Farmer representatives who met him often were irritated with him. He frequently left them with a feeling that he did not intend to convey.[44]

Jerome Frank had many things in common with Tugwell in his economic philosophy and personality, but he also was different in certain ways. Frank did not get along with "the AAA boys." M. L. Wilson, generally known for his genial and compromising spirit, commented:

> Jerome Frank was a bright person, a brilliant and aggressive person, a city person—a person that had a great deal of self-assurance, a person that liked an argument, that talked very easily and very fast, and didn't have too much patience with the person who wasn't smart enough to keep up and be convinced by him.
>
> He was a much higher-geared person than Rex Tugwell. He talked faster, he moved faster, he argued more persistently. He was pretty serious about it all. Rex Tugwell kind of joked and laughed, and even kind of smiled. He wasn't a continuous kind of talker. His conversations and relations with people didn't backstop, and he didn't backstop, but he didn't just step out and push the other fellow off the sidewalk if he differed with his argument. That's Frank—he did. He was born that way, couldn't help but be that way. And that kind of personality wouldn't click at all with the farm boys—very different background, very different point of view.
>
> Jerome Frank had nothing to do with farmers, knew nothing about farmers, knew nothing about farm folkways or anything of that kind.[45]

Apart from personal friendships, loyalties, and common ideologies, other groupings formed that pitted old-line members of the USDA against "the AAA boys." This was inevitable.

Launching the AAA Programs

THE MOST PUBLICIZED OF THE COMMODITY PROGRAMS were those for cotton, corn-hogs, wheat, dairy products, and tobacco. Rice, although important to those who raised it, never aroused as much public interest as did most other commodities in the original programs. The challenge faced by the New Dealers became clearer as the wheels of the administration turned, as the implementation of the various programs began, and as friends and foes watched for results.

The cotton program was the first to be launched because the cotton South contained one-third of the farm population of the country, and nearly 2 million families staked their livelihoods on the staple. Prices averaged 5.7 cents a pound in 1932 and fell to as low as 4.6 cents; and a bale of cotton in 1932 bought about half as many goods as from 1909 to 1914. Worse still, a surplus of twenty-six million bales was on hand, and the pressure to plow cotton under had been mounting.[1]

The head of the cotton section of the AAA was Cully A. Cobb. At one point he had been a serious contender for appointment as secretary of agriculture. A native of Prospect, Tennessee, the son of a preacher, and a graduate of Mississippi A & M, Cobb had been a boys' club teacher, an employee of the Agricultural Extension Service, a high school teacher of agriculture, president and editor of the *Southern Ruralist,* and coeditor of the Georgia–Alabama edition of the *Progressive Farmer.* He felt that the Negro should have been moving along better than he had, but was not rabid on the subject. Cobb was criticized for being a conservative, one-idea man; but M. L. Wilson believed Cobb had a better grasp of conditions in the South than some of his critics. He was concerned with the problems of labor, tenancy, old age, insecurity, health, education, and related problems. Another observer saw a good deal of the revivalist in Cobb, who, when he addressed an audience, would do some weeping on the side "just like an old preacher would do it, and then blow his nose."[2]

Launching the cotton program was complicated by the fact that half the acreage had been planted when the AAA became law on May 12, 1933 and differences prevailed over what to do and how to do it. Wallace had been empowered to do as he saw fit. He believed that the farmers had to produce for a market that existed in the present. To do this, farmers had to have the necessary machinery at their disposal. With this view in mind he decided to plow up cotton in 1933 and withdraw land from cultivation in 1934 and 1935.

News of Wallace's decision revived old fears in both the processors and the growers. The processors complained that it would place cotton at a competitive disadvantage, would create price differentials, and would divert much of the bag business from cotton to paper and jute. They felt it would take business away from the ginners of cotton, the factors, exporters, brokers, and cottonseed millers, increase unemployment, displace tenant families, and stimulate cotton production abroad to compensate for what American growers did not produce. AAA officials countered these charges by saying that the U.S. foreign market could not be damaged because the United States had large stocks on hand to meet unusual requirements when and if needed. The nation enjoyed advantages in cotton production that a temporary reduction in output could not destroy, and the reduction program would end when the foreign demand increased and the carry-over from past years had declined to normal levels. Cotton growers in the Southeast believed the AAA would work to the advantage of the farmers of the Southwest. They blamed overproduction on the growers of the Southwest whose fertile soil and technological advances had spurred them on to larger production, while the poorer soils of the growers in the Southeast kept theirs down. Dairy farmers, too, were worried that the cotton growers might use lands taken out of cotton production for raising dairy products, whose volume had already increased during the 1920s and early 1930s.[3]

Meanwhile, AAA officials busied themselves trying to get as many cotton farmers as possible to sign government contracts. Wallace, Tugwell, Davis, and others in the USDA and the AAA had a better appreciation of the difficulties that were in store for them, and were not the naive simpletons many of their critics tried to make them out to be. It was a matter of acting quickly, decisively, and massively. Any action, even the wrong action, was better than prolonged debate, indecision, and no action.[4]

Roughly, the aim of the AAA was to remove 10 million acres or about 3 million bales from cultivation in 1933 at a cost of $110 million or at about $11 per acre. Contract signers also were given options to buy government-owned cotton at 6 cents a pound in amounts equal to the estimated yields of the land they retired, which meant an opportunity for them to make 4 cents a pound if their options were called for at 10 cents a pound. This, besides rewarding those who cooperated with the government to reduce cultivated acreage, was also aimed to make it difficult for those who refused to curtail their acreage and tried to profit at the expense of neighbors who curtailed theirs.

A farmer who signed a government contract was required to state how much cotton he had planted in 1933 and if it was of "good, fair, or poor quality." He had to state whether his land was fertilized, and if so, give the approximate amount of fertilizer used per acre; record the yield for 1932, where his cotton was ginned, and to whom it was sold; and, assuming that conditions were normal, estimate the amount of lint cotton he might reasonably expect to harvest per acre from his planted acreage in 1933. On a map on the back of his contract, the farmer had to indicate the acres he would take out of production. He further had to agree not to use more fertilizer on the remaining acres than he had used in 1932 and promise, pending an investigation by the secretary of agriculture, that his offer would remain irrevocable until July 31, 1933. Under the plan, farmers were eligible whether they owned the land they farmed or rented it on a cash, share, or other basis. No grower was to take less than 25 or more than 50 percent of his cotton acreage out of production unless he had the approval of the state director of extension, approval that was unlikely to be given.[5]

Obviously this was an enormous undertaking. Some 22,000 local workers were mobilized in 955 counties to help farmers sign contracts. Schools of instruction were held for the workers in many places before the sign-up campaign began. A schedule of news releases was worked out with some 654 daily and 3,500 weekly newspapers and farm magazines, and radio addresses were arranged for delivery over national and local stations. Members of the business community, professional men, and officials of the state cotton cooperatives took active parts in the sign-up campaign. The campaign originally was to end on July 8, but owing to unexpected delays the closing date was extended to July 12, and then to July 19.[6]

The goal had been to take no less than 10 million acres or about 3 million bales of cotton out of production, but roughly 10,400,000 acres, or approximately 4,400,000 bales, were removed. Manufacturers' reports showed that the total sales of fertilizers in the cotton states during June and July 1933 were up over sales for the same months of 1932 by an insignificant 5,126 tons, which indicated the growers were fulfilling their agreements not to use more fertilizers. Slightly more than 1 million contracts, representing 98.5 percent of the total offers, were approved for payment during 1933; and 572,000, or about 56 percent, of these called for cash benefits and options. The obtainable revenue from the processing tax was easy to forecast, steady in volume, inexpensive to collect, and difficult to evade. The tax applied only to the portion of the product consumed at home, did not penalize the exporter, exempted the farmer on the foods he processed for his own use, and was adjustable to changing market conditions. One of the desirable features of the plan, in theory, was that it was designed to control the domestic price of cotton without prejudicing the position of cotton on the world market. It differed from the normal dumping operation in that it was accompanied by acreage reduction.[7]

Unfortunately, the exceptionally favorable weather that brought higher than expected cotton yields, combined with a drop in farm prices after July, a rise in the prices of the goods the farmers had to buy, and delays in sending out benefit payments to the cooperating farmers, sowed the seeds of unrest. Governors in the South reacted to these unexpected developments by asking the president to inflate the currency, suspend the payment of the processing tax, and place a minimum of twenty cents a pound on cotton. But Roosevelt chose, instead, the path of the "professional cotton politician"; he offered the cotton growers a loan of ten cents a pound on their current crop if they would agree to reduce their acreage in 1934 from 35 to 45 percent of the average of the past five years, and to 25 percent in 1935.[8]

The AAA appeared to have learned little from the sad experiences of the Federal Farm Board, which in 1932 offered to lend the producers more than the market value of their cotton. The New Dealers also believed conditions were different now. Under the farm board, loans had been made when prices were declining, with the expectation of halting further declines; but Congress had never given the board the power to force cotton growers to reduce their acreage before granting them loans. In the fall of 1933, however, the government anticipated a rise in prices by lending farmers money on their cotton crops; in fact, prices had advanced by more than 50 percent since the beginning of 1933. More than 4 million bales of cotton had been plowed under, plans for drastic reductions in 1934 and 1935 had been made, the administration was thinking of manipulating the currency with the hope of raising the general price level, and business in general seemed to be recovering. The average price of seven-eighths-inch middling cotton was about ten cents a pound when the loan policy was adopted. Prices had been advancing steadily, then fell, and did not reach the loan value again until mid-January 1934.[9]

Views on the success of the loan program varied. Many held that the ten-cent loan was a success because it enabled farmers to hold their cotton and benefit from the acreage reduction program, the drought, and related factors. Others believed it was anything but a success. Even though cotton prices were about twelve and a half cents a pound from February until July 31, 1934, when the loans were due, the nation still had large quantities of the staple on hand. About $160 million had been lent the producers on about 4.3 million bales of cotton; and at the start of the 1934–1935 marketing season, the government still held about 3 million bales, which was slightly less than the peak holdings of the Federal Farm Board.[10]

By late fall 1933 many processors, middlemen, and other nonfarming groups expressed unhappiness with the cotton program, but fewer complaints were heard from the cotton growers than from the corn-hog farmers and the dairymen. The cotton farmers in November 1933 were getting three and four cents a pound more for their crop than in the previous year, which was fairly good despite the rise in costs. The farmers also got, or were about to get, almost $110 million from the government for reducing their acreage, and they were eligible for government loans on cotton at ten cents a pound.[11]

The dilemma of the corn-hog producers in the Middle West whose hogs reached the markets in large numbers in late May, all of June, and early July at least was equally, if not more, complicated. The weather had been hot, and the storage holdings in fresh pork were increasing rapidly, while the consumer demand had slackened. More distressing was that the corn-hog farmers were unorganized and without a workable program to submit to the administration.[12]

The real beginning in developing a corn-hog program came with the joint discussions of the National Corn-Hog Committee of Twenty-five and officials of the AAA in July, and with the appointment of Albert G. Black as the acting head of the corn-hog section. Owing to the lateness in the season and the anticipated short crop, an emergency program to destroy a portion of the corn crop was unnecessary, but immediate action had to be taken to raise the price of hogs, which had dropped to the lowest level in fifty years.

Two billion pounds of pork were to be removed from the market in 1933–1934 in the following fashion: sell or dispose of to relief agencies such as the Federal Emergency Relief Administration (FERA), with the understanding that the normal purchases of the processors would not be curtailed; convert low-grade hogs and hog products into tankage and lard, and, if necessary, into soap; and increase exports. This program was expected to eliminate 1.8 million pounds in pork, or about 16 percent of the prospective supply, from the normal market and boost the price for the season from 25 to 30 percent. George Peek expected this to bring the hog farmers fully $40 million in additional income over the next several weeks.[13]

Existing machinery was used to place the program into operation. The key to the plan was the contract between the individual packers and the secretary of agriculture that prescribed the conditions under which the packers were to purchase and process the pigs and sows. Only pigs in good health, showing normal growth and no body deformities, were to be accepted, while those of inferior quality were to be purchased at a heavy discount. Inspectors of the USDA and the Bureau of Plant Industry (BPI) decided on the eligibility of the pigs and sows, aided in the buying, supervised the processing, and certified the purchases of the packers, who were reimbursed for the animals purchased and processed. The prices paid by the government were at least double the market price for pigs of compact weight—in fact, an allowance more than double the price was made for the below-average hogs bought during the campaign.[14]

Critics of the emergency hog slaughter were legion. Some denounced it as "pig infanticide" and others as "a birth control program designed for pigs." Still others decried the needless slaughter when so many American families went without meat for most of the year. Some conjured up fears of a pig famine in the immediate future. Farmers who originally welcomed the idea of adjusting production to demand became disenchanted with the complex methods used in placing the program in operation. Texans were irritated when they were excluded from the emergency program because the hogs in their area were in short supply. Newspapers in Saint Louis and Saint Joseph, Missouri, carried false stories of thousands of pigs being dumped into the Missouri River. An Oklahoman advised Wallace that the elimination of garbage feeding of hogs would be more effective in solving the surplus than the killing off of 5 million pigs. Hog producers also complained about speculators, who conspired with terminal market agencies, obtaining permits for the shipment of hogs that farmers themselves were unable to obtain, thus forcing them to dispose of their hogs through the speculators at appreciably lower prices.[15]

Both the processing tax and the processing of hogs posed problems. Ordinarily most processors cured and processed their hams and bacon, but owing to the uncertainty and fears that a heavy tax would be imposed on all pork supplies on hand when the program went into effect, the processors were motivated to sell as much of their production as possible "in the green or raw state" before the tax was imposed. When it came to the processing of hogs, the packers, who originally calculated they would be exempt from the hour limitations of the packers' code (and estimated the number of hogs they could process on this basis), learned that the National Recovery Administration (NRA) would not make an exception for them. The packers, as a consequence, radically reduced the number of hogs they were willing to process; and for a time it appeared as though the emergency program was likely to fail.[16]

The emergency slaughter program was a real challenge to the packers. It was difficult, if not impossible, for them to change the usual packinghouse operations under such short notice for a short-run emergency slaughter program. Pigs under seventy pounds rarely were processed because the packinghouses lacked the needed equipment to handle lightweights. The drought in many states had reduced feed supplies to the point where the smaller animals were mostly skin and bones. Hence pigs weighing less than seventy pounds were converted into grease and fertilizer.[17] More than four-fifths of the 6.5 million pigs and sows purchased by the government during the first program came from the corn-belt states.

On the whole, the products of the corn-hog program were handled sagaciously. More than 1 million pounds of dry salt pork were turned over to the FERA and distributed by February 1, 1934; 22 million pounds of grease were sold through the regular channels of trade late in 1933 at twenty-six cents a pound; and some 12,000 tons of the tank residue were converted into fertilizer tankage. The lard—the most important of the remaining by-products—was kept by the packers, who credited the government for it at the rate of thirty-five cents a pound.[18]

The second emergency hog program had the purpose of supporting prices until such time as the market supplies were reduced through the purchase of 2 million hogs between November 1933 and September 1934, to be processed and distributed to families on relief rolls. In fact, more than 35 million pounds of commercial cuts and nearly 24 million pounds of lard were bought between January 31 and July 19, 1934, for distribution to needy families through the Federal Emergency Relief Corporation (FERC), a subsidiary of the FERA that had been set up for that purpose. Although the AAA gave roughly $1 million for the purchase of pork products for those on relief, its main objective was to relieve the market of excessive supplies, not to dispense relief. Officials of the AAA believed a reasonable quantity of such purchases would help support hog prices, but were skeptical of the wisdom of making relief purchases a key effort.[19]

Evaluating the effects of the emergency campaigns is difficult. The AAA was unable to find a feasible means of raising hog prices in 1933 because of the limited time at its disposal. The increase of $22 million in income gained by the sale of pigs and the receipt of bonus payments on animals sold during the emergency campaign constituted but 10 percent of the gross income of the hog producers, but it was 10 percent more than in 1932. The administration held from the start that the emergency hog-marketing program, the purchase of pork for relief, and the corn-loan programs were temporary expedients aimed to stabilize and, if possible, raise the price of corn and hogs until supplies were brought under control. But the administration also maintained that in the long run the emergency measures would do the producers more harm than good unless they were succeeded immediately by a more permanent program to control production.[20]

Literally thousands of suggestions were received and considered in deciding on a permanent program in the belief that the plan, to be workable, had to come from the corn-hog growers themselves and had to benefit all groups. The decision to reduce the production of corn and hogs promised to strike directly at the adjustment problem. The price relationship between corn and hogs would remain at a level where the value of approximately ten to twelve bushels of corn would be equal to the value of 100 pounds of live hog.[21]

This dual-control system, that is, reducing both the production of corn and hogs, posed problems. It involved determining by what percentage corn and hogs were to be reduced, and setting up the administrative means of reporting the past production records of the farmers, and deciding whether farmers complied with their contracts. There also was the question of adequate finance and deciding how the benefit payments were going to be divided between the two commodities to ensure that the program would be attractive to the farmer who raised many hogs and little corn.[22]

It was agreed that the production of corn should be reduced by some 600 million bushels in 1934; but a dispute arose over the methods of curtailing the production of hogs. The two big issues were: (1) the availability of accurate records of the individual farmer's production in past years to determine what his production should be; and (2) deciding whether the individual farmer actually reduced his production as he had agreed.[23]

The main features of the permanent corn-hog program were made public in the fall of 1933. The producer, under the terms of his contract, was to reduce his corn acreage by not less than 20 percent nor more than 30 percent of his 1932–1933 acreage, and to reduce the number of hogs farrowed and produced for market by 25 percent. Acres under contract to the government were to be used only for planting additional pasture, soil improvement, and unharvested crops to prevent erosion. Finally, the producer had to refrain from increasing the total production of basic commodities, feed crops, or feeder pigs.[24] In return, the government agreed to pay the farmer a corn reduction payment of 30 cents a bushel at set intervals on the estimated yield of the acres rented to him, and a hog reduction fee of five dollars a head on 75 percent of the farmer's base period production.

Announcement of the corn-hog program and the contractual provisions brought a reaction from the dairy and cattle producers, in particular, who feared that unless restrictions were placed on the contracted acres used for hay and pasture, there would be a sharp increase in the production of beef and dairy products.

Even more crucial was the relationship between the landlord and tenant under the program. Some believed that the corn-hog tenant, who was the actual producer, was entitled to more benefits than the landlord, but others felt that it would be difficult to get landlords to cooperate unless the contract was made more attractive to them. The tenant got all the benefit payments under the cash lease, while under the share lease the landlord got the same proportion of the payment as he got of corn and hogs. Changes in the lease that would give the landlord more of the benefits than he was entitled to were not permitted.[25]

Putting the plan into operation proved a more complicated and time-consuming task than had been expected. Much time was spent in establishing corn-hog control associations that reached down to the grass roots, in obtaining contracts, and in adjusting claims. Much of the work of obtaining almost 1.2 million contracts fell on the county agents and committeemen, who endured long delays before they could complete the contracts. Time was lost checking with nonresident landlords, obtaining adequate records, deciding on questions and problems relating to state and federal headquarters, and receiving answers, intepretations, and rulings.

Even more vexing was the delay in making benefit payments. The hope at first was that some of the initial installments would be on their way to the farmers by December 1933, but these deliveries did not reach their peak until September 1934. The second payments, scheduled for November 15, 1934, were made mostly in January 1935, and the third in March and April of 1935.[26]

Contracts that overstated or falsified the base period production, if not corrected, would defeat the acreage reduction program and penalize the producer who submitted an honest report. Some of the overstating was unintentional because few farmers kept good records of their farm business. Most records, if kept at all, were inadequate. On the other hand, it was financially more advantageous to report a higher than a lower base period, and it was natural for farmers to report the highest figure they could remember. Most knew the size of their farms and the size of the fields they planted in corn in 1932 and 1933. Their 1933 acreage could be checked, if necessary, against the stubble in the fields. Unfortunately, a comparable check could not be made on the number of litters farrowed or the hogs raised for market in 1933; hence the reported base period of production for hogs was expected to be in greater error. Most of the needed information was drawn from the files of the USDA, the state census or tax assessment figures, and the U.S. Census for 1930. The establishment of quotas became the responsibility of the Division of Crop and Livestock Estimates in the Bureau of Agricultural Economics.[27]

Announcements of the county quotas in May and June 1934 brought a storm of protests from farmers and committeemen, who denied the implications of "padding." Some county committeemen, believing this was merely the beginning of "a horse trade," demanded increases in their quotas. The more rebellious organized protest meetings to which committeemen from neighboring counties were invited, called on their congressmen to use their influence in obtaining concessions, and appealed to Wallace through the American Farm Bureau Federation.

Many, but not all, of the extension supervisors tended to support the farmers. The supervisors were skeptical of the statistical procedures used in arriving at the quotas and feared they would jeopardize the extension program if they failed to support the producers, as did the county agents, who also tended to see things from the perspective of the farmers. Much was learned from these pioneering efforts in uncovering overstatements. Most, if not all, overstatements were removed without penalizing the producers whose claims were correct. About 1.1 million farmers, representing perhaps not more than 25 percent of all farmers growing corn and 60 to 70 percent of those farrowing hogs, signed agreements. Corn and hog growers in every one of the forty-eight states participated, ranging in number from seven in Maine and ten in Rhode Island to almost 121,000 in Illinois and more than 173,000 in Iowa. As might be expected, the most prominent part was played by the large producers. More than 85 percent of the corn-growing land under contract was in the corn-belt states.[28]

The attempt to resolve the problems of the cotton and corn-hog producers brought new problems to the surface that focused on the shortcomings of the AAA, and indicated that these initial efforts were inadequate. Still, the AAA, with all its limitations, furnished a ray of hope for the larger and middle-class farmers who once feared extinction, and for the cotton tenants and sharecroppers who, for the most part, were ignored. The benefit payments were welcomed by all producers; in fact many felt they were being compensated for participating in the formulation and guidance of farm programs. The methods, practices, and administrative techniques of the AAA were born in an agricultural society that was giving way to the traditions, customs, and folkways of an urban-industrial society.

The wheat program had been thought out more thoroughly than the program for almost every other commodity because of the preliminary work of M. L. Wilson, Mordecai Ezekiel, and the early appointment of A. J. Weaver of the Federal Farm Board, and C. C. Conser, a Montana farmer and stockman, to the wheat section. A detailed plan of field operations, including provisions for wheat production control associations and local responsibility, had been worked out a year before the AAA became law.[29]

Haste, however, seemed unnecessary. The wheat crop of 1933 was the smallest on record since 1894; most American wheat was sown in the fall, and the spring and summer months gave the administration time to organize the reduction programs.[30] Plans to curtail the output in 1933 were shelved, but owing to bumper European harvests, the crops of 1934 and 1935 were reduced by 20 percent.[31]

The procedure used in launching the wheat program was similar to those for cotton and corn-hogs. Farm leaders were invited to Washington where they discussed the wheat situation, drafted recommendations, and then held informal public conferences with wheat growers, handlers, and processors. Four regional program meetings were held in Kansas City, Spokane, Fargo, and Columbus in late June and early July of 1933. The members of the state and agricultural extension staffs were briefed on the basic features of the program. They, in turn, furnished vital information on the special problems the AAA was likely to encounter in the field. The educational campaign outlining the details of the program was carried out in cooperation with the Extension Service. Where county agents were not normally functioning, temporary agents were hired on a three-month basis from a list submitted by the Civil Service Commission.[32]

To qualify for benefits under the AAA program, a grower had to reduce his wheat acreage for 1934 and 1935 by not more than 20 percent of his average for the base period of 1930–1932 and be a member of a wheat production control association whose directorates were chosen by the members. Two-thirds of the first year's allotment benefits were intended originally to be paid about September 15, with the balance to be paid when the acreage planted in 1934 had been fulfilled.[33]

The recruiting campaign to control wheat production was a remarkable one. Some 580,000 of the estimated 1.2 million wheat growers in the country showed an interest in participating; and 500,000—representing over 50 million acres, or 77 percent, of the wheat acreage for the 1930–1932 base period—actually signed contracts. More than 7.5 million acres, or 11.5 percent of the annual average acreage, were pledged for removal from production. Kansas, which planted 3 million more acres than the nearest competing state during 1930–1932, reported 91 percent of its wheat growers signed up. North Dakota, the next ranking state in acreage, had a 93 percent sign-up; Oklahoma had 79; Montana 87; Texas 77; and South Dakota 93.[34]

All was not as tranquil as these figures suggest. The winter wheat farmers of Kansas and other states in the southern tier of the wheat belt, who harvested their crops early and took advantage of the high prices that prevailed then, found themselves in relatively good condition in the late summer of 1933. But the spring wheat farmers of Minnesota, North Dakota, South Dakota, and Wisconsin, whose crops were harvested much later, suffered from crop failures, the drought, and the price drop that occurred in August. Added to these woes was the growing disparity between the prices the farmers received and paid, which they blamed on the NRA. Since the NRA was striving to obtain cost of production, plus a reasonable profit for the manufacturers, by freeing the manufacturers from competition, the wheat farmers felt that they were paying more than they should for their overalls, flour, farm implements, and other needs.[35]

Meanwhile, Milo Reno, the president of the National Farm Holiday Association, warned of a national farm strike unless the provisions of the NRA were extended to agriculture. Cost of production had become the rallying cry of the Farm Holiday Association as it had for the Farmers' Union in the earlier years. The Reno group even drafted a code for the recovery administration that it believed would establish a net income for farm operators, reduce their working hours, eliminate destructive trade practices, and adjust general farm prices to the cost of living. In mid-October Governor William Langer of North Dakota notified President Roosevelt, Secretary Wallace, and Hugh Johnson of the NRA that he, as governor, would act in accordance with a law recently passed by the North Dakota legislature that empowered him to declare an embargo on any farm product selling below the cost of production. Governor Langer said he would call out the National Guard, if necessary, to enforce the embargo. Langer also tried, unsuccessfully, to get the governors of Minnesota, South Dakota, Iowa, and Nebraska to join him.[36]

Meanwhile, attorneys for the four big railroads serving the agricultural Northwest announced they would fight Langer's embargo in the courts of law, which meant a battle with the state administration and the farmers who supported the governor. If the railroads did not resist the embargo and refused to accept shipments of wheat, they would become liable for damages to any shipper for whom they had agreed to provide such services. On the other hand, if they sat back and waited for the grain trade to break the embargo, their yards would be choked with blocked cars, and their companies would be clogged with litigation for liabilities caused by delayed shipments. The presidents of the four railroads informed Langer that, under the provisions of the Interstate Commerce Act, they were compelled to accept wheat for shipment and to transport it. While the office of the adjutant general of North Dakota was making plans to use the National Guard to enforce the embargo, wheat was moving across the border into Minnesota. When Wallace was asked about the embargo, he replied: "I have sympathy but do not admire the judgment."[37]

Later, the embargo also was directed at the grain elevators that bought the farmers' wheat or warehoused it before shipping it out of state. The North Dakota Railroad Commission implemented Langer's mandate with an order to elevators asking them to suspend out-of-state shipments and a threat to revoke their licenses if they failed to comply.[38]

Langer's actions, as expected, proved abortive. Newspaper accounts maintained that North Dakota wheat continued to move into the neighboring states, but Langer insisted: "No wheat moved out of the state." Langer lifted the embargo on wheat when he felt the farmers were getting a "living price," but "clamped down" an embargo on out-of-state beef animal shipments, claiming that the market price for beef was confiscatory.[39]

Developments followed the course predicted. Late in December of 1935, thirty-five grain elevators joined as complainants in a court suit asking for an injunction to prevent the government of North Dakota from enforcing the governor's orders. Then in mid-January 1934, three judges joined in a decision declaring the embargo illegal, saying that the power to regulate interstate commerce rested with Congress and not with the state legislature. Langer's defense for the embargo was based on the state police power and the actions of the state legislature.[40]

The dairy farmers were even less prepared for the AAA than the producers of wheat, corn, and hogs—except for the fluid milk producers, who had limited experiences with individual quotas and classified prices when they were a part of the farm relief crusades of the 1920s. As a group they made less use of the credit and other facilities of the Federal Farm Board than other commodity groups, and they never participated in any lengthy discussions over marketing agreements and licenses. In fact, there was little support among the rank and file dairy farmers for the AAA when it was first proposed. The inclusion of dairy products as one of the basic commodities was a defensive measure adopted by the organized dairy interests, who were unsure of what direction to take.

On the whole the milk producers seemed satisfied with the progress they had made through their cooperative marketing associations until about 1930. When collective bargaining, marketing agreements, and licenses suddenly emerged as proposals during the winter of 1933, few members of the fluid milk cooperatives, and producers who were not members of cooperatives, understood them. When prices began slipping in March 1933 and the milk producers faced stiffer competition, some association managers turned to the AAA as an escape from their difficulties because there were no other state or federal agencies to which they could turn.[41]

The AAA, as a consequence, was not as well equipped to deal with the problems of the fluid milk producers than with those of wheat farmers; no individual association had come forward with any clear-cut ideas about the application of production control techniques to dairy products. In fact, the departmental committee at work on a program for dairy products had reported that production control was impractical. Furthermore, the ideas relating to the application of marketing and licensing techniques to dairy products were even less clear.

Meanwhile, producer and dealer groups in the Chicago area who were alarmed by the delays drafted a marketing agreement and presented it to Wallace on May 12, forcing the administration to move more swiftly than it had planned. Clyde King, a former employee of the Food Administration, an authority on collective bargaining in milk markets in a number of American cities, and a professor of economics in the Wharton School of Finance, University of Pennsylvania, was named first a consultant and then chief of the dairy section of the AAA. Also appointed was Edwin A. Gaumnitz, an economist for the dairy section of the BAE and a student of the economics of milk, butter, cheese, and other manufactured products. Other consultants were called in when needed from various branches of the industry and universities.[42]

The Chicago milk agreement, concluded on July 28, 1933—the first of its kind—stipulated that only cooperatives could be accepted as parties to an agreement. By licensing all buyers in the market, provisions were made for nonmembers of cooperatives. Nonmembers were assured the same price as members.

Other disputed issues revolved around whether the milk marketing agreements would be under the NRA or AAA, the inclusion of the labor provisions of the NRA in the marketing agreement, controlling the production and prices of milk, and the nature of the local administration. Milk producers' associations—especially those in the Chicago area, which had been plagued by labor difficulties—that used a base-rating system to regulate the flow of milk and wanted to be free of restrictions, led the fight to have the agricultural codes under the AAA instead of the NRA.

Control of the production of milk became a reality after a compromise was reached that authorized the use of the base-rating system, provided that the market was to be kept open to new producers. The base-rating or individual farm quota system usually was calculated on the months of lowest milk production on the farm. The greatest objection to it came from the producers in the Chicago milkshed who were dissatisfied with their current or prospective base assignments. Certain authorities within the AAA, such as the consumers' counsel and the legal division, were suspicious of the marketing agreements and viewed them as devices for raising the prices of milk to a monopoly level. Still others believed that the milk market should be left open to new producers while established ones remained free to expand their production if prices warranted.

The milk plan, as originally proposed, denied the producers the option granted to wheat and cotton growers to avoid signing a contract and continue producing as much as they chose. The base-rating system, in use since the Capper–Volstead Act of 1922, had kept within the bounds of the law, and the practice since 1930 had been to carry the old base-ratings over into each new year on the grounds that the use of milk had been declining or was at a standstill. Even though this approach had not been attacked in the courts of law, some believed the day was approaching when it would be. The preference in the dairy section, however, was for the base-rating system already in use rather than for the contract, the processing tax, and benefit payments.

Most of the opposition to the proposal came from the small dealers and a group of milk producers who did not want to be dominated by the large dealers and wished to be free to undersell in the market if they chose. No vigorous opposition came from within the AAA because, as indicated, few in the AAA were well informed about collective bargaining in milk markets. Opposition to resale price-fixing came later from the chain stores and independents, who charged that the wholesale prices for milk sold to stores were altogether too high and that the margins on cash-and-carry milk sales were higher than necessary.

In brief, milk price schedules at this stage were arranged by the AAA and dealers and producer groups that brought the proposed agreement from Chicago to Washington. "It was imposed upon the rest—upon every dealer, store, roadside stand and peddler in the city and its immediate environs—by the issuance of a blanket license that automatically included them whether they wished it or not." The price schedules, if successfully executed, with some exceptions, would have enabled all shippers of milk within the milk-shed, members of cooperatives and nonmembers, to get the same f.o.b. (freight on bill) price for milk of a given grade sold for fluid milk use.

A total of 235 marketing agreements were received by the AAA from May 12 to November 30, 1933, but only fifteen were signed by the end of the year. Meanwhile the offices of lawyers, economists, and members of the legal staff were swamped with interviews that were held morning, noon, and night.[43]

Most marketing agreements for the large consuming centers included the "base-surplus plan" for leveling out the production of milk during the year, assuring the public of sufficient supplies in the season of low production, and rewarding the cooperative farmer with better prices. The amount of milk the dairymen produced during the months of October, November, and December—known as the short season in the industry—served as the base for the ensuing twelve months. The base-price was paid for milk representing the October, November, and December period, and the surplus price was paid for milk produced the rest of the year. Base and surplus prices were determined by the producers' associations and the distributors.[44]

Naturally, the dairy producers were plagued with the same problems as other producers. The prices of the goods the dairy farmers bought rose while the prices they received for butter and cheese fell. A committee representing midwestern milk producers, creameries, cheese factories, and others met on August 17 and urged the secretary of agriculture to take swift action to sustain the prices of butter and cheese. They also made it known that they wanted stabilization of prices with government assistance, not production control.

Wallace replied that some feasible plan for the control of production had to be worked out with the support of industry; and with this in mind, the AAA agreed to advance almost $12 million to remove butter and cheese from the market and keep part of the surplus product out of competitive trade channels. The AAA designed this advance merely as an interim effort to help the industry along until production controls were adopted and made known at the outset that it was not contemplating any surplus buying or stabilization operations as a permanent part of its program.[45]

More serious were the complaints leveled at the milk program. The principal violators were the small dealers who sold under the license price and justified their actions on the grounds that the drafting of the agreement was dominated by the special interests and they had not been given a chance to present their views. The hearings in Chicago, Philadelphia, and Boston brought out longstanding personal and factional grievances, and other preexisting local arrangements that bore on the unsuccessful operation of various phases of the marketing agreements. Eventually the principal producer groups agreed to the need for changes in the agreements and licenses and came forward with amendments of their own.

Matters, however, were not helped much by the administration's cumbersome, time-consuming, and ineffective methods of enforcing the agreements and licenses. Opposition from producers and distributors, large and small, continued. Dairymen with large herds of milk cows and dealers demanded the protection of their constitutional rights. Small dealers often argued that enforcement of a particular license would deprive them of their property "without due process of law." Some large chain stores waged a strenuous campaign against licenses on constitutional grounds and in fairness to consumers who were entitled to savings on purchases of milk made on a "cash-and-carry" basis.

The most serious drawback to the agreements and licenses was that the contracting parties were not sufficiently representative of the industry or the market. Dissenting producers in some areas seemed to represent the majority, and more of the distributors appeared to be against the program than for it. More difficulties arose from the attempt to enforce licenses than from the agreements. Distributors who entered into agreements in general were accustomed to the process, and as a rule they cooperated with the producers' associations in drafting the original proposals. The licenses, however, were aimed at dealers who would not voluntarily enter into agreements. And since there were always enough producers in most markets who opposed the agreements and licenses, it became relatively easy for violators to secure milk. The differences over resale, price-fixing, and producer price policy widened as time elapsed and were related to the greater issue of whether the AAA should place major emphasis on production controls and marketing adjustments, or on raising and sustaining prices without controlling production.[46]

As promised, the administration's new dairy policy, based on restricted output, was announced on January 8, 1934, in part to make the dairy producers understand that the federal government could not go on purchasing butter and cheese to support the prices the producers wanted. Then on March 21 a committee within USDA, after considering more than 100 proposals, made known the plan that regional meetings were going to be held. Dairy farmers would have an opportunity to discuss the program and suggest revisions. Adoption of the program, however, was left up to the farmers.[47]

The underlying philosophy of the plan, which all dairy farmers were eligible to join, was clear: parity prices would be sought only through production control. Farmers who reduced their production from 10 to 20 percent of their 1932–33 quotas would receive benefit payments. The individual farmer was to decide how he was going to reduce his production and was to receive forty cents for each pound of butterfat and a dollar fifty for every 100 pounds of milk. Funds for benefit payments were to come at first from a processing tax of one cent a pound on butterfat that gradually would rise to five cents, and from a compensatory tax on oleomargarine. Administration of the program was entrusted to county production control associations. Supplementary phases included the distribution of milk to underfed children, the transfer of healthy cows from surplus areas to needy farm families having no cows, and furthering plans for the eradication of bovine tuberculosis. Farmers with one or two cows were exempt from participation in the program.

Opposition to the new dairy program proved formidable. Farmers in Wisconsin, the largest dairy state in the nation, voted against the processing tax but for the program. The plan did not even come up for a vote in another prominent dairy state, Minnesota. Conferences on the dairy program at Philadelphia, Syracuse, and Atlanta also showed resistance; sessions in Des Moines, the home of Wallace, and in Indianapolis brought approval.[48]

Among the most vociferous and best-organized critics of the AAA proposal were the National Cooperative Milk Producers' Federation (NCMPF), and the local cooperatives. The dairy farmers, even before the AAA had become law, had expressed great concern over the conversion into feed crops of lands taken out of the production of cotton, corn, tobacco, and wheat. They wanted a far-reaching land classification program that would revert marginal and submarginal lands from cultivation to the public domain. Charles W. Holman, the secretary of the NCMPF, maintained that "the consideration of the quota or allotment principle, acreage reduction or such other control programs" should be "a last resort," and only if the proposals of the NCMPF failed to achieve results.

Holman outlined the NCMPF demands late in 1933 and again at a meeting of the dairy cooperatives in Washington on March 21 and 22, 1934 where the case against the government was developed. Congress in both instances was asked to pass the Brandt plan that called for the government purchase of excess stocks of farm products to be "dumped abroad" or disposed of through relief channels, the losses to be assessed on the producers in the form of an equalization fee similar to the one called for by the McNary–Haugen plan, price stabilization operations, and the reduction of excessive production through a program of leasing submarginal lands. Other specifications of the Brandt plan included imposing tariffs on fats and oils and appropriating money for the elimination of diseased cattle.[49] The AAA committee working on the plan for the control of milk production, however, saw no reason for calling NCMPF leaders into a conference. The problem, as the committee saw it, was to devise an effective program of action, not reconcile conflicting interests.

The reactions of the dairy farmers to production control varied across the country. In the Northeast where the marketing of milk was a dominant consideration, the opposition was strong. The commissioner of agriculture for the State of New York saw no reason why his state should reduce its dairy output when the AAA thus far had only effected higher prices for the things the eastern dairymen bought. As the commissioner put it, why "make the people of New York pay $21,550,000 in processing taxes for only $7,400,000 in benefits." The *American Agriculturalist,* edited by Edward Roe Eastman, a critic of the AAA from the outset, identified the problem as one of underconsumption, not of overproduction, which could be resolved through better marketing and advertising. Still others argued that a uniform plan of reduction was unfair to the cooperatives that had been advising their members to reduce their output over the previous three years.

In Wisconsin, opposition to production control came not so much from the fluid milk cooperatives, which were relatively unorganized, but from the Wisconsin Dairymen's Association. Its members objected to the quota system on the grounds that it was unworkable. The processing tax was condemned as a big burden. The Wisconsin Diarymen's Association preferred the program of Holman and the NCMPF. Representatives of the general farmer organizations in Wisconsin, on the other hand, supported the AAA and endorsed the principle of production control by a vote of more than two to one, but they opposed the processing tax because it would mean lower prices for their products. They felt that other means of financing production control and eliminating diseased and low-producing cattle had to be found. Strong but not overpowering opposition also came from the Twin Cities area of Minnesota, which was the home of some of the powerful producer groups. The Land O' Lakes Creameries and the Twin City Milk Producers Association led the attack through their official publications, the mail, and workers in the field. A clear majority "favored the AAA dairy plan, but with the understanding that it would be followed or supplemented by the Brandt plan as soon as Congress passed the necessary legislation."

Supporters of the AAA program believed that they would benefit from a small reduction of their output. There was favorable opinion to reducing output in a number of states west of the Mississippi River, especially from Des Moines to Dallas, and to some extent in the Rocky Mountain states and the Far West. In the South, positive experience with the cotton and tobacco programs had favorably predisposed most farmers to production control, but even in that region there were some strong pockets of resistance.

The problems of the tobacco growers were perplexing in some respects, but encouraging in others. About 750 million pounds of tobacco, reputedly the largest surplus on record, had been accumulated when the adjustment program got under way in 1933 because of the decline in the use of tobacco at home and abroad and the continued high production. Tobacco was the principal source of livelihood for about 375,000 farmers and an equal number of share-tenants and sharecroppers in twenty-eight states and Puerto Rico, and their income had fallen from $292 million in 1929 to slightly more than $107 million in 1932.[50]

Conditions were more critical among the cigar-tobacco farmers than among the growers of other types of tobacco. Few cigar-tobacco farmers had sold their 1932 crop; the stocks of low-grade tobacco were larger than those of high-grade; prices the previous season were about half their exchange value; and if the crops for 1933 and 1934 had been eliminated completely, there probably would have been a shortage after two years.[51]

John B. Hutson, the chief of the tobacco section, had returned to the United States early in 1933 as the AAA bill was being readied in Congress, after having undertaken a study of tobacco markets in Europe and their effects on the United States. He was assigned to the group that had been discussing what could be done with tobacco under the AAA.[52]

Action in behalf of the farmers who grew cigar tobacco had been delayed until decisions affecting crops with higher priorities such as cotton were reached, despite the fact that growers had filed an application for action before the 1933 tobacco crop was planted. Psychologically, the tobacco growers probably were better prepared to accept production control than were the producers of the other crops. Tobacco production was already controlled to a certain degree throughout the world, and the application of this principle did not appear as revolutionary to American tobacco growers as it did to the producers of other commodities. Many, if not most, growers had been exposed to the philosophy of curtailment in the early decades of the twentieth century, and administration leaders naturally hoped that the producers would respond favorably to the actual practice.[53]

The problems facing the growers and the government were complex. The twenty-five different types of tobacco had to be considered as separate agricultural commodities, with a separate plan formulated for each. Because of changes in the uses and character of the tobacco grown and because current prices for some of the tobacco types were above the parity levels of the prewar base for tobacco, 1919–1929 was chosen as the base period.[54]

Agricultural economists from the states in which the cigar tobaccos were produced, along with administration leaders, were consulted in developing the plan. The consultations were followed by conferences with growers and growers' representatives, and later with manufacturers using cigar-leaf tobacco. Each group's proposal was discussed by the other groups and finally all were brought together into a joint conference. The program that was finally decided upon covered a three-year period; the acreages for 1933, 1934, and 1935 were to be reduced by approximately one-half the 1932 level, and one-half of one year's crop of old-stock low-grade tobacco was to be diverted to noncommercial uses. Eventually a production-control program was agreed upon for all the principal southern-grown tobaccos, including burley and flue-cured tobacco. Early in September, details of a plan for production adjustment were worked out and hopes for a rapid sign-up ran high.[55]

The AAA also accepted the responsibility for trying to secure an immediate increase in price through some form of marketing agreement. A proposed marketing agreement was drafted that, although unacceptable to the tobacco companies, initiated a series of other proposals from which the marketing agreement for flue-cured tobacco finally was developed. Most plans developed thereafter incorporated the same general scheme of operation, with modifications to meet specific situations. Committees representing the agricultural colleges, the growers, and others interested in tobacco thought chiefly in terms of adjusting production and viewed measures such as marketing agreements as having supplementary value.

Once the producers displayed a willingness to adjust production in 1934, the buyers agreed to pay higher prices for the 1933 crop. About 645 million pounds, or nearly half the total 1933 production, were purchased at about $45 million more than if there had been no program in operation. Growers received an additional $16.5 million in rental and benefit payments under the adjustment contracts. The grower's share of the tobacco consumer's dollar, according to government sources, rose from 4½ percent in 1932 to 10 percent in 1933, while the profits of the manufacturers declined from more than 10 percent of the consumer's dollar to about 7 percent in 1933.[56]

The income from the 1934 crop was substantially larger despite the smaller quantity of leaf for sale. The market receipts, totaling $229 million—more than double those of 1932—were exclusive of the rental and benefit payments. The receipts were 25 percent higher than the farm income for the 1933 crop. In part this was because of the improved economic conditions abroad, greater use of the leaf, and a general improvement in the economic health of the nation. The years 1933 to 1935 inclusive, according to government sources, showed that the predepression ratio between farmers' returns and manufacturers' profits had been reestablished.

The benefit payments to the growers at no time exceeded collections from the processing tax. Taxes collected from the various sources from October 1933 through December 1935 totaled about $66.5 million. Benefit payments distributed during the first twenty-seven months to all tobacco growers amounted to $53 million, while administrative expenses bearing on the voluntary programs and the Kerr–Smith Tobacco Act that sought to strengthen them, totaled $4.5 million, bringing the grand total expenditures to almost $58 million.[57]

Grower participation in the tobacco program for 1933–1935 was impressive. Although the 1933 cigar-leaf program began after planting was well under way, 17,668 growers, or about three-fourths of those eligible, signed contracts. In 1934, under all six programs, 284,519 production-adjustment contracts were in effect; the number of growers participating in the various programs in 1935 was 369,465, and their contracts represented about 95 percent of the tobacco base acreage. The Kerr–Smith Tobacco Act passed by Congress in 1934 was designed to prevent growers who did not participate in the voluntary program from sharing in its financial benefits. The act facilitated enforcement of the obligations undertaken by participants, but it was not a major factor in determining the number of sign-ups.[58]

No serious thought, however, was given to the various economic classes of tobacco growers. A blanket program was launched for all of the commodities, without any effort being made to meet the special needs of the small submarginal farmers. Those within the industry knew there had to be a better way. However, the New Deal had to move swiftly. Time was of the essence. There was an urgent need to do something—whether it be effective or ineffective—to convince the tobacco farmers that the administration cared about them and would leave no stone unturned to better their position. It comes as no surprise that such a policy resulted in many tobacco farmers being left out.

In substance, launching these massive programs for cotton, corn-hogs, wheat, dairy products, and tobacco was unparalleled in peacetime America. That the New Dealers had been able to bring together as many producer groups as they did, despite the limitations in the various programs and the resistance encountered in some areas, was a healthy display of democracy in action. Critics pointed to undue pressure being exerted on the farmers by the government to act, but pressures of this sort were hardly an unknown quantity in American life. There were weaknesses, flaws, contradictions, and inconsistencies, but getting farmers and their representatives together to try and resolve their problems through group action was a master achievement and clearly indicated that Americans still had faith in the democratic process.

Dissension within the AAA

APART FROM THE NORMAL RIVALRIES that gnaw at the vitals of any organization effort, the conflicting philosophies, differences over the interpretation of the law, and clashing personalities had serious repercussions on the functioning of the AAA cotton, corn-hog, dairy, and tobacco programs.

Differences inevitably developed between old-line agencies in the USDA like the Bureau of Agricultural Economics (BAE), which was committed to research, education, and service and the AAA, with its personnnel who were activists. The lack of rapport between Secretary of Agriculture Henry A. Wallace and cohead of the AAA George N. Peek (who hoped to become secretary of agriculture himself and who viewed agriculture from a more simplistic perspective than Wallace) did not help matters. Nor did the differences between Peek and his assistants, on the one hand, and Jerome Frank, head of the legal section of the AAA, and his staff on the other, over matters such as the relative importance of marketing agreements and their provisions, the time consumed by Frank and his men in the approval of these agreements, and the failure of the AAA to take effective measures to protect the consumer. Later, a clash broke out between Chester C. Davis, Peek's successor as administrator of the AAA, and Jerome Frank over the interpretation of Section 7 in the AAA regarding landlords who refused to pass benefit payments on to the sharecroppers and tenants. Finally, there was the hostility of some of the colleges of agriculture, their staff officers, and directors of the State Agricultural Extension Service to the AAA programs and federal leadership.

Friction between the AAA and members of the old-line agencies in the USDA developed almost from the beginning. Some assumed that the AAA was a temporary "depression kind of thing" that would disappear after the economy got back on its feet; but there also were those who were convinced that "Rex and Henry" felt there were a lot of people in the USDA who were unsympathetic with the New Deal and new ideas, and something had to be done about them. Mordecai Ezekiel had cautioned Wallace against establishing the AAA as a separate body because this would have given the AAA a free hand to pursue its own course, announce its own policies, and promote its own program, which could place it in conflict with the USDA. Hence the AAA became a part of the USDA, instead of an autonomous unit, and announcements of policy statements and new programs came from the USDA instead of the AAA.[1]

A virtual state of civil war raged within the AAA for almost six months before "the explosion" in late 1933. At the center was Peek, a man of positive views, who liked to order things done. Given his way he would have set up the AAA as a separate agency outside the USDA, and placed far greater, if not exclusive, stress on marketing agreements instead of production controls. Wallace had decided against Peek on marketing agreements as early as June 1933. Chester C. Davis, Howard R. Tolley, and others within the AAA, however, did not have the same faith in marketing agreements that Peek had. But, according to M. L. Wilson, "they thought [since] we're in the Depression . . . and there are a lot of things we've got to do now . . . get purchasing power flowing, . . . things operating, and . . . the economic system in adjustment. Then these agreements and controls will be released." Peek, on the other hand, felt Wallace was a dreamer who listened too much to Rexford Tugwell and Harry Hopkins to be a good secretary of agriculture. He also insisted that as long as he was the coadministrator of the AAA there was going to be nobody between the president and himself, and nobody between the secretary of agriculture and himself.[2]

Peek's position as a coadministrator was at best a difficult one; to complicate matters he was a headstrong man trying to lead two widely divergent groups within his agency. His own group operated on the theory that AAA regulation of the negotiation of industry's contracts had to be limited to seeing that the farmer collected the benefits due him and little else. Frank and Tugwell's group, on the other hand, whose position was favored by Wallace, believed that besides trying to obtain higher prices for the farmers, the agricultural emergency also offered the New Deal a good opportunity to impose social controls on the processing industries when these controls were in the best interests of the consumers.

Peek had never gotten along with Frank, an old adversary, who had been selected general counsel of the AAA before he, himself, had been appointed head of the AAA. The two men first encountered one another in the Moline Plow Works legal proceedings in the 1920s, from which a mutual dislike and distrust for each other developed. Peek was repelled by the idea of having as his general counsel a man with whom he had clashed and from whom he was poles apart in thinking. The immediate cause for the difficulties in the AAA stemmed from the dislike the two men had for each other and the shortage of legal counsel in Frank's office that delayed marketing agreements for indefinite periods of time. Peek complained to the president about this and even made an unsuccessful attempt to have Frank ousted, which only backfired and added fuel to a smouldering controversy.

Peek not only desired to get the codes and agreements through as rapidly as possible (and Tugwell himself did not want to be blamed for delayed action), but Peek kept insisting that the original intention of the AAA was to provide the machinery to run the two-price system and achieve "an American price for American consumption" and a world price for exports. This was the old McNary–Haugen approach. The disagreement erupted when Peek attempted to open up the European market to American butter, which could not compete with the lower-priced European butter.

Peek's strategy to increase butter sales abroad was to order an advance from the AAA of $500,000 of the money raised by the processing tax, thinking this would bring the two-price system into operation. He hoped that this would make the tariff on farm products effective—which, in his opinion, was what "the farm fight" had been all about. But the order to advance funds for the disposal of the surplus butter had to be signed by Wallace, who at the time was at Warm Springs, Georgia. When telephoned by Tugwell, who was acting as secretary of agriculture, Wallace refused to authorize the release of funds requested by Peek because he disapproved subsidizing exports and dumping as a matter of policy.

Early in December Tugwell wrote Wallace about the dispute and sent a copy of the letter to Peek. He explained that the negative decision was based on the theory that agricultural trade could not be improved by selling abroad at a lower price than at home.

> This practice has been condemned in every international conference; it was the subject of special treatment in our recent tariff truce agreement; it is recognized as provocative of retaliation . . . a sound foreign trade must be based on equal exchange between countries. The practice of subsidization is only a method of escaping from the acceptance of imports, it amounts to a bonus to customers to take goods off our hands.

Peek assumed all along Tugwell was the stalking horse for Wallace and that his memorandum was an open declaration of the international point of view that Secretary of State Cordell Hull and Wallace were advocating, as well as a repudiation of the AAA. To Wallace a sound foreign trade meant equal exchange between countries, which Peek said was free trade, as opposed to barter that Peek espoused. "If the marketing agreement and the foreign trade features of the Act [AAA]," wrote Peek a few years later, "were to be dropped and the whole attention centered upon limiting and regimenting production . . . I did not want to administer it. I wanted to be on the outside fighting it.'' Determined to find out from the president just how he wanted the act administered, Peek decided to approach him on the question. ''If he wanted it the Wallace way, I would have to leave. If he wanted it my way, then Mr. Wallace's course was to cooperate.''

Roosevelt adroitly avoided a showdown by telling Peek he wanted both Peek and Wallace in the administration, and thought that he, Peek, ''was especially fitted to work out a foreign trade program.'' Thus Peek resigned as coadministrator of the AAA on December 11, 1933; a number of his AAA employees joined him in his new position, while Fred Lee, his personal attorney, accepted a position with the Federal Alcohol Control Board. Peek's departure meant that the Wallace point of view was going to prevail, as it had from the start; production control, not marketing agreements, was the principal base around which the AAA was going to revolve.[3]

Another controversy developed over the reactions of the BAE with Nils Olsen as the head and the AAA. Tugwell and Wallace, especially Tugwell, had little respect for some of the USDA personnel and believed that some changes were needed.[4]

The Olsen case was a difficult one for Wallace, because Olsen had a deep affection for Henry's father. A native of Illinois, and a graduate of Luther College, Decorah, Iowa and the University of Wisconsin and Harvard where he obtained master's degrees in history and economics, Olsen had been a protege of the elder Wallace and a ghost writer for his book *America's Duty and Debt to the Farmer*. Olsen in later years, however, became a mentor of Arthur Hyde, the secretary of agriculture under Herbert Hoover, and found it difficult to reconcile himself and his agency to the AAA—as was the case with other Republicans in the USDA.[5]
other Republicans in the USDA.[5]

The AAA had a need for a continuous ''fire-alarm'' kind of outlook service to collect, analyze, and interpret economic information on the foreign and domestic markets. Under Hyde and Olsen outlook work had come in for serious criticism and Wallace could not rely on a man who had attempted to curtail such services in the BAE. Wallace, however, could not keep the BAE entirely out of the New Deal, even though he saw to it that Olsen and his staff had nothing to do with the shaping of AAA policy. But even the perfunctory services assigned the BAE resulted in friction. Olsen had agreed in 1933 that he and his staff would classify cotton under the cotton-option phase of the AAA program and compute allotments and secure data for use in the effort to expand the foreign market, with the understanding that the AAA would compensate the BAE for these services. Meanwhile the AAA also decided to create its own staff, taking over personnel from the BAE. As of June 1934, ninety people had been transferred and a request for fourteen more was being considered. The Land Economics Division, a unit of the BAE, reported directly to the AAA in these matters. The BAE in turn was given $850,000 for its labors the first year, but the cooperative arrangement had not been working out as well as had been expected.[6]

The AAA complained, for instance, that its requests for unpublished data and special reports were delayed by the BAE because of the need for special conferences between administrative heads before action could be taken, which made it difficult for the AAA to move swiftly in its action programs. There also were irritating differences on how budget expenses were going to be charged on subjects that fell on the borderline between regular BAE economic service and AAA control work. Worse still were the differences between AAA personnel and most BAE staff members on the objectives and methods to be used in some of the areas of fact-finding and research.[7]

Oscar Stine, the head of the statistical and historical section in the department and a member of the "old school," wrote his former mentor and boss in the BAE, Henry Taylor:

> Until recently the new planners were inclined to be very sensitive to criticism. They did not like to hear about ideas that differed from theirs. If you did not like them you were hopelessly reactionary. Research work was too slow. We were all dummies if we could not answer questions today. Perhaps recent developments have sobered them.

Stine admitted the presence of unusual personnel problems, but believed they could have been worked out if the atmosphere had been "more congenial" during the past year.[8]

Some of the difficulties between the AAA and the BAE on outlook work stemmed from differences in responsibilities, as well as training, methods, and attitudes. The staff of the AAA tended to demand fact-gathering of information that would lead to immediate answers and action. The staff of the BAE, on the other hand, believed in making leisurely investigations not pointing toward any particular control policy; they wanted to remain a research arm of the USDA committed to the truth instead of to a particular program or philosophy. Several BAE leaders, furthermore, believed the AAA was going to be a temporary agency, and were little inclined to give priority to its demands or readily transfer BAE personnel and functions to it.[9]

Such an unfortunate situation developed naturally, if not inevitably, wherever an action agency entered a field adjacent to that of a research and service organization. The earlier counterpart to this had been the Federal Farm Board and the BAE. Farm board personnel discovered that although

they could make use of facts and analyses supplied by the BAE and other research organizations, too much time was consumed in delivering such services. As a consequence, a wide and workable division of labors between the
AAA and the BAE was not satisfactorily achieved.[10]

There was another factor, too. Olsen not only lacked sympathy with
what Wallace and the AAA were trying to do but his authority was
diminishing because the BAE, which he headed, was being overshadowed
by the AAA. Most bureaus were being called upon to give up their best
secretaries and their best administrative assistants and to see that the AAA
got first call on about everything. The older agencies were rankled as much
by the interruption of their work as by the eventual outcome of this
priority.[11]

Relevant to the differences between the AAA and BAE, and the clash
between Peek, Tugwell, and Wallace, were happenings in the office of
General Counsel of the AAA Jerome Frank, where conditions had become
hectic by mid-July 1933. All available space for the legal staff was being
used. Lawyers being hired on a temporary or permanent basis, including
contemporary and future luminaries such as Adolf A. Berle, Jr., and Abe
Fortas, had no desks at which to work; and the need for more lawyers was
pressing. Lee Pressman, Frank's top assistant, warned that unless definite
action was taken immediately the staff would be overwhelmed and a great
deal of inefficiency would result.[12]

One of the first questions raised concerned the role of the office of the
general counsel in matters of AAA policy, and the person to raise it was
Charles Brand, the coadministrator of the AAA and close working colleague of Peek at the time. Frank expressed surprise that Brand raised such
a question and wanted Brand to furnish him with specific instances in which
he, Frank, had been guilty of a transgression. "As far as I am concerned,"
said Frank, "I have studiously avoided any expressions on policy except in
our inner circles. I consider it not my business to express views on questions
of policy to the outside world unless I am asked to do so by someone in
authority." Frank was not a person to be intimidated by anyone in authority, especially if he believed his actions were consistent with his responsibilities and principles. He told Brand that when standards of policy were
announced, lawyers engaged in drafting agreements had to advise representatives of industry if a clause in an agreement they proposed was or was not
in accord with an announced policy and when it complied with the provision
of a statute. This was an obligation of the lawyer. But the lawyer had no
right to go beyond this, except in discussing it with members of the AAA
staff. If the lawyer failed to call such a matter to the attention of the administration and its officers, he would be remiss in the discharge of his
duties.[13]

A certain procedure was followed in drafting marketing agreements and codes during the midsummer of 1933. Whenever a marketing agreement or code was submitted to the AAA, a representative of the interested group appeared before Peek's assistant, Wayne Taylor, who called an informal conference. Other conferences soon followed. Each agreement required the services of a lawyer for about a week or two before it could be whipped into proper shape. Agreements came in at the rate of three to four a day, each requiring a conference. Refinement of the procedure included requiring all who submitted marketing agreements or codes to submit advance copies of their proposals to the members of the AAA, including the lawyers representing the general counsel, to expedite discussion of the legal questions.

Another unresolved issue was whether the legal staff would draft the marketing agreement or code for the group submitting it, or whether the legal staff simply should explain what the agreement should contain and then have the attorney of the group submitting the marketing agreement or code draft the actual document. The earlier practice of presenting a mere outline or semblance of a marketing agreement or code made it incumbent on the already overburdened legal staff of the general counsel to draft the necessary agreement, which was time consuming.[14]

The delays were real, not imaginary, and were to be expected in view of the vastness and uniqueness of the program. Clyde King, the chief of the dairy section, not only complained that his section was being hindered by the lack of sufficient lawyers, but on one occasion demanded "at least three more attorneys who . . . had sufficient experience in the negotiation and drafting of important contracts to take care of the agreements from the time of the hearing until their submission to the Administration for approval." Adlai E. Stevenson, then a special attorney in Frank's office, told of the time he spent attending one or more informal hearings each day, how attending these hearings left little time to prepare a suggested agreement and resulted in the accumulation of unfinished work.[15]

The complaint about the lack of lawyers became chronic with Clyde King. On one occasion he listed a number of trade agreements being held up because of the inability of the dairy section to get a lawyer to redraft them in a form acceptable to Frank, even though they had been drafted by good lawyers. King bluntly warned Frank: "There is a dissatisfaction with this delay from Coast to Coast—a dissatisfaction that I have frequently tried to voice to you. This bottleneck must perforce break down all confidence in our ability to get results." Frank replied to King, "Everything you say in your memorandum . . . is doubtless true. The legal staff is not sufficiently large to permit us to handle the milk agreements as expeditiously as seem necessary." But there were many other agreements, besides those for milk, relating to other commodities and other equally important legal matters left unattended because of the lack of competent lawyers. Frank stated, "I submitted memoranda predicting this would occur, and in the last few weeks, I have said so in writing and orally almost every other day. The responsibility is not mine and I refuse to accept it."[16]

Meanwhile, the general counsel of the AAA and his staff began to move into more sensitive areas. Late in August 1933 Howard Corcoran, an associate attorney, advised Frank that the marketing agreement and code for the cotton industry was bound to encounter resistance because it treated the cotton industry as a public utility and regulated it fairly strictly. Although he was not prepared to vouch for the legality for each clause in the agreement, he thought it was ready to go to a public hearing.[25] Thomas C. Blaisdell, assistant to the general counsel, also informed Frank that he was not completely satisfied with the various clauses being written into the marketing agreements and codes by the parties to these agreements that related to the submission of reports and access to the records of the companies.[18]

Meanwhile King had become more agitated over the delays and asked for the transfer of an attorney to take charge of the legal phases in the enforcement of milk licenses. John H. Lewin, the chief of the licensing and enforcing section in the AAA's legal division, however, asked Frank that "in the interest of unity, coordination and efficiency all the legal work connected with the enforcement of licenses should be performed exclusively by members of [his] section . . ." and that suggestions for enforcement should be transmitted to the office of the general counsel to clear through persons responsible for that work. If each section of the AAA were to determine separately its own policy of enforcement and have independent counsel assigned to it, Lewin believed, "nothing but chaos will result." Lewin further believed it would be wiser to have one member of his section, under his and Frank's supervision, specialize for the time being in the problems of the dairy section as a means of meeting the needs of King. Feelings between King and Frank reached the breaking point soon thereafter and contributed to King's resignation as head of the dairy section. King wrote Frank: "You are a good lawyer. But your psychoanalysis is damn rotten. It smells of the sewer. Come up to my Seminar some Saturday morning."[19]

Competition among the federal agencies for competent lawyers, as well as for philosophical and political considerations, also came to the fore. Lee Pressman, the chief attorney in the general counsel's office and a close personal friend of Frank, contrasted the conditions in their office with those in the Public Works Administration (PWA), the Reconstruction Finance Corporation (RFC), the National Recovery Administration (NRA), and other agencies that were scouring the country for capable attorneys. Whenever these agencies found a good lawyer, continued Pressman, "he is appointed immediately at salaries which we can't hope to match."[20]

The personnel office reported it was unable to proceed with requests for new appointments because of the time lost in locating files and determining what action had been taken. Recommendations for appointments often were returned because the proposed salaries were out of line with the new salary scale, time was lost in determining whether the individual would be willing to accept an appointment at a lower salary, or the recommended salary was considered higher than the nature of the duties or the qualifications of the proposed appointee warranted. Delays also occurred because of inadequate job descriptions for appointment and the failure to obtain the necessary political endorsement. A salary of $4,000 was recommended for Abe Fortas when a maximum of only $2,600 could be justified. In fact the confusion had reached the point where Frank was advised not to submit new requests for appointments until all pending cases had been cleared, even though this meant further delays for the AAA. How could the work of the division proceed at an emergency pace when an inordinate amount of time was spent on appointments?[21]

Peek, Brand, and others who had been unhappy with the way Frank ran his office viewed the personnel situation differently. Peek said, "They pushed their own people into key positions. . . . At one time, Mr. Frank had 130 men on his staff at salaries far above those generally paid in Government Service." Brand and his associates surmised that Frank, perhaps with the assistance of Tugwell and Wallace, circumvented the normal procedure by obtaining clearance from Wallace's office for legal appointments. Brand said on September 12, 1933 that 3,500 appointments had been made since the signing of the AAA on May 12, and that the current staff numbered more than 2,800. He, too, blamed the delays in appointments on the failure of Frank's office to supply all the necessary information on which to base action, and to recommendations for salaries in excess of the rates justifiable for the work to be done, the experience of the applicant, and the compensation paid elsewhere in the government service.

> The 51 attorneys in the law division receive an average yearly compensation of slightly more than $5,300. The average salary of all lawyers in the Department of Justice, I was told today by the Assistant Attorney General, is approximately $4,200.

Strong disapproval, for example, was expressed over the appointment of Lee Pressman as chief attorney at a salary of $6,000, which shortly thereafter was raised to $7,000.[22]

An equally critical situation developed between Frank's office and the representatives of the tobacco industry. The attorneys for the tobacco companies believed their employers were contributing materially to the improvement of the industry when they agreed to buy flue-cured tobacco at about 40 percent above the market price. The attorneys in Frank's office thought they were doing something less than that, and demanded the right to inspect the company books and exert some degree of control over the industry. The tobacco men protested and appealed to Peek, who sympathized with them.

The proposed agreement in this instance was limited to a group of eight tobacco manufacturers who customarily purchased 90 percent of the flue-cured tobacco used in domestic manufactures. It did not include the buyers of the export grades, who normally took about 60 percent of the crop and chose to remain outside the agreement. The buyers of the domestic portion agreed to buy a minimum of 250 million pounds—or about 50 percent of the current crop—between September 25, 1933, and March 31, 1934, at an average of seventeen cents a pound, which was 50 percent more than the price of the previous year. The basic policy of the AAA came into question. Fears that the insertion of the licensing and other provisions into the marketing agreements, including the charts, the remarks about profits, and advertising and related matters, represented an attempt by the administration to assume control over the industry prompted the tobacco companies to defer acceptance of the agreement until the extent of the proposed controls was determined.[23]

Frank said he agreed with Clay Williams, the representative of the tobacco companies, who believed that the proposed agreement as it then stood gave the companies the right to raise the price of tobacco to its maximum, and that by the terms of the agreement the secretary of agriculture was agreeing to refrain from interfering with the companies' right to increase their prices to the maximum. Wallace was within his rights to sign this agreement if he chose. The attorneys for the tobacco companies wanted Wallace to sign it, and so did John B. Hutson, the director of the AAA tobacco program. Frank, however, did not want Wallace to sign such an agreement.[24]

An appeal was directed to Roosevelt, who in this instance approved the position of Peek and suggested that the agreement with the tobacco companies be signed. The AAA was still in the initial stages and the president wanted some record of achievement. Peek estimated that the flue-cured tobacco growers received $122 million for their 1933 crop as compared with $43 million in 1932, and only $9 million of the $122 million came from benefit payments.

After the confrontation over the flue-cured tobacco agreement, Peek made one more desperate attempt to eliminate Frank. Peek wrote Wallace on November 5 that his relations with Frank had become almost impossible, and asked for his removal and the appointment of another general counsel.

Receiving no reply, Peek sent another note to the secretary reminding him of his letter and again demanding the removal of Frank.[25] The first to go, however, was not Frank but Peek.

Peek's successor as head of the AAA was his friend Chester C. Davis, the chief of production for AAA, a realist and a compromiser rather than a reformer or an issuer of edicts. Davis at first did not know whether or not to remain after Peek resigned from the AAA for they had been on very good terms. Davis up to this point had served as a bridge between Wallace and Peek, but he finally came to the conclusion that he could still work with Wallace and not turn his back on his old friend and boss, George Peek.

Peek had been aware that his position as administrator was likely to be offered to Davis, and even talked with him about it before it actually happened. Davis recalled that Peek said to him, "If you take this, you make it a condition of your acceptance that Jerome Frank and some of his boys around him go out. Don't take it unless they do." Davis took the job in part because of his own optimism and in part because of the influence of M. L. Wilson and H. R. Tolley. Years later he recalled regretfully that he did not follow Peek's advice.[26]

Davis by temperament was better suited for the job of administrator. Unlike Peek, who had been inclined to say "yes" and "no" and issue orders in very few words, Davis was more deliberate; and he was easier to approach. He believed that the job of the administrator was to carry out the desires of those who were trying to help the farmers. He believed in getting the story out to the farmers and farm groups through the Extension Service and the committee system. If the people understood what the situation was, they would make the proper decisions; and this principle was the essence of democracy.[27]

CHAPTER SEVEN

Sharecroppers and Tenants

THE SHARECROPPERS AND TENANTS were the closest the United States came to having a peasant class; and in a reformist-oriented period it comes as no surprise that they were the focus of perhaps the most dramatic and explosive phase of AAA history. They fared badly in part because the AAA programs were built around commodities instead of people. Poor farmers who struggled to make a living on the land were not the AAA's prime concern. Many in the agricultural establishment believed there were too many people on the land; and one way of eliminating distress on the farm was by getting people off the land and into the cities. Furthermore, the USDA had never pursued a policy of helping marginal or submarginal farmers, especially in the South where many of the rural folks were blacks and where the larger producers supported the AAA more solidly than producers in other parts of the country.[1]

Chester C. Davis, who found himself in the center of this controversy, knew that the administration of the AAA was going to be difficult; but like his predecessor, George N. Peek, he believed he could manage. He brought with him no thoughts of sweeping reform. He planned to continue with acreage and production controls as in the past; and the AAA was going to continue developing marketing agreements, especially in the milk markets and the specialty products of the West Coast. "I was naive enough," Davis reminisced years later, "not to expect any real difficulties—more than we had. I probably thought there'd be less."[2]

Davis had to deal with the same men as Peek had. There was, of course, Rexford G. Tugwell, with whom Davis disagreed, nominally under the supervision of Wallace but reporting to the president—a situation that must have made the secretary unhappy. Tugwell was a man who Davis felt was "completely out of place in the farm administration. . . . He wasn't a farmer in any sense and just did not have enough grasp of operating problems to make me think his judgement was worth a damn." Davis took no pains to bring Tugwell into the policy meetings of the AAA; in fact he did not care whether he was there or not because he felt Tugwell had little to contribute. Davis, like Peek, believed that Tugwell was attempting to inaugurate policies that were out of line with what the AAA was designed to accomplish.[3]

Davis soon discovered that he had to spend more time in policing what was going on inside the AAA than what was going on out in the field. He saw that Paul Appleby and "Beanie" Baldwin, in particular, enjoyed the business of being "kingmakers." "They wanted to make a President," recalled Davis. "They were beginning that process and they worked on Henry Wallace . . . in 1934."[4]

Davis also had to contend with Jerome Frank and the men around him. He believed that many of the young men were arrogant and offensive in their relations with the public. "They were creating distrust, dislike, and opposition." Davis also felt that "the books and records clause" in the marketing agreements was developed by the consumers' counsel and his supporters, not because these men believed in the clause but because they wanted to sabotage the marketing agreements program. As the spokesperson for a marketing group said, "We will agree to permit the examination of our books and records to the full extent that's necessary to determine anything that's needed to be known about the operation under the marketing agreement." But his group was unwilling to open up its books "to the unlimited extent the clause required."[5]

The most pressing problem facing Davis concerned the relations between the tenants and sharecroppers and their landlords. On February 15, 1934 D. P. Trent, the assistant director of the Commodities Division of the AAA, informed Davis that the large number of letters and telegrams pouring into the offices of the secretary and the cotton production section from all parts of the cotton belt relating to the landlords, tenants, and sharecroppers had become a source of embarrassment. Trent even outlined the options open to the government.[6]

One option was to allow the contracts to stand as they were, make no further efforts to define a share-tenant, and permit the tenants and sharecroppers to carry out the agreements they had made with the landlords. To issue additional instructions simply would confuse matters. A second alternative was to issue more specific regulations and instructions to county committeemen directing them to accept no contracts where they had reason to believe that the tenant was being denied his equitable share of the rental and benefit payments. Or finally the government could, through a special congressional appropriation or means other than the processing tax, throw between $25 and $30 million into the cotton program to be divided between the landowners or landlords and the tenants and sharecroppers on the same basis they shared the crop.[7]

Even though it was advisable for the AAA to try to do something about these charges against the landlords before others entered into the controversy, there is little evidence that the AAA authorities moved with dispatch in counteracting the charges of irregularities. Early in March 1934 Professor William R. Amberson of the College of Medicine, University of Tennessee in Memphis, and a member of the League of Industrial Democracy, wrote Cully Cobb, the director of the cotton section:

> We already have many cases before us in which evictions have been ordered, apparently in direct defiance of the contract. I have seen many of these orders, some delivered several weeks ago. In few cases have evictions yet been made, but many appear imminent. In one case we find that the owner of a large plantation had recently acquired a new tract of land upon which lived 18 share-cropper families. He has evicted nearly all these families, or has brought in negroes to take the land. In one case which we have visited the evicted family has been given temporary asylum in an abandoned shack, but has been denied all access to the land, not even being allowed space for a garden . . . the plantation owner who is responsible for this policy is one of the local committee who oversees the acreage reduction program. Is he above the law? . . . In some cases individual tenants are being given more land . . . others are being denied all land. Large families are being discriminated against in favor of small families. The acres rented by the government are not being turned over to the tenants on the terms contemplated by the contract, if at all. And so on. What can be done about it?[8]

Southerners who were sensitive to these charges responded angrily. The *Memphis Commercial Appeal* accused that "zealots from other sections have long felt they were divinely ordained to uplift the South. . . . Outside uplifters are its pet aversion." Norman Thomas, the New York Socialist, "interviewed a few highly imaginative Negroes and a family or two of what is commonly known as 'white trash,' and upon their statements framed an indictment against the cotton farmers of the south." The town council of Tyronza, Arkansas in a joint statement replied that 90 percent of the landowners and renters in the general area began as sharecroppers, and through industry and thrift rose from the ranks. Only three evictions occurred in the immediate area where sharecroppers farmed more than 20,000 acres. The *Appeal* also claimed more sharecroppers were employed in 1934 than in the previous year.[9]

Late in March 1934 Cully Cobb asked E. A. Miller to submit a statement concerning the charges Harry L. Mitchell filed in behalf of the tenants. Cobb instructed Miller to get to the facts, the supporting records, and the affidavits. But Cobb, upon finding that both Mitchell and his colleague Clay East had opposed the cotton plow-up campaign in 1933 because they believed it was wrong for the government to destroy cotton when so many people needed clothing, minimized the gravity of the charges. Cobb sensed a well-defined political attack, which he had reason to believe would grow stronger, was building against the entire agricultural adjustment program. He also felt that economic progress would be difficult to achieve in the South unless the cotton adjustment program was carried through, debts were cleared, and ownership of more homes made possible for tenants. The best way out of this dilemma was to correct abuses in a manner that would not disturb the cotton program and relations between the landlords and tenants.[10]

Davis asked for cooperation from the chiefs of the various commodity sections in getting to the bottom of tenant charges. Like others in the AAA, he was inclined to believe that the vast majority of the landlords and owners were cooperating magnificently with the cotton adjustment program of 1934–1935, and that violators were few. He found comfort in assuming that the necessary steps to correct injustices and answer critics were being taken.

The investigation of abuses in the cotton program was conducted mainly on an in-house basis. The majority of the members of the committee entrusted with this responsibility were members of the agricultural establishment: the USDA, specifically employees of the AAA; the Agricultural Extension Service; the office of the comptroller of the AAA. Perhaps the only exception was the Legal Division of the AAA, which was headed by Jerome Frank. The Adjustment Committee, a special group in the commodities section, was specifically entrusted with the investigation of the charges against the landowners and landlords. Eight district agents were borrowed from state extension divisions to serve as field representatives; and they spent several days in Washington where policy and procedural matters were outlined to them, and hundreds of complaints given them to study. The chairman of the Adjustment Committee was J. Phil Campbell, formerly director of the Extension Service in Georgia and then a number of the Program Planning Division of the AAA.[11]

The questions asked by the members or representatives of the investigating committee included the extent to which tenants had been displaced by the cotton adjustment program; the degree to which distress in the rural areas causing movements from the farm to the cities was the result of the wages paid by the Civilian Works Administration (CWA); and whether the displacement of tenants went beyond what one might have expected if a cotton adjustment program had not been in operation. Other questions raised were whether the farms and houses vacated by displaced tenants were being occupied by other families or standing idle; the extent to which displacements were due to actions by landlords or landowners; and whether tenants left voluntarily. Still other questions included whether special arrangements had been entered into by landlords and tenants whereby tenants surrendered claims to any or all the rental payments due them and the extent to which this was occurring; and whether share-tenants who qualified as "managing share-tenants" were denied the right to sign contracts and participate in benefit payments as managing share-tenants.[12]

Within a matter of weeks after the duties of the Adjustment Committee had been defined, D. P. Trent stated that the fieldmen had the full cooperation of the AAA county committeemen, the extension workers, and others. On June 25, 1934 the Adjustment Committee reported 617 complaints had been investigated and of these 419 were found to be without foundation, 98 had been adjusted by county committees or county agents, and 85 by field representatives. Most of the unjustified complaints had been filed in Arkansas where most of the adjustments also were made. Rejection of the contract was recommended only in fifteen cases because of the refusal of the concerned parties to comply with requirements.[13]

However, what were satisfactory results to Cully Cobb, the cotton production section, and other members of the AAA from the investigation of the complaints against landowners and landlords were less than satisfactory to Jerome Frank, Victor Christgau, and Alger Hiss. They wanted a clearly defined AAA policy on landlord-tenant problems. They favored formulating a new committee—to be known as the Committee on Landlord-Tenant Relationships—that would be entrusted with farm labor questions arising in other areas such as in the sugar beet and sugarcane contracts. Once such a policy was adopted, a subcommittee would be delegated the authority to conduct investigations of landlord-tenant complaints and decide on the cancellation of contracts, the withholding of payments, and whether or not to recommend prosecutions.[14]

A state-by-state summary of the Adjustment Committee's findings on complaints filed relating to landlord-tenant relationships under contract as of September 1, 1934, was as follows:

Summary of reports received by adjustment committee on investigation of complaints relating to landlord-tenant relationships under cotton contract, September 1934

State	Complaints Investigated	Cases of Unjustified Complaint	Cases Adjusted by County Committee	Cases Adjusted by Field Representative	Contract Recommended Cancelled
Alabama	55	26	11	17	1
Arkansas	477	346	54	66	11
Florida	11	7	1	3	...
Georgia	151	110	24	16	1
Louisiana	38	24	7	7	...
Mississippi	65	54	7	4	...
Missouri	126	86	21	16	3
North Carolina	53	21	14	18	...
Oklahoma	34	16	15	3	...
South Carolina	24	14	3	7	...
Tennessee	52	34	5	11	2
Texas	368	299	65	1	3
Virginia	3	3	...	...	...
Total	1,457	1,040	227	169	21

The Adjustment Committee concluded that the following facts stood out as a result of the investigation of complaints in 320 counties in the thirteen principal cotton-producing states. There had been no wholesale displacement of tenants or sharecroppers in the South. Unemployment in the rural areas had been due to factors other than the acreage reduction program, such as the migration of unemployed from the cities to the farms. There were cases on the very large plantations where both day-hands and sharecroppers were employed and where the workers shifted from one status to the other year after year. Much misunderstanding occurred because of the interpretation of "managing share tenant." On the other hand, there were intentional violations of the contract; and actually it would have been unusual not to have violators among the 1,012,222 who signed reduction contracts. But there also were tenants who attempted to defraud landlords out of the options sent out under the reduction program of 1933.[15]

Although the cases investigated represented only a sampling of the more than one million signed contracts, the conclusion is evident that the violations were not as isolated as some were inclined to believe. The work of the Adjustment Committee, the county committees, and field representatives in adjusting contracts seemed to have a pacifying effect temporarily. Consequently the violations appeared less harsh than they actually were. If the intent and spirit of the law had been observed, there would have been no need for an investigation, for adjustments, or for the cancellation of contracts. Complaints were often not registered by those who had legitimate complaints but were too frightened to complain even after assurances were given that violations would cease.

Meanwhile, two opposing schools of thought—the agrarians versus urban liberals—had emerged within the USDA and the AAA over the handling of complaints involving landlords and tenants. Most southerners in the AAA, such as Cully Cobb and those associated with him, belonged to the agrarian group, as did Chester Davis, who was not a southerner. The most persistent urban liberals were Jerome Frank, who was vigorously, if not vociferously, supported by Frederic C. Howe, the head of the consumers' counsel; Gardner Jackson, Howe's assistant; and Lee Pressman, a close friend and aide of Frank.

The urban liberals maintained that when landowners or landlords entered into a cotton contract for 1934–1935 with the government under the AAA, they agreed to reduce cotton acreage and should be paid for it; in return the landowners promised to keep the same number of sharecroppers or tenants on their farms as they had in 1933 and to share some of the benefits received under the cotton reduction program with the sharecroppers or tenants. The agrarians, on the other hand, viewed the cotton contract for 1934–1935 as an exclusive agreement between the landlord or landowner and the government, with the landlord or landowner reserving the right to lay off sharecroppers or reduce them to hired laborers and pay them wages for the days they worked on the cotton crop.[16]

Cobb naturally opposed the establishment of a special landlord-tenant committee, as he opposed the transfer to it of jurisdiction over landlord-tenant problems. The success or failure of the cotton adjustment program rested with the cotton production section. Responsibility had to go hand in hand with the corresponding authority in the formulation of plans, policies, and the administration of the details of the cotton program. Cobb also insisted that the cotton production section in Washington and in the field was composed of judicious and impartial people who knew the social and economic problems of the cotton states and were acquainted with the terms of the contracts, administrative rulings, and their application to the cotton farms. If the producers, the community, and the county committeemen were relieved of the responsibility of adjusting complaints and gaining complete compliance in the cotton acreage reduction act, the results could be disastrous.[17]

Trent, on the other hand, advised Frank that the members of the cotton section were conscientious and there were honest differences of opinion, but he further added:

> There has been a rather regular systematic effort to delay or forestall most of the efforts . . . to deal with this problem. The investigations which have been conducted under the organization which I was intrusted by the Secretary and Mr. Davis to set up several weeks ago have been carried on very largely without active support from the Cotton Section and in the beginning there was definite opposition to this activity.[18]

R. K. McConnaughey, the acting chief of the benefit contract section, carried the argument a bit further when he concluded that the establishment of a landlord-tenant committee would accomplish precisely what Cobb feared it would do: create a uniformly effective agency that would meet and dispose of questions involving landlords, tenants, and labor. The AAA was entrusted with a responsibility to all classes of farmers to contribute uniformly as far as possible to the general recovery, and the implementation of policies of such a general nature was not the exclusive monopoly of a particular group, commodity, or section.[19]

By the late summer of 1934 Davis was convinced that Jerome Frank, Frederic C. Howe, Rexford Tugwell, Paul Appleby, and "Beanie" Baldwin were in disagreement with what he, Davis, thought was the main task of the AAA. Davis sensed more than ever that this entire group had nothing but

> contempt for the whole land-grant college set-up and the county agents, Extension Service, and other established agencies with which he worked

closely. They were doing what they could in little ways to split them off from the activity of the farm program. They definitely thought the Farm Bureau was playing too large a part in the whole get-up.[20]

The areas of disagreement widened. Cobb, for instance, believed that the form Frank developed for securing a record of the distribution of parity payments was impractical. Few cotton farmers would be able to fill out such a form properly because few had experience with keeping records; and the presumed audit of the completed forms before checks were issued simply would delay the receipt of them by the farmers. As an alternative, the cotton production section devised a simpler form that, combined with brief instructions, would bring the same results in less time and with less confusion.[21]

By late 1934 the situation on some of the plantations in eastern Arkansas had reached crisis proportions. A group of citizens headed by Professor Amberson, and including Clay East, Harry L. Mitchell, and others identified with the newly formed Southern Tenant Farmers' Union (STFU), planned a test case of the landlord-tenant problem in the federal courts. This group had been trying to get the cotton section to investigate complaints on the plantations since March. E. A. Miller, who had been sent out for this purpose, spent a great deal of time with the plantation owners and came back with a statement "whitewashing" the landlords. One event after another convinced those sponsoring the STFU that the cotton section of the AAA belittled all complaints and made no vigorous attempts to investigate them.

The strategy of the STFU was to go to the federal courts, hoping that Secretary Wallace would associate himself with a group of threatened families, "to ask for an injunction against eviction, and for specific performance of the terms of the contract, particularly Section 7." Oscar Johnston, a prominent Mississippi planter, who wrote Section 7 of the AAA, when asked what he meant by it, replied:

> The section pledged the landowner to use good faith in an honest effort to effect the contemplated acreage reduction in such a manner as to occasion the least possible amount of displacement, and to this end required the landowner to prorate the reduction insofar as proration was possible amongst tenants; it required the landowner to maintain insofar as possible, the normal number of tenants and other employees, and required the landowner to permit tenants on the property to continue in the occupancy of their houses, rent free, except in cases where the tenants might so conduct themselves as to become nuisances or as to menace the welfare of the producer; the section requires the landowner to permit the tenant access to his wood land for fuel and permit the tenants to use an adequate proportion of the rented acreage for production of food and feed crops for home consumption and for pasturage of domestically used livestock.

Amberson viewed the Johnston interpretation of Section 7 as a confirmation of his committee's position: "The contract guarantees tenure to all tenants already on a farm, who have not made a nuisance or a menace of themselves." Since this ran counter to the interpretation of the cotton section of the AAA, the only recourse was for the courts to decide. The Amberson committee chose to make a federal case of these complaints because its members profoundly distrusted the state courts of Arkansas.[22]

By November 1934 the eight district agents who had been brought to Washington from the leading cotton states in early spring to serve as investigators and adjustors of tenant and sharecropper complaints had completed their task. W. J. Green was retained in Washington to handle on the average of about 400 letters per month for several months. In December he began receiving an increasing number of complaints from tenants and sharecroppers on the distribution of parity payments.[23]

Late in December 1934 J. Phil Campbell, the chief of the agricultural rehabilitation section and the Adjustment Committee also reported that complaints were increasing; in fact during late November and most of December the Federal Emergency Relief Administration had received a large number of complaints from local agencies that some landlords were unable to provide for their tenants, sharecroppers, and laborers through the winter months. In some areas large numbers of townspeople were on relief as well.

In the spring of 1934 the Rural Rehabilitation Division had received a number of farmers displaced by the reduction program. Three hundred eighty-five displaced tenants were found in one state for whom no substitutions had been made by the landlords. County relief officials had been able to secure the substitution of 255 tenants by threatening the landlords with the loss of their contracts.[24]

Paul Appleby informed Cobb in late December 1934 that after reading the statement signed by Miller he got the impression that the statement was loaded "on the side of the landlords," and that efforts had been made to find out "how not to do something for the tenants." The cotton section had an obligation to provide means of preventing landlords from taking unfair advantage of the lowly tenants and sharecroppers. Appleby added:

> I know of no single problem before the Department more difficult or more important to the continuing success of our program than this one of landlord-tenant equities in the cotton belt, and I repeat that it seems to me to require extraordinary efforts on the part of the Cotton Section to contribute positive plans, rather than evade responsibilities.[25]

Meanwhile, Trent was beginning to have doubts about what was going to happen if the Rural Rehabilitation Division provided aid during the winter months, possibly the entire season, to tenants and sharecroppers facing eviction. Much as he liked the motives behind the proposal, Trent feared this would enable the cotton section and the AAA to avoid taking a definite stand against landlords who violated their contracts. It also would pass over to the Rural Rehabilitation Division an obligation and responsibility that belonged to the AAA. Many thousands of self-respecting tenants and sharecroppers who up to that point had kept off relief rolls might then find it necessary to go on relief.[26]

The fact that the AAA originally was viewed as a short-range emergency program, however, did not discourage some AAA officials from taking a long-range view of the tenant, sharecropper, and farm laborer problems, and from seeking counsel outside the agricultural establishment for their solution. One person whose views were solicited was Frank Tannenbaum, a man with an unusual background and far-reaching interests. Tannenbaum was precisely the kind of person the USDA normally would not seek out for an opinion.

A native of Austria, Tannenbaum came to the United States with his family in 1905 and settled on a farm near Great Barrington, Massachusetts. He held a variety of jobs as a young man, became involved with the Industrial Workers of the World (IWW), and was convicted for disturbing the peace in 1914 by leading homeless and hungry men into churches. He served time in Sing Sing prison where he became a friend of the warden, Thomas Mott Osborne, who was a renowned prison reformer. Osborne recommended him for entrance into Columbia University, from which he graduated a Phi Beta Kappa in 1921.

Tannenbaum served as a correspondent for *Survey Magazine* in Mexico; and during World War I was a sergeant in the cavalry stationed in South Carolina where he became absorbed in slavery and the traditions of the state. He wrote a study on Mexican land reform and earned a doctorate in economics from the Brookings Institution in 1927. He spent the next three years preparing a social and economic survey of Puerto Rico. In 1931 at the invitation of the Mexican government Tannebaum completed a survey of rural education in Mexico. He spent the next two years visiting every Latin American country as a Guggenheim Fellow, and later taught criminology at Cornell University.[27]

Tannenbaum's solution for the landlord-tenant problem of the South was to take over the extensive landholdings of the insurance companies and federal land banks, break them up into small farms, sell them to the sharecroppers and tenants living on the lands, and make the residue available to people without land. As a means of preventing such lands from reverting to the insurance companies and land banks, he would prohibit the resale, mortgage, or lien of the property to any person other than the corporation responsible for this program, require that all lands returned to the corporation be resold within a specified time, limit all sales to specified mortgages, and prohibit sales to persons holding more than the average acreage in this kind of settlement.

Besides helping keep sharecroppers and tenants on the land, Tannenbaum also believed his plan would help the federal land banks and insurance companies convert their current holdings into more liquid assets, slow down the destruction of the "furnishing system" (creditor provides supplies to tenants to be repaid when cotton is harvested), expedite the development of a crop diversification program in the South, assist the USDA with its cotton control program, develop a better rural education program, lessen tensions between blacks and whites, provide a market in the rural South for the cheap electricity being developed by the TVA, and restore to local ownership property being held by outside corporations.[28]

Lewis C. Gray, chief of the land policy section of the Division of Land Planning, who had been drafting plans to assist small farmers to build a sound rural civilization in the South, was asked for his views of the Tannenbaum proposal for land reform. Gray responded with an incisive analysis of the Tannenbaum proposal that displayed a masterful grasp of the history of the South, the plantation system, and contemporary agriculture and the problems it faced in an industrial society. Gray's analysis left little doubt that he was a spokesman for the agricultural establishment.

The cotton farmers, according to Gray, were feeling the effects of the disintegration that the plantation system had been undergoing since 1880; and the AAA accelerated the pace of disintegration that became more rapid after the World War. The disintegration aggravated relations between landlords and tenants, encouraged the spread of mechanization in the alluvial lands of the lower Mississippi valley and the western states, adversely affected cotton production in the older cotton sections of the Southeast, and hastened the depletion of the soil. Also contributing to the painful effects of disintegration were the gradual exhaustion of the timber resources of the South that formerly provided jobs and income in the rural areas; the low price that cotton brought since World War I, which impaired the ability of many landlords, supply merchants, and plantation operators to supply tenants as in the past; and the pull of industrial employment in the cities. With the approach of the Great Depression, conditions in the rural South were further aggravated by the inability of industry to absorb the normal increase in population, the failure of landlords to obtain the needed credit to furnish tenants, the return to the farm of many people who formerly were employed in urban communities, and the acreage reduction program of the AAA.

The Tannenbaum proposal, according to Gray, represented a vigorous presentation of an idea that had been discussed inside and outside the USDA over the previous ten years. During that time relief agencies spasmodically had attempted to put the idea into practice. But this was much too simple and inflexible a proposal to meet the diverse needs of the rural South. It failed to take into account "the great differences among individuals of the tenant class in . . . personal integrity, dependability, thrift, managerial ability, age, race, and general capacity for independent ownership." This line of reasoning dominated the thinking of the agricultural establishment and, in effect, explains why the USDA over the years had done little, if anything, for the sharecropper and tenant classes.

Gray believed few Southern tenants were capable of independent land ownership and fair-sized commercial holdings. Of the ones who were, a considerable portion lived in Texas and Oklahoma. However, the great majority of tenants in the older cotton and tobacco areas were capable of farming small units to raise a considerable part of the family living and small amounts of cotton and tobacco for market. Gray, however, believed such people should be helped to acquire independent ownership through suitable credit comparable to that provided small holders in Ireland and Denmark. But Gray felt that it would be a mistake to attempt to advance the greater proportion of the tenants to ownership in the immediate future.

Gray argued that in the tentative system he proposed, which was costly and contained the barest essentials, there would be need for "supervision, and guidance ranging all the way from little supervision, except to see that the property was adequately maintained and a suitable cropping system observed, to almost complete supervision and direction such as characterized the plantation system in its more intensive form." Specifically, a large proportion of the "ignorant and improvident class of tenants" would require direction. Provisions likewise had to be made for compulsory savings through the deduction of a percentage of the tenant's income to enable him to contribute to the insurance premiums and escape from annual credit advances while making a crop. Tenants should be encouraged to exercise more self-direction, as they displayed a capacity for it, and to strive for ownership.

Provisions also had to be made for a system of cooperative work where the members of the community could produce nonagricultural goods and services on a small basis, such as construct and repair buildings, manufacture furniture, make harnesses and shoes, and tan leather. The goods and services, as far as practicable, were to be made available through direct exchange; labor that previously had been wasted was to be used more judiciously. The old and infirm, who were unable to do heavy farm work, could care for a garden, chickens, a cow, and a pig or two. The numerous wage hands employed as farm laborers, in lumber camps, or other occupations, in most cases could be given leaseholds subject to the general conditions outlined for the farm tenants, while the ne'er-do-wells and chronic drifters had to have a combination of relief and enforced work, probably through work camps and poor farms.

The Battle for the Disinherited

BY EARLY 1935 the plight of the tenant farmer and sharecropper, if altered at all, had deteriorated, and the complaints against the landlords and managers had increased. At the administrative level conditions were taking a turn for the worse. Paul Appleby, Wallace's secretary, was projecting himself deeper into the landlord-tenant controversy, and Jerome Frank and Frederic C. Howe continued as collaborators. Chester C. Davis, Cully Cobb, and associates in the cotton section, on the other hand, were convinced they had done about all they could do with the Adjustment Committee, that the situation was well in hand, and the proposed landlord-tenant committee was a dead issue.

The turn of events failed to shore up the optimism of Davis, Cobb, and the others. William Amberson's predictions were coming true. Not only were the complaints coming in steadily increasing numbers, but a more aggressive stand was being taken by the aggrieved tenants. The Southern Tenant Farmers' Union (STFU) carried forward an organized protest, and tenants became more aggressive with the increase in notices terminating their leases.

On January 2, 1935 H. C. Malcolm, the deputy commissioner of the Arkansas Bureau of Labor and Statistics in Little Rock, informed W. J. Green, the surviving member of the Adjustment Committee, of a claim filed against a "Dr. Spann," a landlord of Altheimer, Arkansas. The complainants said they had been under the impression that the AAA "was designed to benefit everyone . . . raising cotton and [was] not an avenue to enrich the landlord at the expense of the tenant." Spann, the accused, was a member of the county committee investigating complaints against landlords; hence to suggest that the Spann case be turned over to the county

110

committee was like asking Spann to investigate himself. Rarely did one find a sharecropper on a local committee or a county agent who spent much time advising a small farmer.[1]

Meanwhile, the pressure on the cotton section in the AAA was increasing. An article by Amberson originally scheduled for publication in the *Nation* in an early January issue certainly would intensify public concern; Mary Connor Myers, whose unpublished report on conditions in eastern Arkansas was expected to be sympathetic to the tenants and sharecroppers, thought that the impact of the forthcoming article could be softened if Secretary Wallace made a statement to the effect that all substantial complaints of violations of cotton acreage reduction contracts would be thoroughly investigated and appropriate steps would be taken where violations were established.[2]

More significant, however, was the battle brewing within the AAA over Section 7 of the 1934–1935 cotton contract. Mary Connor Myers was in Arkansas to investigate alleged evictions of share-tenants and sharecroppers by the Fairview Farms, of which Hiram Norcross of Tyronza was president.[3]

Cobb had interpreted Section 7 to mean that the landlord was required to keep the same number of tenants as far as possible, but not necessarily the same tenants. "If he (the landlord) makes a change, however, the new tenant must have the same status as the old." Cobb in a report to Davis also said that "inasmuch as our contracts are with landlords and tenants and not between landlords and tenants the contract itself is not involved in the suit."[4]

Frank, upon learning of Cobb's interpretation, replied that a contrary opinion was being prepared which was going to say that "the landlord must not merely keep the same number of tenants but (in the absence of such justification as is referred to in the contract) keep the same tenants." Frank advised that Cobb and W. J. Green be warned "there are grave dangers that, if they write letters giving legal interpretations of contracts, the secretary may be seriously embarrassed, if it turns out that those legal interpretations are erroneous." Frank restated his position to Wallace, adding that a tenant could be adjudged a nuisance or a menace because he helped form or joined a union and thus be forced off the farm.[5]

On January 14 William E. Byrd, Jr., the assistant to the administrator of the AAA, informed Cobb that E. A. Miller of the cotton section had given the above interpretation of Section 7 as early as the spring of 1934, that Frank had not seen it until very recently, and that Alger Hiss, the assistant counsel general, drafted an opinion Frank approved that was "precisely contrary" to the opinion Miller gave Norcross. Cobb was also advised, "I trust . . . you will avoid . . . such embarrassment in the future by seeing to it . . . that no interpretation of contracts or of statutes or rulings or any

such matters are given by anyone in or under the jurisdiction of the Cotton
Section, without first obtaining an opinion from the General Counsel.''
Frank felt that his duties as general counsel were being transgressed upon by
the cotton section, and wanted to determine whether the unauthorized
Cobb interpretation diminished Norcross's legal obligations.[6]

Frank wrote Byrd that Wallace had not authorized Miller to issue a legal interpretation of the contract, and that it was doubtful whether notice of
Norcross's beliefs regarding the contract constituted notice to the secretary.
Norcross was bound by the contract even if he had telephoned Wallace to
tell him he would withdraw from it before the secretary signed it. Norcross
further admitted that the reason the tenants were evicted was because they
formed or joined a union, which, in the opinions of Frank and Hiss, did not
make the tenants a nuisance or a menace within the meaning of Section 7.
Wallace, in other words, was in a position "to take steps legally to enforce
that obligation."[7]

On January 18 Mary Connor Myers wired Frank that she had interviewed the sharecroppers at Fairview and their attorney, C. T. Carpenter,
and "heard one long story [of] human greed." She found Section 7 was
only one of the paragraphs in the 1934–1935 contract being "openly and
generally violated"; and that a state judge privately expressed the view that
enforcement of this law should be an administrative, not a state court, decision. She further found the croppers to be a much higher class of people
than she had expected; all were "pathetically pleased [the] government has
sent someone to listen to them"; and referred to Carpenter as "one of the
finest men [I] have met for ages." Carpenter wrote Frank the following day
that Mrs. Myers was "proceeding with her investigation very earnestly and
. . . in the spirit of a true lawyer . . . exhibiting more patience, care and
discretion in her work than any investigator I have met."[8]

Although Mrs. Myers had been advised not to permit any publicity
about her work, she was unable to avoid it because the *Ward Rogers* case involving a union organizer had attracted newspaper reporters and photogra-
phers to the Tyronza, Jonesboro, and Marked Tree area in Arkansas where
she spent most of her time. Since the reporters talked with officers of the
STFU, she thought it better to explain her presence there than have the officers of the union do this for her.[9]

From the landlords' standpoint, those who signed contracts had been
under the impression they were complying with the letter and spirit of the
law as long as they kept the same number of tenants in 1934 and 1935 as
they had before. Many of the people who helped implement the program
claimed that the landlords, with few exceptions, reasonably lived up to what
they believed were their responsibilities. Movement of tenants from one
farm to the next, year to year, was normal. No one knew the actual number

involved, but in some areas tenants who moved yearly were estimated to be from 10 to 40 and even 50 percent of all tenants. Some, of course, felt that it was neither practicable nor feasible for the administration to prevent a normal moving of tenants. Also, since the charges in the *Norcross* case raised the question of freedom of organization and the right of tenants to join organizations which they believed protected them, the administration should have informed landlords that the joining of a union or the taking part in tenant's organization was not to be considered a nuisance or a menace under Section 7.[10]

Meanwhile, the concern over the communication between Mary Myers and the newspaper reporters persisted. Frank seemed satisfied she was discharging her duties satisfactorily, but again cautioned her not to issue any statements. Frank also suggested to Alfred D. Stedman, head of the information office for the AAA, that he, too, telephone Myers to find out for himself if she had been issuing unnecessary statements. If he thought so, he, Frank, would recall her. He also reminded Stedman that Myers had been sent to him at the request and under written instructions from Byrd, and had been appointed to his staff at the request of the secretary.[11]

Meanwhile, Harry F. Ward, chairman of the American Civil Liberties Union, and Norman Thomas had wired Wallace to send a representative of the USDA to Tyronza to investigate the reported threats of violence against officers of the STFU before they learned that Myers had been sent there.[12] After learning that Myers was in the field, they expressed satisfaction she understood the conditions and would consult with the sharecroppers; but Ward and Thomas also wanted assurances from Wallace that he would support the recommendations of Myers and the organizing efforts of the STFU.[13]

Appleby assured Ward and Thomas that the USDA had a high regard for Myers, who was expected to deliver a comprehensive report of conditions she found. He noted that careful consideration would be given to her findings (he was unsure if she was expected to make recommendations). Appleby also agreed about the desirability of supporting the right of the tenant farmers to organize, but was at a loss as to what the USDA could do to help this.[14]

Late in January 1935, after word spread that a new interpretation of Section 7 of the 1934–1935 cotton contract would be forthcoming that would require the landowners and landlords to keep the same number of tenants in 1935 as they had in 1934, the county agents of nineteen counties in northeastern Arkansas advised Davis such an interpretation would be unenforceable, causing wholesale withdrawal of contracts by landlords, endless litigation, and great embarrassment to those in charge of the program. The county agents further advised that the cotton program would be in danger of being hampered and possibly destroyed by the new interpretation. They urged him to use his influence to prevent such an interpretation from being released.[15]

Davis, as administrator of the AAA, carried a heavy load and felt the pressures—he had a twitching on his face that showed up plainly when he worked hard. His close working associates liked and sympathized with him as a person and a working colleague. He, also, was a man who disliked interference, especially when he felt he was doing a good job. Because he felt he had the confidence of Congress and those who worked for him in the AAA, he resented having the views of Wallace colored by someone who knew less about the problem than he did. By early 1935 Davis believed one of the chief meddlers was Paul Appleby, Wallace's private secretary.[16]

All callers on Wallace had to pass Appleby's desk and he made all the appointments. All of Wallace's mail, and documents he signed, went across Appleby's desk; and Wallace in those days depended on Appleby's recommendations. Davis, on the other hand, had his AAA office across the street; this office, according to Howard Tolley, was in those days as big and important as all the USDA combined. Appleby, in short, sat between Wallace and Davis; Wallace was the number one man, and Chester Davis number two.[17]

The political climate within the AAA had turned for the worse by the end of 1934. According to Davis,

> There was a well-organized although informal group within the Department of Agriculture, mainly . . . in the Triple A legal division, the consumers' counsel, and the Secretary's office . . . planning and trying to instigate policy moves that in my judgement were not intended when Congress enacted the Agricultural Adjustment Act. . . . I became convinced that a lot of it centered in Appleby and Baldwin in the Secretary's office. . . . George Peek had contended with [this] from the beginning . . . which I had discounted.

Davis also estimated by January 1935 about 90 percent of his time and energy was spent on "internal policing and keeping things on the track inside the organization," which was a hard way to make a living.[18]

Davis further suspected that Appleby, Gardner Jackson, and a few others were seeing John L. Lewis, the head of the budding Congress of Industrial Organizations (CIO), and advancing to Wallace in judicious doses the idea of an alliance between the CIO and discontented farmers that could support him for president. Davis thought Wallace was very susceptible to talk of the "high-minded social action course the USDA should take."

Davis, even though he considered himself on good terms with the planners, felt more at home with men such as John Hutson, Jesse Tapp, and others capable of taking a practical problem, coming up with a way to solve or ameliorate it, and getting results. A doer, Davis felt, had to have a good instinct for planning, or he would be ineffective. The idea person, on the other hand, although a necessary part of any organization, frequently got into trouble trying to translate ideas into action. Experience and balance were requisites for obtaining results.

The friends of Wallace prior to his becoming secretary of agriculture and in the early months of his being in the Cabinet were Clifford Gregory of *The Prairie Farmer* and midwest farm leaders who stood shoulder to shoulder with his father when he was secretary. But by late 1934 leaders of the American Farm Bureau Federation (AFBF), the Grange, the cooperatives, and others had sensed a tendency by Wallace to identify himself with the Tugwell–Frank group. Midwest farm spokesmen told Davis of their great concern. "Farm Bureau leaders had a feeling that they were being kept out of Wallace's office. . . . When they were with Henry he was less frank and less comfortable . . . than he had normally been." Eventually these people felt more secure in the office of Davis and never bothered to see Wallace.[19]

Davis also was irritated by the tendency of Appleby to talk with Wallace and others about AAA matters without first discussing them with him. Tolley reported that Appleby had talked over a lot of things with him about the AAA, but Tolley also said he was careful to report his conversations to Davis, because he knew of the feelings that had developed between Davis and Appleby. But this was not done by all people in the AAA, especially those in the office of the consumers' counsel and the Legal Divison.[20]

Davis had been receiving a good deal, if not most, of the credit for what was being done in the AAA, and this may have caused Appleby to conclude that Wallace was not receiving full credit for developing ideas behind the program. Davis not only believed he was doing a good job, but felt that Wallace had too many idealists and dreamers around him who were unfamiliar with the practical problems confronting the AAA, hence making Davis's job as administrator more difficult than it would have been had they given Davis full cooperation. Jerome Frank, Frederic Howe, and others in the urban-liberal group were nothing but a "bunch of city-slickers" who had been brought to the USDA by that "master non-farmer" Rexford G. Tugwell, and never realized what they were trying to do was strange to many in the USDA.[21]

Some of Howe's staff in the consumers' counsel became closely identified with members of the Farmers' Union, the Midland Cooperatives of Minneapolis, and the Finnish Cooperatives of Wisconsin, none of whom had working relations with the AAA. These affiliations, however, enabled the consumers' counsel to say he had some support from the soil in the campaign to curb the processors and middlemen.[22]

Milk was the first to draw the attention of the consumers' counsel.

Hearings were held in the major milksheds of the country to determine prices farmers were receiving and consumers paying, the volume of milk supplies, and what was to be done. Unfortunately, the dairy section became a major battleground and had a series of head administrators.

Frank, Howe, Gardner Jackson, and others clustered around them believed that the cotton and dairy sections had too much influence over the AAA and were affected greatly by marketing agreements. Davis, observed Jackson, was not a New Dealer in the terms that "we young, inexperienced romantics were when we came into the government." Jackson also believed Davis lacked a philosophy on the role of the government and the direction it should take. He played it too much by ear, and some thought Davis "was aiming to . . . undercut and unseat Henry Wallace and take over his job."[23]

The urban-liberal group believed it had a philosophy and a mission to perform. Frank, Tom Blaisdell, Lee Pressman, and Gardner Jackson, largely at the request of Frank and by the arrangements of Jackson, had a "heart to heart, off-the-record talk with [Louis] Brandeis up at his summer home late in the summer of 1934. This was [part of] a very specific design in Jerome's mind, with Thurman Arnold and Wesley Sturges and Lee [Pressman]." Frank and his group wanted the blessings of Brandeis for what they were trying to do, especially the milk program, and the meeting lasted for many hours. Frank and Blaisdell came away encouraged, believing "they would not be knocked out in whatever was going on in the Triple A," if the Brandeis attitude prevailed. Subsequent events, however, proved them wrong.

Jackson claimed what Frank, Howe, he, and others were attempting to do within the AAA was along old-fashioned Jeffersonian lines. Their "book and records" fight against the packers, their efforts to see that the growers were represented fairly in the tobacco marketing agreements, their crusade to prevent the processing tax from being passed on to the consumer, and their campaign to make sure the benefit payments were distributed fairly among the tenants and sharecroppers were all conducted within the capitalist framework. Only when they gave serious consideration to a plan that would have enabled the government to take over an independent packing plant and use it as a yardstick could one claim, conceded Jackson, they were thinking of doing something that was revolutionary or radical.

Another delicate situation arose with the appointment of Einar Jensen, a naturalized Dane and graduate student of John D. Black, as the administrator of the marketing agreement for dairy products in the Boston milkshed. The consumers' counsel office viewed this as a key experimental operation because the dairy farmers of Vermont and New Hampshire, who were organized in a very well-run marketing cooperative, had become highly skeptical about the leadership of the New England Milk Marketing Association headed by Wendell Phillips Davis. Jensen had experience managing a cooperative in his native Denmark and was received with open arms by the dairy farmers.

Jensen found that by classifying milk and increasing consumption through a direct link between the farmers and the biggest chain system in Boston and the New England area he could give the farmers greater returns than they ever had before. Wendell Davis and the processors and distributors retaliated by seeking the dismissal of Jensen in the fall of 1934. At this juncture James A. Farley, postmaster general and patronage boss, interjected himself into the controversy and admitted there was a great deal of pressure to remove Jensen, but asked that his dismissal be held in abeyance until after the November elections. Farley believed that the presence of Jensen in his job until after the election might swing a sizable farm vote for the Democrats in Vermont and New Hampshire.[24]

Wallace delivered a speech early in 1934 about the excessive profits the processors and distributors were making, which irritated Charles Holman and his National Federation of Milk Producers. Reports of federal investigators showed that the profits of many milk producers ranged from 14 to 30 percent of their net plant investment in the previous five years. About that same time the consumers' counsel had been trying to get Mayor Daniel W. Hoan of Milwaukee and his common council to vote for a plan of municipal processing and distribution of milk.[25]

The Frank–Howe forces also were giving special attention to the specialty crops in California whose principal spokesman was Jesse Tapp. The main struggle in this instance was over asparagus. Canners likewise were accused of obtaining altogether too large a margin which again brought the accounts, books, and records of the business controversy into the open. Ironically, shortly before Frank, Howe, Jackson, and the rest were relieved of their positions, the code that Tapp and Davis wanted was disapproved. As Jackson observed, Wallace supported Frank and Howe and his group on the asparagus code one day, then ''canned'' them on the next. The design in the cases of various fruits and other small specialty crops was to squeeze more of the profits of the middleman into the hands of the producers and consumers. There also was the question of determining a ''proper'' and ''just profit.''[26]

The immediate cause for the AAA purge revolved around the new interpretation of Section 7 in the 1934–1935 cotton contract issued by Frank. From Davis's point of view, a telegram precipitated the firing of Frank and others. During Davis's absence Appleby sent a telegram to all state AAA cotton administrators informing them of a new legal opinion to be issued by the USDA that would give a radically different interpretation of Section 7 in the 1934–1935 contract. The telegram actually was sent by Appleby in the name of Secretary Wallace, and signed by Victor Christgau, the deputy and acting administrator of the AAA.

After Davis located and read a copy of the new legal opinion, he argued this was a revolutionary interpretation of Section 7 that would have far-reaching effects. The new interpretation held that all tenants on land covered by the 1934–1935 contract had rights for the duration of the contract identical with those that prevailed when the contract first went into effect. Davis, before doing anything more, checked with the secretary, then discussed the matter with Seth Thomas, the solicitor of the USDA, and his old friend, M. L. Wilson, assistant secretary of agriculture.[27]

To Davis the negotiations leading up to the 1934–1935 contract were of great relevance to the issue at hand. Those who sat in on the initial deliberations of the contract had been deadlocked after six weeks of discussion in trying to determine how best to protect the interests of the tenants. In fact the approval and issuance of the contract had been held up by this dispute, despite the pressure to get the contract out into the field. Davis believed that Section 7 was the best compromise that could be worked out under the circumstances. At no time during the discussions, noted Davis, did Alger Hiss, who sat in on these discussions and was a member of the Frank–Howe faction and who later initialed the telegram releasing the new interpretation, "ever suggest or recommend that a provision be inserted to require the contract signers to assume . . . legal liability to retain on the farm, in status as tenants, the identical tenants who were on the land when the contract went into effect."

The provisions of Section 7 also had been explained thoroughly to the cotton growers by the representatives of the USDA before they signed the contracts, and more than a million of them accepted the terms of the contract in the light of these explanations. The meaning of the contract, according to Davis, "was clearly understood and not publicly questioned during the sign-up campaign or in the first year of operations under the contract." Although Section 7 sought to maintain as many cotton workers as in 1933 on the farm, with a minimum of displacement, "no contract signer understood it to require him to retain as tenants the same individuals as in 1933. . . . Had such [an] interpretation been placed on the section in the beginning as now proposed, there would have been no sign-up." This is why Davis said he read the legal opinion "with amazement and alarm."

Davis told Wallace of the probable effects of the new interpretation of Section 7, that it had been sent out without having his approval, and that he could not continue to live with the situation that had developed within the USDA. Davis also cautioned Wallace that "if this goes into effect it will set off forces that will drive you out of the Cabinet. You won't be able to stay." Events proved Davis a poor prognosticator, but he and Wallace agreed to meet again to discuss the subject.

Davis next sought out M. L. Wilson, his "father confessor, advisor, and friend" of more than twenty years standing, who had guided him in some of the most crucial decisions he ever made. M. L. was very serious about what was happening, had seen more clearly perhaps the inevitable course that had developed, and agreed to the procedure Davis proposed. "He did not try to . . . modify it in any way. He said he guessed that was what had been done. I came away feeling that I had his moral support, and I guess that is what I wanted more than anything else."

After he decided what he would do, Davis conferred with Seth Thomas. He asked Thomas whether he would be ready and willing to take over the legal responsibilities of the AAA in "a day's notice or less," and Thomas said "Yes." Later Davis recalled,

> Solicitor Thomas and John P. Wenchel, his deputy, were both quite clear that the organic law creating the Department of Agriculture unqualifiedly placed the responsibility for all legal activities in the Department upon the Solicitor, and that in setting up an independent general counsel in the Triple A we were not complying with the law.

Davis now was more determined than ever that the legal functions would be taken over by the solicitor "without causing a ripple of disturbance in the operation of the Triple A. And a lot of free-wheeling young lawyers would be subject to Department discipline they hadn't had before."

After conferring with Wallace on February 4, Davis came away convinced that he would have a free hand in discharging those who had been interfering with the functioning of the AAA. A few of the key men were mentioned, but they did not add up to the total of those who left.

> I named Jerome Frank. It was under his general shelter that a cluster of trouble-makers had assembled . . . the actions in his division which I called disruptive and disloyal could not have been taken without his approval. He was part of it. He was the head and heart. Lee Pressman was active and aggressive. He was considered the number two man in the general counsel's office. I was determined that I did not want any more of either of them.

Davis also wanted the resignations of Frederic Howe and Gardner Jackson, his assistant, for the same reasons. In the legal division he named Francis Shea, who had been head of the opinions section, and told Wallace he was not going to retain Victor Christgau as deputy administrator of the AAA if the heads of the important sections of the AAA backed him up. Davis likewise told Wallace that Appleby and Baldwin in his office "were in this up to their necks, and if they were working under me and I had the authority, I would fire them too."

Although Davis left his conference convinced that he had the unqualified support of the secretary for his proposed actions, months later he learned that the secretary had changed his mind after the reorganization had been completed, but he never learned why.

Davis started out February 5, the day of the firings, with a number of interviews, beginning with Frank and Howe. Frank, according to Davis, was not particularly surprised by the dismissals, but he wanted to know "why." To which Davis replied, as he reminisced years later, it was because of the dishonest legal opinion that had "brought us to the breaking point," and "the continuous strain of policing hostile and embarrassing activities within the Department." Frank pressed Davis for his "full reasons" and Davis recalled saying something like this:

> We've worked together for a long time. I've had the chance to watch you, and I think you are an outright revolutionary, whether you realize it or not. You are using the AAA in every way you can to stir up all the forces you can . . . in favor of political and other actions towards the ends you seek, which I am quite sure by now are not the ends sought in the Agricultural Adjustment Act. The Secretary has agreed that it has to end, and this is the way to do it.

Pressman came in to see Davis after Frank had spoken to him, and his reaction was surprising. Pressman in effect admitted that Davis was doing the right thing and expressed surprise he had not done this earlier. He was curious, however, about his own removal.

> But I want to ask you, why me? Haven't I been cooperative? Haven't I been carrying the load around here and doing everything possible? I think the action you're taking is alright, but I just ask you not to include me. I don't think I belong in it.

Davis stood firm and told Pressman he was out.

Davis showed more compassion in dealing with Howe and Christgau. However, he informed Howe he had been negligent as the consumers' counsel in allowing some of his subordinates to "run the show" and in not controlling them. Since Howe had financial problems, Davis told him he would try and find him another job. Christgau's case bothered Davis because he liked the man and the worst thing that could be said about him was that he had been "stupid." So he asked a "jury of his peers" to study the case and advise him what they thought should be done with Christgau. The unanimous opinion was that he be retained but not as deputy administrator of the AAA.

Davis did not ask for the resignation of Alger Hiss, a hardworking conscientious servant in whom Davis had a lot of faith, and who at the time had been on leave without pay working for the Senate Munitions Investigations Committee. Davis discovered later much to his consternation that after reading the legal opinion which had been drafted by Margaret Chapman, Hiss came down from his office on the Hill to approve it. "If anyone in the Department had reason to know what the language of section seven meant and was intended to mean," recalled Davis, "it was Alger Hiss who had participated in the discussion of it for weeks, helped draft it, and signed it."

Determined to get to the bottom of the matter Davis called Hiss soon after the events of February 5 and asked him:

> Alger, you know as well as I do that this new section 7 interpretation is a dishonest legal opinion. Why in the hell did you approve it? Of all the men in the legal division you are in the best position to know that it is dishonest.

His response was that "the language can be interpreted the way the opinion proposes." Davis replied,

> Of course it can if you want to torture the language, but you know damn well it doesn't mean that and was never intended to. You sat through every meeting we had. You know how the contract was explained to the producers, and how it was interpreted for a full year. Why in the hell did you do it, I want to know?[28]

Although Hiss was not fired, he did resign shortly thereafter, as did a few others.

Alfred Stedman, the AAA press officer, advised Davis that at the press conference they should stand together on their press statement and state that the reorganization was "made in the interests . . . of smoothness and efficiency in operation"; and the reorganization of the AAA would make for a closer working relationship with the office of the secretary "first, through the consolidation of the legal work in the Solicitor's office, and second, through the work of the operating council, headed by Secretary Wallace and yourself [Davis]." Stedman likewise thought it advisable to avoid defining a specific issue, especially one that suggested a split along radical and conservative lines; and that anything said about the need for being surrounded by men with training in agricultural problems should be counterbalanced with a specific statement of recognition of the ability and hard work of Jerome Frank.[29]

Meanwhile, the "purged" members of the AAA congregated in the offices of Frank and Pressman and sought assistance from the higher authorities. Tugwell, who was away when Frank was relieved of his duties, flew back to Washington shortly after being informed of what happened.[30] Wallace said he would see two members of the discharged group, but not all; and Frank and Hiss were the ones to see him. Frank's thesis was that Chester Davis had acted on his own as a means of displacing Wallace as secretary of agriculture; and if true, Frank and the others planned to resist it.

Frank and Hiss reported that as they entered Wallace's office the secretary came forward from behind his desk with tears in his eyes and hands outstretched to Frank, saying that he had to do it or words to that effect. Wallace praised all of them saying what great fighters they had been for the good cause, but he could not face them after what had happened.[31]

Tugwell, the man on whom Frank, Howe, and others looked upon for advice and support, years later claimed that he never had had any great interest in the struggle, and always wanted to resign but stayed because Wallace wanted him. Tugwell also feared that if all these people resigned it would "look like [a] liberal desertion of the administration," and recommended that any new job offered Frank had to "look like a better one than he now has." "The whole Department," continued the under secretary, "is seething and I am afraid my own situation may become impossible unless things quiet down . . . if possible an issue of principle ought to be avoided by convincing Frank his services are really needed elsewhere and that his past efforts were appreciated."[32]

Tugwell, after talking with Wallace about it, went to see the president immediately and advised him that the firing of Frank was a betrayal of everything the New Dealers had been working for, that Frank and his group were trying to protect the president and something had to be done. Roosevelt promised he would do something for Frank and got him another job. Tugwell further was of the belief that the entire episode was part and parcel of a studied plan of Davis "to rid the Department of all liberals and give the reactionary farm leaders full control of policy; . . . meaning, of course, full satisfaction to all the processors with whom we had been dealing since most of the farm leaders [were] owned body and soul by the processors."[33]

Politics undoubtedly was the deciding factor in the firing of Jerome Frank and his collaborators. Wallace had to keep strength behind him, and he wanted support from farm leaders who were dissatisfied with Tugwell and other "radicals" in the USDA. Tugwell admitted farm leaders had no confidence in him and as a consequence were turning against Wallace. "A Secretary of Agriculture who doesn't have the confidence of the agricultural community is in a pretty bad way," said Tugwell; but he also felt that a secretary could keep the confidence of the agricultural community "and still keep his policy." "He gave up his policy," said Tugwell. "It was more failure of leadership than anything else. It was letting himself be pushed around by what I thought were pretty sinister forces."[34]

According to Drew Pearson and Robert S. Allen, the roving journalists, the growing belief in the big eastern industrial centers was that the

AAA, not the drought, had been primarily responsible for the rising living costs.

> The Roosevelt administration has played directly into the hands of those fomenting this idea, by discharging Jerome Frank, Gardner Jackson and Lee Pressman—who fought for the interests of the consumer and claimed that he was being squeezed between the farmer on the one hand and the big processors on the other . . . the AAA purge . . . created a distinctly unfavorable impression in consumer centers. This feeling was not reflected in the West or South where the AAA had powerful popular support.[35]

Meanwhile, a spirit of complacency set in after the purge. As long as Frank, his group, and the people in the consumers' counsel office were in the AAA, there was a questioning of the effectiveness of the program, a great deal of debating and discussions, and demands for changes. But after the firings, more people in the AAA expressed satisfaction with the programs in operation. The public began to think of agricultural adjustment primarily as a program of writing benefit checks to farmers and making loans. Many had grown tired after their experiences with the depression, the campaign of 1932, the coming of the New Deal, and the establishment of the AAA and the numerous other agencies. When the New Dealers took office, "There was new blood, new ideas, new thoughts . . . the desire . . . [by] government to do things that it never would face before. There [also] was a willingness to legislate expeditiously. . . . That was in 1933." By 1935 most people who had pushed and argued a point of view and a particular program saw it implemented or rejected and as a consequence left the government. "Any organization, any agency—public or private—tends to ossify, get hardening of the arteries, settle down, not want to do anything new." "I'd seen it happen," recalled Howard R. Tolley, "with surprising rapidity in the Department of Agriculture in the AAA."[36]

Davis was unaware that the events of February 5, 1935 had affected his relations with Wallace. He felt, in fact, that they worked harmoniously in the succeeding months to secure amendments in the AAA and passage of the Soil Conservation and Domestic Allotment Act. But while friendly and cooperative, they were not as sympathetic as previously. Wallace, Davis believed, was showing signs of the pressure to lead him into politics, the constant work "going on around Henry to convince him that he was the Messiah for the under-privileged, and that in that role and along that route a glorious political future lay before him."[37]

Opposition to the AAA Mounts

THE DROP IN COTTON PRICES in March 1935, the mounting opposition to the processing tax, the strenuous efforts to make the AAA function more smoothly, the May 1935 march of farmers to Washington, D.C., the planning of alternative and supplementary programs, the campaign to assure the American public that the farmers were not benefiting at its expense taxed the physical and human resources of AAA personnel and indicated that the firing of Jerome Frank and his collaborators had not lessened the pressures. Matters were aggravated by the Supreme Court decision of January 6, 1936 declaring the AAA unconstitutional. New significance was given to ideas and plans that AAA leaders had been considering throughout 1935.

Wallace and his associates were thinking about the workability of zoning laws for land settlement comparable to those in the cities. They were contemplating changes in land holdings that were too small or too large to farm profitably, and the creation of public agencies to encourage family farming in cases where the creditors had taken over large tracts of land or where plantation owners no longer could operate their holdings under old standards.[1]

Meanwhile, complaints kept coming in from blacks, which for the most part were ignored, and from consumers—both black and white—which administrators tried to answer. The blacks protested about discrimination and their inability to make a living because of the political structure of the South. In response to the consumers, administration leaders argued that farm prices had risen only 6 percent above the prewar levels by August 1935 while the prices of the items the farmers bought climbed 26 percent; hence the consumers did not suffer because of the AAA. It was true that the unemployed found it difficult to meet their living costs, but the remedy was jobs, not farm prices below a fair exchange value.[2]

Wallace further maintained that the rise in farm income had a healthy effect on industrial income. Industrial payrolls and the average earnings of the employed since 1933 had increased at about the same rate as farm income by late 1935. USDA sources, for instance, indicated the shipment of industrial goods into rural areas had increased in proportion to the growth in rural income. Four of every five persons reemployed in urban industry since the spring of 1933, continued Wallace, owed the recovery of their jobs to improvements in farm conditions. Farm recovery started earlier than industrial recovery, but there was evidence that urban industry benefited from this immediately. Automobile sales on farms and in towns of less than 10,000 people in 1934 totaled 833,000 as compared with 602,000 in 1933, an increase of 231,000 sales or 38 percent; but in cities of more than 10,000 people, the sale of automobiles in 1934 was 1,055,000 as against 892,000 in 1933, an increase of 163,000 or only 18 percent.

By mid-July 1935 Wallace was beginning to focus more attention on conservation as the hope of the future and on bringing the farmers a more equitable share of the national income. He was unsure when and how this switch from acreage reduction to conservation could be made, but he felt a longtime program with benefit payments for conservation through better crop rotation and the conversion of more lands to legumes, meadow, and pasture would help check soil erosion, production problems, and, probably, surpluses.[3]

The Soil Conservation Service (SCS) that was transferred to the USDA took on added significance after the *Hoosac Mills* decision in 1936 outlawed the processing tax. The AAA had been working on a program for the constructive use of land taken out of cash crop cultivation. In doing so it indirectly caused more Southerners to shift to livestock production and thus create more competition for producers in the Northwest. The main difference between the SCS and AAA approach was that the SCS sought to bring about better land use through the model state laws of the soil conservation districts by taking acreage out of cultivation as a means of curtailing production.[4]

One contract per farm was still another idea talked about in 1934, especially by H. R. Tolley. Instead of having one contract for the farmer to adjust his wheat acreage and another for his corn, if there were two crops on the farm, the farmer would have one contract for both crops. In the fall of 1935 the USDA finally publicized its plan of placing all cooperating farmers under a single contract to eliminate red tape, encourage farmers to shift to crops better suited to their soil and nearest markets, and provide a more flexible plan for them to adjust their production to changing yearly demands.[6]

Wallace saw no conflict in striving for efficiency and controlling production at the same time. Since the government devoted many years of research to improve types of seeds, discover better methods of fertilizing, soil control, and scientific efficiency, it was absurd for farmers to work long hours to produce crops they could raise in less time. Naturally the administration was sensitive to criticisms of its agricultural control programs and at times responded to critics. On one occasion Wallace lashed out at a critic by saying, "It is false sentimentality for a true-believer in the old-fashioned profit system . . . to urge the American farmer to produce until the last hungry Chinaman is fed and the last naked Hindu is clothed." Wallace suggested that the true believer "begin with the really great sinners, the men who close down factories and throw labor out of work . . . we are all victims of a system which placed a premium on scarcity rather than abundance." Wallace informed a correspondent that the administration never favored a program of scarcity, but "it opposed consistently the accumulation of unsalable surpluses in excess of amounts needed for maximum consumption, ample carry-over for emergencies, and all probable exports."[7]

Meanwhile the twelve-cent-a-pound loan policy on cotton which the administration hoped would prevent cotton prices from falling below that level came under heavy fire following the price collapse of March 11, 1935. Senator "Cotton Ed" Smith of South Carolina requested that the Senate conduct an investigation of the USDA. Form letters of protest kept coming to Wallace from persons who in the past made a good living working with cotton compresses along the waterfront of Galveston, but now were working on a part-time basis for less take-home pay, because there was no cotton for them to handle and little else they could do. Wallace also received many letters in support of the cotton program that suggested they, too, had been inspired by some central source because they were identical in content.[8]

The constitutionality of all AAA programs was questioned with greater vigor during 1935. The issues raised, even though the nature of the attacks varied, included the excise taxes collected on the processed commodities and used to pay farmers who agreed to adjust their acreages; the marketing agreement and order program that bound the distributors not to engage in unfair marketing practices, regulated the marketing, and fixed the minimum prices paid on milk and milk products; and finally the Bankhead Cotton Act, the Kerr Tobacco Act of 1934, and the Potato Act of 1935, which authorized marketing allotments and imposed a special tax on marketing in excess of the allotments.[9]

The advocates of the processing tax had given a great deal of painstaking study to this and other forms of taxation, and believed the processing tax was about as fair and effective a tax as could have been imposed and administered. The intention was that the AAA benefit payments would be paid farmers well in advance of the time the taxes were collected, and definite provisions had been made with the Treasury Department to advance money for this purpose that would be repaid with the processng taxes collected later. The theory behind making benefit payments well ahead of the collection of the processing taxes was that this would help restore business activity, buying power, and price levels sooner than if the benefit payments were paid after the taxes were collected.

Unfortunately, the AAA found it far more difficult to check individual farm contracts, establish bases, and check compliance than had been anticipated; hence it took much more time to get the benefit payment checks to the farmers. In fact the disbursement of payments ran behind instead of ahead of the collection of taxes. The hope, however, was that the administration would carry through the disbursements more rapidly the second year; but the fact tax collections ran $150 million ahead of benefit payments in late October 1934 meant that the AAA had failed to provide the intended stimulus.[10]

Mordecai Ezekiel also was unhappy when he discovered that many in the AAA assumed that the cotton tax would continue in 1935–1936 at the going rate. If the administration had hopes of obtaining judicial approval of the AAA, it had to prepare at once to change the existing cotton tax at the beginning of the next season on the basis of the going parity price and farm price levels. Ezekiel also preferred Congress to provide a deficiency appropriation to make up for deficits incurred from a lowering of the tax, than run the danger of having a legal overthrow of the processing tax itself. From an administrative standpoint AAA leaders believed that the processing tax on cotton was working reasonably well. With improvements the tax was expected to work even smoother. It continued for a year after the reduction program ended.[11]

Meanwhile, the constitutionality of the processing tax. on cotton and the corresponding floor taxes was being challenged in the courts. The receivers of the Hoosac Mills Corporation in the case of *Franklin Process Company* vs *Hoosac Mills* refused to honor the claim of the collector of the Internal Revenue Service on the grounds that the AAA taxes were unconstitutional. Although the decision upheld the constitutionality of the AAA, the right of the plaintiffs to appeal this decision, allowed on January 23, 1934, posed a series of problems for the AAA and the USDA.

For several reasons the strategy of the USDA was to bypass the Circuit Court of Appeals and take the cases directly to the U.S. Supreme Court. Some $705 million in processing taxes had been collected by February 28, 1935, and the payments actually made to the farmers by December 31, 1934 amounted to about $534 million. Payments of nearly $1 billion were to be made during the fiscal years of 1935 and 1936 from the processing taxes collected. If the AAA was declared unconstitutional, the effect on the budget would be serious and become increasingly difficult. The consumers who paid the taxes would not be reimbursed, and the processors would pocket an unconscionable gain. In other words, the consequences of an unfavorable decision would be greatly lessened if such a decision was made early.

There were other practical reasons for an early decision. The receivers of the Hoosac Mills Corporation had not paid any processing taxes since October 8, 1933. Many processors who paid their taxes complained about this and it was becoming more difficult to explain satisfactorily why the court refused to order payment of the taxes on the grounds there was uncertainty regarding the constitutionality of the AAA.[12]

The opposition of the cotton mill interests to the tax up to early 1935 had not gone much beyond the passage of resolutions of protest, the publication of newspaper articles, conversations, and a few attacks in the courts. Because of the acute conditions among the cotton growers and the fact that public sentiment favored an action program, defeat of the Agricultural Adjustment Act could bring about the defeat of the growers' own textile code and provisions for limiting the output, and perhaps lead to the adoption of another agricultural program more objectionable than the one in operation.

Still, the cotton textile interests considered the processing tax a distinct burden. They believed that the tax, combined with the higher price of manufacture resulting from the cotton-textile code and the cost of raw material, raised cotton good prices to a level that was out of line with general commodity prices. They also charged that the tax placed cotton at a competitive disadvantage with rayon, which did not have to pay a tax. The response to the rayon argument was that the quantity of rayon used in the United States in 1935 was equivalent to about 7 percent of the cotton used. However, when it could be demonstrated that a competitive article such as rayon was taking the market away from cotton because it did not have to pay a processing tax, the AAA provided that a compensatory tax would have to be levied on rayon. Thus far a shift from cotton to rayon had not been demonstrated and a tax was not imposed on rayon.[13]

The textile industry then consisted of about 1,200 units and was suffering from excessive competition, poor coordination between production and sales, excessive stocks, and high operating costs. Matters also had been aggravated for the industry by the fact that the textile mills in the South enjoyed certain competitive advantages over those of New England. Spindles in operation in New England, for instance, had decreased at an average of 800,000 spindles a year from February 1923 to February 1933 when the processing tax was nonexistent. From August 1, 1933 to April 1, 1935, when the processing tax was in existence, the cotton spindles, ironically, decreased at an average rate of less than 245,000 a year. The problems of the cotton mills in 1935, in other words, were much the same as they had been in 1933, before the AAA became law and regardless of the price of cotton. In fact it might even be argued that the processing tax slowed down the rate in the decrease of spindles per year, that the tax was passed on to the ultimate consumer and was not a significant factor in the plight of the textile mills, and that the removal of the tax could not materially benefit the cotton spinning and weaving mills.[14]

The textile interests, however, refused to accept the conclusions of Wallace on the processing tax. They did not claim the processing tax alone had been responsible for their plight but that it had become a factor in their present condition.[15]

The AAA felt hampered in its efforts to get its side of the story on the processing tax before the public because of the restrictions placed on the use of publicity men and speakers. The agency was confined to issuing releases telling what the AAA was doing and speeches delivered in an incidental way by officials whose time was spent mostly on administrative matters. The AAA, as a result, depended on the actions of interested citizens.[16]

And the supporters of the AAA did express themselves. Merchants, farmers, politicians, and others, especially in the South, assailed the New England cotton textile interests, the political opposition, the processors, the large cotton merchants, and others who wanted to deny the farmers protection. The AAA, in their opinion, represented about the only wholesale attack being waged successfully against low farm prices and low income. The farmers wanted self-sustaining and permanent protective tariffs like the industrialists had, and the processing tax was one way of achieving this.[17]

As the opposition to the processing tax hardened and the charges and countercharges multiplied, Clifford H. Day of Plainview, Texas planned to head a march to Washington May 14 as a means of expressing the farmers' appreciation to the federal government for all the AAA had done for them. Years later Chester C. Davis remarked: "This march on Washington was not in behalf of any amendments or any particular legislation. It wasn't asking for anything. It wasn't Farm Bureau. It was Cully Cobb." Davis recalled Cobb coming in to see him one morning and saying, "You know Chestah . . . the people from the cotton states would like to send some folks down to Washington just to come down there to call on the President, call on the Secretary, call on others, just to express their appreciation of what's been done for them, and not to ask for anything." This, according to Davis, was the genesis of the "so-called march on Washington." Davis claimed he warned Cobb that this was "loaded with dynamite," but as presented it was not nearly as big as it finally turned out to be. "The bulk of it was in the South and Cobb was the grand commander of it." Cobb's belief was that "nothing could be more calculated to impress Congressmen that a bunch of farmers coming down to say 'Thank you for what you've done.' "[18]

Wallace said he first heard of the proposed visit to Washington in an Associated Press story about April 17, but disavowed having anything to do with it. Later Ed O'Neal, the president of the AFBF, telephoned Wallace that some farmers were coming to Washington from his home state, Alabama, who wanted to see the president and asked Wallace to make an appointment for them. Wallace informed O'Neal that the president would be happy to see the farmers, but the USDA had no authentic information about a general meeting of farmers being planned in Washington.

After the meeting, however, Wallace wrote: "Many farmers told me personally . . . they wanted to thank the government for what had been done . . . to help them through the adjustment program." Since the processor groups maintained strong lobbies in Washington for years, there was "nothing reprehensible about . . . farmers making their voices heard in the capital along with those of the processors' lobbies."[19]

Once the farmers reached Washington, their leader, Day, appealed to Wallace and Davis for help because he and his associates knew little about the city, and because more farmers came than had been expected. Accommodations were found through the aid of the Washington Board of Trade. There were other complications, too. The hall originally engaged for the meeting turned out to be too small for the crowd that assembled, and with the help of officials of the USDA and AAA, Constitution Hall was obtained for the purpose.

Accusations soon began circulating that the federal government had "bought and paid" for the farmers' meeting. In answering Senator Daniel O. Hastings, Republican of Delaware, Wallace quoted from a letter Davis had written to Senator Joseph T. Robinson of Arkansas on the same question. The AAA, said Wallace, had neither questioned the right of the farmers to come to Washington nor their right to petition as provided for by the Constitution. Nor for that matter did the AAA deny the farmers the right or discourage them from visiting the capital. On the other hand, the AAA neither sponsored, financed, nor permitted county agents or production control associations to subsidize the farmers' visit.

Officials of the USDA, however, wired extension directors in the states that sent farmer delegates to Washington asking them whether state extension funds were used to finance the trip, whether state extension officers participated in organizing the farmers or giving them instructions to participate, whether county agents had any hand in this, and how many agents accompanied the farmers to Washington.

State extension directors who replied by May 24 said that extension funds had not been used for the trip, and that the farmers raised the money among themselves and through contributions made by local businessmen and friends. No extension director indicated his office had given instructions to county agents to promote the visit. Of the more than 1,300 county agents in the country, the directors of the thirty states reporting indicated there were less than 100 county agents from these states among the 4,500 or so farmers who came to Washington. This figure of 100, however, did not include county agents from Texas, which sent one of the largest farmer delegations, and from a few other states that had not reported.[20]

On May 27, 1935 the U.S. Supreme Court handed down the *Schechter* decision invalidating the National Recovery Act on the grounds that it constituted an unlawful delegation of legislative power. On the basis of the *Schechter* decision, the Circuit Court of Appeals apparently reversed the *Franklin Process Company* vs *Hoosac Mills* decision of 1934 that originally held the processing tax valid and declared the tax unconstitutional on the grounds that it had been imposed by an unconstitutional delegation of legislative power.[21]

Once the *Schechter* decision was handed down, the congressional committees considering changes in the AAA revised the proposed amendments to simplify the administration of the act, make possible the implementation of the proposed "ever-normal granary plan," and define more explicitly the standards to be used in guiding the administration of the adjustment programs and overcoming the contention that the AAA delegated legislative powers. Congress passed the revised amendments.[22]

Meanwhile the *Schechter* and *Hoosac Mills* (1934) decisions had encouraged many processors to assume that the processing tax ultimately would be declared unconstitutional, and more than 1,100 suits were filed to prevent its enforcement. By the end of September 1935 these lawsuits prevented the collection of about $100 million in processing taxes.[23]

The legal position of the federal government in the processing taxes was that they were excise taxes "uniform in their operation both geographically and in their incidence upon all processors in the same class, and levied under the tax power granted to Congress in article 1, section 8, clause 1 of the Federal constitution." Use of sums equal to the proceeds of the processing taxes for benefit payments to farmers who agreed to adjust their production also was a proper exercise of the general spending power of Congress based on the section that said "Congress shall have power to pay and collect . . . excises to . . . provide for the . . . general welfare of the United States."

The appropriations, in the opinion of the government attorneys, were for "the general welfare," since the AAA was held indispensable to the recovery of American agriculture and the general economy. The "processing tax benefit payment program" was exercising the taxing and spending powers expressly granted it by the Constitution, had a real and substantial relation to the object sought, and respected due process of law.[24]

Furthermore, Congress in authorizing the secretary to enter into marketing agreements and enforce them through administrative orders was exercising the power granted under article 1, section 8, clause 3 of the Constitution to regulate commerce with foreign nations and among the several states. Similarly, the Bankhead Cotton Act and the Kerr Tobacco Act of 1934 and the Potato Act of 1935 were exercises in the congressional power to regulate interstate and foreign commerce.[25] The U.S. Senate also took cognizance of the *Schechter* and *Hoosac Mills* decisions and by an overwhelming vote of sixty-four to fifteen passed amendments to the AAA.

Congress in effect legalized and ratified every rate of the processing tax from the day of the passage of the AAA, May 12, 1933, to the day the amendments became law as "fully to all intents and purposes as if each such tax had been made effective and the rate thereof fixed specifically by prior act of Congress." Congress likewise fixed the rates of the processing tax to December 31, 1937 with the provision that if any modification was held invalid, the rate fixed by Congress would be restored and continued. Rental and benefit payments and the making of marketing agreements also were fully legalized and ratified.[26]

By the end of 1935 Wallace believed that the USDA had done a good job in helping restore the economic health of agriculture; supplies had been brought into better balance with shrunken markets and farm surpluses were disappearing. Production of twelve important crops had declined by more than one-third between 1932 and 1934, and farm prices had risen. Unfortunately cotton still was available in quantities beyond immediate needs, but grain and livestock supplies no longer were excessive. Stocks of certain types of tobacco also were large, while the supply of dairy products was more in line with effective demand. Prices of farm products had climbed to 108 percent of the prewar levels, while in the calendar year of 1932 they were about 65 percent. However, the shrinkages in output that were excessive for many commodities, Wallace conceded, had occurred mostly as a result of the drought of 1934 and less because of the AAA. It would be wrong, therefore, to assume that the need for crop adjustment had disappeared, because the tendencies toward excessive production were still in evidence, and would become more visible if foreign demand remained stagnant and the weather returned to normal.[27]

This meant that what defects remained in the emergency adjustment efforts had to be eliminated if production was to be controlled on a more permanent basis. The emergency adjustment contracts of 1933, for instance, were based on past production of the individual farmers; this prevented adjustments made necessary by changing economic, physical, and climatic conditions and left many farmers who approved of the program unhappy. As a result, farmers who responded quickly to the pleas for reduced demand were frozen into a historic mold, in violation of efficient production.[28]

Greater flexibility occurred during the second adjustment season and the farmers had more freedom in combining their various crop enterprises, but the AAA retained the commodity approach until a study was made of the problems involved. In making long-range adjustments it appeared more desirable for the AAA to develop a regional program that would avoid conflicts between adjustment quotas and good land use principles, balanced farming, and sound farm management. Unless this was done it would be difficult to combine fair treatment of the individual farmers with the necessary changes in localizing the production of crops.

Conditions that helped produce the great surpluses of 1929 no longer were present in 1935; but the stoppage of production controls, barring the prospects of low tariff barriers, could throw the farm economy into chaos again. Foreign lending by the United States literally had come to a halt since 1929; foreign nations deliberately were excluding American goods from their markets, and the prices farmers received no longer justified greater production. Administration leaders by and large believed that the days of unlimited farm production had come to an end for the American farmers. If they returned, they would return as a result of the natural recovery from the drought and the inherent drive of the farmers to produce as much as possible.[29]

A rational approach in finding a solution to this dilemma was to determine how many acres were required to satisfy the domestic and export needs of the United States, something difficult to calculate. Concerted action by all the farmers was needed because it was beyond the individual farmer acting alone. Clearly the annual harvest from 360 and 365 million acres between 1928 and 1932 was beyond the foreign and domestic requirements of the United States in 1935.

Wallace believed that the estimated 285 to 290 acres of land used from 1925 to 1929 in satisfying the domestic requirements of the United States, when the nation was relatively prosperous, was a sounder acreage base from which to begin calculating the needs of the country. Another 25 million harvested acres would supply the population of 1935 with nonfood products. In other words roughly 310 million acres were needed to supply the food and nonfood requirements of the American people in 1935. These estimates took into account that the acreage requirements for exports had declined from 84 million in 1920-1921 to 39 million in 1933-1934 and were still declining; that foreign trade was being blocked by tariffs, quotas, embargoes, quarantines, and similar restrictions, and administration leaders could not count on an increase in export demand.[30]

Readjustment of the acreage could be achieved in one of several ways: remove from cultivation certain lands which conservatively could idle from 10 to 25 million acres; shift land from intensive crops such as cotton, corn, and wheat to pasture, hay, and forage; and retire about 50 million acres in submarginal lands.[31] Moreover crop adjustment on a regional basis as conceived in 1934-1935 by the AAA could be conducted on a commodity basis to some extent because of the distribution of the principal crops, but at the same time rotation practices and production also could be encouraged in a manner that permitted an efficient use of machinery, tillage methods, and fields. As a consequence the adjustments were not to be similar for all farmers regardless of where they lived, whether they specialized in the production of certain crops or raised them as part of their rotation practices.

The Program Planning Division, as a means of helping adapt the AAA program to the various regional or local requirements, divided the country into twelve major agricultural regions. The hope was to centralize adjustment planning with the help of the cooperating farmers and the state agencies. Once the desired volume of production had been decided upon, the problem was to divide the total of the important farm commodities among the different regions with an eye on long-range as well as immediate benefits, and then allocate the production equitably among the individual farmers.[32]

Getting farmers to look far in advance in the heat of the competitive struggle posed problems. For a central authority to impose a cut-and-dried plan on the farmers might have been unrealistic, but the alternatives were even less appealing. One alternative was to return to the old free-for-all system and another was to retain the commodity approach. A relapse into blind unrestrained competition of old might have been unthinkable to many, but retention of a strictly commodity approach in crop planning also was fraught with the possibilities of individual and regional dissatisfaction. Basically, the problem was deciding which method was to be used in controlling production.

The USDA in making the first move toward the regional approach sought the cooperation of the state agricultural experiment stations; they had been less active in adjustment work and in gaining a better description of the regional differences in farming in their respective states. Information such as the size of the farms, the distribution of crops by areas within the states, the kinds of farming engaged in, the state of soil conservation, and the relation of all these factors to farm income, information that was at the disposal of the state agricultural experiment stations, could be of help to the AAA. Regional conferences to formulate recommendations on a state, regional, and national basis and promote good land use were held during the first half of March 1935.[33]

By late August and early September 1935 the states had reached tentative conclusions on what the desirable adjustments were to be within their respective areas, and the conferences coordinated these recommendations into regional reports. Adjustments in the corn belt centered around the feed grain–livestock problem and the ratio of feed to grass and other crops to be used to conserve the land and yield the maximum net returns. In the small grain area where wheat was the center of unrest, the problem was how an overextended cultivated area could be adjusted to the markets in prospect.

In the range states it was largely a matter of differentiating the lands that best could be used for grazing and other purposes, and the restoration of the productive capacity of the range. In the cotton and tobacco areas the problem was one of determining the acreages to be maintained without damaging soil resources and oversupplying the market. In the dairy region the problem was one of deciding on a production and marketing policy consistent with the demand of the home market, and blending this in with what was happening elsewhere.[34]

AAA spokesmen believed the program they were advocating and implementing contributed to a good use of the land. The program, they felt, permitted individual farmers to employ systems best adapted to their farms. Emphasis at first had been on curtailing production; coupled with the droughts of 1933 and 1934, this reduced the agricultural supplies of the nation to nearly normal levels. Then the emphasis shifted to crop adjustment. This shift allowed some increases in production and changes in the cropping systems because good farm management and land use was an integral part of farm adjustment. True enough the shift from flat percentage reductions to differential adjustments made the job more complicated; but it was fairer, more scientific, and enlisted the cooperation of farmers in constructive efforts.

AAA leaders recognized the importance of moving cautiously before adopting new programs or discarding ones in operation. The AAA believed it wise to build on the framework already developed and to retain those features that withstood the test of practice. The incorporation of new principles into action programs of necessity had to be gradual, but with an understanding that the steps being taken would carry the farmers only a part of the way.[35]

But the steps undertaken by the AAA in 1935 to shift from outright reductions to a more constructive use of farm resources and eliminate the constitutional defects in the AAA unfortunately were inadequate to save it from demolition by the U.S. Supreme Court in a six to three decision. "Agricultural production, if it exists at all, must under the Constitution, remain with the states rather than the federal government," said the court. Reduction of agricultural production under the AAA was not voluntary; and if it were, it still would be beyond the power of the federal government to reduce the acreage and control production.[36]

The problems facing the AAA as a result of the adverse court decision were staggering. Collection of processing taxes and the disbursal of benefit checks by the Treasury stopped, and the AAA needed $250 million to meet obligations to farmers who had fulfilled their crop reduction contracts. Since its inception the AAA had paid out $1.2 billion; the tax receipts amounted to about $1 billion; between $200 and $300 million in taxes were tied up by injunctions granted in lower courts; and various processors planned suits to regain the taxes they had already paid. Furthermore, the 6,400 employees of the AAA, most of them in Washington, were worried about their future, and many were making plans to return home.

Farmer reaction, except in Ames, Iowa, the home of Iowa State College where six life-sized dummies dressed in black were hanged in effigy, was surprisingly mild. The disappointment in the corn belt, however, was great. Many Southerners likewise were puzzled and confused, but violence did not break out. The farm vote could easily decide the November election, and the bulk of the farmers were for the AAA. Republican politicians, much as they rejoiced inwardly, as they did when the "NRA was Schechtered," outwardly were not jubilant after the Court had spoken.

The president displayed this same taciturn attitude. At the Jackson Day dinner in Washington, two days after the Court handed down its decision, Roosevelt disposed of the AAA decision as follows:

> I know you will not be surprised by lack of comment on my part tonight on the decision by the Supreme Court two days ago. I cannot render offhand judgment without studying with utmost care two of the most momentous decisions ever rendered in a case before the Supreme Court of the United States. . . . It is enough to say that the attainment of justice for American agriculture remains an immediate constant objective.[37]

The months from February 6, 1935 through January 6, 1936 were months of exploration, planning, and uneasiness. An apprehensive administration explored and coped with problems plaguing the farmers with an intensity that was unparalleled in farm relief annals. Indications were that the economic nationalism of the early AAA years was beginning to bend, and that the AAA was not the static, straitjacket type of operation it first appeared to be. New Dealers were trying to put to practical use the findings of years of research by farm economists, land use experts, and other specialists. At the theoretical and planning levels, at least, this was an unusual period in the history of agricultural reform.

The Search for Foreign Markets: 1934-1936

THE PREPONDERANCE OF ATTENTION given acreage controls, benefit payments, the pig killings, the sharecroppers and tenants, caused many to overlook the other less dramatic but significant phases of the New Deal such as the efforts to reopen the world markets to farm products. Acreage controls and benefit payments were viewed as a sort of temporary bridge across the depression until Europe again began taking some of the surpluses of the American farmers off their hands. By early 1934, if not earlier, the New Deal manifested a desire to recapture some if not all of its former foreign market and make it a part of its long-range program for agriculture.[1]

Two contradictory positions had shaped up. Henry A. Wallace, to the surprise of some, espoused a sophisticated, possibly ill-timed, philosophy of world trade. George Peek, who became special adviser to the president on international trade after resigning as administrator of the AAA, had a more simplistic view of foreign markets. As it turned out Peek became more of a problem for the State Department, in which he was deposited by Roosevelt without consulting Secretary of State Cordell Hull, than to Wallace, who was glad to have him out of the USDA.

The U.S. Tariff Commission, Cabinet members, and the AAA studied the possibilities of negotiating trade treaties during 1933. John Lee Coulter, a former member of the Tariff Commission and long associated with agriculture, cautioned Peek that flat reductions in tariffs "on all articles from all countries to all countries" would have serious repercussions, and that a more effective approach would be through direct negotiations on specific articles of trade. This meant the writing of reciprocal trade agreements and then modifying the rules applicable to a particular article from a particular country or countries.[2]

Peek stressed what appeared to him to be two major approaches to the problem. One was emergency and short range: to seek mutually advantageous "deals" between this and other countries. For instance Peek would explore the possibilites of selling wheat to China and pork to Russia; and negotiate, in other cases, barter agreements as a means of obviating exchange difficulties. A second and long-range approach required thorough examination of the political, economic, and other considerations affecting trade between the United States and other countries and the negotiation of tariff and other concessions as a means of removing the existing trade barriers.

By early 1934 the prospects of expanding foreign trade were being explored by an interdepartmental committee that had been at work for several months, a small functioning unit of the AAA, and other governmental agencies. Peek agreed with the president's decision to designate a special committee to coordinate all governmental activities on foreign trade. The Executive Committee on Commercial Policy was formed, and an officer of the State Department was entrusted with the responsibility of supervising the drafting of a coherent government policy on trade. Peek was asked to advise the members of his agency to consult with the State Department official in charge before they took any action that directly affected export and import trade.[3] William Phillips, the under secretary of state, became the first chairman of the Executive Committee on Commercial Policy. His duty was to serve as "the regular channel of communication with all foreign governments on all policy matters affecting American export and import trade." Shortly thereafter, Professor Francis B. Sayre, assistant secretary of state, became the permanent chairman.

Peek, to no one's surprise, was infuriated by the appointments to the committee. He believed the committee "was dominated by Professor Sayre and his associates in the State Department" and was almost devoid of businessmen and financiers with practical experience; he also complained that his recommendation to establish a foreign trade administration was "completely disregarded."[4] Peek wanted trade bargaining operating on a bilateral basis with pure barter deals negotiated whenever profitable, a discarding of the unconditional most-favored-nation clause in trade agreements, and a return to the most-favored-nation policy of pre–World War I days. Implicit in all this was Peek's belief that the depression basically was a domestic problem stemming from the disparity between farm and industrial income.

> Give the American farmer and industrial worker the full benefit of the domestic market, so that we can remain more nearly on a self-sustaining basis. . . . We should abandon the unconditional most-favored-nation policy and regain our bargaining power. . . . We should trade

selectively both as to imports and exports, dealing country by country, and if necessary, as in the case of cotton, commodity by commodity.[5]

Wallace disagreed with Peek. Wallace's fear of "compulsory control of farming" perhaps contributed as much as anything else to his return to his original position on the tariff: lowering the tariff would forestall the regimentation of agriculture. This became clear in *America Must Choose,* the pamphlet he wrote for the Foreign Policy Association, an organization of "sophisticated citizens" with local chapters in major cities of the country.[6]

Wallace in *America Must Choose* noted that much as the new social controls may be disliked, they were here to stay and would grow on a national and international scale. He leaned toward internationalism, but he knew that the United States would not adopt such a position unless it was prepared to import nearly a billion dollars worth more goods than it had in 1929; and he asked for a thorough consideration of the alternatives, the finding of a new leadership, and a common will to support "a planned and statesmanlike purpose." New Deal efforts to combat the depression would break down, he warned, unless inspired by men of "a larger vision than the hard-driving profit motives of the past."

> Our people on the street and on the soil must change their attitude concerning the nature of man . . . and human society. They must . . . be willing to pay the price to attain it. They must have the intelligence and will power to turn down simple solutions appealing to the short-time selfish motives of a particular class.

A campaign of education and reason was needed to achieve a middle-ground policy.[7]

The public response to *America Must Choose* was remarkable; by late February 1934 the first edition of 40,000 copies was practically exhausted. The Foreign Policy Association, which undertook the campaign of public education on economic nationalism, also proposed a nationwide series of public discussions, and consulted Wallace before making any hard and fast commitments. Wallace was asked to launch the campaign of public education on economic nationalism by posing the question on the radio and then leaving the discussions to others who would follow him. This approach was suggested on the theory that the masses could not be reached through the traditional political channels because of their partisanship, and because government agencies were handicapped by the popular belief that their motives were partisan, too.[8]

Wallace emphasized this theme in his public statements, newspaper interviews, and conversations with men in high places throughout 1934 and 1935. James B. Conant, the president of Harvard University, complimented him warmly on his *America Must Choose* pamphlet, and Harvard University later awarded him an honorary degree for his statesmanlike qualities. Wallace also delivered an important address before the American Farm Bureau (AFBF) in Nashville in late 1934 in which he departed from his prepared text and spoke eloquently about reciprocal trade agreements, the restoration of foreign markets, and on *America Must Choose*. M. L. Wilson, who sat on the speakers' platform with him, observed that Wallace had been inspired by the ovation he got from the audience.[9]

The substance of the Wallace argument for reopening world markets, which he believed had to become part of the New Deal farm adjustment program, was that success of any program depended to a great extent on how much it advanced the national interest. The farmers could not advance the national interest on their own because they lacked sheer numerical strength; and if they possessed the strength, it would be very unwise for them to try and employ this power as a weapon. A liberal import policy was needed, even if it inspired opposition from producers who believed such a policy would hurt them. The lower tariffs that would follow would help all people who purchased a variety of goods, including salaried employees and wage earners. Lower tariffs inevitably would require painful adjustments for the less efficient industries, but in the long run such adjustments would be less painful than the economic disruption that inevitably would follow if agriculture failed to regain its foreign market. Eventually even those in the previously tariff-sheltered industries would receive some benefits. Initially, however, a liberal import policy would benefit the consumers and the major producers of export goods.[10]

Progress in the reciprocal trade program was hampered by a lack of realization by the public that the penalties of trade exclusion were greater than penalties of trade inclusion. The agricultural problem was a national one that called for the sharing of responsibilities. City dwellers blamed the AAA for crop limitations, when the original cause of the limitations was the refusal of the nation to allow agriculture to regain its foreign markets. The United States failed to import goods in sufficient quantities to enable foreigners to buy American farm products. Hence, the time had come for nonfarm groups to show less concern about the possible injuries that could result from tariff readjustments and realize that encouragement of foreign trade might create new employment opportunities.[11]

Although it appeared on the surface as though agriculture alone suffered from a high tariff policy, the truth of the matter was that some of the urban industries, as well as those branches of agriculture that were on an export basis, also failed to benefit from the tariff. Many urban industries depended for their prosperity on the foreign market, which they were unprepared to share with other sectors of the economy. Accepting foreign imports for American exports would increase the supply of commodities within the country, but to benefit the farmers the imports must be non-competitive, nonfarm goods. Such a policy was unacceptable to many manufacturers.[12]

The United States' refusal to accept imports for exports had an adverse effect on production and employment at home, and limited the production of goods we were best equipped to produce. Unemployment in rural and urban communities resulted largely from the paralysis in U.S. export trade and pressures on the prices of the products of sheltered industries. A reduction in farm production brought a drop in farm employment, immobilized farm capital and land, weakened the capital structure of agriculture, reduced farm owners to tenants, sharecroppers to wage hands, and created a surplus of farm labor that was compelled to seek relief. Government and business refusal to take imports for exports changed the distribution of unemployment and increased rural unemployment. The protection of one industry harmed the other, and limited the gain of the protected industries.[13]

Wallace in effect was trying to tell the nation that the expansion of international trade would stimulate production, boost national income, increase per capita spending, create a better balance between consumption and distribution, give the farmer a large share of the national income, and raise living standards.[14]

The administration finally decided on March 2, 1934, when the president asked Congress for authority, to enter into executive commercial agreements with foreign countries for the purpose of removing impediments to trade. Roosevelt proposed to use this authority "within carefully guided limits" to modify the existing duties and import restrictions in a manner that would benefit both agriculture and industry. He also stated that discussions carried on with the governments of Spain and Italy ended after they reached an advanced stage.[15]

Meanwhile, the controversy over reciprocal trade agreements continued. Hull, like Wallace, was much more concerned with the general revival of foreign trade than with the exact balance of trade the United States had with an individual country; while Peek held that the country that imported more than it sold to another country would have to settle its balance with money payments that would result in a net loss to the nation. Peek demanded that production bars be taken down because they fomented social unrest and increased unemployment. Governor Floyd Olson of Minnesota and other middle western political leaders sided with Peek in this controversy.[16]

In effect, while Peek was proposing that the United States play the game the other countries were playing and try and get as large a share of the market as possible, Hull was proposing a change in the rules of the game so that instead of imposing more restrictions on international trade, the countries of the world should shift back gradually to a freer exchange of goods.[17]

The trouble with the Peek proposals, as Chester Davis observed, was that the United States would have to pay too high a price for what would amount to "the small dribble" of export business. When the United States, for instance, considered the opportunity to sell butter to Great Britain at lower than the domestic price, the government found that it was better business to buy the butter outright and give it to the needy of the country. And this was precisely what occurred. The Italian silk negotiations also involved a subsidy to buy Italian silk at a price that would compete with Japanese silk in the U.S. market, notwithstanding the fact that Japan was a good customer for cotton.[18]

Overcoming the apprehensions of those who feared the United States would enter into tariff-bargaining agreements with politically unstable countries was another problem. Mordecai Ezekiel informed an inquiring citizen that the USDA was involved in negotiations only with those countries who enjoyed "reasonably stable political conditions over a considerable period of time" and from whom "continuity of action under the agreement can be expected." Unfortunately a good deal of the political and economic activity of the world then was based on grounds that were "not fully rational." "It is only by taking people as they are," continued Ezekiel, "and not as we would like to have them be that realistic work can be done in this field."[19]

Early indications were that the benefits from the proposed trade agreements were going to be fewer than had been hoped for and the obstacles to gaining anything more were formidable. Wallace wrote Francis B. Sayre, the assistant secretary of state, early in 1935 that the proposed trade agreement with Belgium contained no significant concessions on farm products. The concessions on fresh and dried fruits were appreciated, but those on pork and lard were minimal compared to what the hog export market in the United States enjoyed when these products were on the free list. Belgium refused to make concessions on wheat, but Belgium in those days provided but a small market for American wheat and its import restrictions on wheat were mild. The only real agricultural beneficiary was California. The agreement contained nothing to secure the agricultural support of the Middle West in sufficient force to offset attacks from the industrialists who would be affected. Leslie A. Wheeler of the USDA complained to Wallace that maybe the government would have been more successful in efforts to gain concessions if agricultural specialists who knew the details of the Belgian restrictions, and understood the agricultural relations between Belgium and other countries, had been invited to participate in the negotiations.[20]

Meanwhile, the opposition to the reciprocal trade agreements was mounting. On March 21, 1935 Wallace expressed the hope to the State Department that announcements for increasing the apple quota—whether

THE NEW DEAL AS ILLUSTRATED BY "DING" DARLING

JAY NORWOOD "DING" DARLING was a nationally renowned political cartoonist for the Des Moines *Register* whose work was syndicated for nearly a third of a century by the New York *Herald Tribune*. He won two Pulitzer Prizes for his cartooning, his work played daily to an audience of millions, and "Ding"—a contraction of the cartoonist's last name—became a household word in the twenties and thirties.

Darling was born in 1876 in Norwood, Michigan, but he grew up in Sioux City, Iowa, and considered himself an Iowan throughout the remainder of his life, including his forty-nine years as a professional cartoonist.

He began cartooning for the Sioux City *Journal* in 1900 and joined the Des Moines *Register and Leader* in 1906. He drew for the New York *Globe* from late 1911 to early 1913. The only other interruption of his *Register* career came in 1934 and 1935 after Franklin D. Roosevelt appointed Darling chief of the U.S. Biological Survey, forerunner of the Fish and Wildlife Service.

Darling was a conservative Republican whose cartoons reflected his distrust of the New Deal and his dislike of FDR. Darling was also a personal friend and supporter of Iowan Herbert Hoover and had been a frequent visitor at Camp Rapidan and the Hoover White House.

Henry A. Wallace, Roosevelt's secretary of agriculture, was a longtime friend of Darling. The two had labored together in the Iowa Republican vineyard before Wallace's conversion. Wallace recommended to Roosevelt that Darling be appointed chief of the Biological Survey—then a part of the Department of Agriculture—because of his record as a mover and shaker on behalf of soil, water, and wildlife conservation. In 1935 Darling left his $100,000 position to become chief of the Biological Survey at $8,000 per annum; and, in the bargain, he joined the New Deal administration, whose aims he so distrusted.

Darling was in an excellent position to comment on the New Deal and its influence on agriculture. He was headquartered in Des Moines, surrounded by some of the finest farmland and some of the most productive farmers in the world. He was a nationally recognized, well-read, and well-traveled figure who nevertheless was convinced that "Iowans think more to the square inch than New Yorkers think to the square mile." He had studied and commented publicly on the nation's agricultural dilemmas for a generation before his friend, Hoover, was swept from the presidency.

Darling retired from political cartooning in 1949, at seventy-three years of age, but he continued to exercise his influence on behalf of politics, conservation, and other interests. Among his other accomplishments he founded and served as the first president of the National Wildlife Federation. He and his friend, Walt Disney, were to have served as co-chairmen of National Wildlife Week in 1962, but Darling died a few weeks before the event at the age of eighty-five.

The following cartoons comment upon some of agriculture's problems and the New Deal's responses to them. The cartoons have been reproduced from engraver's proofs given by Darling to his friend and colleague, the late John M. Henry. Henry, in turn, donated the vast collection to the Cowles Library at Drake University. The following examples are presented through the courtesy of the Library and Jim Leonardo of its Government Documents section.

David L. Lendt

Remember Your Shipwrecked Brothers
JANUARY 14, 1933

**Seems As Though
Something Ought to
Start Pretty Soon**

FEBRUARY 13, 1933

**Two Pairs of Pants and
a Pair of Suspenders**

APRIL 4, 1933

**Some Folks Won't
Follow Leadership
When They Have It**
APRIL 14, 1933

**All Ready for the Big
Ride**
MAY 2, 1933

Off to the Economic War

AUGUST 23, 1933

The Holiday Boys Help with the Milking

OCTOBER 26, 1933

Two Families That Ought to Know Each Other Better

NOVEMBER 8, 1933

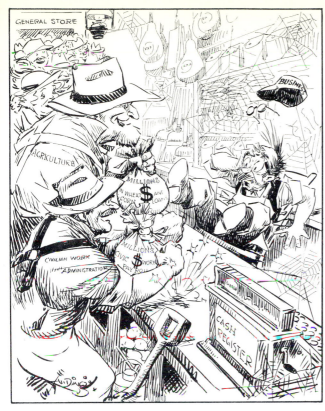

Hey! Wake Up. There's a Cash Customer in the Store

DECEMBER 7, 1933

Readdressing the Christmas Present

DECEMBER 14, 1933

And So One Thing Leads to Another—

DECEMBER 20, 1935

**Never Mind the Political
Souvenirs, Get a Doctor**

JANUARY 7, 1936

**Well, of All People to
Complain About
"Economy of Scarcity"**

MARCH 19, 1936

**Oh What Will the
Harvest Be?**

JULY 31, 1936

**The Only Critter on the
Farm That Seems to
Thrive on Drought and
Grasshoppers**

AUGUST 12, 1936

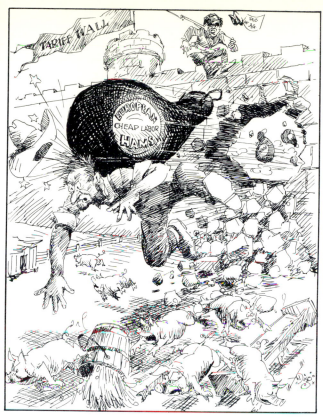

There's a Hole in the Breastworks

APRIL 14, 1937

The Farm Problem Can Wait for the Next Car

JUNE 2, 1937

Close Harmony

SEPTEMBER 13, 1937

The Kidnaping—Or More and More Democracy

NOVEMBER 21, 1937

"Who's Afraid of the Big Bad Wolf?"
DECEMBER 7, 1937

Out of Control
JULY 14, 1938

Darn It

OCTOBER 11, 1938

Crop Control or Vote Control?

OCTOBER 19, 1938

Horatio Guards the Bridge

APRIL 1, 1939

Barn Yard Trouble

APRIL 15, 1940

**Home from the Seven
Years Hunting Trip**
AUGUST 30, 1940

The Hidden Mystery
NOVEMBER 1, 1941

made by the French government or ours—would place as little emphasis as possible on the wheat phase of the negotiations. He observed,

> All imports of foreign foodstuffs this season are arousing intense political opposition within this country and any flat announcement that an arrangement had been made to import French wheat into this country might create so much opposition as to result in action blocking the agreement.[21]

Failure to obtain greater concessions on American wheat naturally came as a great disappointment because American negotiators had made earnest efforts to obtain them. Negotiators found foreign resistance to concessions on wheat, especially flour, strong and insurmountable. Under existing conditions foreign governments felt compelled to grow and mill as much wheat as possible at home; and even when they were unable to grow enough wheat they were anxious to maintain and, if possible, expand their facilities for milling wheat at home. There was considerable resistance in Europe to the reduction of duties and other barriers against all farm products produced in quantities within their borders. However, the resistance in the cases of wheat and flour was unyielding. Efforts to obtain an abatement on the existing restrictions on wheat and flour in Belgium and a reduction of the Brazilian duty on flour were unavailing. A concession, however, was obtained on flour in the Cuban treaty that was expected to be of value to the millers of the Southwest.

The task for the American negotiators would have been made easier if the American industries anxious to obtain more trade had made known in advance what concessions they were willing to make in exchange for the reopening of these markets. But this kind of cooperation was slow in coming, if it came at all.[22]

Senator Arthur Capper of Kansas asked why none of the trade agreements concluded by the spring of 1935, except that with Cuba, contained concessions for wheat and flour. The main explanation was that American wheat prices, owing largely to the inclement weather of 1934, were substantially above world prices, which made it very difficult for higher-priced wheat to compete with flour made from a lower-priced foreign product. Furthermore, foreign wheat production capabilities and flour-milling facilities had expanded considerably since World War I. In fact it appeared unlikely that the United States could expect concessions on wheat flour even if future concessions on wheat were possible.

The situation in the Latin American countries that had become principal outlets for U.S. flour and expected future concessions was somewhat different. The treaty with Cuba was very encouraging. Failure to persuade

Brazil to reduce its duties was largely the result of its duties being not unreasonably high. Haiti, which depended on revenue derived from custom receipts on wheat flour, was unwilling to jeopardize this important source of revenue.[23]

Apprehension over what the trade agreements would do to the domestic market of the farmers was causing many to lose their confidence in the New Deal. Clifford V. Gregory, the editor of the influential *Prairie Farmer* of Chicago, wrote Wallace in November 1935 at the behest of Ed O'Neal, the president of the American Farm Bureau Federation, about Wallace's forthcoming speech at the Chicago convention where he was to speak on the Canadian Trade Agreement. The Canadian agreement and other pending agreements were creating "the first definite rift between farmers and the present administration," and Gregory believed that the secretary would have to meet the issues squarely and discuss every phase frankly if he was going to minimize the effects of this rift.

Farmers were concerned not so much over the quantity of Canadian wheat and other products that would be coming into the country, but over the effects the treaty might have on the adjustment program that had been tied almost exclusively to the domestic market. Did this mean that the crop adjustment policies of the AAA now would have to be reconciled with foreign trade? The AAA, as originally conceived and implemented, was nationalistic in orientation; it was based on the adjustment of production for the domestic market. Consequently, when farmers were reducing their acreage to bring production in line with domestic demand, they wanted to know what the argument was for sharing the domestic market with foreign producers.

Gregory advised Wallace to give a concrete answer to this and other questions. The answers would be better understood by the delegates if Wallace talked in terms of acreages. The farmers wanted to know what the probable results of the trade pacts would be on their acreages. What, for example, would the probable results of the Canadian agreement be? To what extent would the result in increasing activities offset the disadvantages of growing foreign competition in their own markets? Why did the trade pacts fail to lower tariffs in places where the real inequities existed, such as steel and aluminum that were produced by highly "monopolized" industries? The "farm folks" and Gregory, who had grave doubts about American foreign trade policy in agriculture, wanted to be convinced they were wrong, or else given the opportunity to convince Wallace and Hull that a change in foreign policy was in order.[24]

Wallace informed the delegates attending the AFBF convention that the real and continuing problem of agriculture was not how to stop the small trickle of farm imports from entering the country, but how to move America's great surpluses into the foreign markets. The unusually short crops of corn and small grains of the previous three or four years resulting from the abnormal weather had obscured the picture and the farmers were unsure what the surpluses were going to do to prices within the next year or so.[25] Wallace added that some very real gains had been registered; rates had been reduced on seed potatoes, clover, seed, and feeder cattle which American farmers used in substantial quantities as a result of the Canadian agreement.

Substantial reductions also were realized on pork and lard in the British agreement, which Wallace hoped would aid in regaining a larger share of the pork market. The American share of that market had dropped from 21 percent in 1932 to 8 percent, while that of Canada had risen. The next Canadian agreement, as a consequence, enabled American pork to enter Canada as a replacement for the pork exported by Canada to Britain. In other words, the large corn crop of 1935 and the prospects of increased hog production and shipping larger quantities of American pork to Canada became of major importance.

Wallace likewise cited the important benefits expected for the fruit and vegetable producers of the Pacific Coast states, Colorado, the South, and to some extent the northeastern states. Even grain growers hounded by fears of new Canadian competition were expected to benefit because Canadian duties were reduced on practically all grains and grain products, in some cases below 1929 levels. Americans who worried that their government's adjustment program would be wrecked by the Canadian agreement were assured by a clause in the agreement that the imports of a commodity could be limited if either country attempted to control the production or marketing of any commodity.

Wallace further estimated that if U.S. exports were increased as a result of the Canadian agreement by $300 million, about $150 million would go into payrolls and bring substantial income gains to the farmers. USDA studies indicated that a $150 million increase in payrolls could add from $5 to $6 million to the incomes of livestock producers in Illinois, Wisconsin, Minnesota, Nebraska, Missouri, Iowa, and Ohio—the farmers most worried about the concessions granted to Canadian cattle, calves, cream, and cheese. Wallace did such a thorough job of convincing the delegates of the AFBF, who had been dubious about the value of the reciprocal trade agreements, that the convention endorsed both the principle behind the treaties and the act authorizing their negotiation.[26]

The reaction of the dairy farmers toward the Canadian trade treaty varied. Those in the agricultural Northwest, for instance, were worried in early 1936 more about the future of the AAA than about the treaty. A general indifference prevailed in Montana and North Dakota, because the producers in these states were more dependent on grain than dairy products. The delegates of the Cooperative Pool of Brown County, Wisconsin charged the trade treaties had a demoralizing effect on the cheese factories, made it impossible for them to compete with the condenseries owned by the large corporations, and asked the federal government to help relieve them by purchasing 10 million pounds of cheese. Wallace, of course, was quick to deny that the trade agreements "almost wrecked the country's dairy industry."[27]

The USDA also attempted to pacify those concerned with the tariff on cattle by showing that there was a close relationship between the incomes from livestock and livestock products and the wages of industrial workers. Cattle imports had never been large except in years of relatively high prices and usually occurred at the low point in the production cycle. In 1928 for instance, a low point in production, the United States imported 524,000 head of cattle.

Cattle raisers in the southwestern part of the United States were particularly concerned about the effects the Canadian treaty would have on Mexican imports. Import records over a long period of years, however, showed that Mexico had never shipped any appreciable quantity of cattle weighing more than 700 pounds into the United States, and there was little likelihood of it doing so in the immediate future. Range and marketing conditions in northern Mexico discouraged the feeding of cattle in excess of 700 pounds, at least in early 1936. The quota of cattle to be imported annually from Canada represented but a small percentage of the total number of American cows and was unlikely to have any influence on the American price level. Furthermore, the concessions on cattle imported from Canada would prove advantageous to American dairymen adjacent to the Canadian dairy region by allowing them to secure replacements for their herds at somewhat lower costs.[28]

By mid-1936 sufficient progress had been made in studying the effects of trade treaties on American farm products in the brief period they were in effect to enable analysts to draw some conclusions. The total value of all competitive and noncompetitive agricultural imports in 1935 was placed at $1,106 million. Of these, the imports considered competitive to U.S. products were valued at $623 million; excluding sugar and distilled spirits, they were valued at $456 million. These figures, although showing a greater value than the imports of the immediately preceding years when the prices and purchasing power were lower, actually were considerably smaller than the figures for the competitive agricultural imports of the predepression years.

The increase in competitive imports in most cases could be traced to the effects of the drought of 1934, but these imports made up a very small part of the shortage from the drought, which resulted in a reduction of 50 million tons of the total U.S. feed supply. Likewise, the total imports of beef in all forms represented only 13 percent of the decline in federally inspected slaughter of cattle and calves between 1934 and 1935. Most other imports made up even smaller percentages of the reduction in normal supplies. Corn imports in 1935 represented only 1.7 percent of U.S. average production; oats 0.8 percent; wheat 3.2 percent; and barley 4.7 percent. Only rye imports were relatively high, amounting to about 25 percent of the average production because of crop failures in 1934 and 1935 and the increased demand for rye caused by the repeal of the prohibition laws.

Interestingly, the prices received by farmers were higher in periods of larger imports. The average price for wheat in the calendar years of 1934 and 1935 was 84 cents a bushel, as compared with 67 cents in 1933 and 38 cents in 1932. The average farm price of corn in the marketing year 1934–1935 was 83 cents a bushel as compared with 52 cents for the same period in 1933–1934 and 32 cents in 1932–1933. The farm prices of oats in the crop year 1934–1935, when imports were substantial, was 48 cents a bushel; and the average in the 1935–1936 season, when imports were negligible, was 28.5 cents a bushel. The farm price of rye was 71.3 cents a bushel during the marketing year 1934–1935, when imports were large, and only 38 cents a bushel in 1935–1936, when the United States had practically no imports.

In short, the reciprocal trade treaties had no significant bearing whatsoever on the increase in agricultural imports during 1935 when compared with agricultural imports in 1934, a year before the treaties were in effect. The treaty with Cuba, the only one in effect for all of 1935, brought no significant increase in the importation of competitive agricultural products; but the export of farm products showed significant gains. Lard exports in 1935 were more than twice as large as in 1933; export of potatoes in 1935 was about six times as large as in 1933; and export of cleaned rice was more than twenty-five times as large.

Trade agreements were in effect with Belgium, Haiti, and Sweden during part of 1935, but none contained any significant concessions on agricultural products imported by the United States. These countries, however, made substantial reductions in their import restrictions of American farm products.

A study of the Canadian trade treaty for the two months of 1936 showed that American agricultural exports into Canada benefited more than Canadian agricultural exports into the United States. Rice exports, for instance, totaled 5.4 million pounds during the first two months of 1936 as compared with 1.6 million pounds in the same two months of 1935, a gain of 230 percent. Grapefruit exports totaled 113,000 boxes as compared with 79,000 boxes in the same two months of 1935, a gain of 44 percent; and egg exports rose from a negligible 3,000 dozen in the first two months of 1935 as compared with more than 50,000 dozen in 1936.

Agricultural exports in general had been staging some kind of recovery since mid-1935. The principal export gains were made by cotton whose shipments totaled 4.8 million bales from August 1935 to March 1936, as compared with 3.5 million bales for the same period the previous year, or a gain of 35 percent. Exports in leaf tobacco from July 1935 through February 1936 amounted to 327,000 pounds, an increase of 18 percent over the same period of 1934–1935. Rice exports between July 1935 and February 1936 totaled 83 million pounds, an increase of almost 85 percent over the same months of 1934–1935. Fresh, dried, and canned fruits also registered substantial gains, but pork, lard, and wheat exports remained low because the drought of 1934 kept production low. In the case of wheat, the continued poor weather conditions of 1935 also contributed.[29]

Early in August 1936 Chester C. Davis, who in the meantime had been appointed by President Roosevelt to make a survey of world trade conditions, following his resignation as administrator of the AAA, submitted a report on international agricultural policies based on his observations and conversations in England, Holland, Germany, Sweden, Denmark, Czechoslovakia, Austria, Hungary, Italy, and France over a two-month period. Davis's findings more or less confirmed what seasoned observers reported earlier.[30]

Western European countries were advocating policies of national self-sufficiency in food and feeds, and were willing to accept the higher costs of tariffs, quotas, exchange controls, and restrictions on imports necessitated by preparations for war. Economists and many European statesmen also deplored the excessive nationalism into which their countries were drawn, approved in principle what the United States was trying to do, and expressed hope they could work back to a freer system of general trade; but no one had any idea when this would become feasible.

Spokesmen for countries that sought to control their trade through special bilateral agreements said they had been driven to these practices by countries whose trade had been important to them and who had been employing such methods. European countries, it became obvious, came closer to meeting their requirements in wheat than cotton because the wheat acreages of most continental countries in the spring of 1936 were at a level that would supply average domestic requirements. Being unable to raise cotton within their borders, these countries relied on substitutes that were considerably more expensive than cotton.

Davis was convinced that trade treaties offered hope for increasing U.S. agricultural exports. He saw little hope for rebuilding foreign trade with export subsidies in the foreseeable future. Export subsidies could be useful to meet special problems with special crops at special times, but reliance on them at the present time could be disastrous. The United States could not "jimmy" more exports into European countries, unless it bought proportionately as it expanded sales, no matter what subsidizing or high pressure techniques were applied to induce these countries to take more American goods. Complete self-sufficiency, on the other hand, was impossible for every country that had been an important market for U.S. products, and there still was a potential market for goods produced in exportable quantities. However, the ability of the United States to capitalize on this market was contingent on its willingness to accept more European goods and services. If countries could fill their needs with trade balances elsewhere, they were not going to use capital or investments in the United States for purchases.

Davis realized that the urge for self-sufficiency was more "deep-seated" in the case of agricultural than industrial products. The nations that bought American manufactured goods were industrialized to a small extent, and were willing to accept manufactured goods from the United States in exchange for certain raw materials not produced there. Mass production had enabled some American manufacturers—the automobile makers being a prime example—to produce products of a higher quality and at lower prices than other countries.[31]

Those in command of New Deal farm policy, in effect, were more influenced by the views of Cordell Hull and the reciprocal trade program he advocated than the views of George Peek whose influence on Roosevelt continued well into 1935. Peek, while serving as special advisor on trade to the president, made his vociferous presence felt in interdepartmental executive committee meetings through protests, constant bickering, and the initiation of irrelevant studies that retarded the program. Peek in fact continued to attack the program from the outside after he left the administration. The agency Peek headed was not retained after he left office. Foreign trade specialists all along felt that much of the material published by the Peek organization was biased and misleading.[32]

Meanwhile, the trade treaties became as much a part of the New Deal's broader policies in agriculture as the AAA had been from the beginning, and the need to reconcile differences between the two was seen. If the AAA was an obstacle to the progress of the trade program, it was only to the extent that the tariffs had to be modified to protect the AAA. The political pressures built up against the trade program in agricultural circles came from sources other than the AAA.[33]

Wallace not only praised the work of the State Department in the negotiation of these treaties, but was quoted in the spring of 1936 as saying:

> I would rather trust the State Department with the handling of foreign trade problems of agriculture than I would a Congress whether it be Republican or Democrat. I believe the farmer has obtained real benefits from the reciprocal trade agreement policy.[34]

The War on Rural Poverty

MOST TOP OFFICIALS OF THE AAA CONCEDED that the agency had done little to help the marginal and submarginal farmers. As Howard R. Tolley, the successor of Chester C. Davis as administrator, put it: "Our contracts were mostly with those . . . farther up the ladder—the landlords, the ordinary large farmers, rather than the small. . . . The landlords and the large farmers were the ones who had the organization, and . . . the ones who were vocal."[1]

Tolley's observations more or less sum up the attitude that prevailed toward the rural poor, not only in the AAA and the USDA, but in rural society in general. This helps explain why relief for the poor had made greater progress in the cities, especially in the East, where the poor and their needs were more visible, greater repositories of wealth existed, and where men and women with resources were willing to do something in their behalf as early as the mid-nineteenth century. In the rural areas, on the other hand, a comparable consciousness was slow in developing.[2] Some of the preliminary phases for social work in rural communities were developed in Iowa, Massachusetts, and New York as late as the second decade of the twentieth century.

Relief work in the rural areas took a radically different course from that in the cities. Not only was the population in the rural communities scattered so that the more affluent often did not know who the rural poor were and where they lived, but the prevalent attitude when such information became known was that these people simply did not manage well. Rural people as a rule preferred to express their sentiments personally and critically, instead of through formal institutions. The reactions of those in distress often was one of emotion that subsided quickly, and the need for trained personnel to deal with people in such situations rarely was appreciated. Progress in the development of rural public welfare agencies by 1933, as a consequence, had been confined primarily to child welfare, public hygiene, public health, caring for the blind, the aged, and the pensioners. Preparations for a major depression at the local, county, and state levels were even less advanced in the rural areas than in the urban.[3]

That rural poverty was more widespread in the early 1930s than most people realized should come as no surprise. Roughly 2,500 of the 3,000 counties in the United States had populations that were more than 50 percent rural. Reports from 166 counties, chiefly agricultural and containing no large industrial towns or cities, showed that in July 1933 one in ten of all families obtained relief from public funds. Larger percentages of families were on relief in the predominantly rural sections of the South Atlantic, the East South Central, and the West South Central states. Reports from 70 counties in these areas based on more than 250,000 families showed that over 37,000 families, or 15 in each 100, received relief in July 1934.[4]

The situation worsened in 1934. Approximately 1.7 million rural families, comprising between 6.5 and 7 million people, came under the care of emergency relief organizations. These numbers included residents of smaller industrial communities, but the bulk were farmers, tenants, sharecroppers, farm laborers, and those in occupations that directly served the farm population. Likewise included were families in which the father was dead or incapacitated, and mothers provided for under state laws.[5]

The farmers' needs can be appreciated if one realizes that they did not live on a cash-and-carry basis as the wage-earners did. Hard times stripped the farmer of both capital and a job, because the farmer could not work without land, work animals, seed, plow, cows, and poultry. If he lost his farm or lacked means of financing a going farm, he could not benefit from the AAA.

The farmer had to go to town to obtain relief, if he was eligible for it, whether it was in the form of money, food, or a public work project. Relief supplies in many areas had to be delivered great distances, "on horseback in the mountains, by boat in the bayou country." Farmers near the end of their resources had fewer alternatives than city workers. "They had no near neighbors, no casual charity, no help from lodge or union, and fewer jobs."[6]

A new activity, such as providing aid for the rural poor, called for establishment of a new independent agency. The reasoning was that personnel in old-line agencies might be unsympathetic or unenthusiastic about initiating and implementing new programs. Roosevelt probably thought there would be less friction and scrambling among departments and established government agencies if these new activities were placed in the hands of a new independent agency instead of the USDA.[7]

Because the newly created Resettlement Administration (RA) attracted liberals and social activists, it became the target of New Deal critics and others who disliked the direction such a program was taking. The RA "carried on the ideas and philosophy of the old Consumers' Counsel" after the purge of February 5, 1935, said Tolley. "It became a rallying point although it was not exclusively that by any means." Many employed by the RA did not care for the AAA, and vice versa. However, L. C. Gray and those working with him in the land and tenant programs were also in the RA. Carl C. Taylor, a rural sociologist and agrarian liberal, but far from the Tugwell–Frank type, "showed up there too," as did Will Alexander, Tugwell's assistant and later head of the Farm Security Administration (FSA).[8]

Assistance programs posed problems because of their uniqueness and the fact that many who dealt with them were traditionalists. M. L. Wilson in his reminiscences presents a graphic account of the administrative problems confronting the RA as experienced by Elmer Starch, the regional director of the Denver office. The RA administrators in Starch's region were county agents and college people.

> Our biggest problem was the bankers . . . the eternal everlasting burden of bankers [said Elmer Starch]. Every bank in the country was busted; so there were a million unemployed bankers around. We kept getting old-time bankers in the organization. Rehabilitation and this business of giving credit on the basis of reorganized units, based on all these book-learning things, just didn't appeal to them. So they sifted out of the deal rapidly. [At the opposite extreme were] the pure social theorists. Yes, a whole slug of them . . . [who probably had been brought in by Tugwell]. They had ideas about the magic of cooperation, and how the unit should be cooperative. Somehow they thought that would run the yield up and people would earn more than ever before. They were thinking of cooperative homesteads. They contributed quite a little, but there was a tremendous clash all the way.[9]

Four governmental agencies: the Federal Emergency Relief Administration (FERA), the Subsistence Homesteads Project in the Department of the Interior, the Land Program of the FERA, and the Land Policy Section of the AAA, were established to deal with the question of rural poverty before the RA and the federal works programs came into being. Meanwhile, the growng concern with agricultural reform and rural problems stimulated the growth of studies in farm economics, rural sociology, and related disciplines. The detailed findings of trained scholars in turn provided the serious students with an abundance of information on agriculture that otherwise would have been unavailable.[10]

Acute conditions called for immediate relief. The enactment of the Federal Emergency Relief Act on May 12, 1933 provided for FERA and authorized expenditures of $500 million. Relief grants under the act were made available to the states on a matching basis of $1 of federal funds for every $3 of local, state, and federal funds spent on relief in the state the preceding quarter of the year. By November 1933 some 1.3 million cases or 11 percent of all rural families obtained federal relief.[11]

Other types of assistance took the following form. The FERA announced in August 1933 that between 200 to 300 million pounds of meat obtained through the AAA would be placed into the hands of state Emergency Relief Administrations for distribution in areas where relief standards were low; then came the announcement that dairy, poultry products, and cotton were to become available soon. Later, persons not on public relief rolls but in need of help became eligible for farm surplus goods, including families receiving mother's aid and old age assistance, clients of private family welfare societies, and the like. Large numbers of rural families were removed from the relief rolls by December 1933 because of employment on the Civil Works Administration (CWA) projects; but relief increased throughout 1935. Nearly 1.8 million cases or about 14 percent of all rural families were on relief by August 1934.[12]

Early in the spring of 1934 an announcement stipulated that on April 1 a rural rehabilitation program would replace civil works and direct relief in rural areas and towns with less than 5,000 people, and the needy had to reapply. New work projects would enable the relief recipients to exchange their labor for consumer or capital goods, and relief was denied any family failing to have a home garden if it possessed facilities for one. Those in the drought areas were told that thereafter relief programs would be based on individual needs and cash payments for work performed on approved projects; the hours of work were not to exceed thirty hours per week at the prevailing wage rate, and at not less than thirty cents an hour. Late in June 1934 the FERA also authorized the purchase of 250 thousand bales of cotton to be used in making mattresses and comforters for distribution as surplus commodities; and about one million were produced by the time the project came to an end. Rural relief case loads reached an all-time peak in January 1935 when nearly 16 percent of all rural families were on relief and when Roosevelt announced, "The Federal Government must and shall quit this business of relief" and work must be found "for all able-bodied but destitute workers."[13]

The Appalachian–Ozark and the Great Lakes cutover areas were among the most severely affected by the depression. About one-sixth of all rural families in the Appalachian–Ozark district were on relief in October 1933; and about one-fifth in 1934–1935, which was well above the national average. Relief rolls in the Great Lakes cutover region climbed from one-fifth the rural families in October 1933 to almost one-third in October 1934 and two-fifths the rural population in February 1935.

Conditions were even more depressing in the spring wheat, winter wheat, ranching, and cotton states because of the drought in 1934. Ten percent of rural families in the spring wheat area were on relief in October 1933; 32 percent in 1934; 34 percent in February 1935; but only 14 percent in October 1935 because of rural rehabilitation, better farming conditions, and administrative changes. Similar sharp increases and decreases in the relief rates occurred in the winter wheat, ranching, and western cotton areas. In the eastern cotton areas more than 12 percent of the families were on relief in October 1933, a proportion exceeded only by the Appalachian–Ozark and Great Lakes cutover areas. Rural rehabilitation here, too, was partially responsible for the steady removal of families from relief.[14]

Conditions were different in the relatively prosperous corn belt, hay, and dairy areas where the proportion of farm families on relief always was below the average. Less than one-eighth the rural population in these areas was on relief at the peak of the relief load in February 1935, and in October 1935 only 3 percent in the corn belt, and 6 percent in the hay and dairy areas.[15]

Work relief assignments in the southern states followed the established pattern. Fewer blacks got work relief, especially in the eastern cotton area where two-thirds of the white farmers and less than half of the blacks were on relief. Blacks in all categories got lower wages than whites; and relief grants were the smallest in the Appalachian–Ozark and cotton areas where the living standards were lower. Fewer black clients received capital goods, and blacks in general received smaller advances in capital and subsistence goods than whites.[16]

Agricultural reformers had to take into account the fact that the farmers had been the victims of agricultural maladjustments of long standing and bad climatic conditions, as well as the depression. Programs for the conservation of the natural and physical resources and control of surplus production, to be effective, had to be adaptable to the needs of people in different parts of the country. A proposal to combine farming with industrial employment, for instance, was limited by the location and the available hours of work. The retirement of submarginal lands from cultivation was a necessity in many areas, but financial and legal obstacles stood in the way of accomplishing this. Reform of the tenant system and curbs on the growth of tenancy likewise were essential in some parts of the country if crops were going to be diversified, soil conserved, and cooperative marketing encouraged.

Nor was this all that had to be taken into account. Guided migration out of poor lands had become a basic need for the impoverished farmer. The government could not move people out of the blighted areas arbitrarily, but it could offer advice to those who wished to leave land on which they could not support themselves. Cooperation in the marketing of crops and the purchasing of farm needs, a common ownership of machinery and lands, recognizing the need for higher standards of living, and improvements in educational and other institutional needs such as a better distribution of funds for health, education, and public welfare agencies likewise would help reduce the imbalance that persisted between rural areas and the centers of urban-industrial and financial concentration. Measures for a stronger agricultural society further had to be geared to a long-range program instead of immediate gains. Finally, federal support and coordination on a national scale was required along with a continuing course of action uninterrupted by sudden shifts in policy comparable to that which characterized the relief and rehabilitation programs.[17]

One program theoretically designed to help reconstruct rural America called for subsistence homesteads. Its prime advocate was Milburn L. Wilson, the first head of the wheat section in the AAA, then director of the Division of Subsistence Homesteads, and finally assistant and then under secretary of agriculture. The philosophical roots of subsistence homesteads can be traced back to the communitarian experiments of nineteenth-century Americans such as the Shakers, Rappites, members of New Harmony, the Oneida community, and others. But Wilson attributed his interest in them in part to the graduate studies he took at the University of Wisconsin, where he was exposed to the teaching of Richard T. Ely, John R. Commons, and Edward A. Ross, lectures he heard in anthropology in which Freudian concepts helped explain behavior and social change, and his residency at the faculty club where he met younger faculty members and discussed a wide variety of relevant subjects with them.[18]

Wilson also was inspired by the accomplishments of Brigham Young who settled his band of Mormons on the plateaus between the Great Salt Lake and the mountains, and where villages were laid out in blocs of 2.2 acres as a means of protecting themselves from the Indians. Later sugar beet factories and milk condenseries helped create a wage-earning class and enabled those living on 2.2 acres to work from 100 to 150 days a year at the prevailing wage rate, and enjoy a life that was difficult to duplicate.[19]

Subsistence farming, also known as "part-time farming," was practiced in Connecticut and other colonies before the American Revolution. The communitarians were part-time farmers. Farmers in the mountains, the cutover lands, and regions adjacent to industry outside the rich areas of agricultural production likewise did some subsistence or part-time farming. After World War I people of small means from urban areas began to acquire suburban tracts near cities in the hope of combining suburban living with city employment. Subsistence homesteads were discussed at the Chicago land utilization conference in 1931. Henry I. Harriman, president of the U.S. Chamber of Commerce, was interested in them; so was Gerard Swope, president of General Electric. Bernard Baruch thought that the southern textile industry should have been organized in this fashion. Bernarr Macfadden, the health faddist and publisher of *Liberty,* was still another advocate.[20]

Wilson believed the Americans could move in the direction of subsistence homesteads because of cheap electricity, rapid communication, and the automobile. He envisaged a community in which industry would be in the center with families on subsistence homesteads instead of town lots for ten or fifteen miles in each direction. The resulting village life could also enable the ambitious to express themselves in woodworking and other handicrafts.[21]

Despite the initial enthusiasm, the subsistence homesteads program got off to an inauspicious start and soon became the target of heavy criticism. The National Recovery Administration (NRA) made $25 million available in June 1933 for the purchase of subsistence homesteads and the redistribution of the population in industrial areas. In August an executive order authorized the creation of the Division of Subsistence Homesteads to provide some direction for a "back-to-the-land" movement. The money was earmarked to assist people in industrial areas where unemployment was heavy, and the stranded, disorganized, and poorly located farmers. Early in the spring of 1934, however, research funds for the program were stopped and the remaining monies reallocated to specific projects in areas in which the projects were to be developed.

Unfortunately, the policies of the Division of Subsistence Homesteads failed to keep abreast of the new back-to-the-land movement and patterns of part-time farming. The necessary preliminary research never was completed. Programs were hindered or wrecked by legal technicalities, administrative confusion, and misdirection. To complicate matters, Rexford Tugwell, whose name often was linked with the program, never liked the general concept of subsistence homesteads. He was apprehensive about the industrial support behind them, and feared that the projects would be converted into company towns.[22]

One big question at first was whether the homestead projects were going to be planned, built, managed, and administered exclusively by the federal government or as a partnership between the federal and local governments. Mrs. Roosevelt liked the idea of some local responsibility; so did Louis Howe, a close friend of Mrs. Roosevelt, the advisory committee, and Senator John Bankhead of Alabama who said this was the way he always wanted it. Local responsibility offered more flexibility. But Secretary of the Interior Harold Ickes, who had to approve expenditures, was busy, not much interested in subsistence projects, and took a long time before he finally said, "No." Wilson reminisced, "Ickes came from Chicago; he didn't trust people; he feared graft; and he would not compromise." The subsistence homesteads project had to be a 100 percent federal project.

Ickes also felt that the subsistence homesteads program had to have a hard-boiled businessman, a builder and a contractor, as its head. Such a program had to be closely related to public works and the person heading it had to work with Ickes. Wilson naturally wondered where this was going to leave him as director. Ickes's administrative assistant finally told Wilson he could develop the social services.[23]

Tugwell agreed with Ickes that subsistence homesteads should be a federal project because this was the only way it would work. Wilson, however, felt that Ickes never understood the rural side of the program, and the breach between the two was because of differences over policy and to some extent philosophy. Wilson's days as director of the subsistence homesteads project were limited. On June 21, 1934 Wallace told reporters he wanted Wilson to succeed Tugwell, who was being designated under secretary of agriculture, as assistant secretary of agriculture. Wilson assumed his new post on July 1.[24]

Ickes was irritated over costs, singling out the project at Reedsville, West Virginia for criticism. "The theory was that we would be able to set up families on subsistence homesteads at a family cost of from $2,000 to $3,000 and here we have already run above $10,000 per family. I am afraid we are going to be in for some justifiable criticism." Ickes reported to Roosevelt that M. L. Wilson was "not a good executive" and the subsistence homesteads project "got off to a very bad start" under him. Despite the fact that Charles Pynchon, an experienced businessman, was brought in as the general manager of the program, the situation "seemed to be getting more and more into the hole."[25]

Late in 1933 Carl C. Taylor observed that no one had come up with a good definition of a subsistence homestead or what it should be. In 1934 Taylor said, "I do not believe . . . the confusion has cleared much in the last twelve months."[26]

The creation of the RA by executive order on April 20, 1935, and the appointment of Rexford G. Tugwell as its director were influenced by at least three factors: (1) the FERA as administered by Harry Hopkins was more urban-industrial than rural oriented and the farmers were not faring as well under it as they should have; (2) the belief that farmers and rural projects would be better served if they were placed under the jurisdiction of an agency that would concentrate on their needs; and (3) Tugwell was interested in the program and it was thought expedient to put him in charge. As a consequence, part of FERA, the Division of Rural Rehabilitation, the Division of Subsistence Homesteads, and the land policy section of the AAA came under the jurisdiction of the RA.[27]

The prescribed functions of the RA, according to its first annual report, were:

> To administer approved projects involving resettlement of destitute or

low-income families from rural and urban areas, including the establishment, maintenance, and operation, in such connection, of communities in rural suburban areas.

To initiate and administer a program of approved projects with respect to soil erosion, steam pollution, seacoast erosion, reforestation, and flood control.

To make loans as authorized under the said Emergency Relief Appropriation Act of 1933 to finance, in whole or in part, the repurchase of farm lands and necessary equipment by farmers, farm tenants, croppers, or farm laborers.

Rural rehabilitation had made slight progress under the FERA by the time the RA took over this responsibility in June 1935. Only twenty-nine communities were started, and for more than half nothing beyond the purchase of land had been accomplished. Most of the work under FERA consisted of giving aid to farmers who lacked the means of carrying on their work. The plan after the RA took over was to continue the state administrative arrangement initiated by FERA, but a ruling by the comptroller general of the United States made this impossible. Rural rehabilitation, as a result, was centralized in twelve regional offices, and RA policies were more sharply defined.

The loan policies of RA and FERA differed. The FERA made rehabilitation loans to all needy farmers; and often the differences were few between those who received loans, loans and grants, and only grants. The RA, on the other hand, drew a distinction between standard and emergency loans. Standard loans, usually given in sums of between $300 and $400, were based on the farm-and-home management plan drawn up by the farm family with the help of a field staff member. The family, by following a series of efficient farming methods, was expected to be able to raise most of its own food, feed for its livestock, and two or more cash crops for market. The field workers who helped work out these plans were trained farm-management specialists and home economists who brought to the farm family knowledge of the new farming and homemaking practices that the state agricultural colleges and the extension services had been developing. The FERA made limited use of this phase of the program because of the lack of money, trained personnel, and time.

The theory behind the assistance program was that the farmer had to have enough good land and some practical knowledge of the newer ways of farming if he was going to develop sound farm and home management practices. Unfortunately, hundreds of farmers had little fertile land or experience; hence it was impossible for them to devise a plan that would provide enough to eat, clothe and house themselves, and still enable them to repay their loans. Thus the RA made emergency loans to such farmers with the expectation that the family would progress to the point where it would be eligible to obtain a standard loan. The grant program under the RA, on the other hand, was used to augment the emergency loans. Farmers in the hard-hit drought areas who had little chance whatsoever of repaying their loans continued to receive outright grants. The RA, in other words, was covering the same ground as the FERA, but in a different way.

Rural rehabilitation was expanded during the winter of 1935–1936. However, a shift in rural relief began with the coming of the Works Progress Administration (WPA), which started to fill the vacuum created with the phasing out of the FERA. While the FERA made grants to families on the basis of need, to keep them alive (these often were supplemented by wages from private sources that were too small to furnish adequate family support), the WPA paid wages and hired only the totally unemployed. The WPA made no grants to those unable to find work as the FERA had done. The shift from federal work and direct relief to federal jobs and local relief was achieved by the end of 1935. Farmers in need and not employed by the WPA or cared for by the RA became the responsibility of local and state relief agencies—and this continued until the outbreak of World War II and the demise of the New Deal.[28]

The need for a proper use of the land program, which land economists had emphasized for years, finally was driven home dramatically by the dust storms, droughts, and floods. Land planning consultants indicated that at least 100 million acres of land in agricultural use were submarginal and should be retired. The FERA planned to acquire 20 million acres; a total of $78 million became available for this purpose, but relief requirements unfortunately caused $50 million of these funds to be rescinded. After the RA took over the program another $20 million were authorized for land purchases, which meant that $48 million now were available for purchases. As a result, a program of 206 active projects, involving the purchase of 9.3 million acres of submarginal land that could be converted to grazing, public forests, parks, recreational areas, wildlife sanctuaries, Indian reservations, and other uses, got under way.

Land use specialists cooperated closely with agricultural experiment stations, state planning boards, conservation commissions, and other state agencies in these efforts. Matters such as the economic status of the land occupants, the conditions of the soil and vegetation, and land needs for public purposes also were considered before a final decision was made on the development of a project. The relationship of the proposed land-use project to the adjacent towns and cities, local public opinion, the attitudes of various state officials, the costs, and the prospects of providing employment were explored.

Although acquisition of land was slow, the progress under the RA was greater than under the FERA. A total of 9.7 million acres were under options by April 15, 1936, and options on almost 8.5 of the 9.7 million acres, costing more than $36 million, had become legal commitments. More than $42 million of the $48 million available for the program were encumbered. This was a far cry from the 100 million acres originally recommended for retirement from use.[29]

The RA had completed eighteen of the thirty-three projects taken from the Division of Subsistence Homesteads by April 30, 1936. Construction was in progress on eleven others and final plans were being prepared on the remaining four.[30]

The new resettlement projects initiated by the RA were of several kinds. Farm unit projects were interspersed among existing farms by the so-called "infiltration process" in thirty-six cases in the New England and middle western states where the farm unit pattern was well established and it was difficult to secure large blocs of land. In other instances the infiltration process was modified so that the purchased farms were grouped within existing rural communities and the services sponsored by the RA.

Thirty-five projects were to be of the "close community" type in which the land assembled was in one bloc. The land in most cases was to be divided according to standard practices and the farm homes located on individual tracts. Cooperative organizations were to buy, market, process, and supply utility services.

Three labor camps in California were to provide 4,000 to 5,000 itinerant families during the season with hot and cold showers, flush toilets, washtubs, and in some cases gas plates. California was a state in which 57 percent of those making a living in agriculture were farm laborers living under extremely bad conditions.

The RA was contemplating the development altogether of about 140 rural resettlement projects, including the former subsistence homestead projects, at a total cost of $92 million. Eighteen of these were completed in May 1936, and thirty-nine more were under construction. The RA also hoped to reach an estimated 2 million youths who under predepression conditions would have moved to town for work but now found themselves on the farm with no security and little hope for the future. RA officials were so optimistic about the outcome of the program that in 1936 the RA reported:

> The present program will demonstrate . . . that resettlement is a
> profitable undertaking where families are moved from poor land to
> good land, are sold farms that are large enough to yield a satisfactory
> gross income under supervision, and where 3-percent money enables
> the purchaser to enjoy immediately a higher standard of living.[31]

The RA also undertook the development of suburban resettlement demonstration projects, after a program of eight such projects costing $68 million had been approved by the president in 1935, in the vicinities of Berwyn, Maryland; Bound Brook, New Jersey; Milwaukee, Wisconsin; and Cincinnati, Ohio. These projects provided the living facilities and utilities common to cities together with farms, gardens, wooded areas, and recreational facilties.

The first significant attack on the RA came in December 1935. Merritt Lane, the counsel for Franklin Township in Somerset County, New Jersey, filed suit in the Federal District Court of Newark to halt the Bound Brook greenbelt project. The suit charged that the Emergency Relief Appropriation Act of 1935, which provided the RA with most of its funds, represented an unlawful delegation of powers by Congress, violated state rights, deprived local property owners of property without due process of law, removed property from the tax rolls without the consent of the township, and was unconstitutional.[32]

The district court upheld the complaint, and the RA immediately appealed the case in the U.S. Court of Appeals for the District of Columbia. The Appeals court in a 3 to 2 decision upheld the lower court and enjoined the RA from proceeding on the Bound Brook project on the grounds that the Emergency Relief Appropriation Act of 1935 did not contain "a word or syllable authorizing the resettlement of destitute or low-income families, not did it provide for the organization of a resettlement administration for the purpose of establishing model communities." The RA, after learning that this decision applied only to the Bound Brook project, planned to go ahead with three other resettlement projects, subject of course to the final decision of the Supreme Court. The *New York Times* reported that the RA would not appeal the Bound Brook decision on the theory it would be better to lose one greenbelt than all three.[33]

The Bound Brook decision, however, heightened the attack on Tugwell, "Rex the Red," "the dreamer," and on the RA. "Too much theory and too many professors," said Representative Clifford R. Hope of Kansas. The agency was overstaffed and the employees were paid too much. According to the *New York Times*, the RA had 12,089 organized jobs for 5,172 relief workers, and the directing staff was paid twice as much as the relief workers. The inevitable charge of bureaucratic bungling and waste that grew out of incidents such as a check sent, through clerical error, to an Arkansas farmer who applied for aid also was there.[34]

Conservative farm groups found fault with the migratory farm workers camps. In California commercial growers and the local chambers of commerce charged that the camps would become hotbeds of radical agitation. The Associated Farmers, an organization of large corporate farmers, bankers, and landowners which was organized after the field strike of 1933 to suppress "communist" agitation in the fields and orchards, and the State Chamber of Commerce organized a quiet but effective campaign against the camps.[35]

Complaints that the policies of the AAA and the RA were inconsistent, contradictory, and irresponsible were heard repeatedly. For instance while the AAA sought to prevent the expansion of cash crops, the RA sought to place more people on the land to earn a better living. Needy farmers complained that the largest part of the RA's program was based on the assumption that only worthy families would be helped, and to be deemed worthy one had to have security for a loan. Meanwhile, the Republicans claimed that the RA was lending money on "insecure loans." In late October 1936 Tugwell stated that more than three-fourths of the rehabilitation loans had been repaid, and that in his opinion the great majority of farmers under the rehabilitation program would repay their debts in full. A report published by the University of Pennsylvania in the summer of 1936 disputed the hypothesis that the decentralization of industry could serve as a major solution to the problems of stranded rural populations, and warned of the dangers of creating company towns or towns without sources of cash income. Studies of population redistribution in 200 industrial counties showed that the percentage of manufacturing jobs in these counties had remained the same between 1899 and 1933.[36]

The RA also faced insurmountable financial obstacles. Supporting funds had to come from those allotted the president for relief purposes the first and second years, and Congress refused to make the RA a respectable and permanent addition to "the family of federal organizations."

Tugwell believed that the RA probably would have been more acceptable if it had experienced a more gradual and seasoned growth. This would have reduced the administrative difficulties and made them more manageable.[37] RA officials had been under the misapprehension that two generations of agitation in behalf of conservation had prepared people for land-use programs and the retirement of land from commercial purposes. But they were wrong. The critics "let us know that this was a fancy idea developed by intellectuals. It was wholly impractical; and they refused to have anything to do with it," said Tugwell.

The well-to-do farm people, furthermore, were convinced that poverty was the result of "shiftlessness and incompetence" that could not be overcome by any program. This conclusion, they insisted, was based on intimate, irrefutable firsthand evidence which was the only kind worth considering. Such attitudes were brought to bear on congressmen through the testimony of farmer organizations and lobbying techniques. The more prosperous farmers paid dues to these organizations, thereby contributing to the salaries of their lobbyists, and their views prevailed.

The entire system of social relations also was a factor. If the tenants, sharecroppers, or agricultural laborers for whom these programs were intended became more independent, as the RA threatened to make them, "they would be hard to deal with. If they moved away, the labor market would be tightened. If they became owners they also became competitors. If something had to be done, the last of the three alternatives was preferable." Ownership at least would give those who climbed up the ladder the outlook of the proprietors. Hence the farm-tenant purchase program was approved, which was all that survived of the RA activities.

A basic reason for the eventual defeat of the entire program was that the rural poor the RA sought to help were among the least influential voices in the country. They lacked experienced leaders, had few funds to contribute to political parties, and had hardly any voters in the poll-tax states. The only friend the RA had was the Farmers' Union, whose strength was considerably weaker than that of the more affluent farmer organizations that opposed the RA.

Likewise, the corollary programs the RA was asked to administer—such as the grants and loans extended after the drought of 1934, the subsidiary medical services, and the payment of poll taxes—infuriated critics. Matters took a turn for the worse after the Division of Subsistence Homesteads, which already was under fire, was transferred to the RA. Then there were the troubles of the Division of Suburban Resettlement whose projects were supposed to reflect good planning and decent construction, and eventually supplant the crowded neighborhoods and the shabbily built houses offered by the real estate promoters. The RA came under such savage attacks that plans for sixty projects had to be abandoned. The three remaining projects never were finished and eventually were given up to speculators.

Congress knew that the RA had little political support and Democratic politicians hoped the entire operation could be junked. They were worried over the effects the RA would have on the presidential election of 1936, and Tugwell and his associates were asked to remain quiet during the campaign. The sweeping victory by Roosevelt in 1936 did little good, and the RA was among the first to suffer in the upsurge. The president was defeated in the humiliating fight over the Supreme Court, and during the next few years many New Deal agencies were emasculated in the bitter struggle between the executive and legislative branches of the government.[38]

The Farm Security Administration

THE AGITATION OF 1935 AND 1936 in behalf of the tenants, sharecroppers, and agricultural laborers, the inability of the Resettlement Administration (RA) to ease their plight to any appreciable extent, and the persistence of politicians, public-spirited citizens, church groups, the Southern Tenant Farmers' Union (STFU), liberal publications, Socialists, and farm extension leaders, combined with the general publicity the disadvantaged groups received, helped arouse public interest in them, and left the impression that some far-reaching legislation finally was going to be passed.

Nineteen thirty-six was a presidential election year. Early in June a group of Democratic House members suggested to James A. Farley, the chairman of the Democratic National Committee, that a plank on farm tenancy be included in the party platform that year. The Republicans, who assembled in convention before the Democrats, promised, among other things, "to protect and foster the family type of farm," adopt a national land-use program, provide ample farm credits at low rates of interest, and withdraw nonproductive lands from cultivation, but they maintained a discreet silence on tenants, sharecroppers, and farm laborers. The Democratic platform mentioned farm tenancy and rural rehabilitation, but came forward with nothing more specific.[1]

Roosevelt wrote Senator John Bankhead on September 17, "An enduring agricultural civilization must be built on the firm foundation of homes and farm ownership," and "the welfare of the nation and of farm people involves improvement of the farm tenancy situation." The farm tenancy question could not be resolved overnight, continued the president, but farm ownership could grow with government aid as in Ireland and Denmark by giving tenants with an ability to manage land an opportunity to buy farms on longtime terms at moderate rates of interest. Roosevelt asked Bankhead to meet with Representative Marvin Jones, chairman of the House Agricultural Committee, to prepare plans which would help the administration tackle the question of farm tenancy. The president wanted to meet with Jones early in December to complete the recommendations to Congress.[2]

Meanwhile, the administrative machinery began to work. In October a group comprised largely of representatives of the USDA met and agreed that each member should formulate some ideas on the principles that should govern the proposed Bankhead bill and its administration. Resettlement Administration representatives did not participate in these discussions to give the members of this new group the opportunity to come forward with their proposals independently; then the two groups would be brought together to pool their suggestions. The only exception was L. C. Gray, who attended the initial meeting to serve as a bridge between the two groups.[3]

In early November Roosevelt referred Wallace to a letter he received from Morris L. Cooke, Rural Electrification administrator. Cooke proposed the formation of a committee to prepare a report summarizing available data on the tenancy problem in anticipation of forthcoming legislation. Henry A. Wallace and Rexford G. Tugwell believed that such a report should be prepared under the general auspices of the National Resources Committee, and that the prestige of the report would be enhanced if its special committee consisted of persons with an extensive knowledge of the problem and a sympathetic interest in finding constructive solutions. On November 16 Roosevelt informed Wallace he was appointing him chairman of the Special Committee on Farm Tenancy, and L. C. Gray, executive secretary and technical director.[4]

Complaints soon were voiced over the composition of the committee. Clarence Poe, the influential editor of the *Progressive Farmer,* wired Wallace and L. C. Gray that the subcommittee was "dangerously one-sided" because no person from the South was included in it. A Floridian protested that a black woman, Mary McLeod Bethune, was appointed, but no white person from Florida. (Bethune was director of the Division of Negro Affairs in the National Youth Administration.) Fears also were raised that the committee would give too much weight to group farming.[5]

The arguments against tenancy and for more farm ownership were repeated with monotonous regularity. Wallace emphasized at the opening committee session that three of every four farmers who had been owners in 1880 saw their equities decline over the succeeding years until they amounted, on the average, to less than half their total value. While owner-farmers were being converted into tenants slowly, the equities of those who had not been reduced to tenancy were being chiseled away. The survival of an agricultural civilization depended on giving greater security to farm families working the land with ownership, security of tenure, or both. At the time, the American people seemed prepared to support any reasonable program to reverse the tide of tenancy. Late in 1936 the American Institute of Public Opinion reported that 83 percent of the people interviewed approved of a government program that would enable farmers to buy the farms they were renting.[6]

As a means of arousing as much interest and public support as possible, the committee on farm tenancy agreed to hold public hearings in the cotton and corn belts, the Great Plains, and the Pacific Coast states. Announcements of the scheduled hearings were sent in advance to the governors of the various states, asking them to appear in person or send representatives and encourage all properly qualified persons to present their views.[7]

This procedure had a contagious effect. Discussion groups on farm tenancy had sprung up all over the country by early January 1937. The USDA, to facilitate matters, prepared a series of information bulletins written in an easygoing style that called attention to the various points of view and left it up to the individuals or groups of persons to decide which position they agreed with. About two-thirds of the Extension Services appointed state directors to assist the farmers in discussing the social and economic issues involved.[8] The regional hearings brought some relevant information to the surface. A field information specialist for the AAA, R. L. Burgess, said the San Francisco hearings did a lot of good, but that he expected criticism to filter back to Washington from some of the large California growers who felt it was a mistake to allow certain types of small farmers to testify. Burgess felt that ". . . the large growers, corporation farmers and land speculators of this region have not shown themselves very loyally devoted to the AAA program." Burgess likewise believed it was urgent that

> the rank and file of farmers, the farm laborers, and the general public . . . not get the impression that the AAA and the Department of Agriculture as a whole is absolutely tied up with the corporation farms and with certain organizations and agencies generally felt to be rightly or wrongly closely associated with the "big interests."

According to Burgess, some representatives of the big growers were "among the most consistent opponents and sabotagers [sic] of the AAA and Department policy out here." The manager of one of the large corporations boasted he hired spies to learn about AAA affairs relating to milk and other commodities. The hearings, nevertheless, reminded these big growers that they also were citizens of the United States as well as feudal lords in their own domain, and a feeling emerged that in the future they would be more cautious in the conduct of their heretofore flagrant policies.

The hearings also emphasized the necessity for cooperation between the RA and the AAA. Despite the mistakes of some RA officials, generally speaking all farmers, not just the large operators, were given the opportunity to benefit from government policy. Meanwhile the RA had to realize the advantages to be gained from diplomacy and pragmatism, virtues that were better exemplified by the AAA than the RA. The focus was on the farm management approach of the AAA and the land-use approach of the RA.[9]

Meanwhile, a series of far-reaching suggestions, solicited and unsolicited, were received by the President's Special Committee on Farm Tenancy, which represented a wide spectrum of opinion. Jonathan Garst, RA director for the states of California, Nevada, Utah, and Arizona, informed Tugwell that any program to better the lot of the disadvantaged groups had to take into account that two types of agriculture predominated in the Far West: the range and the irrigated. A family could scarcely maintain itself on a range farm with less than 200 cows or an equivalent number of sheep, which at the prevailing prices would cost about $6,000 and a land investment for grazing that meant additional expenditures of $50 per cow or $10,000. These capital needs made it desirable for the range lands to be owned by the government with controlled grazing by lease comparable to that provided by the Forestry Service and the Taylor Grazing Commission.

Farming on irrigated lands, on the other hand, was restricted to areas in which there was water and relatively level land. Irrigation in practically all instances required commercial rather than subsistence farming. Large mechanized, industrialized farms predominated in California and Arizona where much of the land was devoted to specialized crops competing with the small, independently owned and operated farms.

Some benefits might accrue to the small farmer in the areas in which the small unit was the logical type of farming, such as in Utah, which had many small farms, by providing him with the means of becoming an owner. Aiding the small farmer to buy land was advisable if ownership actually increased his security and income.[10]

Garst in effect was saying that agriculture in the Far West faced two alternatives: one was industrialized corporation farming in which farm laborers would organize and force wages up to living scale by fighting against their employers; the other was group farming. If the man who worked the ground obtained the benefits of mechanization, commercialization, security, and occupancy, and a farm home through group farming, progress would be made in resolving this problem. Garst believed that perpetuating or increasing individual small ownership of the land in this region would be a move backward instead of forward.

Garst's plan for group farming in the states of the Far West was to place fifty-six houses along either side of about one mile of road, centering them at a road junction. He would attach two acres of land to each house and place the remainder in the control of the association. If an individual wanted to farm forty acres himself he would be leased a forty-acre plot in a corner where it would not interfere with the larger groupings. If two wished to farm eighty acres together, they could lease that much in common; and if sixteen wished to farm a section, the leases could be arranged so that they, too, would have such a group. The big question was whether the proposed legislation would permit group purchases and farming.[11] Garst also suggested part-time farming—the hope being that the part-time farmers and farm laborers intended for settlement on these projects would lease land for group operations.

Security of tenure for operators, according to Garst, could be had by allowing them to keep the improvements on the farms and buildings by granting those actually in need loans at something like 2 percent interest on a sixty-year basis. Since profit was not a consideration, this land could be tied up in the same fashion as the subsistence homesteads so that the sales could be made back to the government until the period of amortization ran out. If $2 million a year was made available annually for such a program in his region, loans of $250 could be made to 8,000 farmers, and land purchased from the thirty self-help agricultural cooperatives that had been started in California under the FERA.

Obviously this kind of assistance was going to embitter farmers who had been making their own way and borrowing from the Federal Land Bank. Garst thought this bitterness might be lessened or avoided if this subsidy was granted through subsidized housing or by having the government carry the cost of aid through supervision and the granting of low-cost loans to cooperative ventures.

The National Committee on Rural Social Planning (NCRSP)—of which Gardner Jackson was chairman and Norman Thomas, the candidate of the Socialist party for president in 1932, Representatives Thomas R. Amlie of Wisconsin and Vito Marcantonio of New York, Senator Gerald P. Nye of North Dakota, Walter White of the National Association for the Advancement of Colored People (NAACP), and rural sociologists Carle C. Zimmerman of Harvard and Rupert B. Vance of the University of North Carolina were sponsors—came forward with recommendations similar to those of Garst, but with a southern focus, and with the essentials for drafting a comprehensive bill.

The NCRSP emphasized that in the South differences in agricultural practices and the social and economic conditions of the rural population were too varied to come forward with a simple and uniform method of attack. Matters were also complicated by the problems of race and the suppression of civil liberties. There also was the danger that the United States would revert to the "horse and buggy" economy of the smaller European countries with their small individual peasant holdings, lacking the most efficient, up-to-date techniques, equipment, and marketing facilities. At best such a program would anchor millions of the rural people in the South to a subsistence or a near subsistence level.[12]

In the opinion of the NCRSP the Bankhead bill, S2367, recognized the complexity of the tenancy problem, but was inadequate because the measure was designed to convert sharecroppers, tenants, and farm laborers into small landowners and ultimately create an American peasant class. The NCRSP doubted that a program of individual farm ownership, however comprehensive, would eliminate permanently the evils of tenancy that existed in the cotton, tobacco, rice, and sugar areas, and quoted from a statement of the STFU on the inadequacies of the small isolated tracts:

> If the prospective new farm owners are to make something more than a mere subsistence living, and if the cultural level of the people is to be raised, a new type of farm organization will be necessary. That organization must perforce be a communal or village farm economy. . . . The large plantation has an economic justification which we neglect at our peril. Particularly where there is a century old tradition of plantation collectivism . . . the fundamental readjustment which is needed is in the character of the large farm.[13]

If the NCRSP believed that a majority of the sharecroppers, tenants, and farm laborers would fare better under the community type of farming, it also recognized many farmers would prefer small holdings of their own, and that such desires would continue until some agency undertook an educational campaign to dispel the romantic notion regarding the individualism of the farmers.

Such individual farms, however, had to have the size, fertility, and equipment to enable their operators to pay their annuities from their annual incomes, secure for themselves and families adequate livings, and pay decent wages; and all persons from eligible groups had equal rights to these farms regardless of race, color, creed, politics, or farmer organization ties. Such owners also had to be protected from absentee landlords, land speculators, and others who made it a business of "farming the farmers." Finally, precautions had to be taken to prevent banks, insurance companies, and other landlords from dumping their most worthless holdings onto the government, which in turn would find itself compelled to unload such properties on unsuspecting tenants.

The advantages of longtime leasing that left the title to the land in the hands of the government also had to be considered. Such a system could be more flexible than one based on the ownership of the land, without sacrificing practices essential to the maintenance of the soil and the restoration of its fertility. This would make it possible for isolated tenant tracts to be merged gradually and permit a steady increase in the establishment of farm communities best suited to the cultural and economic backwardness of large sections of the rural population, and provide protection from land speculators and inflated land values.

More pointed and dramatic were the recommendations of the STFU, whose officers wrote the president "two years of terror and violence" had convinced their members that it would be more advisable for the United States to concern itself with the 90 percent who would not gain from the RA and rural rehabilitation within the next few years than with the 10 percent who would. The following program of action was proposed:

1. Federal support of the constitutional right of the officers and members of the STFU to organize and conduct educational campaigns free from interference or molestation by any groups.
2. Federal legislation that would outlaw sharecropper contracts that charged outrageous rates of interest on accounts for goods of inferior quality, and compel the issuance of final settlements honestly arrived at.
3. Ban contracts between the federal government and the landowners that would require a sharecropper, tenant, or farm laborer to buy his supplies from a commissary store, and federal assistance in a campaign to abolish commissaries through appropriate state legislation.
4. Government loans to sharecroppers and tenants at low rates of interest without waiver of landlords' liens, and the advance of loans directly to the sharecroppers and tenants.
5. Written contracts between landlords and tenants or sharecroppers to protect all parties concerned.
6. Contract disputes to be referred to county and state arbitration boards made up of representatives of the interested parties.
7. Cooperation between state labor departments or responsible state agencies with the federal government in seeing that contracts were properly fulfilled.
8. Require a new type of contract between landlords, tenants, and sharecroppers that ran from three to five years and made for greater security in land tenure.[14]

The STFU, like the NCRSP, recognized that most farmers wanted to own their farms, but believed that a substantial percentage were willing to attempt cooperative operations on large tracts of land in line with the trend toward mechanization in the cotton-growing areas. Most farmers, if not all, according to the STFU, favored cooperative enterprises even where the land was individually owned. Realizing, however, that proposals to own land in fee simple or group farming were going to encounter opposition, the STFU believed that the federal government should consider the possibility of guaranteeing tenure on government lands to cooperative groups through long-term leases. A broadened program was suggested on the theory that some farmers would succeed by one method and some by others. The education of disadvantaged classes would be further facilitated if their homes were located in small villages near the lands they farmed, whether operated collectively or individually.

The recommendations of a subcommittee of the Southern Policy Association were more modified in tone in comparison with those of the STFU and the NCRSP. The report of the subcommittee of the Southern Policy Association, headed by Professor Charles S. Johnson, who was the director of the Department of Social Science at Fisk University, and including historian H. Clarence Nixon of Tulane University, Arthur F. Raper, research secretary of the Commission on Interracial Cooperation, and Rupert B. Vance of the Institute for Research in Social Science, University of North Carolina, was unique in that each member submitted his own report.

The needs of the farmers in the southeastern states where the greatest percentage of the land was misused and eroded, tenancy rates were high, farm income the lowest, subsistence the most meager, diets among the poorest, production costs and population ratios the highest, farming methods the crudest, and adaptability to large-scale mechanization and production very difficult, were different from the needs of the farmers in the Delta area and the Southwest. Johnson believed that the program envisioned by the Bankhead–Jones Act was in line with programs advanced by European countries faced with similar tenancy problems. He also saw the need for an agricultural program based on the purchase of land by the government and assistance to the tenants and sharecroppers in the acquisition of this land with the necessary farm dwellings, stock, and equipment, and less on the continuation of cotton as the sole commercial crop.

Johnson further understood that such a program would benefit about 5 percent of the farmers in the Old South; hence other measures were necessary. Government loans to small producers who had been unable to obtain them through the credit merchants; aids to ownership through certain types of homestead exemptions; help to agricultural cooperatives to purchase large tracts of land for operation on a profit-sharing basis; minimum wage laws for farm laborers and the inclusion of them in the provisions for Social Security; development of a regional "authority in agriculture" comparable to the TVA, with lands owned by the government and operated on a participating basis by agricultural workers that could serve as a yardstick in determining a fair return for farm labor and demonstrate the benefits of a balanced agriculture, soil protection, and cooperative production were all necessary if most of the farmers were to be helped. Johnson also asked for tariff adjustments, the extension of government grants to land-grant agricultural institutions, demonstration agents and vocational agriculture teachers, and an increase in the number of such agents to make possible a broad program of adult education for farm workers in the essentials of agricultural life.[15]

H. Clarence Nixon agreed that the principles of the old Bankhead–Jones farm tenant bill should be adhered to, but felt that the details of the bill itself should be revised. Farm ownership had to be expanded on a gradual basis with emphasis on the selectivity of the farmers and the land, and supervision for a temporary period. Like Johnson he realized that hardly more than 5 percent of the tenant farmers and farm laborers could be included in the program, but it was important that the 5 percent be aided under the plan.

Nixon reiterated the recommendations of others: long-term leases that provided the tenants with more secure tenure, land conservation, a constructive land policy for farmers who might become owners, the improvement of property once means had been discovered for developing farmers to be staked in land ownership; production credit for tenants or owner-operators who were in need of working capital, livestock, farm machinery, and equipment, but were a good risk; cooperative ownership and enterprise for small farmers who otherwise were incapable of holding their own; flexible regulations to enforce balanced farming; and soil improvement.[16]

Arthur Raper believed it important for the legislators to remember that the best lands in the South were owned by the cotton plantation interests, the plantation system had its economic background in slavery, and this was the area in which farm ownership had to be increased. Legislation had to be provided with specific provisions for adequate medical services, educational facilities, scientific and supervisory personnel, and protection for tenants and would-be owners to participate in farm and labor unions and producer and consumer cooperatives. Raper also stressed programs for erosion, crop and soil improvement, crop production and emergency crop loan services, production control, and political farm blocs. Farm tenancy legislation had to provide for the expansion and refinement of the rural rehabilitation program, experimentation with rural resettlement farm colonies, and aid to tenants in selected areas to obtain land ownership, individually or collectively, through methods comparable to those of Denmark and other European countries anxious to increase farm ownership.[17]

Rupert B. Vance believed the old Bankhead–Jones bill, not the RA, had to be the point of departure.

> Any attempt to salvage the Resettlement Administration by change in alphabetical arrangement would be most unfortunate. If taking over the physical assets of RA means taking over their conflicts of authority, their infeasible overhead, the dictatorial techniques of certain project managers, etc., the whole thing is . . . doomed from the start.

Land ownership was no guarantee against speculation, mortgage, or loss of farms. An arrangement that granted the farmers all possible rights—legal and economic—afforded by ownership and prevented the alienation of title by use of a longtime government lease was preferable. Subsistence farming was almost imperative as a means of sustaining rural life. Cooperative and perhaps collective farming also had a place in American society, providing the experts chosen to manage these projects did not become more dictatorial than the former plantation managers.

Vance also thought that in areas where blacks constituted from 70 to 90 percent of the population, shifting them from tenancy to ownership would mean, if carried through, the practical evacuation of the white population. The white landlords in these areas behaved something like the British colonial servants; they remained in a fairly alien environment as long as they exercised social and economic direction. If they were deprived of these functions, they would abandon the "Black Belts" to govern themselves or be governed from the state capitol.[18]

Vance's views were the views of the members of the subcommittee of the Southern Policy Association and were more consistent with those of the social activists in the New Deal as opposed to those of the southern agricultural establishment and the USDA.

The suggestions of C. E. Brehm, the director of extension services in Tennessee, reflected the farm management approach and the sentiments of the agricultural power structure. He stressed differences in mental and physical capacities, managerial abilities, and other qualifications that explained why some people became farm owners, and others remained tenants.

> If it were possible to give every tenant at the present time a sufficient amount of land to support his family, and give his family complete title to it, with the next generation we would have the same problem . . . a large percentage of the children of the present generation would be tenants, and within twenty years a large percentage of even the present generation would be tenants.[19]

Something overlooked, however, was the fact that tenancy was not necessarily a sign of poverty. A study of farm tenancy in Tennessee, for instance, indicated there was less tenancy in the mountains and poorer land counties than in the better land areas. Poor land with a low yielding capacity did not necessarily bring on tenancy, but wild fluctuations in the prices of agricultural commodities and the ability to borrow money on good land did. Unfortunate events in the lives of men and women also were factors in keeping many in the tenant class. Many farmers possessed the ability to become owners, except for illness, accidents, deaths in the family, and the inevitable burdens that followed.[20]

Brehm also emphasized what others had said. The plan allowing tenants to purchase farms on long-term loans at low rates of interest should be started in a small way. Tenants had to be selected carefully and supervised rather closely to see that good farm and home management practices were established. Tenancy and its consequent evils did not develop in a year and could not be cured in a year.

Edward A. O'Neal, the gregarious head of the AFBF who seldom waited to be asked what he thought about a particular farm issue, said that a fair price system and parity of income for the farmers would do more to prevent the loss of farm income than any other factor, and restated what others had said about elevating a tenant to ownership status through government assistance.[21]

Mary McLeod Bethune argued that federal supervision was necessary if 700,000 blacks in the South were to be given the opportunity to acquire land or become a part of the rehabilitation program. She suggested that a clause be written into the proposed legislation to guarantee unprotected blacks on the lowest rung of the economic ladder full participation in the homestead and rehabilitation programs—clauses comparable to those by the Public Works Administration (PWA) housing division and the National Youth Administration (NYA) school aid program, which stipulated that "the number of young men and women of any racial group given aid shall not represent a smaller proportion of the total number aided than the proportion this racial group represents of the total population."

Bethune believed that need should be the only criterion for participation in such a program, but recognized that traditional local attitudes posed a serious obstacle. The strong arm of the federal government had to be used if black farmers were to receive justice in the settlement of tenant-landlord differences, emergencies, and housing questions in states where the franchise and civil liberties were denied them. Extensive federal support, equitably allocated, also was needed to supply adequate schools, farm and home extension agents, vocational teachers of agriculture and home economics, boys and girls club work, rehabilitation programs, cooperative organizations, libraries, and health clinics.[22]

M. Katherine Bennett, the vice-president of the Council of Women for Home Missions, believed that the government had to assume some financial responsibility for the migratory farm workers on the Pacific Coast who were badly housed, underpaid, and whose children were deprived of schooling, the security of a stable life, and threatened by bad moral influences. She suggested that the farm tenancy report urge laws that included "a minimum standard of decent living, careful segregation of families and unmarried men and women, decent toilet facilities, adequate water and cooking facilities."[23]

The views expressed were relevant to the fate of the RA and the successor organization, the Farm Security Administration (FSA), around which the new legislation was to be built. A great deal depended on the intent of Congress, and the new administrator and his policies, if the growing clamor for the assistance of the underprivileged farmers was to be placated.

Rexford G. Tugwell found himself in an almost hopelessly tangled situation at the RA, his record marred by poor public relations, a seething band of political opponents, a conviction that he had become a distinct political liability to the New Deal, a complicated marital situation, and resentment in some quarters because the RA, which dealt with a large body of farmers, had been kept out of the USDA and entrusted to individuals in whom the agricultural establishment had little faith. Wallace, if we are to accept the word of Will Alexander, Tugwell's deputy, and others, had been very unhappy with this organizational structure.[24]

Will Alexander, the man Tugwell named his deputy because he believed it would be better to have him inside the RA than outside, succeeded Tugwell. Alexander said he had no previous notice of his being chosen. "The first I saw of it was in the newspapers. It was a curious way to do it." The question of what would happen to the RA was announced in December 1936 when Wallace said that the agency was being transferred to the USDA.

Alexander portrays a discouraging picture of the RA at the time he assumed command.

> It was a mess. They'd just been dumping everything in it. Administratively it was an impossible kind of thing. . . . We had inherited Subsistence Homesteads and . . . these suburban greenbelt things that within themselves called for a highly technical, specialized kind of wisdom to operate. . . . I was interested in doing something for the masses of people at the bottom of agriculture. So I wasn't there under any illusions. [Alexander knew he would] clean out all that publicity crowd we had there and get a plan for telling this story in a thousand communities in America—to the newspapers and bankers and businessmen—and interpret to the grass roots what it was we were doing so we would have some sympathy.[25]

The RA, with Will Alexander at the helm, continued "everything, with some exceptions." No more greenbelts were going to be built; they were Tugwell's idea, and they had been severely criticized. Many believed in the greenbelts, but the new administration maintained that "three was as many as we could get away with." The "songs and the ceramics" also were eliminated because Grace Falke, the administrative assistant to (and future wife of) Tugwell, left.

Others feared that the RA would be scuttled after it was transferred to the USDA because it would be more exposed to the attacks of the unfriendly AFBF and the Extension Service. Alexander, on the contrary, felt that the RA had the support and goodwill of Wallace, Paul Appleby, Milton Eisenhower, and M. L. Wilson, of whom he said, "There never was a fairer man. We went into an atmosphere of friendliness,'' continued Alexander, ''and they were much more friendly to us after we got into the department than they had been when we were on the outside. I think we ought to have been in the department in the beginning.''

One of the most disturbing personalities in the department and representative of those who were hostile, according to Alexander, was Assistant Secretary of Agriculture Grover Hill, "a stupid fella," a political protege and friend of Representative Marvin Jones of Texas, whose appointment was viewed as a political payment to Jones for all he had done for the USDA. Hill on one occasion told Alexander he wanted a justification for everything going on in the RA, that "he was going to keep his eye on us. He was tangled up . . . as a fly on a piece of sticky fly paper. . . . He was skeptical about it all, and said very frankly he was voicing the stuff he'd heard.''[26]

The farm tenancy question was discussed, analyzed, and weighed at great length in the committee hearings, Congress, and the press during the first half of 1937, more than in any previous period in history. The Special Committee on Farm Tenancy submitted its report to the president on February 13, 1937, and three days later Roosevelt told Congress, "The agricultural ladder, on which an energetic, young man might ascend from hired man to tenant to independent owner, is no longer serving its purpose." The authorities failed to bring this to the attention of the general public as they should have done years ago; the agricultural ladder had ceased to fulfill its mythical function for many, if not most, tenants years ago; in fact those who questioned the validity of this hypothesis often were branded as nonbelievers in the promise of farm life, apostates, and enemies of the family farm.[27]

Principal debate on that portion of the bill that became part of the Bankhead–Jones Act began in the House on June 29, and differences over the adequacy of the approach recommended and what it was going to do became evident almost immediately. Representative William Lemke of North Dakota was dismayed by the meagerness of the loan authorization of the bill and said, "I am surprised to hear so much fuss about nothing. If ever a mountain labored and produced a mouse this bill is it . . . this bill is a joke and a camouflage." Congressman Clifford Hope of Kansas felt otherwise.

> There is something to be said on behalf of a careful and cautious approach. We have 2,800,000 farm tenants. If we were to spend only $5,000 in putting each one of them on a farm, it would mean the expenditure of $14,000,000,000.[28]

Following debates on a series of amendments, the Jones bill was approved in the House by a roll call vote of 308 to 25.

The Senate debates on the Bankhead portion of the Bankhead–Jones bill began on the first of July. One of the biggest complaints voiced was that interest rates to the tenants were lower than those paid by the owners—altogether too small. Tom Connally of Texas offered an amendment to increase appropriations the first year to $50 million, but the Senate at the urging of Bankhead voted it down. At the end, however, the House version of the bill prevailed. It provided loans to eligible applicants who would select and purchase their farms outright. The Senate version had authorized the Farmers' Home Corporation to purchase and lease land to prospective purchasers for probationary periods up to five years. Roosevelt signed the measure on July 22, 1937.[29]

Passage of the Bankhead–Jones Act made several things clear. Congressional and administrative circles showed little sympathy for cooperative or communal farm activity. Those who planned the tenant purchase program deliberately avoided the group approach, and the law did likewise. Meanwhile difficulties in administering the resettlement projects mounted, and public sentiment crystallized rapidly against this kind of undertaking.

One of the lessons learned well was that it was unwise to try and install borrowers on farms too small to enable them to earn a living and retire their debts. Lemke was correct when he said that the Bankhead–Jones Act was little more than "a sop" to the farmers, with promises of more money to come if all worked well. "Somewhere between twenty-five hundred and three thousand farms can be financed out of the proposed appropriation, and this could be on the average about one for each agricultural county in the country."[30]

Converting a bill into law was one thing, establishing the machinery for the law to function and achieve its objectives was another. When Paul Maris assumed his duties as director of the new Tenant Purchase Division on September 7, 1937 his job was to lend $10 million to qualified tenants, farm laborers, and sharecroppers before June 30, 1938 in a manner consistent with the spirit and letter of the law. A staff had to be recruited and its activities coordinated with those of the personnel in the Farm Security Administration. The funds were inadequate and loans could not be made in all counties; no decisions had been reached on how these loans were going to be made or not made; and loans could be made only after the county committee appointed by the secretary approved them. Basic guidelines were needed by the field workers, even with the decentralization. Failure to make use of the provided funds would cast doubt on the workability of the law or the competence of the administrators, perhaps both, and harm the future of the program. Three weeks passed before the president signed the bill, and another two months before the secretary assigned the functions vested by the act to the FSA administrator. By June 30, 1938 some 1,879 loans had been made and more than $9 million of the appropriated $10 million obligated.

Although the name of the RA was changed to the FSA and RA personnel were retained on the staff of the agency, there was a noticeable shift in orientation. The resettlement and community housing activities were to be phased out gradually in favor of a massive rural rehabilitation effort, whose real goal, as the name implied, was going to be greater security in farm tenure. Even though the scale of its activities soon exceeded that of the RA, the FSA moved more quietly. Its activities were less novel or spectacular; and for a time it appeared as though the FSA would enjoy a more tenable position.[31]

On the whole the prospects of overhauling the tenancy structure of the United States and introducing wholesale reforms were slim. The niggardly provisions of the Bankhead–Jones Act, the war clouds hanging over Europe, the hostility of the AFBF and the agricultural establishment to sweeping land reforms were overriding factors. Tenancy had not been created overnight and was not going to be eliminated overnight. The eventual involvement of the United States in the war, the growing need for manpower in the factories, the military, and the fields, and the rising wages soon helped obscure the plight of the rural disadvantaged. Over the next few years hundreds of thousands abandoned the rural areas for the cities where they found gainful employment, and later were joined by others who had been equally unsuccessful in making a living on the land. The Bankhead–Jones Act was not calculated to stem the tide of migration to the cities, and it didn't.

The Black Farmer under the New Deal

WHENEVER ANYONE SUGGESTED that black farmers were confronted with more difficult problems than the white farmer, the customary reply was that the USDA served the needs of all, regardless of race, color, or creed. This reply, however, was unacceptable to the black farmers, the overwhelming majority of whom lived in the South and knew that the farm programs in their region were in the firm control of members of the southern power structure.

Most blacks were farmers or had recently left the farm. The almost 883,000 black farmers in the United States in 1930 constituted 14 percent of all farmers in the country. In 1935 more than 9 million of the almost 12 million blacks in the United States lived in the South, and 6 million of those lived in the rural areas. They lived in rural slums and wrestled for the bare essentials of life from steadily deteriorating fields. They were deprived of the expectations of a just reward for their labors and the pride of ownership and had little prospect of extricating themselves from their wretched conditions without help from the federal government.[1]

The blacks and their white allies, who before the New Deal confined themselves to campaigns for equality in civil rights, now began pressing for the appointment of a black advisor or advisors in the USDA, the employment of more black county agents and home demonstration workers in areas with heavy concentrations of blacks, the creation of special credit facilities, the conversion of more black tenants into farm owners, the establishment of black resettlement projects, more responsible positions for blacks, and greater use of the black press.[2]

One of the first requests was for a special bureau in the USDA to represent the "voiceless and voteless," the "hitherto largely overlooked, forgot-

Note: Although the term *Negro* was current in the 1930s, *black* has been widely adopted in modern parlance. The latter term has been employed in this chapter and throughout *The American Farmer and the New Deal*.

ten," "colored farmers." Racial attitudes, complained N. C. Bruce, president of the little-known National Jeffersonian Cooperative League, left the blacks unrepresented on boards, commissions, and directorates created for the relief of all groups. Representative Fred H. Hildebrandt of South Dakota was among those seeking the formation of a bureau of black farmers. Benjamin F. Hubert, the president of Georgia State Agricultural College, reminded Wallace that the large number of blacks in farming entitled them to "some direct representation on the various Boards and Commissions that have to do with Rural Life." The Office of Indian Affairs in the Department of the Interior and the Division of Negro Education in the Office of Education were examples of what could be done.[3]

Rexford Tugwell was one of the USDA officials highly skeptical of such proposals. He informed one advocate that "our services are intended . . . for all American farmers, and to draw a color line would be to discriminate unduly. We have in our Extension Service carried on some special activities for Negroes. . . . Probably this is as far as we should go." He wrote Congressman Hildebrandt that a bureau dealing exclusively with the problems of black farmers would cut across the work of every other bureau in the USDA, such as the Bureau of Plant Industry, the Bureau of Entomology, and the Bureau of Agricultural Economics.[4]

As for the Indians, said Tugwell, the conditions among them were different from those of the blacks. The Indian population had become a ward of the government, and the Office of Indian Affairs was created out of the need to supervise government contacts with them. Such a relationship, however, never existed between the government and the blacks. As for the Division of Negro Education, the school systems in most states in the South were segregated; hence a separate division was established to deal with the black schools. However, there was no comparable segregation of blacks, whites, or other races in agricultural production; and no basis for the establishment of a separate contact with black farmers.[5]

Wallace firmly believed that the Extension Service at the state and federal levels was in the best position to render the needed assistance and, along with Tugwell, he was unsympathetic to the idea of a separate bureau for black farmers. Even if it was desirable from an administrative standpoint to segregate work with blacks into a separate bureau, the administration would have to have congressional sanction for this. Wallace even contended that blacks would respond unfavorably to the idea of segregating their interests for special handling.[6]

W. F. Reden, who favored the creation of a special bureau, reminded Tugwell that the much feared patronizing and discriminatory treatment that would result from a special bureau for the blacks had been happening in the USDA all along. "A check up on the states having A & M Colleges . . . will show that the Negro colleges received very little. . . . The Negro tenant and cotton farmer are practically in the same condition as the Indian who has a bureau to look after his interest." Reden ridiculed the idea there was "no discrimination in the Department of Agriculture," said that any race that farmed "an area greater than the combined land area of Maryland, New Jersey, Vermont, and West Virginia" was entitled to direct representation in the USDA, and warned that the Communists were organizing black farmers. The USDA, like other government agencies, did not have specific figures on the number of blacks it employed, but several years earlier a survey showed it had 1,086 black employees. The number, Reden believed, had increased since then, but he did not know by how much.[7]

Pressure, meanwhile, continued for more black county agents and personnel in the bureaus of Home Economics and Agricultural Economics. J. P. Davis, the executive secretary of the Negro Industrial League, asked for the appointment of a black farm demonstration agent in Marion County, Texas. Marion County in 1930, according to the Census for Agriculture, had 1,558 farms, 1,085 of them operated by blacks and 473 by whites. Black operators farmed 60,221 acres and the whites 40,281; all told, the black population of Marion County was 6,456, and the white 3,915. In Jefferson County, Texas, a 60-year-old white demonstration agent without any formal education concentrated exclusively on the white farmers. Thus the many advantages to be derived from the aid furnished by the USDA were lost to the black farmers of that county. Wallace, in perfunctory bureaucratic fashion, informed Davis, however, that under present circumstances there was little likelihood of adding new agents, even though many of the counties were in a position to do their share; federal and state funds were only sufficient to maintain those agents now employed.[8]

Pressure from blacks apparently persuaded Cully Cobb, after discussing matters with C. W. Warburton, director of the Extension Service, to call a conference of black state leaders in Washington at the earliest possible opportunity in the belief that every effort should be made to give black interests the fullest consideration in the formulation and execution of all plans.[9]

When a special black farm credit bureau was proposed, Wallace replied that agricultural credit was the responsibility of the Farm Credit Administration (FCA), which had absorbed all federal agencies dealing with farm credit, including the Federal Land Banks, the Intermediate Credit Banks, the Regional Agricultural Credit Corporation, and the Crop Production Offices formerly operated by the USDA. Paul Appleby in response to the inquiry on credit said that the USDA had been making seed loans to blacks annually since 1929, and although the records did not distinguish between black and white farmers, the loans given the black farmers probably constituted about 40 percent of all seed loans in the South, and the repayments had been excellent.[10]

Clark Foreman, advisor on the economic status of Negroes in the Interior Department, wrote Wallace early in 1934 that it seemed important to have an interdepartmental review of this question, and at the suggestion of Harold Ickes asked Wallace to designate someone in the USDA to sit on this committee, so that the blacks would receive fair consideration. C. W. Warburton of the Extension Service recommended J. A. Evans as his first choice, C. L. Chambers as his second, and E. H. Shinn as his third. John P. Davis, this time as executive secretary of the Joint Committee on National Recovery, wrote Wallace early in the spring of 1934, "The problem is becoming more and more aggravated and deserves personal attention by you." Appleby replied that the USDA had two separate studies of the problem under way: one by an interdepartmental committee, and another by two or three groups in the department; and that the most expeditious thing for Davis to do was to take this up with Calvin B. Hoover, who was the special representative of Wallace in this field and already had made two reports.[11]

Subsistence Homesteads was one of the programs to attract the attention of blacks. Bruce L. Melvin, supervisor of black workers in Subsistence Homesteads, Department of the Interior, asked R. R. Wright, Jr., president of Wilberforce University of Ohio, to consider the needs of his university with those of an area near Dayton where a project for blacks was under way. In midsummer 1934 Melvin wrote Wright asking him to look at this question in a purely objective manner, keeping in mind the long-range interests of the people of his state. That fall, however, Wright was informed that the original grant of $25 million would make it impossible to consider any new subsistence projects, including one for Wilberforce; efforts were being concentrated on five projects in which blacks were to participate near Tuskegee, Orangeburg (South Carolina), Newport News (Virginia), Dayton, and Philadelphia.[12]

Meanwhile, several chapters of the National Association for the Advancement of Colored People and individual blacks protested that the reclassification of cotton gin employees as agricultural, instead of industrial, workers deprived them of benefits under the NRA. Roy Wilkins of the NAACP informed Wallace that cotton gin work was highly mechanized and industrial labor, and if this reclassification went into effect, 62,000 blacks would be deprived of NRA benefits. Wilkins did not receive a clear-cut answer to his letter, but the NAACP had reason to believe that Cully Cobb had taken the lead in reclassifying the cotton gin workers as agricultural workers.[13]

Administration officials were hard pressed for answers and the ones they often gave were hypothetical and unsatisfactory. When William V. Sanders, the executive secretary of the National Association of Teachers in Colored Schools, asked what good the agricultural programs were doing for the blacks, Milo Perkins replied the "American Negroes, like other citizens, have already benefited considerably.'' The approximately 880,000 blacks engaged in farming were helped directly through the rental and benefit payments they received for their participation in the adjustment program, and the higher prices they got for their products. Blacks in the cities and towns benefited indirectly from the increased employment ''resulting from the rehabilitation of farmers as consumers of industrial products.'' Since all but 12,000 of the 880,000 black farmers in the United States farmed in the South, it was inevitable that they must have benefited from the increased incomes farmers in these states received in 1933 and 1934. When Walter White, the secretary of the NAACP, suggested late in the winter of 1935 that the USDA create a labor board within its ranks, Appleby replied that precautions were being taken to see that justice was done participants in the adjustment programs, and the fact there were more white than black tenant farmers in the country indicated that injustice could not apply to one group without also applying to the other. Appleby was convinced that conditions were infinitely better in 1935 for black and white farmers in the cotton states than they had been in 1933, and cited the National Federation of Colored Farmers at Charleston, Missouri, which unanimously endorsed the cotton program and expressed appreciation for what the administration was doing for the black farmers.[14]

Black criticisms of the New Deal took other directions as well. The *Pittsburgh Courier,* a leading black newspaper, reminded Roosevelt in an open letter in 1935 that black people voted for him in 1932 in the face of every conceivable argument advanced against him and his party. Yet the AAA and some relief agencies continued unequal practices against blacks after he got into office. The *Courier* supported Roosevelt and the Democratic party again in 1936, but continued to complain about discrimination, and the little the New Deal had done to end it. Roosevelt ''expressed shock over the beatings of Jews abroad but not over lynching of Negroes at home,'' continued the *Courier.* ''Mr. Roosevelt could have at least deplored the fact that Negroes are pariahs within the shadow of the White House but he preferred to make speeches condemning the dictators for doing the same thing to Jews, Catholics and others abroad.'' Others demanded that black physicians, dentists, and pharmacists be permitted to participate in medical relief work among blacks ''so far as economic limitations and the maintenance of efficient service would allow.''[15]

The administration was caught between cross fires. Officials of the USDA, for instance, had to explain to inquiring congressmen and senators, pressed by their constituents for explanations, why they were paying so much attention to blacks. Howard R. Tolley once had to explain to Senator Robert J. Bulkley of Ohio why the AAA sponsored a meeting of black editors in 1937, despite the fact that AAA programs depended for their effectiveness on the degree to which farmers—blacks and whites—understood them. The AAA expected to elicit suggestions from the black editors in this conference on how to improve the administration of the program and understanding among blacks.[16]

In fact, the administration had been making gestures along these lines earlier. Black farmers and extension workers formed themselves into a permanent committee in the spring of 1936 to aid in planning the active participation and the fullest possible cooperation of blacks with the long-range agricultural programs. The black county agent, whenever possible and practical, was to be recognized by the local or county advisor on matters affecting black farmers in a new program, and he was to associate with him as a representative of the committee. Director Cully Cobb was asked to make special mention of this to state AAA officials. For a time, even the prospects of enlarging the black extension forces under the provisions of the Bankhead–Jones Act were encouraging.

The blacks, however, did not cease their complaints. In 1937 Charles S. Brown, a student of agricultural problems as they related to blacks, charged that the USDA continued to be insensitive to the interests of an important minority, spent too much time placating vocal and wealthy "reactionary forces," instigated benefit payments without the benefit of a single black farmer or spokesman, failed to protect the welfare of the blacks, and charged that its claim of helping all farmers was an empty, meaningless gesture. Nobody expected the economic advisor of the president of General Motors to represent the interests of the workers, but the USDA permitted white spokesmen to represent black farmers.

The allocation of funds for agricultural research was another grievance. There were 116 black colleges in the United States, continued Brown, most of whose curricula emphasized agriculture, and in the South all public schools serving blacks were required to emphasize agriculture and the manual arts. One black institution of higher learning in Washington, D.C., was partially supported by the federal government with adequate equipment, but it received no aid in establishing agricultural research facilities.[17]

The USDA, said Brown, was vulnerable from still another standpoint. Approximately one-third of the blacks in the United States lived on farms and suffered from mass illiteracy and poverty. Still, the USDA, the AAA, the Farm Security Administration (FSA), and the Soil Conservation Service (SCS) deemed themselves competent to administer fairly all the agricultural laws and to handle racial issues that frequently arose without the services of a single expert on black affairs. The USDA pretended to be fair on the race question, while the Interior Department, the WPA, the Labor Department, the Civilian Conservation Corps (CCC), the Commerce Department, and the Public Health Department all had blacks as advisors. "Your Department has no one," protested Brown to Wallace, "nor do the subsidiary administrations under your guidance." There was "no poverty of Negro talent," but rather an abundance of it.

C. W. Warburton, head of the Extension Service, advised J. D. Le Cron, an assistant to Wallace, on how best to handle the Brown letter. Le Cron was told to first obtain information from the SCS, FSA, AAA, the Extension Service, and the office of Experiment Stations on what they were doing to serve blacks. Once he had the necessary information in hand he wrote Brown, "Your statement that neither the Department of Agriculture nor any of its subsidiary administrations has any Negro advisers is not correct," he countered. "The Agricultural Adjustment Administration . . . has in its employ three outstanding colored people, Messrs. James P. Davis . . . A. L. Holsey, and Mrs. Jennie B. Moton." Le Cron added that the Cooperative Extension Service employed 235 black county agricultural agents and 186 black county home demonstration agents in the twelve states of the South, who were supervised by sixteen black state leaders and assistant state leaders, and eleven state leaders in home demonstration work. Two blacks were employed for more than twenty years to give supervision to black extension work. The RA and the FSA had the advice and counsel of Joseph H. B. Evans, a black and a specialist in race relations; the SCS was helping and receiving the cooperation of many blacks in demonstration projects and camp areas. Late in 1937 the SCS was working on a plan for a soil conservation program for the 1700-acre farm of the Tuskegee Institute, and earlier that year representatives of the AAA and the Extension Service held a three-week training course for black extension workers at the college.[18]

Shortly after Brown leveled his criticisms at the USDA, John W. Davis, president of West Virginia State College and Institute, submitted a copy of a letter drafted by the presidents of the black land grant colleges to Wallace complaining that the black colleges had not been receiving their fair share of money for teaching, research, extension services, and the various programs the administration had launched to better the status of the farmers.

Wallace, in replying to Davis, stated that the federal government under the Hatch Act of 1887, the original experiment station act, provided financial assistance to agricultural experiment stations affiliated with land grant colleges in each state. Legislatures normally allocated agricultural research funds to a state college or university in states with agricultural experiment stations. The USDA was interested in the development of one strong research institution in each state, believing that far better results would be obtained from one station in each state, adequately financed, equipped, and manned, than from a division of funds among several stations. The results of this research were available to all people, regardless of race or creed. However, the USDA did not feel that federal funds designed for agricultural research should be used to increase the teaching efficiency of college staffs.

The legislature of each state under the Smith-Lever Act of 1914 determined the recipient of federal funds for extension, and named the land grant college as the recipient of the funds. The importance of extension work among blacks was recognized from the beginning, and in the states where they constituted a considerable portion of the population, funds were set aside for black agents. Such agents usually were graduates of black land grant colleges. Under the New Deal the expansion of the black extension forces was accomplished largely with state and federal funds, because in many counties it was difficult to obtain county money for the employment of black county agents. Granted that the allocation of funds for black extension work had not been in proportion to the relative number of black and white families, especially in those counties in which black agents were not employed. Wallace insisted, however, that black farmers were always free to consult with white extension agents.

Furthermore, continued Wallace, other New Deal agencies tried to aid black farmers. Special efforts were made to keep the black agents informed about the AAA program so that black farmers could participate intelligently; and in the South the AAA, the RA, and the FSA employed several blacks to assist in the field. The personnel on black settlement projects were selected from black candidates, and expectations in the early stages were that the work of the FSA was going to expand in this direction.[19]

Reliable studies of the extent and comparative quality of assistance rendered black farmers by white extension workers are unavailable, but the fragmentary evidence available shores up the complaints of blacks. After studying a "Report of the Work of the Arkansas Extension Service with Tenants and Sharecroppers, 1936," Mordecai Ezekiel concluded that "as a whole a disproportionately large part of the work of the Extension Service is done with white owners and . . . a disproportionately small part with colored tenants and croppers." The most intensive work with black tenants and croppers was in farm demonstrations where they had their full proportionate share of assistance. The next most effective work was with the 4-H Clubs. When it came to visits by agents and attendance at extension meetings, only 7 to 8 percent of the total work reached the black tenants and croppers who composed 24 percent of all farmers in the state. At the opposite extreme, 50 percent of all farm visits by agents were made to white owners and managers who represented only 35½ percent of all farmers in the states. Ezekiel concluded that despite efforts to expand black extension work in the state, the black tenants and croppers still received a small proportion of the direct activities of the Arkansas Extension Service.[20]

Perhaps the status of the black county agents before World War II is best summed up by historian Gladys Baker who concludes that the New Deal programs did not change the character of the work performed by the black county agents as it had that of the white county agents. The black county agent was used in explaining the programs to his fellow farmers, and in some states to measure the land under the supervision of his white colleagues. Rarely was he given any administrative or supervisory authority. Black county agents could not report cases of unfairness in the distribution of payments under the AAA program in some states simply because it was unsafe for them to do so. Blacks sometimes were allowed to vote for committeemen under the AAA, but never to make nominations. Their presence and voting was more or less mandatory to make a strong showing in favor of the program. Stimulating attendance at the votes was one of the tasks of the black county agent.[21]

Farm tenancy in the South never was primarily a problem involving blacks. Five-eighths of the 1.8 million tenant families in 1930 and nearly two-thirds of the slightly more than 1.8 million tenant farmers in 1935 were white. Tenancy among white families increased between 1920 and 1930 by 200,000, while tenancy among black families decreased by 2,000. The "whitening" of farm tenancy continued at an accelerated pace between 1930 and 1935; meanwhile the number of white families increased by 110,000, while the number of black families declined by 69,000. The land tenure system, which in the eyes of many blacks, as reported by Rupert Vance, was designed "to train, supervise and keep the Negro 'in his place,'" in effect was training, supervising, and keeping about twice as many white families in their place."[22]

While some proposed that the federal government establish black farm communities and settlements on which the disadvantaged blacks could be placed to make a living, others were suggesting the return of thousands of blacks from the North to the farms of the South as a means of reducing unemployment in the cities. The latter plan called for the federal government or philanthropic agencies to buy up small farms of thirty or forty acres, equip them with houses, barns, stables, mules, farm implements, foodstuffs for stock, and rations for farmers for six months. The occupants of these farms were to be placed under competent superintendents and charged an annual rent for the lands—which in due course would equal the cost of investment. When the total cost of the investment was paid off in the form of rentals, the farmer would be deeded the farmland as a fee simple, with the expectation that the nation would never again have to worry about the unemployment of the black man. He would not become a ward of the government like the Indian on the reservation, but an independent landowner living in colonies inhabited by his own people.[23]

Two questions often asked about the economic future of black families were: should they be encouraged to remain in agriculture, and if so, what additional efforts had to be made to enable them to operate more efficiently? In the industrial centers, the black male theoretically enjoyed to a certain extent "a larger and fuller life for himself and his family," better educational opportunities for his children, new avenues of self-expression, access to the ballot, recreational facilities, and more sources of cultural enrichment. Congested urban conditions, the high cost of living, exploitation by real estate sharks and landlords, the temptations of city life, and the fact that black men were likely to be the last to be hired and the first to be fired, on the other hand, nullified many of these advantages.[24]

Houston G. Schweich, one of the blacks to ponder this question, concluded it would be more advantageous for blacks to remain on the farm, and for those in industrial centers to return to the land, for several reasons. The majority were "peasant people" and although discipline was necessary for permanent progress, living conditions on a farm were more healthful. Furthermore the prospects of becoming homeowners were more within reach of blacks in the country than of those in the city. Blacks, Schweich maintained, were unable to compete for jobs in the cities, and suffered more in periods of depression. He concluded that, with the anticipated decentralization of industry, part-time employment would become more available in rural communities.

However, black farm communities and agricultural institutions had to be built in areas of the South in which the black population was large. A plan was needed for federally supervised model black farm communities to enable the largest possible number to learn practical farming by actual observation, a national farmer organization to encourage cooperative producing, buying, and marketing, well-trained county agents and home economics demonstrators, rural credit unions to help establish credit and teach blacks how to use it wisely, and building and loan associations to promote thrift and the advantages of home ownership. Such a program could be coordinated with the activities of the Inter-Racial Commission, the Rosenwald Fund, the Urban League, the NAACP, and other organizations interested in the welfare of blacks.[25]

An argument advanced, especially by the large white landowners, against a system of peasant ownership was that the tenant was incapable or unwilling to assume the risks involved. Yet, ironically, under the AAA the government actually assumed most of the landowners' risks and shifted them onto the tenants. The owners were protected from overproduction by fixed quotas with rents for their retired lands, while the tenants, whose share was pitifully small or nil, carried most of the reduced acreage burden. The risks of price fluctuation for the owners were met with loans of ten cents a pound or more that helped maintain prices; and the government credit production corporations and the FCA offered them credit at a rate unavailable to the tenant unless the landlord waived his first lien on the crop. The owner's likelihood of losing the equity in his farm also was lessened by the opportunities available to him to refinance and scale down his debts in conference with his creditors. However, the various debt reconciliation commissions made few, if any, attempts, at least in the beginning, to get the landlords to scale down debts owed them by croppers and share-tenants. The only way a tenant could escape assuming risks under the AAA and the existing system, in other words, was by becoming a landowner.

Another argument against the development of a system of small landowning farmers in the South was the amount of supervision that would be needed for tenant farmers, black and white, who aspired to become landowners. Unlike cotton farming, which was routine work, livestock growing, subsistence farming, and the production of fruits, vegetables, and special crops required supervision and some managerial abilities. Many, if not most, members of the tenant class simply lacked these qualities; and the large landowners or plantation managers were unprepared to provide supervision to help prepare such tenants for ownership. Advocates of small landownership such as Vance believed that the needed supervision could be provided by county farm agents scattered throughout the South who knew subsistence farming. In the long run small landownership would be less costly to producers and consumers than the prevailing system of landlordism propped up by an economy based on scarcity and concealed subsidies.[26]

When someone asked Wallace why the total number of sharecroppers dropped 8 percent, divided equally between white and black operators, while the total of all operators increased 6 to 7 percent, and why the total of all black operators declined by 8 percent and that of white operators increased by about 10 percent from 1930 to 1935, he was told that several factors had been at work.[27] The increase in white farm ownership, especially in the Appalachian highlands of West Virginia, Kentucky, and Tennessee, and totaling about 28 percent of the overall increase in the South, had been chiefly in small, rough, unfertile farms and resulted partly from the movement of city families to abandoned farms in the area. A large part of the gain also was due to persons who ordinarily lived in rural areas and worked in the coal mines but turned to subsistence farming in periods of unemployment. Increases in full ownership by whites in other parts of the South also were heaviest in the poor sections of the uplands for similar reasons. The smaller increases of ownership in good farming areas, on the other hand, resulted from absentee landowners returning to work land they had been renting out or had permitted to lie idle.

The unusually large net decrease in sharecroppers, both white and black, was owing to several important factors whose relative influence was difficult to determine. Before 1933, during the worst part of the depression, it was difficult for farm owners to obtain adequate credit to furnish their normal number of sharecroppers; hence they reduced them to wage hands. The shift to wage hands, in some instances, probably had been motivated by the various relief programs that made it possible for wage hands to obtain part-time employment away from the farm. The lack of opportunities for the normal movement of white youth from the farms to the cities forced many to remain on the farm. The sons of many white owners, especially, became small farm operators by displacing sharecroppers.

There were other explanations, also. The readjustment program tended to hold back the increase in the number of sharecroppers, as did the substitution of machines for sharecroppers in the level areas of the South. Since black tenants had greater difficulty than whites in maintaining their operating capital during the depression, they were more likely to be reduced to wage hands. In short, many black operators were "squeezed out" more readily than white operators during the highly competitive period from 1930 to 1936 for a combination of interrelated social and economic factors.[27]

Community projects were developed in areas where the percentage of black families was extremely large, and special efforts were made to secure the location of these projects near land grant colleges. Studies also were made in the early stages of projects that included all-black communities, such as Mound Bayou, Mississippi, and Boley, Oklahoma, which had shrunk during the depression. Although it is not known if there were positive results, revitalizing and converting these areas into thriving agricultural communities was the goal.

Five months after the Resettlement Administration was launched, four projects providing for black participation had been approved by Rexford Tugwell: Bricks, North Carolina—200 families; Orangeburg, South Carolina—100 families; Tuskegee, Alabama—158 families; and Phillips County, Arkansas—140 families. Black families were included in the development of Monticello, Georgia and the Tillery Farms of North Carolina. Regional directors investigated areas for additional projects in Mississippi, Oklahoma, Texas, and Louisiana.

Black participation in the RA programs included workers and those receiving benefits as resettled or rehabilitated families. The policy of the agency was to distribute its black employees throughout the RA instead of placing them into separate units. A breakdown of the 102 blacks employed by the RA five months after it was started shows them in the following occupations: thirty in building and custodial services; thirty-six messengers; five chauffeurs; one garage foreman; twelve clerks; nine stenographers and typists; eight professional employees, including project analysts, architects, engineers, and draftsmen; and one administrator. Thirty percent of the employed were in clerical and professional positions.[28]

The FSA, which later encountered bitter opposition from the American Farm Bureau Federation, undertook an extensive program of aid and rehabilitation of black families; and by mid-1939 the FSA had extended about 50,000 rehabilitation loans to them. More than 1,000 black farm families were living in thirty-one homestead communities in January 1939. Blacks were participating in "rental cooperatives" through which groups of tenants leased large tracts of land with FSA loans to operate them on a cooperative basis. By this time the USDA believed the FSA was beginning to do a great deal to better the status of black farm families in the South.[29]

Black spokesmen, however, were convinced that the New Deal had not done enough for their people. On December 8, 1938, Walter White wired Wallace that the NAACP was happy to learn he was going to speak at a meeting called by Mayor Fiorello La Guardia of New York at Carnegie Hall to protest the oppression of minorities in Europe. White and the NAACP also expressed hope that, while in the process of denouncing barbarism in Germany, Wallace would also call upon the American people to

> clean up our own back yard. Since Congress adjourned seven lynchings have disgraced America. Of the more than 1,000 [lynchers] not one has been arrested, much less punished. This seventh lynching brings the total number of lynchings in the United States since 1882 to 5,120. In 99 percent of these lynchings no lyncher has been punished. German, Italian and Japanese newspapers are featuring stories and photographs of American lynchings as reasons for laughing at American protests against oppressions of minorities in those countries. Discrimination in employment, education, right to use public accommodations, and disfranchisement in the United States, especially of Negroes, provide basis for foreign bigots to hurl charges of hypocrisy at legitimate American protests against conditions abroad.[30]

The New Deal on the Great Plains

IN ATTEMPTING TO RESOLVE THE PLIGHT of the farmers on the Great Plains, the New Dealers realized that besides having to contend with the destructive forces of nature, they faced problems of communication and education, winning over those fearful of basic changes, and resolving conflicts between local and state authorities on the one hand and federal authorities on the other.[1]

The disasters that overtook the Great Plains in 1934 and 1936 were widely publicized by feature writers, columnists, politicians, and others. What were not given equal exposure were the sustained efforts to help cushion the effects of one-crop farming by small farmers who lacked the needed capital, technical equipment, and managerial abilities to support themselves; to cut costs through the consolidation of overlapping governmental units; to discourage "suitcase" farming and rekindle an interest among farmers in community affairs; to redirect the farming practices of marginal and submarginal farmers whose methods were more suitable to the humid than the semiarid areas; to prevent the overstocking of the range with cattle; to make better use of the land in relation to water; and to prepare the farmers for the dry years and bad harvests that often followed wet years and good harvests.[2]

The programs on the Great Plains, as elsewhere in the country, were of two kinds: those arising from the immediate needs of the population, and those of a long-range nature that already have been described. In the first category were the programs to purchase cattle that had been afflicted by the drought, and direct relief to the needy in the form of food and seed; and in the second, programs for submarginal land purchases and resettlement, land-use readjustments, shelterbelt plantings, soil conservation, the ever-normal granary, and crop insurance.[3]

The returns to the Great Plains farmers for their energies were less than the returns to farmers in other parts of the country for comparable efforts. In some Great Plains counties the cost of federal aid ran as high as $200 per capita from April 1933 through June 1936. The net increments of the relief population for the entire country between 1933–1934 and 1934–1935 were 4 percent; but for New Mexico they were 19.2 percent; South Dakota, 17.6 percent; Oklahoma, 11.3 percent; and North Dakota, 10.9 percent. Twenty percent of all farmers in the spring wheat area (North Dakota, South Dakota, Montana, and portions of Minnesota) received relief in June 1935, and another 8 percent were in the process of rehabilitation.

Rural rehabilitation work under the Federal Emergency Relief Administration (FERA) sought to make it possible for persons to sustain themselves through their own efforts. Goods and subsistence money distributed to families were given a cash value against recipients' accounts on a non–interest bearing basis—to be repaid with work, cash, or kind. Needy families in the drought stricken areas received assistance from the state Emergency Relief Administrations by the end of February 1935, and rural rehabilitation work began on March 1, 1935. A ruling from the office of the comptroller general that decreed funds available under the FERA had to be disbursed by the federal government meant that the entire machinery through which rural rehabilitation work was being channeled had to be reorganized and centralized.[4]

One of the first acts was to relieve distressed cattle farmers by buying their starving animals, aiding them to maintain their foundation herds, digging or deepening wells, and giving them employment. The AAA, FERA, the Farm Credit Administration (FCA), and other federal agencies lent a helping hand in trying to meet this crisis. Benefit payments from crop adjustments, funds for the control of livestock diseases, and modifications in planting restrictions under AAA contracts that encouraged the production of more forage helped tide many farmers through this critical period.[5]

Of the 8.3 million cattle purchased between June 4, 1934, when the cattle buying program began and January 31, 1935, when it ended, nearly 25 percent were acquired in Texas and more than 20 percent in North and South Dakota; the remainder in seventeen of the other eighteen states west of the Mississippi River, Illinois, and Florida. Purchases were continuous in Texas, but heaviest in the Dakotas. The farmers sold roughly about 40 percent of their stock at the time of appraisal. About 18 percent of the purchased animals were condemned, the proportion ranging from 40 percent in Oklahoma and 34 percent in Texas to less than 3 percent in Kansas, Minnesota, and a number of other states. The proportion of condemned cattle also was high in New Mexico, and states not in the Great Plains, such as Utah and Louisiana. Condemnation of cattle, as in the case of hogs, was based on whether or not they could stand shipment.

Cattle were purchased faster than they could be disposed of in an emergency program of this kind. About 1.6 million cattle were shipped to the Federal Surplus Relief Corporation (FSRC) to graze in the eastern and southern states until they could be slaughtered; another 1.8 million were turned over to the state relief organizations; and a few thousand to the Indian Service for distribution among the Indian reservations. As a result of drought purchases and commercial marketings, dairy cattle and calves in 1934 were reduced by 2.2 million head or 6 percent, and all beef cattle by 5.5 million or 17 percent.[6]

The farmers, on the whole, were satisfied with the prices received for their low grade animals; $10 or $12 was a liberal payment for a thin or emaciated animal unlikely to survive a trip to market. The maximum total payment for cattle two years or older was more than $20 per head, while the average price for cows, other than those kept for milk, was about $17 at the time the purchases began.

Purchase of the drought cattle became possible through the use of Jones–Connally funds and a provision in the Emergency Cattle Agreement that bound the producer to cooperate in future adjustment or reduction programs. This part of the agreement was denounced by critics as "deplorable and inexcusable." AAA officials, however, considered this provision essential if purchases were to begin immediately under the Jones–Connally Act, and portions of the payments were to go to the producer instead of the mortgage or lien holder.

The controversial provision was inserted in the agreement because of the uncertainty over the outcome of the drought and cattle-buying program. If the rains came and emergency purchases were discontinued, the shelved program might have to be revived or a new one devised; and if this happened the producers and the cattle-buying program would be faced with a dilemma. Producers who received premium prices for their cattle during the drought would not be entitled to further payments for the reduction of their herds, certainly not as much as those who were forced to sell during the emergency.

Purchases by the government kept price levels in the commercial market higher than they would have been in 1934. Federally inspected cattle killed that year, exclusive of those slaughtered by the government, totaled 16 million head or 18 percent more than in 1933, the largest on record. An additional 2.5 or 3 million head would have been slaughtered under federal inspection if no purchases had been made by the government, and few of the 1.3 million condemned cattle would have gone to market. If one took into account the resulting low market prices, many of the remaining 6.5

million head would not have been slaughtered under government inspection. Prices, instead of rising after midsummer, could have declined to a level slightly above the cost of marketing the poorer grades and conceivably remained at that level until the liquidation had run its course in 1935. The cattle industry in 1934 faced the worst crisis in history, and probably would have been in worse shape had it not been for the drought purchases by the government.

The percentage of farmers participating in the program was an index of the degree to which farmers supported the program. A study by states indicates that the Great Plains farmers were among the strongest advocates of the AAA. North Dakota and South Dakota, respectively, with estimated percentages of 87.5 and 79.8 of farmers participating, led all other states in supporting the program. Nebraska was next with an estimated 69 percent farmer participation, then Texas with 64.5, and Oklahoma with 61 percent. Only Mississippi and South Carolina equalled or surpassed some of the Great Plains in AAA participation. The complaint that the AAA helped the larger producers more than the marginal producers who were faced with bankruptcy does not obscure the fact that the Great Plains farmers received some aid when they needed it desperately.[7]

Among the questionable beneficiaries of the AAA were the tenants. Since the complaints about not receiving a fair share of the benefit payments were heard from tenants in the South more than elsewhere in the country, it is reasonable to assume that the tenants in the northern Great Plains fared better. In North and South Dakota 93 and 84 percent of the tenants, respectively, participated in the AAA programs; in Kansas 78 percent; Nebraska 75 percent; Oklahoma and Texas 64 percent. Again the record was equalled, if not exceeded, by the tenants who officially participated in the South. South Carolina led the states of the South with 84 percent participation, North Carolina recorded 82 percent participation, Mississippi 81 percent, Alabama 74 percent, Arkansas and Georgia 71 percent, and Louisiana 66 percent.

Owner participation was equally formidable in the Great Plains states. North and South Dakota again led the procession with 79 and 70 percent owner participation, respectively, Nebraska followed with 66 percent, Kansas with 62 percent, Oklahoma 61 percent, and Texas 58 percent. Owner participation in the South also equalled, if it did not exceed, that in the Great Plains. In Alabama and Georgia 71 percent of the owners participated; in South Carolina 63 percent; Louisiana and Mississippi 60 percent; Arkansas 54 percent; and Tennessee 53 percent.[8]

The government acquired submarginal lands in the Great Plains to make changes in the types of farming practiced instead of withdrawing the land from production completely. The "submarginal" or "marginal" label was misleading, according to L. C. Gray, because little of the land in the

Great Plains was submarginal in the sense that it was not adapted to agriculture of some kind under proper conditions. The ill effects of the inefficient units had been obscured in the fifteen years prior to 1930 by adequate rainfall and higher prices when compared with the inadequate rainfall and the lower prices of the 1930s. Too much emphasis, for example, had been placed in the eastern half of the Great Plains on wheat as a cash crop, or on a combination of sheep ranching and sporadic efforts at wheat growing.

Studies and experience brought out that the farmers who concentrated on wheat had to place greater reliance on cattle and feed crops. In range areas there was less emphasis on grazing lands and, where practicable, more on forage crops. Such readjustments, unfortunately, were impeded by land tenure patterns that developed out of the various homestead acts and the checkerboard grants by the railroads. Foreclosures, abandoned lands, sales, tax delinquency laws, and tenancy also influenced tenure pattern formations.

Farmers who made the readjustments on their own did so through the purchase, renting, or use of abandoned lands that were available in many parts of the Great Plains. However, it was difficult to enlarge a farm in a financially impoverished area. Absentee owners, as a rule, were interested in renting their lands for income purposes only until they could sell them. They were not eager to make improvements or lease their lands for periods long enough to encourage tenants to make improvements of their own. When the rains or good prices returned, the owners tended to divide their land instead of selling or renting it at a fee that would justify range use. In relatively good years, absentee owners often flocked back to raise a crop or two of wheat. In doing so they often exposed the land to wind erosion instead of allowing it to grow grass. There was little incentive to avoid overgrazing on lands rented under short-term leases for range purposes. The capital required to return arable land to grass and provide the requisite fencing and water supplies also was an obstacle to the reestablishment of farming.[9]

Submarginal land purchases were initiated in the late winter of 1934 under the terms of the National Recovery Administration (NRA) when $25 million were appropriated and later by emergency allocations that brought the total up to about $40 million. Some of these funds were diverted to the purchase of land for migratory waterfowl refuges, recreational purposes, and Indian use; hence only $27 million was available for agricultural readjustment projects. Only $9 million of the available monies for land purchases were used on the Great Plains, even though Congress had given the land acquisition program a more durable foundation under the Bankhead–Jones Act. Still, projects were established within definite boundary lines for planning, acquiring, and developing the purchases to be made, instead of making purchases sporadically.

Twenty projects had been established under the old program, totaling about 13.9 million acres before the Bankhead–Jones Act went into effect, and 3.7 million of these were purchased. Additional acquisitions increased the total purchased or under contract to more than 6.4 million acres, which was about two-thirds the combined areas of Massachusetts, Connecticut, and Rhode Island. The purchase of a given acreage in the Great Plains made it possible to exert a strong influence over an area several times the size of the purchased area.

In a typical western Great Plains project, publicly owned land was interspersed with land owned by states, railways, and corporations. Control of these lands could be acquired through the formation of cooperative grazing associations. Lease rights were obtained to these scattered units, but public purchase was necessary for the more strategically located tracts that could not be leased.

Through the purchase of 61,000 of a total of 91,000 acres for one of two projects in western North Dakota, it was possible to thin out the population and establish holdings large enough to permit a range economy or a range economy supplemented by forage production. Of the eighty operators who originally managed units averaging 1,100 acres, thirty-eight operated units averaging 2,400 acres each by late 1938 and showed an improvement in their financial status and ability to get along without government relief. Most of the forty-two operators who left the specific area did so because they were relocated elsewhere within the general region. Fifteen established themselves on nonirrigated farms within the county or state; two abandoned farming, worked as laborers nearby, and became chronic relief recipients; and fourteen moved to other states. Economies also were realized in the costs of maintaining schools and roads.

Land purchased under the land utilization program was leased to cooperative grazing associations in western North Dakota, Wyoming, and Colorado. The local cooperative grazing association and the secretary of agriculture in each instance entered into an agreement that stipulated the carrying capacity of the land, which was not to be exceeded, or the land used for any other purpose. Lands also were leased directly to individual operators to become part of their operating units. Some lands were converted into fenced community pastures and made available to individuals who had permits to graze an appropriate number of animals. In all instances, leases and permits were subject to restrictions aimed to improve and maintain reserves on the range.

In the "Dust Bowl" of the southern Great Plains, the need was to check wind erosion. There the administration placed more emphasis on the purchase of "nuisance land" or land exposed to sand and dust that harmed other land and became a source of discomfort to the residents of the region. Often such lands were held by absentee owners who assumed no responsibility in caring for their lands or abating the nuisance, or rented them to "suitcase" farmers who failed to grow a protective cover on the land.

L. C. Gray was among those who believed that more than the public acquisition of land was needed to resolve the problems of the Great Plains and cited the recurring periods of rainfall and high prices. In his opinion, there were other alternatives. Rural zoning could be used and perhaps found more effective, if the public would tolerate it. More systematic efforts also could be made to discourage would-be settlers by warning them of the hazards they faced, by refusing them credit, and by denying them relief payments and other subsidies if they deliberately refused to employ sound methods of land use and settlement. Or the area under lease and control of the cooperative grazing districts could be expanded gradually, thereby reducing the area subject to speculative settlement and cultivation. In fact, Gray felt, the formation of cooperative grazing districts offered one of the most effective ways of applying the public purchase program.

One of the most controversial programs was the Shelterbelt Project, officially known as the Prairie States Forestry Project, whose purpose was to ameliorate drought conditions, protect the crops and livestock, reduce dust storms, and provide the people of the stricken areas with employment. Designed to furnish a maximum of relief for the people of the region, financed almost exclusively with relief funds, and subjected to the uncertainties that faced all projects based on this kind of funding, the Shelterbelt Project endured a precarious existence until the WPA closed it down.[10]

There were ample precedents for the Shelterbelt Project here and abroad. German Mennonites who emigrated to the Russian steppes in the late eighteenth century planted shelterbelts that later were extended thousands of miles. "Shelterbelt" was used as an expression as early as 1833, if not sooner, to denote the idea of controlling wind erosion through the use of trees. In 1898 members of the American Forestry Association asked for the formation of a federal commission to consider the feasibility of constructing windbreaks in the Great Plains to "regulate the surface of air currents" and conserve precipitation needed for grain production. Farmers in Kansas began planting single row Osage orange hedges as early as 1865. Interest in tree planting at the federal level manifested itself again in 1904 with the passage of the Kincaid Act, and in 1916 with the inclusion of demonstrational tree planting as part of the program of the Northern Great Plains Field Station near Mandan, North Dakota.[11]

A comprehensive study of the climate, soils, groundwater, vegetation, land use, and kinds of trees that proved successful was undertaken in the Great Plains before actual work on the Shelterbelt Project began under the

New Deal. Data on plantings were studied and information sought from foreign countries that claimed their grain yields had increased from shelterbelt planting. Once this information was obtained, shelterbelt boundaries were determined, the species of the trees to be planted were selected, and techniques established.[12]

Hardly had the Shelterbelt Project been announced in July 1934 before rival camps began to form. Many of the differences stemmed from political preferences and past experiences. Foresters were regarded as deficient in professional qualifications by many engineers and scientists, and the task of gaining popular support for forestry projects, in the opinion of some, was made more difficult by sponsoring this kind of a project. The front page publicity revived prejudices. What particularly aroused some professional foresters was the official pronouncement that "man can ameliorate the effects of the weather on a large scale, just as he can around his home." Professor Fay G. Clark of the Montana School of Forestry wrote H. H. Chapman, president of the Society of American Foresters, that practically all the shelterbelts and woodlots in northeastern Montana and western North Dakota were dead from the lack of water. Branding the Shelterbelt Project "a political pork barrel" and something "doomed to failure before it starts," Clark warned the professional foresters, who were viewed as "rattle-brained theorists," they were in danger of losing the integrity and confidence they had earned after many years of labor, if they sponsored such a project.[13]

Roosevelt created the Shelterbelt Zone, by executive order, over an area that extended from the Canadian border into the Texas Panhandle. A solid belt of trees that was 100 miles wide had been projected, but actually the trees were planted in areas of from twenty-five to forty acres in each 640-acre section. Shelterbelt strips 165 feet wide and from a quarter to one mile in length, requiring less than 3 percent of the zoned area, were planted at one-mile intervals. Each strip, consisting of from seventeen to twenty-one rows of trees, was planted at right angles to the direction of the prevailing winds. The outer rows consisted of shrubs and low-growing trees with tall trees in the center.

The purpose of the Shelterbelt Project was to prevent soil blowing, conserve the moisture, stabilize the productivity of the land, and make one of the most important agricultural regions of the country a better and more profitable place to live. The aim of the shelterbelts definitely was not to withdraw any considerable portion of the Great Plains from agriculture and transform it into a forest.

The financial, aesthetic, and scientific reasons given for the shelterbelts were persuasive. Livestock protected in the winter by shelterbelts brought savings on feed and reduced animal losses from added exposure to the cold. The timber provided fuel and other products for farm use in areas where wood was scarce and offered suitable habitats for birds and other forms of wildlife. Birds were a principal check against destructive insects that destroyed crops, the theory being the more trees the more birds there would be and the less damage to crops by insects. Furthermore, farms with shelterbelts and groves commanded higher prices in the marketplace than those without them. The scientific study of trees also could be advanced by such a project. The government, for instance, could learn more about the trees planted on the Great Plains before the New Deal came into office. Farmers ordinarily were not good foresters, and a certain degree of forestry knowledge and skill was necessary to plant and manage trees successfully. From 1916 to 1933 the field station of the Bureau of Plant Industry at Mandan, North Dakota cooperated with farmers in the western part of the Great Plains in establishing more than 2,700 shelterbelts. This area was west of the zone considered favorable for tree growth, but the average survival rate for these plantings at the end of the period was 70 percent. Success in the planting of trees hinged upon the selection of the proper place for planting, careful selection of the species and seed source, use of proper planting and spacing methods, and the right kind of care. The application of these principles varied from locality to locality, especially in areas as large as the Great Plains where a wide variety of problems in tree culture were evident.[14]

Fortunately, the Shelterbelt Project did not become a hot political issue in 1936. Administration leaders who had taken the brunt of the earlier criticism were heartened by the friendlier attitude shown by planning boards, the President's Drought Relief Commission, Federal Land Bank representatives, merchants, insurance companies, farmers, and an increasing number of congressmen in both political parties.

The decision of the *New York Times* to send a photographer out to the Shelterbelt Project in 1936 had far-reaching effects. His photographs and accompanying favorable commentary in a two-page rotogravure layout on August 30, 1936 constituted endorsement of the project by the *New York Times* and had a tremendous influence on other eastern newspapers. In 1938 the same photographer visited the project again and the retakes published with the originals showed the growth of the shelterbelts over the two-year period. Hamilton Owens, the editor of the *Baltimore Sun,* also made a trip to Kansas and was moved by the fact that the farmers "proved that trees can be made to grow in all save the most forlorn areas and . . . make this parched and windswept land look a little more inviting.[15]

Findings of a systematic survey of 1,079 belts in ninety-three counties undertaken in 1944, ten years after the Shelterbelt Project was launched, and representing 3.6 percent of the belts planted, confirmed the optimistic note sounded earlier. The survey brought out the interest of the farmers and ranchers in the program, the better than expected survival and growth of the trees, the importance of adequate cultivation, and the silvical and management problems they presented. Some 78.4 percent of the belts were rated as good or better, and only 10 percent as unsatisfactory. Benefits included landscape improvements, wind erosion control, and snow traps along the highways; protection of farmsteads, gardens, orchards, and feedlots; havens for game and song birds; wild fruit for preserves; fence posts and small plots for use on the farm; and new districts in the soil conservation program.[16]

Erosion control began in 1933 under Harold Ickes as an emergency public works project to relieve unemployment. Rexford Tugwell attributed the growing interest in it to the "empire-building compulsion" of Ickes, and to the influence of Hugh Hammond Bennett's campaign on the dangers of erosion. The USDA had not developed a program of direct assistance to conserve soil and water, despite the fact that much had been written on soil conservation before 1933 and practical plans for building terraces had been devised. Experiments and demonstrations had been conducted between 1914 and 1933 by the Extension Service in Alabama, Texas, and Iowa, and this work had been extended to practically all states by 1936. C. W. Warburton took special pride in the work done in the Southern Great Plains with the federal emergency funds administered by the state extension directors. The earlier work of the Texas politicians also helped the movement along.[17]

Researchers are more sure of why the Soil Erosion Service (SES) was transferred to the USDA in 1935 than they are of why it had been set up in the Department of Interior in 1933. After the dust storms and the drought of 1934, the American people demanded relief that would lessen the effects of such tragedies in the future. Unfortunately, the USDA had to accept a program and an administration of soil erosion control that it inherited.

The damage from wind erosion in 1934 was spread over a billion acres of land stretching from Texas to North Dakota. Cultivation and overgrazing had helped deplete the land of its humus, pulverized the soil, and exposed vast areas to gusts of wind that swept across the Great Plains. The small, light particles of dry soil that were blown high into the air drifted great distances, and the coarser and less productive particles rolled along the surface until they were stopped by some obstruction. Sometimes they buried crops, fences, and buildings, especially in areas in which the annual rainfall was less than twenty-five inches.[18]

The SES undertook another soil erosion survey in 1935, at the request of various states and agencies, of almost 25,000 square miles of the wind erosion areas of Colorado, Kansas, Oklahoma, and Texas. The new survey was more intensive than the one in 1934. It was based on the theory that accurate information was essential for the ultimate stabilization and protection of the land; therefore it did not single out the Great Plains for special attention, and it disregarded established boundary lines.[19]

A preliminary report was issued by the subcommittee of the Land Policy Committee that had been appointed to consider a coordinated program to deal with wind erosion. It indicated that of the large number of acres and counties affected, 3.5 million acres were in twenty-five counties of Texas; 600,000 acres in twelve counties of New Mexico; 1.3 million acres in three counties of Oklahoma; 1.4 million acres in twenty-seven counties of Colorado; and 10 million acres in forty-four counties of Kansas.[20] About the only thing that could be done immediately was to list all land not protected by a soil cover, except the most sandy soil for which nothing was to be done then because stirring the soil in a dry state would increase its tendency to drift. After the listed areas had acquired sufficient moisture, germination, and growth, then a thick-growing variety of sorghum could be planted. For the heavier unprotected soils, complete or strip listing was expected to be effective on all except the more severely affected areas. Strip planting in lister furrows with a thick sorghum would provide a low windbreak and the sorghum stalks left standing and ungrazed through the winter would prevent soil blowing. If sufficient moisture was available for crop growth, the strips between the sorghum could be planted with Sudan grass or other spring crops or left fallow for wheat seeding the following fall, subject of course to the production control contracts of the AAA. The sorghum stalks would catch and hold snow that fell during the winter and provide a windbreak through the winter and early spring if there was insufficient moisture at the time to prevent soil blowing.

When the subcommittee made its preliminary report on April 9, 1935 the winds were blowing in certain areas of Nebraska, and unless good rains fell in the near future, wind erosion was expected to spread into Nebraska, eastern Wyoming, Montana, and North and South Dakota in the immediate future. More time also was needed to consider a longtime plan for wind erosion control in the southern Great Plains and coordinate the various efforts in the USDA. Drafting a plan at the time was difficult because the SES had been transferred to the USDA, and because of the uncertainties that prevailed regarding its functions and relationship with the other branches of the department.[21]

In mid-April 1935 M. L. Wilson made a trip to five of the affected states to study the problem of soil erosion firsthand. He met with Governor Alfred M. Landon of Kansas, and representatives of Colorado, New Mexico, Texas, and Oklahoma, to obtain a report on the extent of erosion damage. Later soil erosion experts, agronomists, and policymakers suggested possible methods of minimizing erosion in the immediate future and the adoption of a longtime policy of control. Wilson's visit was timely because the storm made travel difficult, and he, Landon, and other prominent figures arrived late. "One must see these dust storms," said Wilson, "to realize their severity and to appreciate the discomfort they cause to residents."

No mere written report could have had the impact upon administrators that Wilson's visit in western Kansas created.[22]

The drought of 1934 emphasized the importance of maintaining adequate farm reserves in the Great Plains and other regions subject to the hazards of weather. The development of a more specialized agriculture that deemphasized food reserves and stressed money only increased the need for farm reserves. This question received considerable attention from Wallace when he was with *Wallace's Farmer,* and he revived the idea in an address delivered in Bismarck, North Dakota on June 6, 1935.[23]

Wallace favored an "ever-normal granary plan" from the beginning, but the storage of reserves, he believed, had to be linked with the control of production. Wallace made special efforts to assure private interests that the ever-normal granary plan would not harm them. Indeed, it would guarantee private traders that stored goods that could be disruptive would not be released suddenly, and it would give due regard to prevailing market conditions while keeping the public informed about the storage problem. He affirmed that "The AAA . . . has played square with business. It will continue to play square. It will not spring any surprises on the market."[24]

The proposal, however, was opposed from the start by the private grain trade, which had less experience with and tolerance for such programs than did the cotton trade, which had dealt with them for years. Frightening headines that the ever-normal granary plan would "break the back of agriculture" or that Wallace was "setting out to undermine the interests of the country elevators and other grain dealing interests" were heard repeatedly but were unwarranted, wrote J. D. Le Cron in behalf of Wallace. The *National Grain Journal* editorially commented that the plan was a threat to the grain trade, farm prosperity, and the farmer, and it urged those readers engaged in the grain trade to write their representatives in Washington. "This is your country. Do your part."[25]

The ever-normal granary plan and the commodity loan approach were integrated with soil conservation after the Soil Conservation and Domestic Allotment Act (SCDAA) replaced the AAA, and the emphasis shifted from production control to soil conservation. When the supply of the commodity during any year was larger than what had been determined as normal, loans would be made to the producers of this commodity on the basis of the supplies held in storage. Such loans were expected to keep the surplus portion of the crop in storage for future use and prevent the price to the producer from falling to a lower level. If, however, there was a bumper crop in one or a succession of years or a decline in demand resulting in a granary overflow, provisions would be made to store in the soil instead of the bin. To achieve this, producers could be offered conditional payments in addition to their regular conservation benefits on the theory this second payment would conserve and build up the fertility for future years when supplies were below

normal. If a succession of good years led to extreme surpluses, further production control would be undertaken as a last-ditch operation. In effect, as
the stocks increased, the ever-normal granary plan would be applied in three
progressive stages: commodity loans, storage in the ground by cooperating
farmers, and compulsory and universal production controls. As the stocks
decreased, the controls would be removed in reverse order. If the plan
worked smoothly, a rough balance of supply and demand would be maintained.[26]

Edwin G. Nourse, Joseph S. Davis, and John D. Black, the authors of
Three Years of the Agricultural Adjustment Administration, were among
the skeptics whose apprehensions were based on a study of market conditions and past experiences. They questioned the argument that prices were
"unduly" depressed in years of heavy production and reminded the ever-
normal granary advocates that previous attempts by government agencies,
cooperatives, individuals, and others to withhold supplies from the market
for one period or another often resulted in deterioration, storage, and
financial charges that made such operations more costly than had been anticipated. Such activities also tended to inject "a disturbing influence of
unknown significance into the marketing system" with unfortunate consequences.

Furthermore, Nourse, Davis, and Black charged that the anticipated
benefits of the ever-normal granary were grossly exaggerated. Comparing
the plan with "the biblical story of Joseph in the land of the Pharaohs" was
an oversimplification, if not naivete. The world's supply of food in the
1930s was produced over a wide geographical area that was linked with efficient systems of commerce and transportation, and there was a strong
tendency for the reduced production of some crops in some regions to be
more or less compensated for by the enlarged production of other crops in
the same or other regions. The year-to-year variations in the world output
of food products were small as a whole in comparison with the variations in
the output of particular crops or of particular regions, and extremely small
in comparison with variations in specific crops in specific regions. Then,
too, large quantities of potential food products for human use were ordinarily fed to animals, diverted to industrial uses, or wasted; and these
constituted large invisible reserves that could be drawn upon in case of
need. Consumers likewise were accustomed to continuous adjustments in
food consumption in terms of available supplies, and commerce assisted
them in making these adjustments. Therefore, adequate insurance against
oppressive food shortages in the United States was provided for without the
presence of a special system of reserves, despite agricultural tariffs and new
quota provisions that erected partial barriers to the flow of emergency supplies into the country.

Professor Joseph Boyle of Cornell University, a leading conservative economist at that time, also warned that all historic experiments in withholding crops had been failures, graft often developed in the management of such granaries, and the private grain trade was wiser and more dependable in such matters than the federal government. Boyle, too, cited the repeated attempts of the Federal Farm Board to withhold supplies from the market when they should have been sold. Even if economists and statisticians were capable of making scientific projections into the future, they could not always be relied upon to tell the truth when political issues were involved.[27]

Crop insurance was another phase of New Deal farm policy to attract attention in the Great Plains. It was a subject of interest in Japan during the late 1880s, and efforts first were made to protect the farmers of the United States by such a plan during World War I and the years that followed.[28] The idea then was for the federal government to assist private companies in providing this kind of protection, instead of having the federal government itself sponsor such a program. But extended periods of drought, successive years of crop and animal losses, and low income had driven home the need for greater protection as quickly as possible. Meanwhile, the USDA as a result of its experiences with the AAA programs had acquired a great deal of essential information on the annual yields of wheat on individual farms in the country, and with this information in hand the crop insurance program did not seem as big and difficult a task as it had once appeared.

Wallace, Alf Landon, and Senator James Pope of Idaho expressed themselves in favor of crop insurance; and shortly before the election of 1936 Roosevelt designated Wallace as chairman of the President's Committee on Crop Insurance. Roosevelt was impressed by the work of the USDA in developing sound actuarial principles in protecting farmers against such hazards. Late in 1936 a group headed by Myron W. Thatcher of the Farmers' National Grain Corporation, a keen student of the wheat trade, a powerful lobbyist, and an influential figure in the Farmers' Union, recommended that crop insurance be established first only for wheat on an experimental basis; and if successful with wheat, then it could be extended to other crops.[29]

Provisions finally were incorporated into the AAA of 1938 for the Federal Crop Insurance Corporation (FCIC) with a capitalization of $1 million; and the crop insurance program was launched in Omaha, Nebraska on April 19 and 20, 1938. Crop insurance on wheat was offered on either 75 or 50 percent of the average yield of the individual farm; but few applied for 50 percent coverage. Applicants, to be eligible during the first two years, were required to practice conservation and not extend their acreage beyond the permitted allotments for the farm. Earnings under conservation practices were granted to be used for the payment of insurance premiums and to encourage greater participation in the program; in fact about 95 percent of all premiums in 1940 and 1941 were paid with such advances. Coverage increased in the low-risk, low-premium areas in 1942, but decreased in the high-risk, high-premium areas. Crop insurance was extended to cotton in 1942 and for the first time in 1943 there were three-year contracts for wheat.

Unfortunately, the losses of the Federal Crop Insurance Corporation were heavy for the first four years. The indemnities paid from 1939 through 1942 exceeded the premiums, and Congress in view of these losses called an abrupt halt to the program. However Congress, with the support of the administration, enacted a new and enlarged crop insurance program in December 1944.

The Report of the Great Plains Committee, released in 1936, recommended a three-pronged beginning at the federal, state, and local levels. (1) At the federal level it advised: surveys of the best uses of the land, water, and other natural resources; the purchase of scattered farms and other appropriate lands in areas suitable for grazing; control of the purchased lands in accordance with the objectives of the general rehabilitation work; increases in the size of farms; adoption of measures for the resettlement of families suffering from droughts and dust storms; control of destructive insect pests and the development of other resources that would contribute to the economic welfare of the people. (2) At the state level it urged: survey as promptly as possible all laws pertaining to tenancy, leasing, taxing, and tax delinquency with the view of instituting needed reforms; pass enabling legislation permitting counties to zone land in terms of its proper use; encourage the formation of grazing associations; aid the formation of soil conservation districts to control the erosion of arable lands; avoid the resale of tax delinquent lands to private individuals and make them available for coordinated use through cooperative grazing associations; facilitate efforts to consolidate local governments that would cut the costs of schools, roads, and other public services without the loss of their efficiency; revise the taxation system so that it would take into account the current or average income from the land; aid the development and use of water resources; "promote ownership and permanent occupancy (of the land), and . . . make more equitable the position of those who continue as tenants." (3) At the local level communities were urged to: enlarge the size of the family farm or ranch; avoid the single crop and restore the "balanced farm"; each season adopt crops that would grow best in the amount of moisture in the soil at planting time; create feed and seed reserves against dry years through the use of the pit silo; adopt soil conservation practices; utilize springs, wells, and other local sources of water supply; and plant trees and shrubs as windbreaks.[30]

Some recommendations of the Great Plains Committee were inaugurated, but persisting distress in many areas made full implementation impossible. The effects of the drought were felt throughout 1937 and 1938, particularly in the northern Great Plains, where the specially created Northern Great Plains Committee tried to develop a program that would provide more than temporary relief. Again the results were minimal. The National Planning Resources Board in 1940 conceded:

> There is comparatively little to show in the way of long-term rehabilitation for the huge sums spent there by the Federal Government in recent years. The problem of land-use readjustment . . . in the Great Plains . . . the Northern Great Plains and the Southern Great Plains alike, still remain the most difficult agricultural problem of its kind in the United States.[31]

With prophetic foresight the Northern Great Plains Committee warned,

> Progress in fundamental readjustments, slow at best, might be stopped and much of what has been accomplished . . . undone by a prolonged European war. A sharp rise in the price of wheat, accompanied perhaps by the false promise of a series of generous rains, might tempt the Plainsmen again to cultivate in the hope of speculative gain. Constant vigilance will be needed to safeguard the progress already made, and to make continued progress.[32]

Experience bore out that the size and efficiency of the farm had more to do with the survival and success of the farm in the Great Plains than did social legislation, and that more public and community action was both necessary and possible to resolve the problems in the region. The AAA, the Farm Credit Act of 1933 that established the Production Credit Associations, the Bank of Cooperatives, the Federal Intermediate Credit Bank, and the revised Federal Land Bank–National Farm Loan Associations undoubtedly were of material assistance to the larger farmers and ranchers, but they merely put off the day when the small inefficient producers were eliminated. As the Northern Great Plains Committee predicted, the outbreak of the war, the need for increased food production to supply the United States and its allies, and the migration of many rural people to the cities (and their replacement by new arrivals, who knew little about farming and soil conservation) tended to undo much, if not all, of what the New Dealers sought to accomplish.

Rural electrification and soil conservation had more lasting results. Less than 8 percent of the farms in the Great Plains had electricity in 1930, but as a result of the REA and the lines built by the private utilities, often in competition with the REA, more than 90 percent of all farms in the Great Plains were lighted by electricity in 1960.[33]

The Battle for Rural Electrification

THE CAMPAIGN TO ELECTRIFY THE FARMS was prompted largely by the unwillingness of the private utilities to furnish these services to more farmers. It was further encouraged by the administration's ability to capitalize on the public clamor for federal support of such services. The New Deal, through the Rural Electrification Administration, established a solid foundation for furnishing electricity to rural areas before the United States entered World War II.

Living conditions on most farms as late as 1933 were comparable to those of a preindustrial society. Rural people endured hardship and drudgery in much the same way as their ancestors had in the eighteenth and nineteenth centuries. The household was generally without running water, electric lights, or a refrigerator. Cleaning the farmhouse, washing clothes, and other domestic chores were performed with primitive equipment. Water was laboriously drawn from wells, carried to receptacles in the houses, and heated on wood or coal stoves. Of the 6.3 million farms in the United States in 1930 only 571,000 had electric lights and 531,000 had running water. Roughly one farm in ten had electric service in 1933.[1]

The availability of electricity on the farm prior to 1933 varied from region to region. The Far West, primarily the states of California, Utah, and Washington with 58, 53, and 41 percent of their farms electrified, was the best supplied. A factor in this was the widespread use of irrigation practices in these states, which required large amounts of electric power. The New England area with 36.4 percent of its farms electrified was the next best supplied. The density of farms per mile in New England and their proximity to

The material in this chapter was provided by Clayton Brown, associate professor of history, Texas Christian University, Forth Worth, Texas. He has since published *Electricity for Rural America*, Greenwood Press, 1980.

the cities helped determine the costs of service, and accounted for the wider use of electricity in the region. In the East North Central and West North Central states, respectively, 13.4 and 6.5 percent of the farms had electricity; the South had even fewer electrified farms. Only 3.5 percent of the farms in the South Atlantic states had electric service, in Arkansas and Louisiana only one farm in a hundred, and in Mississippi the ratio was even lower.[2]

The private utilities showed a minimum of interest in developing the rural market. Through their trade association, the National Electric Light Association (NELA), they created a Committee on the Relation of Electricity to Agriculture (CREA) in 1923 to promote the use of electricity in the rural areas. Members of the CREA were representatives of the colleges, government agencies, the electric industry, professional engineering societies, and homemakers' organizations.[3] Although its members were convinced that rural electrification was an assignment for the private utilities to undertake, and committees were established in twenty-five states to carry on the work of the parent body, the private utilities soon lost the confidence of the advocates of rural electrification.[4] Many of the state committees were poorly organized and lacked enthusiasm. As a consequence the average state CREA electrified about 100 farms; and in some states CREA was nothing but a "paper organization." The CREA, for the most part, became an agency for the promotion of research and publicity, and never dealt directly with the cost of electric service, which was a critical obstacle in the electrification of the rural areas.

The cost of building distribution lines in the rural areas was about $2,000 per mile, and the revenues received by the power companies in the rural areas were about one-fifth the return on the same investment in an urban area. Farmers who wanted electricity normally had to pay a deposit of $1,000 or the cost of building an extension line to their home, which most could not afford to pay. Farmers who enjoyed electric service either lived close to the power line or used enough electric energy, as on the irrigated farms of the West, to attract the power companies.[5]

Cost, however, was not always the only inhibiting factor. Companies in many instances refused to serve farmers within reasonable distances from power lines; in other cases companies refused service even when the farmer agreed to bear the brunt of the expense in building the extension line. The attitude of the utilities was that the rural market was too risky, causing farmers to look to the federal government for leadership.[6]

In North Carolina, providing electricity to farmers had become a public responsibility before the New Deal acted. Rural electrification began as early as 1919, if not sooner, after an educational campaign was launched urging farmers to furnish their homes with electrical equipment and organize electric cooperatives whenever private companies refused to serve them. Farmers, with the assistance of members of the Department of Rural Economics and Sociology at the University of North Carolina, established a cooperative in Cleveland County in 1925, and others soon joined the campaign. J. C. B. Ehringhaus, the newly elected governor, after a decade of agitation, urged in 1932 that rural electrification be made a public responsibility and asked for a state program to build rural power lines. In April 1935, one month before the creation of the REA, the North Carolina legislature established the North Carolina Rural Electric Authority, which served as an intermediary between the REA and the farmers.[7]

Meanwhile, pressure to bring electricity to the farms had been mounting in other states. Neighboring South Carolina, after twice failing to obtain financial support from the federal government, established its own Rural Electrification Authority also before the REA came into being. In Virginia, an advisory group consisting of representatives of the Federal Emergency Relief Administration, the Virginia Polytechnic Institute, and electric companies in the state recommended the formation of a nonprofit corporation in 1935 to build lines, and administer and sell electric energy to the state. These efforts were to have some influence on Washington. Morris L. Cooke, the first REA administrator, suggested that the work of Virginia was a logical beginning for any federal undertaking in rural electrification.[8]

Farmers in Idaho, Iowa, Wisconsin, and Kansas likewise had been active in trying to develop programs of rural electrification. In 1920 a group of Idaho farmers organized an electric cooperative and purchased energy from the state's reclamation service plant; and a comparable situation prevailed in Wisconsin where twenty-five farmers built their own lines and bought power wholesale. In April 1919 a group of forty-eight farmers in Namaha County, Kansas organized a transmission company to provide electric service to its members, and in Iowa thirteen farmer electrical cooperatives were active by 1935.[9]

Electrical cooperatives in most states were similar to those in Iowa, Kansas, Wisconsin, and Idaho. They were few in number, isolated, and rendered service usually to the most successful farmers in a prosperous area. The common practice had been for farmers to organize and build the cooperative and then turn it over to the electric companies to maintain and operate. Since long-term, low-cost funding was needed and was not within the reach of the average farmer, the cooperative was unable to finance rural electrification on a wide scale. Clearly this was an area the federal government had to project itself into if the farms of the nation were to have electricity.

The farmers' cause was championed by a nonfarmer, Morris L. Cooke, a practicing consulting engineer in Philadelphia who gained the reputation of a reformer following his victorious fight with the Philadelphia Electric Company for lower utility rates. Cooke believed that average citizens, as well as commercial interests, were entitled to enjoy the energy resources of the nation at low cost. He became "the father of rural electrification." As chairman of a committee appointed by Governor Gifford Pinchot of Pennsylvania in 1923, he helped author the Giant Power Survey, which, although having no immediate effect, helped publicize him as a crusader for rural electrification. As his biographer put it, here was "another example of the engineer acting as a plowman cutting a furrow through virgin soil for others to follow."[10]

Cooke's concern with rural electrification coincided with that of Franklin D. Roosevelt, whose interest went back to the 1920s when he bought a cottage in Warm Springs, Georgia. The two men worked together. As governor of New York Roosevelt had appointed Cooke to the New York Power Authority, which had been created especially to develop the Saint Lawrence River as a source of low-cost power. During the presidential campaign of 1932 Cooke helped draft the "Portland Power Speech" which outlined Roosevelt's position on public power.[11] Roosevelt's election in 1932 meant that rural electrification had been accepted at the highest government level. The views of Roosevelt, Cooke, and their advisors were supported by a public that expressed animosity toward the public utilities companies during the 1930s. The vexing problem that remained was to draw up a practical plan to implement this policy.

Cooke had to content himself by making a limited trial run of public rural electrification through the TVA until 1935. Cooke was aided by the pressure applied on the federal government by the states for assistance in building their own systems. Cooke, also, was enough of a realist to understand that the electric industry was in the best position to handle the generation of power, the construction of lines, and other practical needs of a rural electrification program. There likewise was the possibility of working through the local cooperatives or of using state agencies and municipalities as middlemen. Fortunately, the question of whether rural electrification by the federal government would work was resolved by the TVA, which fostered the first large-scale public enterprise that brought electricity to the farm. The problem was solved, according to David Lilienthal, a director of the TVA, when a committee of Corinth, Mississippi businessmen and leading farmers met with a TVA committee. The result was "the birth of the Alcorn County Electric Cooperative. . . . Corinth and her farm neighbors set out to electrify the whole country. Such was the unpretentious beginning of farm electricity co-ops. . . ."[12]

Alcorn County was typically southern, and represented the depression cotton-growing South; it was located in the poverty-ridden northeastern part of Mississippi, had a high percentage of blacks and tenants, and a low per capita income. If the TVA experiment succeeded in Alcorn County, rural electrification on a national scale was possible. Operations of the

Alcorn Coop began in June 1934 after the cooperative entered into a contract with the TVA. Power was purchased from the TVA at wholesale rates, and redistributed to members at cost. Events progressed smoothly. Members of the cooperative began to enjoy modern conveniences that in the past had been unavailable to them, such as electric lamps, pumps, ranges, and refrigerators. Town merchants reaped a bonanza from the sale of electrical appliances. Within the first six months of operation, the cooperative had a gross revenue of more than $38,000 and a net income in excess of $14,000 after the deduction of taxes, interest, and depreciation. At this rate the cooperative could pay its indebtedness to the TVA in slightly more than five years instead of the twelve to fourteen that originally had been calculated. This was all done with electric rates being 50 percent lower than those of the private utilities operating in the same area.[13]

Since one of the big obstacles to rural electrification had been the original cost of electrical appliances and the lack of purchasing power by the potential users, the Electric Home and Farm Authority (EHFA) was created on an emergency basis by executive authority in December 1933 to overcome this hurdle. Strictly on an experimental basis, the EHFA program was confined to those areas in Mississippi, Alabama, Georgia, and Tennessee served by the TVA.[14]

The EHFA was unique in that it helped farmers buy household equipment, entered into contracts with appliance manufacturers, and designed standardized low cost electric ranges, water heaters, and refrigerators specifically for this program. The farmer becoming a part of this program signed a purchase agreement with a participating retailer, made a small down payment, and the EHFA paid the balance—for which it later billed the farmer. The unpaid balance owed the EHFA was paid through regular monthly billings stretched over a three- or four-year period at a low rate of interest. After collecting the payments, the cooperative turned them over to the EHFA. This made it possible for the farmer to obtain electrical equipment quickly and easily, and farmers receiving service from the utility companies shortly thereafter were allowed to participate in the program. Electrical appliance sales shot up 300 percent in the Tennessee basin. The EHFA was so successful that in 1935 the program was extended to cover all the states and even serve urban areas.[15]

Meanwhile, several points were becoming clear. TVA and the EHFA were well received because they helped farmers escape from many of the backbreaking experiences of farm life. Farms in seventeen counties of Alabama, Mississippi, Tennessee, and Georgia were the first to be electrified with federal help. The Alcorn Coop experiences demonstrated that the extra use farmers made of electrical equipment—more than city dwellers—helped offset the extra cost of building rural lines. Since cooperatives were feasible financially and the farmers with federal guidance were found capable of managing them, they gained new respect as the logical instruments to carry out the larger program.[16] The trial run in the Tennessee valley gave the New Dealers greater hope for electrifying agriculture than might otherwise have been the case.[17]

Meanwhile, Cooke recommended at every available opportunity that the federal government commit itself to the electrification of the farms of the nation. On several occasions he suggested that this might be a joint public-private undertaking, but government leadership was at the heart of every proposal he made. Cooke had a good understanding of what electricity could mean to 50 million Americans. As chairman of the Mississippi Valley Committee (MVC), created especially by the president to study the potential use of the natural resources of the Mississippi River basin, Cooke drew specific attention to the waste of human resources. He submitted a report to the president in February 1934 that asked for a federal electrification program to operate through self-liquidating cooperatives, with federal funds to lend, build rural lines at low cost, and provide technical, engineering, and management advice when needed.[18]

Cooke wanted to avoid competition with the private utilities and urged that the cooperatives restrict service to areas not already served by the electric companies. Also, instead of indicting the private utilities for failing to develop rural electrification, he seemed to absolve them of criticism. "Large average use of electricity on farms, especially in the initial stages, seemingly requires planning and investment beyond the capacity of a private company to initiate. Perhaps only the power and force of the Government can master the initial problem."[19] His report circulated through the administration and helped make certain "the federal government would see that rural electrification was made an essential feature in our economy." On January 4, 1935, Roosevelt requested $5 billion from Congress for public works, a request that included money for the construction of power lines in the rural areas and relief to the unemployed. About $100 million of the $4.8 billion authorized by Congress was for rural electrification. Roosevelt created the Rural Electrification Administration (REA) by executive decree on May 11, 1935, and Cooke was appointed administrator.

Cooke wrestled with practical plans of making the REA effective. The most perplexing questions involved the place that the electric industry was going to have in this vast undertaking, and how the cooperatives through which the program was to be carried out were to be selected. Originally, Cooke had been empowered to lend or grant money to private corporations, municipal districts, cooperatives, and public bodies for the construction of rural cooperatives.

Shortly after the REA was created, Roosevelt issued several new executive orders in an effort to coordinate and streamline the employment of labor, and the disbursement of relief funds by the federal agencies. He stipulated that 90 percent of the labor be taken from relief rolls and at least 25 percent of the funds be spent on employment. But the construction of electric lines required skilled labor—which was unlikely to be found in persons on relief—and the expenditure of large sums of money on equipment and materials. Cooke, as a consequence, could not fulfill the requirements set forth in the executive order, and spending 25 percent of the REA funds on labor became impossible. Simultaneously, the comptroller general issued a new ruling that prohibited the lending of relief funds by any agency. The president, to overcome these obstacles, issued a special order that gave the REA exclusive right to lend money on a self-liquidating basis and freed it from the provisions concerning relief labor. These changes converted the REA into "an orderly lending program on an interest bearing, self-liquidating basis," and Cooke was now left with the decision of who was to receive a loan.[20]

Cooke kept in mind there was a place for private enterprise in the REA. The private companies had the experience, equipment, and personnel to build rural power lines; and he felt it quite logical for the REA to lend the private utilities money and allow them to serve the farms. He therefore invited their representatives to meet with him in Washington on May 20, 1935, hoping that they would be moved by a new sense of public responsibility and the prospects of borrowing at the low rate of 3 percent and the other generous terms offered by the REA. Utility representatives attended, and following the meeting they appointed a special committee of executives to survey "the approximate extent to which further development of rural electrification may be promptly effected in cooperation with the REA."[21]

The utilities committee, after studying the matter for two months, asked the REA for a loan to the electric companies of more than $238 million to connect 351,000 prospective rural customers in 1935–1936. The utilities, according to the industry report, considered "the immediate urge for rural electrification as a social rather than an economical problem. The problem of the farmer is not one of rates, but of financing the wiring and purchasing of customers" and "there are very few farms requiring electricity for major farm operations that are not now served."[22] This report was accepted as a classic example of the disregard the private utilities had for the farmers, and had an unfavorable reception.

Public power advocates wanted to know how the electric industry could conclude that only a few remaining farms were without electricity when just 10 percent of the nation's farms had such service. These critics were aghast when they heard private utility claims that farmers received preferential treatment and could afford to wire their homes and buy appliances, when instead the facts indicated they paid the highest rates. Cooke responded that rates were at the heart of providing electricity for the farms of America, and that the rates of the private utilities had been the chief obstacle in promoting rural electrification.[23] Relations between the REA and the private utilities began to cool slowly after this, and eventually broke off.

The utilities from the beginning had been reluctant about taking part in the rural electrification program; some of their executives felt the REA would develop into "another New Deal failure" and did not want the industry to be identified with it. Others were critical of the friendly attitude Cooke displayed toward the electric cooperatives. The final break came in the fall of 1935 when Cooke rejected the application of the Wisconsin Power and Light Company for a $260,000 loan to finance the construction of 200 miles of rural power lines on the grounds that the rates submitted in the application were exorbitant and farmers could not afford them. When the Wisconsin Power and Light Company refused to revise its rates and resubmit its application, a wave of public resentment broke out. Thereafter open hostility was evident between the electric power companies who did not participate in the program and the REA.[24]

The Wheeler–Rayburn bill, the famous utility holding company measure fought in Congress with White House support, was one reason for the decline in goodwill between the REA and the electric industry. Seldom before had any administration been locked in fierce battle with a special interest group. Senator George Norris, a close associate of Cooke, opposed utility participation in the REA program. He argued that the lending of money to the companies could not be defended on grounds of either justice or honesty, but he was not the principal reason why the private utilities did not receive money from the REA. The breakdown resulted from the failure of Cooke and the utility companies to reach an understanding on the rate schedules.[25]

Cooke and his staff, on the basis of these and other experiences, met in Washington on June 5, 1935 with persons who were not associated with the electric industry, but were interested in rural electrification. Some of the delegates at this meeting had doubts about the feasibility of using cooperatives on a wider scale,[26] but pressure was brought to bear to use them. Judson King, the crusading head of the National Popular Government League—a militant public power organization—insisted that public bodies be given "the first right to this federal money."[27] The American Farm Bureau Federation and the National Grange asked for a national power program that used cooperatives or public power districts. Requests from local farm groups to organize as corporate bodies to help bring electricity into their homes, and the antiutilities sentiment that swept the country in the 1930s also influenced the REA to work through local organizations.

Since some farms received power from municipal power plants, Cooke saw the municipalities as a possible means through which to work; and proposals to electrify farms through municipal plants were presented at a conference of municipal and REA spokesmen in Kansas City, Missouri on November 7 and 8.[28] For the most part the municipal representatives were more concerned with higher rates for urban dwellers as a result of lines built in the countryside surrounding the town, questions of jurisdiction over territories with potential rural sales, and possible legal entanglements between the cities and their respective state legislatures than they were with the needs of the farmers. After Cooke saw that the delegates at the Kansas City meeting had little enthusiasm for the REA proposal, he concluded that the cooperatives were his only answer.

The triumph of the cooperatives was evident in November 1935 when the REA announced its first series of loans for rural electric lines; eleven went to individuals, seven to cooperatives, one to a municipal power line, and one of the few to an electric power company. Before December 1935 farm cooperatives forged to the forefront as the principal borrowers under the REA program.[29]

Cooke, in a report to the National Emergency Council in the fall of 1935, however, emphasized that the government was not moving fast enough with the electrification program, resulting in public dissatisfaction. He suggested that part of the problem was the REA's temporary status as an agency.[30] Senator Norris, the "father of the TVA" and the champion of public power, was the logical person to seize the initiative in making the REA a more effective organization. Norris and Cooke had kept in close contact since Muscle Shoals days, and remained close friends throughout the New Deal period. Norris knew first hand what life was like on a farm without electricity. He knew the drudgery of drawing water from the well and the inconvenience of kerosene lanterns for lighting. Early in 1936 Norris introduced a bill in the Senate to make the REA a regular agency with an appropriation of $100 million a year for ten years, and Sam Rayburn of Texas introduced a similar measure in the House. Rayburn, like Norris, had lived on a farm and understood the longing of the farmers for modern conveniences. The farmers in fact would have had difficulty finding a more zealous and powerful ally for rural electrification than Rayburn, the majority leader in the House, who was in a powerful position to push his favorite legislation.

Norris's bill met only token opposition in the Senate, in part because of the popularity of the REA in the rural districts, and the apparent unwillingness of the utility interests to oppose it because of the widespread hostility toward them. Roosevelt, however, considered the Norris request of $100 million to be spent each year for the next ten years too steep and persuaded him to accept a lower total figure of $420 million spread over a ten-year period. Otherwise, no major revisions were made in the Senate bill.

In the House, the bill underwent two major changes. Norris emphatically wanted the utilities excluded from receiving REA loans because they had refused to provide farms with electricity. In his opinion, they did not deserve to participate. Rayburn, on the other hand, felt that the private interests should be allowed to participate. If the farmers failed to qualify for loans in some areas, at least they should be able to look to the electric companies as an alternative. The House version of the bill also said the rate of interest on the loans was to be no less than 3 percent, while the Senate version wanted the rate to be no more than 3 percent. The changes in the House bill were a fundamental issue when the two zealots of rural electrification met.[31]

The collision between the two came in the conference room. Norris wanted the rate frozen at 3 percent because this was what money cost in 1936 and was the logical rate, while Rayburn wanted a flexible rate, fearing that a fixed rate would open the door to the REA for a subsidy once the economy took a turn for the better and interest rates exceeded 3 percent. Rayburn further wanted the program to be self-sufficient, while Norris believed the REA deserved a subsidy. For a time it appeared as though the REA measure was dead.

Norris announced that further meetings were futile and that he was going to make electrification as a wholly public enterprise an issue in the fall elections.[32] Representative John Rankin, also a member of the conference committee and advocate of public rural electrification, pleaded with Norris to be patient, agreed with him on the exclusion of the utilities from participation in the program, and asked for time to get the other House conferees to come around to his way of thinking. After considerable persuasion, Rankin got Norris to promise to try again.

Cooke had been watching the battle and felt that the REA bill at best had an even chance for approval. Participation by private utilities was pretty much an academic issue, since the companies were not applying for loans. Cooke, however, did suggest to Rayburn that the rate of interest "be no more than the average rate of interest payable by the United States on its obligations." This meant that the recipients of REA loans would get capital at a lower rate than the utilities, since U.S. Treasury securities in 1936 had a lower interest yield than electric utility bonds. If Norris balked on the House proposal on utility participation, Cooke warned the bill would fail; but he had a hunch that Norris would give in.[33]

When the conference committee met again, a mood of compromise was evident. When Cooke's recommendation on the rate of interest was brought up, Norris agreed; and he also agreed on utility participation by allowing "persons and corporations" to be eligible after preference had been given cooperatives and municipalities. The Senate and House both accepted the compromise, and the REA became law on May 11, 1936; the president signed the measure on May 21, and Cooke was confirmed by the Senate as administrator on May 26.

The REA, by the act, was converted from an agency with emergency status created by executive order to an agency created by Congress, which gave it a sense of permanence and greater stability. Loans under its provisions were to be made primarily to cooperatives for a period of twenty-five years on a self-liquidating basis. A second type of loan, inspired by the success of the Electric Home and Farm Authority, provided families in need of money with assistance to buy appliances and wire their homes. For each of the first two years the Reconstruction Finance Corporation (RFC) was to supply the REA with $50 million and for the next eight years Congress was authorized to appropriate funds up to $40 million per year. It was therefore an agency with at least a ten-year life span.[34]

The states were to receive loans on the basis of how much rural electrification each lacked. A state that had very little rural electricity such as Georgia, with fewer than 3 percent of its farms electrified, would be entitled to a larger loan than California, with 54 percent of its farms electrified. To qualify for a loan, a local group first had to incorporate as a legal cooperative according to state law, place a small deposit from a minimum number of members, normally 100, and file an application with the REA. The idea was to attack the crisis of rural electrification where the need was greatest.

Contrary to popular belief, the REA accepted an application for rural electrification only if the proposed cooperative demonstrated clear evidence of economic feasibility. The cooperative had to guarantee "area coverage" of all farmers under its jurisdiction, including the poor. Area coverage was an important principle of the REA. Whereas the private utilities had ignored the low revenue rural customers, the advocates of rural electrification insisted the rural poor deserved electric service. The REA exercised close control over the cooperative after it was started. Engineering and management details were supervised, the accounting data of each cooperative were audited annually, and veto power was maintained over the selection of the project manager. During the first year, field officials of the REA, officers of the Grange and the AFBF, and congressmen spurred on by the prospects of finding loyal and helpful constituents who would aid them in their political campaigns helped in organizing cooperatives. After 1937 the REA concentrated on providing technical and management assistance to the cooperatives.[35]

When the private utilities finally recognized the threat of competition in the rural market, some moved quickly into a particular area and built "spite lines" that served the more lucrative rural customers in the hope of heading off the REA. By law the REA could not serve an area already provided with electricity by a power company.[36]

Most spite lines were built between 1937 and 1940 and represented the principal form of opposition. The spite lines harassed the cooperatives, but did not permanently damage or set back the REA. Cooperatives in such instances tried as often as possible to compromise these conflicts of jurisdiction with the private utilities. Often disputes were settled in court or through state public service commissions, and on occasion a cooperative bought the lines of a company in a particular community. By 1940, however, the private utilities stopped building spite lines, and the relationship between the REA and the electric companies took on a more cordial tone. The most lucrative areas had been developed either by the REA or the private companies by that time, and the conflicts over jurisdiction were resolved. Meanwhile, the REA also had won several important court cases that discouraged spite line activity.[37]

Servicing of rural areas by the private utilities increased after the REA began its operations. The pressure of competition from the REA spurred them on into recognizing belatedly the value of the rural market. Private utilities served 976,000 farms or rural dwellings in late 1936 when rural electrification was just getting started. By June 30, 1941 they furnished almost 1.25 million farms and rural homes with electricity. Private industry accounted for 58 percent of all farms receiving service from central stations on the eve of World War II, and its rates were competitive with those of the REA.

The nature of the service rendered by the private utilities to their rural customers also expanded. Some companies launched promotional sales programs to encourage the purchase of refrigerators, radios, washing machines, and other appliances. The Georgia Power Company initiated a sales plan comparable to that of the Electric Home and Farm Authority that made long-term appliance loans possible, rented refrigerators for eighteen dollars a year, and gave the customer the option of applying rental payments toward the purchase of the refrigerator.[38]

Statistics, however, bear out that the REA surpassed the private utilities in serving the farms. As of June 30, 1941 the REA had more than 780,000 subscribers in forty-five states, which represented an increase of almost 774,000 farms served by the agency since the end of 1936. During this same period the private utilities added more than 269,000 rural customers, which indicates that the real thrust of rural electrification came from the federal government, not private industry. The REA spent more than $1 billion over these years, of which more than $18 million went for loans on appliances and electrical equipment to REA members. The repayment record of the cooperatives was outstanding. A total of almost $11 million was due in interest and principal on REA loans by the end of the fiscal year 1941, and only $125,000 of that amount was overdue. This was accomplished despite the low rates charged by the cooperatives.[39]

The success of the rural electrification program was assured by the time the New Deal came to an end. It was both sound financially and self-sufficient, and the opposition of the private utilities had ceased. The REA working together with the private utilities raised the percentage of farms provided with central station service from the 10 percent it had been in 1936 to 35 percent by April 1941. The pace of the REA slowed down drastically after the United States entered World War II, but was resumed with breathtaking speed in 1946.

Public electrification improved crop and livestock production, permitted wider use of machinery, reduced labor costs, and enabled the farmers to use modern, efficient techniques of farming. Much of the backbreaking toil and drudgery was eliminated, and reliance on the "coal oil" lanterns ended. Farmers' wives and daughters, freed from many daily chores, found time for other pursuits. Usable indoor time for the farm family was lengthened by two to four hours daily. Farm homes became cleaner and brighter. Social discussions, more reading, and greater interest by children in their schoolwork were stimulated; and farm life became more comfortable and satisfying. Electric lights, more than anything else, meant deliverance from the dark. They symbolized a turning point in the lives of many rural Americans.[40]

Electricity, by enabling farmers to have their own pumping systems, and thus indoor plumbing, led to the elimination of most outdoor privies (the old symbol of rural living); facilitated the spread of refrigeration and the storage of perishable foods, which in turn helped combat pellagra, a disease caused by deficiencies in vitamins A, B, and D; and brought the farmer into closer contact with the outside world through the use of the radio. Country folks began to have much the same entertainment and educational programs as the majority of urban Americans, and became more aware of events affecting their lives. Special radio broadcasts informed farmers of weather conditions, brought to them crop reports, commodity prices, and other information useful in the farm business.[41]

Rural education especially benefited from public electrification. Electric power brought the dark, drab classrooms to an end, even though it did not abolish the one-room schoolhouse. The quality of the pupils' reading and neatness and order in the classroom improved. Adolescents learned how to use electrical equipment such as cream separators, pumps, tools, electric ranges, cold storage units, electric sewing machines, and other home aids; in short, vocational training was upgraded.[42]

One industry that was revolutionized through the use of electricity was poultry farming. New equipment for hatching brooding chicks could now be operated with electricity; and night lights materially increased the number of eggs the hens laid, an important factor to egg producers in the fall and winter months when the price of eggs was high. A fully automated poultry farm could produce 50,000 broilers per year with one man operating it. In fact, poultry farming became so popular in some areas of the South that it replaced cotton farming as the chief means of livelihood.[43]

The rise in rural industries that had been predicted by the proponents of public electrification had partly taken place when the New Deal came to an end. Some 3,500 small industries, including sawmills, food and milk processing plants, canneries, citrus packing and shipping plants, cotton gins and oil presses, grain elevators, tree and shrub nurseries, slaughterhouses, game and fur farms, lumber yards, planing mills, and machine shops, received electric power from cooperatives in 1940; and these figures did not include industries served by private power. These industries provided opportunities for farmers unable to depend entirely on agriculture for a living and brought about a degree of industrial decentralization and a diversified economy that was sorely needed.[44]

Though rural electrification made possible a fuller and more rewarding life on the farm, it never succeeded in stemming the flow of people from the farms to the cities; nor did it resolve the disparity between income and expenses. Perhaps the New Deal did not go far enough in helping make more of the comforts and conveniences generally associated with urban living available to the rural inhabitants. Yet it was only after the New Deal undertook the development of the rural market for electricity that the private utilities, who up to then served only the more prosperous farmers, took a more serious interest in the rural market and made conveniences and comforts available to low income farmers as well. The REA, in short, stands out as one of the most significant contributions of the New Deal to the farmers and to the nation.

The Election of 1936 and the Farmers

THE NEW DEALERS WERE HOPEFUL, but also much concerned, about the election that fall. The intradepartmental conflicts over the sharecroppers and tenants and the external pressures weighed heavily on the administration, notwithstanding the remarks to the contrary. The concern over the nature of the Republican counterattack and the reaction of the press, which, for the most part, was hostile, was genuine. Patronage-minded Democrats posed a problem for Henry Wallace, who wanted the USDA to have a nonpartisan image of being committed to the welfare of all the farmers. The Supreme Court decision that invalidated the AAA was a prime issue in the campaign along with agriculture, especially in the West. The selection of Alf Landon of Kansas as the Republican standard-bearer was proof to many wary Democrats that the Republicans hoped to penetrate the agricultural heartland.

M. L. Wilson observed that although the Republicans in the East started out with a vigorous campaign lambasting the AAA, on the assumption the farmers resented being regimented and told how much they could raise, the party soon discovered this line of attack was accomplishing little. Wilson also heard reports of a Republican strategy to offer a substitute for the AAA that was simpler to administer, gave the farmers more money, and eliminated contracts, but he believed the mass of farmers wanted something more tangible in exchange for the Roosevelt–Wallace agricultural programs before they would switch their votes.[1]

Lewis S. Clarke, the president of an Omaha investment firm and an original supporter of the New Deal, informed Wilson that Nebraska farmers responded favorably in the corn-hog vote and this was causing Republicans in his state to sit up and take notice. "If they are smart it seems to me, they will approve the AAA plan and let it go at that and not try and mess around trying to find something to take its place.'' The wheat and corn farmers, despite the rust and drought, were ''a whole lot better off than a year ago.'' The greatest complaint of the farmers was the red tape, not the program itself. Wilson replied that Wallace wanted to reduce the red tape and develop a higher degree of local administration, but the comptroller general of the United States insisted that each check was a regular expenditure of the U.S. government, and the AAA had to comply with all rules, regulations, and procedures governing public expenditures. This was extremely difficult to explain to the farmers, but it was easy to understand why they were critical of such a situation.[2]

In January 1936 Mordecai Ezekiel found time to ''amuse'' himself by studying the *Literary Digest* poll on the popularity of New Deal policies. The value of such a poll, he held, depended on the questions asked and the absence of bias in the sample. The *Digest* sample, however, showed clear evidence of bias because the list of names the ballot was mailed to included one of every eighteen who voted for Hoover in 1932, one of every twenty-five who voted for Roosevelt, and one of every thirty who voted for Norman Thomas or others that year. In other words, the Hoover voters were overrepresented in the sample by 20 to 40 percent, except in the South. If the whole country had voted in 1932 the way this 5 percent voted, then the electoral college vote would have been 288–243, not the actual result, 472–59. The high-income, propertied, conservative classes were overrepresented in the sample, and the low-income, dissatisfied, and liberal classes underrepresented. The sample suggested that only 37.3 percent approved of New Deal policies, and 52.7 percent opposed them. The question asked by the *Digest* sample was ''Do you now approve the acts and policies of the Roosevelt New Deal to date?'' This was a far cry from asking ''Will you vote for or against Roosevelt in the next election?''[3]

Ezekiel's analysis of the *Literary Digest* poll was sent to Drew Pearson, co-author along with Robert S. Allen of the widely syndicated column ''Washington Merry-Go-Round,'' hoping that he would publish it. Pearson wrote back, however,

> Bob Allen and I have been trying to figure out ways of using it, but, inasmuch as we pretty well publicized our own poll on Roosevelt, which had the effect of showing up the *Literary Digest* poll, and a bunch of our editors were protesting we were too pro-New Deal, it was rather difficult . . . to write anything more on the same subject.[4]

Following an inquiry by the USDA of the methods used by the American Institute of Public Opinion in sampling voters across the country, the editorial director of the Institute informed Wilson that names for the mailed ballots were taken at random from city directories, lists of registered voters, telephone directories, automobile owners, and other lists. Different names were used for each mailing, but the same kind of cross section was used in each instance; and interviewers were instructed where to go and what type of voter to interview. Genuine efforts were made to see to it that the sample was representative. Ballots had to come back from each state in proportion to the voting population of the monthly political barometers and correct proportions were maintained in each state in the returned ballots for those who had come of voting age since 1932, between rural and urban dwellers, and among all groups—notably people at the relief level and those who in 1932 voted for Roosevelt, Hoover, Thomas, and others. Each type of ballot was a check on the other.

Interviews were necessary to get adequate responses from persons near or at the relief level; 250 interviewers were being used in June 1936. Interviews and mailed ballots were counted, and between 100,000 and 200,000 respondents were reached for each issue of the Institute. The average for mailed ballots returned ran from 5 to 40 percent, depending on the income level, on whether the ballots were sent out by postcard, third-class mail, first-class mail, or airmail, and on interest in the question.[5]

The role that employees of the USDA played in the election became an obvious concern of Democrats and Republicans. The desire at first had been to bring aid to the farmers on a strictly nonpartisan basis, but this idea began to erode. Wallace returned from a Cabinet meeting with a memo saying that the USDA should issue instructions limiting the activities of non–Civil Service appointees in the same manner Civil Service employees were limited. W. W. Stockberger, director of personnel in the USDA, issued such instructions as early as March 1935.

> Employees, while retaining the right to vote and to express privately their opinion on political subjects, are forbidden to take an active part in political management or in political campaigns. This also applies to temporary employees, employees on leave or absence with or without pay, substitutes, and laborers. Political activity in city, county, state, or national elections, whether primary or regular, or in behalf of any party or candidate, or any measure to be voted upon, is prohibited.[6]

Representative S. D. McReynolds of Tennessee, who got a copy of the Stockberger memorandum, was "mad as hell," said Paul Appleby. "He came over and jumped on Dr. Stockberger, and gave Julien [N. Friant] the works. He came in to see the Secretary, who was then in Secretary [of Commerce Daniel C.] Roper's office, and subsequently called him on the phone and asked that this should be rescinded." Stockberger soon discovered that no other department had issued comparable instructions, which meant that the USDA had gone out in the front line and was "taking the heat for it." McReynolds argued that if this order stood, then they might just as well discontinue all patronage, but revocation of the order, on the other hand, was fraught with embarrassment to the administration.[7]

The administration had disapproved strongly of the use of production associations to further the political ambitions of anyone, or mixing the affairs of these associations with local politics. On April 27, 1934 Chester Davis and C. W. Warburton in a policy statement said, "The production control programs and the county production control associations have been carried on without any regard to partisan politics and it is desirable and necessary that . . . [they] be kept entirely free from . . . any appearance of political favoritism." Anyone officially connected with a production control association who had become a candidate for public office had to be relieved of his committee membership or official connection with the association. These associations suspended their activities on January 6, 1936 after the Supreme Court rendered its decision. But after legislation was approved providing for payment to farmers who had fulfilled their contracts under the AAA, production associations were reactivated for the purpose of issuing payments. However, the policy enunciated by the USDA under the first AAA was going to apply, at least in theory, to whatever program and associations were set up under the new legislation.[8]

The behavior of Governor Clyde Tingley of New Mexico was typical of the kind of pressures exerted on the USDA. Tingley had traveled about 12,000 miles organizing Roosevelt-Garner Clubs in his state, and was able to cooperate with federal agencies in the development of their programs, except the Soil Conservation Service (SCS), which he found aggravating. About 75 percent of the several hundred employees of the SCS in the spring of 1936 did not even realize Roosevelt was a candidate for reelection. Several hundred more were going to be hired, some from relief rolls and some not. The SCS had given authority to Alejandro Gonzales, one of the leading Republicans of Sandoval County, to recommend men for employment, instead of consulting with persons friendly to the administration. Tingley felt this kind of indifference was injurious to the interests of the Democratic party in the coming election.[9]

The SCS was placed under Civil Service by an act of Congress in December 1935. Civil Service rules and regulations were very stringent in prohibiting political activity by workers or political discrimination by their superiors as in the case of WPA. From Washington, however, it did not appear that Gonzales was serving the interests of the Republican party; the SCS needed twenty-five men quickly "as a mobile planting crew to be used in Rio Grande projects, such men to be completely conversant with planting operations, men who did not object to travel, to camping on the job, and to furnishing subsistence for as long a period as a month in advance.'' Gonzales was consulted because he was a successful farmer in the Rio Grande Valley, had suggestions to offer, and was a member of the Board of Education of Sandoval County, which was one of the conservation districts. Gonzales was also on the advisory board of the Resettlement Administration. Inquiry further revealed that ten of the twenty-five men hired were Democrats, nine were Republicans, and the political affiliations of the other six were unknown. Henry A. Wallace assured Governor Tingley that he would ask the SCS to refrain from getting further suggestions from Gonzales, and that anyone found engaged in political activity would be dismissed.[10]

The pressure increased as the time of the Democratic National Convention neared. E. J. MacMillan, director of the speakers' bureau of the Democratic National Committee, approached a number of men, including Albert G. Black, Cully Cobb, and Claude Wickard, about taking part in the forthcoming political campaign. After some intimated that Wallace was unwilling to have them participate, MacMillan wrote to Wallace directly to find out why. "I am sure that this is not in accordance with your wishes," wrote MacMillan, "for it is entirely at variance with the attitude assumed by the heads of other departments under President Roosevelt." His beliefs were that the administration should have the services of those best able to defend the agricultural policies of the administration. It seemed inappropriate to rely solely on the members of Congress who had acted upon suggestions of the experts in the USDA and voted for measures that constituted the agricultural program of the administration.[11]

Appleby wrote MacMillan that "it would be a political mistake as well as an administrative mistake" for men such as Black "to engage in direct campaign speaking." Black could properly accept invitations to speak before agricultural groups on subjects related to the work of his bureau, but only when the invitation came from such groups. It would be politically dangerous to inject career men such as Black into open campaigning.[12]

The Republicans assembling in Cleveland on June 9 more or less rehashed what they had been saying before. The farm problem was a social and economic, not a partisan, problem. Their platform promised "to protect and foster the family-type farm, traditional in American life, and to promote policies which will bring about an adustment of agriculture to meet the needs of domestic and foreign markets," and to utilize federal benefit payments only when consistent with a balanced budget. The Republicans also stressed a program of abundance instead of scarcity; land-use development on a national scale; protection and restoration of the land resources of the nation; new industrial uses for farm products; protection for the farmer against the importation of all livestock, dairy, and agricultural products, substitutes and derivatives; ample farm credit at lower rates of interest; reasonable benefit payments to family-type farmers upon the domestically consumed portion of crops of which there were exportable surpluses; encouragement to cooperatives; and repeal of the Reciprocal Trade Agreement Law and the substitution of government assistance in disposing of surpluses by bargaining selectively with countries for exports and imports.[13]

Alfred M. Landon of Topeka, Kansas was nominated for president according to *Business Week* because "this man was their kind of person, possessing the homely Calvin Coolidge virtues, the old-fashioned, covered wagon, typical prairie state idea of thrift and economy, recognition of property as well as human rights." Ogden D. Mills summed up Republican strategy thus: "We must assume that the East is safe. We must carry enough Western states to make these Eastern electoral votes good if we can get them." Pressure for "soft money" was growing, also. The Republicans were "anxious to beat Roosevelt . . . eager to sacrifice anything—almost—to be sure of winning. And they had been thoroughly sold on the idea that the West—the farm regions—would be afraid that a speedy return to gold would work toward lowering farm prices."[14]

The Democrats who met in Philadelphia on June 23 repeated what they had been telling the farmers and the nation the past four years. They said they had taken the farmer off the road to ruin, returned him to freedom and prosperity, and planned to keep him there. The platform summarized what the New Deal had done to raise farm income, reduce farm debts, restore fertility to the land, check erosion, and bring electricity and good roads to the farmers. Building a reserve supply of goods to insure fair prices to consumers was stressed along with a fair profit to the farmers, the purchase and retirement of 10 million acres of submarginal land, and assistance to those attempting to eke out an existence from it.[15]

All indications were that Wallace and those closest to him did most of the work in drafting the Democratic platform on agriculture. One person who apparently had little to do with it was "Cotton Ed" Smith, the chairman of the Senate Committee on Agriculture. As the *Memphis Commercial Appeal* put it bluntly:

> What . . . made him [Smith] boil was that here was the chairman of the Senate Committee on Agriculture, not only available but eager to be drafted for advice and counsel on the agricultural plank in the platform, but had read in the papers on the way up that Secretary Wallace and Chester Davis had prepared the plank to what the administration conceives to be to the entire satisfaction of the farmers of the country. Stupid as he is reputed to be, and as he frequently appears, Senator Smith was able to appreciate the fact that he had been passed up and snubbed. Some of the South Carolinians were fearful that he would not apprehend the full import of the intent, but he did.[16]

Wallace was embittered by the Republican position on agriculture and this bitterness increased as election day drew near. In a letter to Burridge D. Butler, the publisher of *The Prairie Farmer,* Wallace accused the Republicans of double-talk and being captives of the big interests: the munitions manufacturers, the holding companies, and other corporate interests represented by the Liberty League, including the biggest tariff beneficiaries, and some of the processors. The Republican platform promised to exclude imports, increase exports, and collect foreign debts, which was as impossible to do as jumping to the moon. These groups had no interest in the welfare of the farmers. The "young Turks" in the councils of Alf Landon were "window dressing" whose presence there was aimed to split the northern from the southern farmer, and destroy the unity shown by the farmers over the past three years. The Supreme Court decision on the AAA did not represent the views of the farmers because they did not consider these programs coercive as charged. They voted overwhelmingly for the wheat, cotton, tobacco, and corn-hog programs, and the Democratic platform reflected this.[17]

Crop insurance was the latest proposal advanced by Wallace during the presidential election year. This was in line with the ever-normal granary plan of Wallace for storing up the surplus in times of plenty to have it available in periods of drought or crop failure. The automatic regulating feature of the ever-normal granary plan, of which crop insurance was a part, had not been worked out.[18]

The Republicans apparently had overestimated the prospects of victory in 1936 or believed they would carry the farm states without much of a serious effort. Roy Yarnell, editor of *Capper's Farmer,* however, was not among the confident. He wrote Landon:

> I'd like to add my voice to the voices of others who have urged you to get out in the so-called "sticks" and do some campaigning from the platform of your train. You campaigned that way when you ran for Governor and the voters liked it. . . . People want to see you and know you and hear you face to face . . . the Republican party must offer agriculture as definite and as appealing a farm program as the Democrats. . . . The Republican party must get punch in its farm program.[19]

The overoptimism that Yarnell complained about was reflected in the correspondence of Representative Clifford R. Hope of Kansas, the ranking Republican on the House Committee on Agriculture and director of the Farm Division of the Republican National Committee. Hope wrote a friend early in August, "There is a definite swing toward Landon in the middle west and if it continues, there is no question at all but that he will carry all the states out here. Reports from the East indicate that his strength is increasing there also."[20]

For a number of weeks after the Cleveland convention, the Republicans did very little but criticize the Democrats. As late as August 6 Hope wrote a congressional hopeful in Wisconsin, "I expect to be in Chicago all next week for the purpose of . . . setting up an organization to handle the agricultural end of the campaign. The matter is now in the formative stages." Charles W. Holman, the secretary of the powerful National Cooperative Milk Producers' Federation, throughout his travels between the East and the Middle West found an insistent demand that Landon discuss the issues, "get down to brass tacks, etc.," and that criticism without advocacy of something better was creating sympathy for Roosevelt. Frank Knox, the candidate for vice-president, was not doing much good for agriculture. Farmers resented his attitude on reciprocal trade, and considered his speeches those of a plutocrat. Farmers wanted to know Landon's position on monetary policy, the disposal of surpluses, and protection for the farmers. The dairy farmers, especially, wanted a pronouncement on what he was going to do to control bovine diseases. Frank Maher, an attorney in Fort Dodge, Iowa complained to Senator [Arthur] Capper of Kansas that Senator Lester J. Dickinson of Iowa had assured Landon that an agricultural program wasn't necessary to carry Iowa. All he would have to do was to criticize Roosevelt. Maher warned that "Iowans are waiting for the Governor's program. They were told by the Cleveland convention that the candidate would give his views. He has not done so, and we are losing strength fast in the State. We are not going to carry Iowa unless a program is put up by our candidate."[21]

Apparently the pressure on Landon to speak directly on the farm issues and tell the farmers what he would do for them if he were elected president bore some fruit. He delivered two major speeches in September in the Middle West that attracted national attention. On September 22 in Des Moines Landon told Iowa farmers the Republican platform was pledged to aid the farmers who had been ruined by the drought, protect the income of the farm family, preserve the soil and other natural resources, and defend the farmers and the rest of the nation from ruinous debts and land-use policies. He also promised to give the American farmers what George N. Peek had once pledged: an American instead of a foreign price for their products, and the equivalent of an effective tariff. Crop insurance, which had not been included in the Republican platform, likewise was promised.

Landon said that most Republicans cooperated with the AAA in the initial stages, on the theory this was an emergency measure that would end in due time; but they rebelled when they discovered the New Deal "was trying to stretch the Triple A into a means for the permanent control of American agriculture from Washington." So far as Landon was concerned, the administration had no farm policy; the Soil Conservation and Domestic Allotment Act of 1936 was "a subterfuge." He considered soil conservation the essence of his farm program, something that Kansas had been a pioneer

in developing. He promised under his administration the federal government would cooperate with the states to do what Kansans had been doing,
and this would not be at the expense of the dairy and livestock producers.
He emphasized that the Republican concern was with the "family-type
farm" and not the large corporate enterprises; and pledged "to extend
within the limits of sound finance adequate credit at reasonable rates, to
capable tenants and experienced farmers, for the purchase or refinancing of
farm homes."[22]

In his second major farm address on September 25 in Minneapolis, one
of the citadels of farm cooperatives and a dairy center, he concentrated on
the reciprocal trade program and how badly this was affecting the American
farmer. Landon also said that he believed in reciprocal trade in principle
because it offered benefits to the nations involved; but the current program,
after being in operation for two years, was doing the farmers more harm
than good. It delayed recovery, and sold them down the river. He further
blamed "the confused and destructive policies of the administration for
farm products having the smallest proportion of our foreign trade in the
history of the nation."[23]

The Democrats and USDA officials viewed these attacks on the reciprocal trade program as irresponsible, not based on facts.[24] Wallace, whose
distaste for Landon was strong but restrained, accused the Republicans of
wanting to destroy the conservation program. Some of Wallace's associates
felt that, owing to the supposedly nonpartisan character of the agricultural
programs, the secretary should confine himself to speaking on the operation
of the plan and allow the facts to speak for themselves. His speeches in the
past had confined themselves generally to the agricultural situation and
plans for the future. But now Wallace decided to change his stance.

Landon's attack, Wallace realized, came at a time of widespread suffering from the drought. Farmers were relying on small supplies of drought-
resistant grass and forage crops under the conservation program to carry
them through the coming winter. The need to protect soil from erosion and
exhaustion had been demonstrated, and AAA conferences were being held
in the western states to develop a range program and extend the benefits of
conservation to them. Of even greater significance to Wallace was that John
D. M. Hamilton, the national chairman of the Republican party, coupled
his attack on the soil and conservation program with a sweeping denuncia-
tion of the AAA. The Soil Conservation and Domestic Allotment Act of
1936 was at the foundation of the government's long-range agricultural program, and the determination of the Republicans to destroy this was proof
they were opposed to any effective national program for agriculture.[25]

Wallace also foresaw cuts in farm prices of from one-fourth to one-
third, ending in a depression worse than in 1932, if Landon's tariff
equivalent proposal outlined in Des Moines was carried out. He said, "The

greedy and ignorant forces behind the national Republican party have not learned the lesson of 1932.'' Wallace accused Landon of insincerity in proposing crop insurance, saying that, if given his way, Landon probably would have the protection of the farmers' crops handled entirely by private insurance companies. His proposal for a federal warehouse law was unconstitutional in light of a recent court decision. Landon's farm record as governor of Kansas was unfavorable when compared with that of Roosevelt when he was governor of New York. ''Frankly,'' said Wallace, ''no one knows anything outstanding that Governor Landon has done for the Kansas farmer or for the cause of conservation in Kansas.'' There was little reason to expect that the farm record of Landon would be any better than those of Harding, Coolidge, or Hoover. The same men stood behind him. ''In slightly different terms he is proposing the same policies.'' ''Ninety-eight out of 100 big bankers are for Landon. Ninety-eight out of 100 big corporations are for Landon.'' The Republicans had learned nothing from the depression; they wanted to do away with soil conservation and production controls when the obligations of 1936 were paid off. Like his predecessors Landon believed in a monetary policy that would lead to deflation; while he was making promises to the farmers in the West he also was making a systematic effort in the East to get housewives to demand an immediate return of retail food prices to 1932 levels.

There was no way of assessing how much effect Landon had on the farmers as a result of his speeches in Des Moines and Minneapolis, and Wallace and the Democrats continued to be worried about the farm vote in the Middle West. Wallace wanted to wage another intensive campaign in October and try to line up as many farm states as possible. Roosevelt sentiment was strong in Wisconsin and Minnesota, states with strong Progressive and Farmer-Labor party traditions, but the New Dealers took nothing for granted.

In Wisconsin a Roosevelt ''all-party farm organization'' was perfected, and Paul Weis, once a bitter foe of the AAA and leader of the attack on the 1934 dairy program, became its permanent chairman. None of the original Roosevelt and dairy program supporters, however, were on the executive committee; but the effort was motivated by a Progressive allegiance to Roosevelt. E. R. McIntyre of the *Wisconsin Agriculturalist and Farmer,* one of the leading farm periodicals in the state, believed that the Roosevelt all-party farm organization group would help fight off the Union ticket of William Lemke in the state. McIntyre also hoped that the friends of Roosevelt in Washington would not be misled into believing that the men running his campaign had been devoted followers of the agricultural program, because they had not.[26]

Minnesota was one state in which Wallace believed he should have at least one important speaking engagement before the election. Paul Appleby thought it might prove effective if Governor Elmer Benson, Congressman Ernest Lundeen, and two prominent Minnesota Democrats sufficiently representative of the two important elements of the party appeared on the platform at the same time the secretary spoke. Appleby also thought it best to leave all arrangements in the hands of Benson, and if a meeting could be arranged for October 26, they could count on Secretary Wallace.[27]

In North Dakota efforts were made to get C. C. Talbott, president of the North Dakota Farmers' Union, to campaign for Roosevelt and Wallace. Talbott, however, advised Appleby that his being president of a non-political organization made it imperative for him not to take part in any political campaign. "We have a candidate for governor who is actively supporting Mr. Landon, and we have a national secretary and president who are actively supporting Mr. Lemke. Were I to take any active part in the political campaign, we would probably destroy our organization and its effectiveness in the future." Talbott hoped that Appleby understood that the national officers of the Farmers' Union had retarded the programs of the organization during this entire administration, and many in the Farmers' Union wanted to elect a new set of officers who could be counted on to work for the best interests of the farmers. Talbott wanted to raise this issue in the forthcoming national convention of the Farmers' Union and would not be in a strong position to do so if he took an active part in this campaign. He felt he could do more good if he advised members of the committee from time to time, than if he became an active campaigner.[28]

Of all Cabinet members, Wallace, an original nonpartisan selection, was bearing the most political responsibility in the campaign of 1936; he was shoved forward as the number two man, and his powers of persuasion were continuously being exerted in the agricultural areas, where the real battle was between him and the Republican nominee. Wallace was aware that the opinions of his father had had little weight in the Harding administration when he was secretary of agriculture. Wallace realized that his political future was at stake, regardless of the outcome of the election, if he failed to carry the farm states for Roosevelt. If Roosevelt was reelected but lost the home ground of Wallace—the prairie states—the secretary was sure to face demotion as a presidential adviser. Wallace was expected to have a solid political future only if he won these states, according to those who had been watching the transformation of Wallace from a nonpartisan into a politician.

The role that the USDA and the various New Deal agencies were playing in the election of 1936, as indicated, had become a topic of concern. As best as could be determined, there was no widespread use of county soil conservation associations in the campaign. In the South where they were most political, there was no need for them to become more active. AAA employees at the administrative level in Washington devoted a part of their time in the preparation of campaign material for Wallace and made reports on their political observations when they returned from trips; and AAA economic advisors were utilized. The AAA, according to one theory, was willing to participate in a little quiet political activity, providing there was no chance of being caught. In the 1934 elections, AAA administrator Chester Davis could tell congressmen who wanted benefit payments rushed to their districts before the election to be quiet and wait for the regular order. But in 1936 efforts were made to get a small percentage of the payments out before election as a token of the bountiful returns yet to come. Southerners in high administrative positions, of whom there were a significant number, in particular were in favor of an open-ended aggressive campaign to support Roosevelt and give Wallace a vote of confidence. Westerners, on the other hand, who had not forgotten the early nonpartisan nature of the agricultural programs, were more reluctant.[29]

The New Dealers, whether one agreed with them or not, developed a cogent argument in support of what they were doing for the farmers. They emphasized the relative importance of the prosperity of the farmer to that of the nation as a whole. The more the farmer sold, the more money he had with which to buy the products of the city workers. Four of every ten persons returning to industrial jobs in 1936 and the 60 percent increase in the shipment of manufactured products from the industrial East to the South and the West were attributed to the $2.5 billion rise in farm income between 1932 and 1935. Roosevelt, they argued, restored the value of the farmer's dollar by devaluing the gold content of the dollar, and caused the price of cotton to shoot up two and a half cents a pound, of wheat to thirty cents, and that of corn to double. They stopped raising crops for a foreign market that no longer existed, but did not cut production below the needs of the people at home. While the AAA, aided by the drought, cut the production of wheat by 33 percent, cotton by 25 percent, and corn by 52 percent between 1932 and 1935, between 1930 and 1932 the captains of American industry cut steel production by 66 percent, iron by 72 percent, copper by 61 percent, and motor cars by 59 percent.[30]

The AAA, moreover, had the power to increase production as well as to decrease it; as a result of short crops in 1934, the AAA in 1935 sought an increase of more than 5 million acres in the production of wheat. The existing wheat shortage had been due to the drought exclusively, not the AAA, because the plantings in 1936 were 10 percent larger than for the average 1928–1932 period and in 1935. The whole idea was one of "elastic control" to bring supply and demand into balance.

The reciprocal trade pacts also were strongly defended. Agreements with fourteen countries already had increased America's foreign trade by 47 percent, and the farmer was entitled to his share of federal protection until his country's agricultural export trade was more fully revived.[31]

Equally strong was the defense of the contract arrangements between the AAA and the farmers. All of the 3 million farmers who cooperated with the AAA did so of their own free will; in 1935 more than 90 percent of the contracting tobacco, corn, hog, and wheat farmers voted to continue AAA control because this phase of the program was carried out by state, county, and local committees, instead of by "foreigners" in the USDA and Washington. Committees of farmers, selected by farmers and familiar with the land of their neighbors, signed up those who wished to cooperate, set allotments, and supervised the entire process with as little outside help as possible, which gave the farmers the feeling they were marching toward a common goal together. Once the Supreme Court ruled that the AAA was unconstitutional (early in 1936), the New Deal pushed through the Soil Conservation and Domestic Allotment Act, which emphasized soil conservation and continued in a constitutional way many of the purposes of the old AAA.

Credit also was claimed for the work of the RA, which took more than a quarter of a million farmers off the FERA rolls. That agency focused on the small loans to farmers for livestock, feed, and equipment, and the low-interest loans to purchase or lease homes on resettlement projects, the advice rendered on use of equipment and the wiser use of the land, and the aid the drought-stricken farmers received in July 1936. New Dealers also cited what the Farm Credit Administration (FCA) did for the debt-worried farmers, half a million of whom were enabled to save their homes, and the more than a million feed loans and advances to save the harvest. Also stressed was the work of the cooperative associations through which the farmer could procure liberal long- or short-term credit from the Federal Land Banks.

All these farm programs and benefits meshed together into a national recovery program, said the New Dealers, who claimed credit for the $2.5 billion rise in farm income over the previous three years, the increase in farm property values by nearly $3 billion, and the 27 percent increase in farm wages. For those who charged this increase in income was the indirect result of benefit payments, the New Dealers replied that the important factor was the higher farm prices; the bounty payments accounted for only 17 percent of the increase in the farmers' gross income.[32]

The Republicans, on the other hand, found themselves in a more difficult position. With little tangible proof of what they had done for the farmers, they could only claim they would do a better job than the Democrats, and continue to charge that Roosevelt had no fixed agricultural program, and did not have the interest in the West that he had in 1932. The New Deal sweep of the farm states in 1936 stunned the Republicans when they realized the extent of their defeat.[33]

Years later M. L. Wilson reminisced about why the farmers voted for

Roosevelt in 1936. They felt directly the effects of the payments they were receiving from the AAA; the Supreme Court decision early that year was interpreted by many as the court's deliberate attempt to take away their AAA benefits. The propaganda of the Liberty League against the New Deal sounded as though it had been released by Wall Street, a mortal enemy of the farmers. The droughts of 1934 and 1936 affected large numbers of people, and the efforts of the federal government to aid the stricken people deeply impressed the farmers. The AFBF was solidly behind the administration, the farmers' committees were a great help, the Democrats were united, and the opposition was ineffective. The Republican party was completely "down at the heels," the slogans used against Hoover proved effective, and Landon was a weak candidate.[34]

The results of the election gave the administration renewed confidence in itself and its farm policy, and it deemed this a mandate from the voters to go ahead and start an "ever-normal granary," practice soil conservation, authorize crop loans, offer crop insurance to protect the wheat farmers from the drought, and empower the secretary of agriculture to assign national acreage allotments and subsidies to producers of staples. The vote also indicated the farmers wanted the federal government to play a positive role in protecting their interests. Wallace himself came out of the election very secure politically, which warmed the hearts of his closest associates and others awaiting the opportunity to advance his political future.[35]

CHAPTER SEVENTEEN

The AAA, 1936-1939

THE AAA, STILL AMONG THE MOST PUBLICIZED, if not *the* most publicized of all New Deal agencies to aid the farmers, continued to give most of its assistance to the more substantial middle class farmers, despite the public clamor for additional assistance to the low-income groups. Southern politicians who dominated the House and Senate agricultural committees and their allies in the Middle West helped assure this. Once Roosevelt was reelected and the immediate future of Wallace seemed secure, the agricultural phases of the New Deal began to take on greater political overtones. Especially clear to the astute observer was that Wallace's reformist enthusiasm had eroded, and those closest to him were busy advancing his candidacy for the presidency.[1]

No reasons were given for the resignation of Chester C. Davis as administrator of the AAA in 1936. Davis, suffice it to say, had worked hard as administrator of the AAA, tired of the vigorous pace he had to maintain, and experienced more than his share of difficulties with Henry A. Wallace, Paul Appleby, and others who disagreed with some of his actions. Howard R. Tolley, his successor, had resigned from the AAA in 1935 to accept a position with the University of California, but returned to Washington after the resignation of Davis and became the acting and then the permanent head of the AAA.[2]

The Supreme Court decision in January 1936 invalidating the production control features of the AAA had prompted Congress to move swiftly in order to cushion the effects that the sudden stoppage of the adjustment program would have had on the farmers. New legislation was needed to clear away the wreckage left behind and Congress reacted by repealing the Kerr Tobacco Act, the Bankhead Cotton Act, and the Potato Act, then approved the Supplemental Appropriation Act of 1936 that made more than $296 million available for the obligations incurred by the AAA by January 6,

1936. Such action was mandatory because the court decision ended the collection of the processing taxes.[3]

The Soil Conservation and Domestic Allotment Act (SCDAA) of 1936 was designed as a substitute for the AAA. Sections 7 to 17 inclusive of the new measure were enacted within eight weeks after the Supreme Court decision, and provided the basis for the conservation program. With this the AAA entered a second phase, one that placed emphasis on an increase in farm income through land use and farm practices that conserved and built up the soil. Adjustments in the production and marketing of crops practiced under the old AAA were deemphasized. The new legislation in a way sought to carry out the objectives of the AAA in a constitutional manner. Soil conservation practices had been encouraged by the AAA from the beginning, but the emergency from 1933 to 1935 relegated these practices to a subordinate position. In 1936, however, soil conservation became fundamental to long-range farm policy and was a primary part of the adjustment program.[4]

Payments under the SCDAA were based on the willingness of farmers to cooperate voluntarily in the use of their land, the extent of the adjustments and the productivity of the land on which soil conservation practices were used, the volume of certain domestically consumed crops, or a combination of these alternatives. Originally payments were limited to $500 million annually and were to be paid until such time as effective state agencies for such purposes had been established or until January 1, 1938. An amendment in 1937, however, extended federal aid to January 1, 1942.

When Tolley became acting administrator of the AAA in March 1936, he found the same old group he left behind in September 1935, but with "a regenerated spirit." Meanwhile, a definite program for the administration of the SCDAA had to be worked out, and the main task was to get this program out into the hands of the farmers and have them sign contracts before planting time.

Up to this point everything had been done in Washington. The entire staff, except for the state and county committeemen, was stationed there. All farmer contracts were verified in Washington and checks written and mailed there. Now an office had to be opened in each of the states in which contracts with the farmers were to be made, verified, and checked for compliance. Then, benefit or conservation checks, as they were called, would be written.

The SCDAA also was empowered to write one check per farm. Crops were catalogued as depleting, soil building, and soil conserving by the USDA. The farmer was offered one contract if he worked out a plan with his local committeeman to reduce the acreage of the soil depleting crops and increase that of the soil conserving and soil building crops. A farmer also could use recommended commercial fertilizers to improve his pasture and soil building crops and be reimbursed at the end of the season. This arrangement inevitably led to a consideration of the cropping system for the entire farm before a contract with the farmer was negotiated, which would have been difficult under the old arrangement when separate contracts were given for each crop.

The work of the SCDAA inevitably assumed more of a regional complexion. Because there was one contract per farm, there was no reason to have the agency divided into wheat, cotton, corn-hog, tobacco, and other sections, as was the case in the first AAA. The crops were grown in certain areas: wheat in what under the new arrangement came to be known as the Western Division, cotton in the Southern Division, tobacco in the East Central Division, corn and hogs in the North Central Division, and a general variety of products in the Northeast Division. Agricultural adjustment activity had been minimal in the Northeast, which was devoted primarily to dairying, truck, and general farming.[5]

Much of 1937 was spent trying to perfect legislation and the administration of the SCDAA. Officials in Washington often conferred among themselves and with representatives of the state colleges and county committeemen about the SCDAA being a farmers' program for the benefit of farmers. They talked about the differences from region to region, state to state, and county to county, and about rules formulated in Washington being unsuited to the diverse conditions in the country. Wallace, M. L. Wilson, and Tolley often talked about "farmer participation," "democratic participation," and "citizen participation" in the operation of the agricultural program. Administration leaders had been sensitive to charges that the farmers' programs were "authoritarian," "totalitarian," and "FDR politics."

Pains were taken to see to it that committeemen were elected, and that ideas and suggestions relative to the contents of the program and method of operation were welcomed. Experts outside the administrative level were asked to travel around the country and talk with farmers, committeemen, and townspeople about the program, ask them what they thought about it, report their findings, and recommend changes. Complacency and bureaucracy had started to seep into the state and local levels as it had into the national.[6]

State and local administrators often thought they knew what had to be done and how to do it. On the other hand they seemed to pay little attention to the problems of the individual farmers, and even in 1936 and 1937 they generally accepted the view that their only purpose was to write checks and make payments. Discussion groups, as a consequence, were organized to explore farmer attitudes and opinions. Regular reports of what was on their minds began coming into Washington from all parts of the country.

The SCDAA stated that after two full years of operation at the federal level, that is, in 1938, the program would become a state grant-in-aid program comparable to the Smith–Lever Act that established the Extension Service, the Morrill Act, and other college-related programs. The federal government would then enter into a contract with the state governments, and the states would assume the lead in administering the program. This arrangement, however, never went into effect because the AAA of 1938 superceded the SCDAA of 1936. "The opposition was too strong. It also became apparent that a good many of the states wouldn't pass the needed enabling legislation."[7]

Meanwhile, the USDA drafted a model soil conservation district law. A soil conservation district, according to this proposal, could become a civil subdivision. It could have relations with the state or federal governments if the landowners of a particular area voted for it by referendum. The general idea was to give the farmers a greater voice at the local level. This model law had a land-use provision which said that whenever two-thirds of the landowners of a district voted, they would or would not use the district in a certain way, their decision would bind all landowners in the district. On the theory that the heads of local organizations wanted decentralization, Roosevelt sent a copy of this model law to the governor of every state with a special letter suggesting its adoption by the state legislature.

Bringing the Resettlement Administration (RA), which the Farm Security Administration had absorbed, into the USDA meant bigger and fiercer battles, and bigger and sharper divisions, despite the air of friendliness proclaimed by Will Alexander, the RA's head. The FSA by virtue of seeking to aid low-income farmers had become a sort of place of refuge for old "AAAers" who disliked the AAA because they believed it still catered primarily to the commercial farmers. Those who remained faithful to the AAA believed the FSA was aiding failures, misfits, and incompetents. There also was the Soil Conservation Service (SCS), with its conservation districts representing "democracy at work," which like the FSA was viewed as a rival of the AAA. Samuel B. Bledsoe, chief of the Press Service, Office of Information, USDA, recalled, "You had to be around to feel it, but there was a feeling in many places against the ordinary commercial interests. It was a feeling of escape from exploitation and economic cares."[8]

Tolley, himself, first felt the inadequacy of the job the AAA was doing in the fall of 1936 after he returned from a trip to the South with Tugwell, Wallace, and Will Alexander. Tolley said,

> On that trip I got a feeling and an understanding that I never had before of the status and problems of the low-income farm people in that

part of the country. In the AAA our contracts were mostly with those
. . . farther up the ladder—the landlord, the ordinary large farmer,
rather than the small farmers. The landlords and the large farmers were
the ones who had the organization, and they were the ones who were
vocal.[9]

There also was antagonism between the FSA and the Farm Credit Administration (FCA), which at first had been outside the USDA. The FSA made loans under the provisions of the Bankhead–Jones Act to help farmers "get on their feet." FSA activities were activities that the FCA was unwilling to undertake; some in the FCA charged that the FSA extended loans to people who did not know how to use them properly, while the FSA charged that the FCA made no genuine effort to help those who needed help the most and ministered only to the better-placed and wealthier farmers.

Then, too, there was friction between the FSA and the Extension Service. Those associated with the FSA believed that the extension agents showed little interest in the low-income farmers; while the agents, in turn, accused the FSA of invading their territory and doing part of or all of their job. In fact, in many places the land-grant colleges were showing antagonism toward the FSA, the SCS, and the AAA. The land-grant colleges reasoned that since they were the old established institutions, all or most of these activities should have been channeled through them.

Meanwhile, the administration once again experienced difficulties in achieving the desired balance between acreage restriction and production. Payments for the improvement of farming practices by "fixing up" pastures, building terraces, and plowing up the contours were doing well by mid-1937, but they were doing little to keep down production. Wheat and corn farmers with smaller acreages, better cultivation methods, and the use of more fertilizers, raised as many crops as before. Wheat and corn production had been influenced very little by the adjustment program by the end of 1937; but cotton and tobacco were greatly affected by it, even though indications were that the cotton yield was increasing. AAA officials, therefore, were concluding that the adjustment program had not been very effective in 1936 and 1937.

Tolley, Alfred D. Stedman, Jesse Tapp, John Hutson, and others believed that the AAA report for 1937 had to be an accurate and careful account of how much had been accomplished since the SCDAA had been in effect. Thus they sought to determine the strengths and weaknesses of the programs, and how they could be improved for the best interests of agriculture and the general public. Harold Rowe, a member of the research staff at the Brookings Institution—which had appraised the first AAA—was hired to help prepare this report. Rowe studied changes in production and their causes, increases in the yield per acre, shifts in prices and agricultural income, and the attitude of the farmers toward the program. Tolley was proud of the report; so were those who had a hand in preparing it, because they thought they were telling the truth.

The findings were submitted to Wallace who kept them until Tolley learned that the secretary was unhappy with them. Wallace feared that the report would furnish "meat for the opposition," and mentioned some congressmen and senators who would complain that the USDA had not done as well as it should have. The report pointed out again that the benefits had not gone to the low-income farmers as much as they should have. Tolley, however, realized that it was up to the secretary to determine whether the report was to be published. Wallace decided to send it in for publication.

Tolley further realized that it was a problem keeping "the good old spirit" going among the people in Washington and in the field. Whenever new legislation was being considered and hearings held, the enthusiasm was up; but in general the same self-satisfaction and ossification he sensed back in 1935 seemed to be seeping in. Little was being done to make things better. Many were following the line charted by interest groups, general farmer organizations, and the cooperatives.

The divisions widened throughout 1937–1938. There were those, as indicated, who believed that the best program could be developed if the people whom the program was designed to help could have a voice in deciding what these programs were to be, and how they should be administered in a particular locality and farm. The AAA administrator, according to this group, should discharge his responsibilities as agreed upon with the local people in the way they wanted them carried out, and consistent with the existing legislation. Stress was to be on grass roots participation and the way labor unions accomplished things. M. L. Wilson was the ranking member of the USDA who believed in decentralization and the democratic process.

An opposing group believed that the best way the government could help the farmers was for Congress to pass a law, issue a decree, cut down the acreage, and fix prices, with authority and control remaining at the federal level. This group was impatient with the slow process of citizen participation. Many who favored centralization and the exercise of authority had been original backers of the AAA and what preceded it during the 1920s and the early 1930s. They had come to the AAA in the early days as local administrators and as chairmen of state committees. The American Farm Bureau Federation (AFBF), for example, had men on its board who believed that decentralization was not in the best interests of the farmers, and that the best thing to do was to get a law passed and issue orders. There was a considerable amount of such sentiment in the USDA among those who had southern roots and were close to the administration. John Hutson and those identified with the tobacco growers also were sympathetic to the centralized approach. Cully Cobb exhausted his patience over this particular issue and resigned in mid-1937. The Bankhead Cotton Control Act certainly reflected this approach.

The enactment of the AAA of 1938 meant that the adjustment program entered a third phase, which reflected a middle course between the programs authorized in 1933 (AAA), and those authorized in 1936 (SCDAA). This middle course resulted from a realization that the droughts of 1934 and 1936 had obscured the actual value of the programs. The droughts, from a legislative standpoint, tended to emphasize that the permanent solution lay in conservation rather than in the acreage or marketing approach. This view had been encouraged by the liquidation of the original AAA and the enactment of the SCDAA.

Then the unusually favorable growing conditions of 1937 and the prospects of excellent crops in 1938 exposed the shortcomings of the conservation approach in years of bumper crops; and attention focused on a broader program based on the control of larger reserves through storage. The droughts of 1934 and 1936 had driven home the need for larger supplies of wheat and corn for food and feed, an idea embodied in the ever-normal granary plan that was the starting point of the new legislation. The AAA of 1938, in effect, had a double role: provide a larger supply of reserves in periods of drought, and protect the farmer from ruinous surpluses by the control of interstate marketing instead of by the control of production as in the original AAA. The idea of reserves that attracted attention in 1937 and 1938 was used to a limited extent in 1933 and 1934 when the farmers were enabled with government loans to carry their corn from a period of extreme surplus to one of extreme drought; but Wallace also acknowledged his indebtedness to the Chinese for the idea as well. Wallace, as expected, met outright opposition, if not derision, from those who neither liked the plan nor the AAA. Once the ever-normal granary plan got through Congress it became a primary part of the AAA of 1938.[10]

The ever-normal granary plan became a partisan issue. The part of the act calling for loans to the farmers was assailed as price-fixing and vote-buying, which to a certain degree it was; in fact any proposal that said loan rates depended on the size of the stocks on hand became a leading question in agricultural politics. Some wanted the loan rate to be at parity because anything below that was wrong; but 90 percent of parity became the top for any commodity except on cotton loans, which could go as high as 95 percent. According to Tolley, FDR's personal interest in cotton probably had something to do with the 95 percent level.[11]

Wallace derived a great deal of personal satisfaction from the contributions of the ever-normal granary plan. Shortly after World War II broke out in 1939 he informed the American housewives that it was unnecessary for them to run to the grocery stores from fear of food shortages; the ever-normal granary had ample supplies of wheat, cotton, and corn on hand,

and the nation was secure in a period of war as it was in a period of drought. The plentiful supplies of the ever-normal granary also made possible extensive Lend-Lease loans to the British before the United States entered the war in 1941.[12]

Another problem was the rivalry between the federal government and the land grant colleges. When the federal government launched the AAA, some of the colleges objected because they believed that the colleges should have taken the program out to the people. Meanwhile, the USDA decided that since a different approach would be needed in each state, having the colleges participate would be too time-consuming. Almost every state had a land grant college and each college head and his associates felt that his state had a problem that was different from those of their neighbors; and a great deal of time would be spent discussing a single question before an acceptable answer was found for all.

Some college presidents, on the other hand, wanted all the government assistance they could obtain for their respective schools, but they did not want the federal government telling them how to spend their money or run their institutions. The federal government was unwilling to relinquish control—at least to the degree that some of the college administrators had asked—and an endless series of debates took place. Some colleges even tried to influence policy in the USDA on the theory that their representatives knew more about local conditions than officials in Washington, which was true in some cases. According to Wallace assistant Rudolph M. "Spike" Evans, after "more practical people" started to run the program, the members of the USDA learned a lot more about conditions, and the agitation ceased.

During the summer of 1937 Evans spent a great deal of time with representatives of the various land grant colleges and personnel in the USDA trying to develop a more satisfactory basis of cooperation between the two. At the same time an effort was being made to fit the SCS, which to some degree was duplicating the work of the Forest Service in planting trees and furnishing educational services, into the USDA.[13]

The need for better understanding and closer cooperation between the USDA and the state agencies, especially the land grant colleges, also was apparent. New planning and arrangements to guide this collaborative effort were needed. In fact in 1936 the Association of Land Grant Colleges and Universities (ALGCU) appointed a committee on federal-state relations to work with a USDA committee on this question. A series of joint meetings were held, and finally on July 8, 1938 at Mt. Weather, Virginia an acceptable agreement was reached.[14]

Under the Mt. Weather Agreement land-use planning was to be integrated with the action program. The farmers were to become the basis of the system, participate in local planning, and bring their knowledge of conditions at the local level to bear on the national programs. The state extension services, on the other hand, were to create agricultural land-use planning committees as part of the agricultural program building committees, whose work would be correlated on a statewide basis by a state agricultural land-use program or policy committee. In theory this was to help tie the direct line of administration reaching from the USDA to the farmer and thus help democratize the national farm program.

Analysis and land-use planning at the community level was to be carried through from the county and state to the national level, which presupposed planning by the USDA and the local and state committees. Whatever planning had been done up to this point had been confined largely to the coordination at the administrative level of planning by the action agencies.[15]

The Mt. Weather Agreement proposal to establish a land-use planning committee in each county comprising at least ten farmers, the county agent, and an official of the local action agency fanned the flames of a new discontent. The arrangements at the state level were similar to those at the county level, in that the extension director became the chairman of the state committee comprised of farmers and a state official from each action agency. As a consequence, the Extension Service, which once had been the only agency in the USDA with a field force, now found itself "outnumbered at both county and state levels by representatives of the better financed and at times more vigorous newcomers." Later these committees came under vigorous attack from the AFBF, which feared they were developing into a rival organization.[16]

A feeling had developed, perhaps more pronounced than ever before, that since this was a farmers' program and the need for college professors and "brain-trusters" had passed, the time had come for the farmers to run their own programs. More of those who once had been local committeemen now were becoming state committeemen, and those who had been state committeemen were becoming regional directors. One such person was Rudolph M. "Spike" Evans, who had been associated with the AAA in Iowa, then came to Washington to be another of Wallace's assistants, and finally became administrator of the AAA.

Tolley believed the people in administrative policymaking seemed to be interested in receiving checks and getting largesse from the government, not in agricultural readjustment and in the betterment of the conditions of the tenants and farm laborers. The general feeling was:

> Now at last we have this law that we needed—the AAA of 1938. We've got the political set-up that will keep it going so that [we] who are in will get what's coming to us. That would be the best thing. We don't care for any more innovations and we don't want any more of this high-powered planning. We'll continue this way.

Many of these administrators also began to look to Henry Wallace as the next president of the United States. "And Henry Wallace," said Tolley, ". . . began to look at this group as the people who would enable him to be President. While he was writing to the 'yogiman' and looking for 'devils' and so on, he at the same time was cultivating this group of agrarian fundamentalists."[17]

Meanwhile, events took an additional turn for the worse. By the late summer and early fall of 1938 cotton and wheat were selling for uncomfortably low prices, and vast surpluses had accumulated. The tobacco growers were bitterly dissatisfied with their acreage allotments, and the farm income for 1938 was expected to be lower than in 1937. News columnists Joseph Alsop and Robert Kintner observed, "After five years of continuous effort by Henry Wallace, the farm situation is just about as bad as it can be."[18]

Reports of a seething farm rebellion were also circulating. A farm speech prepared for New Deal primary candidates in Georgia omitted the name of Henry Wallace for fear of booing from the audience. Anti–New Deal newspapers such as the *Chicago Tribune* featured stories about farm revolts in Indiana, Kansas, Nebraska, Illinois, and other middle western states, and left the impression that a widespread farm revolt was imminent. To complicate matters Wallace and the administration were caught between the farmers' clamor for high prices and the consumers' threat not to pay them. Wallace and his associates worked continuously on the most democratic system they could devise to achieve a sensible compromise, but they had not succeeded by the fall of 1938.[19]

A 1938 poll on "Farmer Opinions on Best and Worst Parts of the New Deal" in the cotton and corn belts, and the northern tier of states including North Dakota, South Dakota, Minnesota, Wisconsin, and Michigan, indicated that:

> The AAA farm programs were most frequently named as the best part of the New Deal in every region, by all degrees of education, and those favorable or neutral to the New Deal, but not by those opposed. Legislation stabilizing the banking system was second for the whole group, followed in order by Rural Electrification, the Civilian Conservation Corps, and better farm credits.

One striking feature of the poll was the high proportion—18.1 percent—of the farmers in the "north region," mostly in Minnesota, Wisconsin, and Michigan, who saw nothing good in the New Deal; and the high proportion—32.1 percent—of the cotton-belt farmers who thought the stabilization of the banks was the best part of the New Deal program. Farmers agreed that relief or the WPA was the worst part of the New Deal. Government spending, the unbalanced budget, and the increasing national debt were a poor second, followed by war preparations, too friendly a policy toward organized labor, and the AAA programs. Roughly half the objections to the farm program were over the whole idea, and the other half over the delays, details, or methods of administration.

Many northern dairy farmers thought the New Deal was not worth the cost. They were worried about the reciprocal trade treaties, which they honestly believed increased farm imports. The corn-belt farmers, on the other hand, were more concerned with the imminence of war and the legalization of liquor sales. Southern farmers strongly objected to relief and were more antilabor than farmers in the other regions. The objections to relief in all regions were due partly to the increased costs of farm labor. According to generally accepted belief, hard work and thrift were rural virtues, and relief given on the basis of need instead of work placed a premium on improvidence and was a moral affront to the average farmer. Complaints also were voiced that relief employees did not work hard enough and lived too well. Farmers in general were defenders of the traditional virtues.

Banking legislation, rural electrification, the Civilian Conservation Corps, and better farm credits were the first choices of nearly a third of the farmers polled. Those who condemned the New Deal often did so without offering a rational explanation for their views. College men tended to list reciprocal trade agreements as constituting the best part of the New Deal, while men with a grade school education tended to regard such agreements as the worst.[20]

The reorganization of the USDA in 1938 came at a rather unfortunate time. How much this had been inspired by dissatisfaction with the operations of the AAA, the farmers' protests in the spring and summer of 1938, sagging farm prices, fear of defeat in the congressional elections that fall, and the political ambitions of Henry Wallace and those around him may never be known. But such a reorganization had been under consideration for a period of time and was a well-kept secret. Among the uninformed was H. R. Tolley, administrator of the AAA, who was stung by it more than anyone else because he had always thought of himself as a loyal and faithful lieutenant of the secretary and looked upon his transfer to the Bureau of Agricultural Economics as a demotion.

Sentiment, however, had been building up against Tolley as AAA administrator. Some originated with staunch New Dealers such as Senator Joseph F. Guffey of Pennsylvania, who shortly after the election of 1936 wrote Wallace that it was not always possible for a busy man like Wallace to keep his hands on everything his subordinates were doing, but was quick to add, "There had been a very great lack of cooperation since Mr. Chester Davis retired as Administrator." Too many reactionaries, in his opinion, were administering the AAA; Roosevelt had done more for the farmers than for labor, but labor seemed to be more appreciative than the farmers for what the New Deal was doing for them. Guffey also stated that continued good relations between Capitol Hill and the USDA depended to a considerable extent on a change in the manner in which some of Wallace's subordinates were carrying out the farm program.[21]

Others criticized Tolley because he had been a professor, was too academic as an economist, did not have enough of a farm background, weighed things too much, too long, was too reflective, and had dealt with government employees most of his life. "You know," said Samuel Bledsoe, "if you know too much sometimes it can be just as bad as not knowing anything. Lots of times it helps you not to know very much. Then you can made decisions, and lots of times they are the right decisions."[22]

The big issue was whether to have practical farmers in command of an action program or whether to lean on the more professional types such as the Extension Service and the farm management groups. The farmers themselves had a strong preference for the practical farmer types, and the land grant colleges for the other. The feeling had grown that those who knew farmers and could talk to them were needed more than ever in the agricultural action programs.[23]

Many New Dealers feared that once the farmers were in better economic shape they would return to the Republican party, and that the only reason they voted Democratic was because of the effectiveness of the AAA and other programs. The more politically oriented within the administration recognized that the committee system with its state, county, and local committees was an amazing arrangement, even though they did not talk about it or emphasize it.[24]

Tolley was convinced that his transferal from the AAA to the BAE was part of the grand design to make Henry Wallace president of the United States. Wallace, reminisced Tolley,

> felt the need consciously or subconsciously of an organization among farm people to back his candidacy when the time came. This great farmers group, farm committeemen, state, county, and local, was the making of such an organization. It couldn't become such an organization unless something direct and deliberate were done about it. There were people who were sponsoring it and talking to Henry Wallace about it. I don't know who was doing this—maybe "Spike" Evans. I never was told . . . maybe Paul H. Appleby, maybe any number of people in the Triple-A or directly connected with it—committeemen and so on. . . . Any or all of them might very well have said or suggested that maybe somebody with political ambitions, political desires, and so on, should be head of this organization now, preparatory for two years hence, and Henry Wallace finally agreed.[25]

Among those to resign following the reorganization of the AAA and BAE, in protest to the way in which this reorganization was accomplished, were: Alfred D. Stedman, who was scheduled to remain as assistant administrator of the AAA but instead returned to his old job as Washington reporter of the *Pioneer Press* and *St. Paul Dispatch* at half the salary he had been getting with the AAA; Jesse Tapp, also an assistant administrator of the AAA, who would have gone over into the new marketing and regulatory unit; and F. R. Wilcox, director of Marketing and Marketing Research Division.

Wallace explained that the reorganization was necessary to unify the work of the local and state planning units and integrate them on a national basis and to aid the proper functioning of the many new activities that Congress had authorized in recent years. Such an integration became urgent after the Mt. Weather Agreement committed the colleges and the USDA to the principles of democratic procedures and gave the farmers a voice in the formation, correlation, and localization of the agricultural programs. An expanded BAE, with Tolley as head of the general planning, was to establish part of the machinery to integrate state and local with general planning and to be responsible for the program formulation activities of the USDA.[26]

Middle western newspapers viewed this as the most drastic shakeup of a major government department since Roosevelt took office, and observed that the reorganization was announced after Wallace took a tour of the states in the Southwest and Middle West to study the reactions of the farmers to the 1938 agricultural programs. Cotton farmers had a record supply of 25 million bales, more than double the 11 million bales used by the domestic mills and the export market the previous year; and farmers complained that prices were 25 percent lower than in 1937 despite the fact that 7 million acres had been removed from production that year. Wheat prices were 50 percent below 1937 and a record supply of 1.1 billion bushels was on hand.[27] The *Chicago Tribune,* a vitriolic foe of the New Deal, described the reorganization as an effort to strengthen the tottering control of the USDA over the farmers because it feared the loss of large blocs of house seats in the corn and wheat states in the November elections. A statement issued by a conference of cotton growers and southern congressmen a week before the reorganization was announced declared the plight of the cotton farmers to be as bad as ever and ''put the administration on its toes.''[28]

Wallace had good reason to be worried because the heavy loss of supporting congressmen in the corn and wheat states of the Middle West reflected dissatisfaction with low farm prices and AAA controls. Democratic losses were greater numerically in the industrial states, but in the wheat and corn states the losses in terms of percentage were more severe. To Wallace it seemed clear that the election results indicated farmers in the corn and wheat sections wanted something positive done to help their income. The big question was how this could be done constructively.[29]

Meanwhile more than forty bills embracing monetary changes, export subsidies, rigid price-fixing, subsidies on domestic consumption, unlimited production, tariff reduction, and other related topics were being prepared for introduction as soon as Congress convened. The AFBF, the Grange, and the Farmers' Union, the big three general farmer organizations, were agreed they did not want an outright repeal of the AAA, and also appeared close to agreement on monetary reform. The Grange wanted a reasonable profit based on the cost of production, "exactly as all other lines of business demand," but "with an insistence that individual farmers be allowed to work out their own affairs without government interference or restrictions." The Farmers' Union, on the other hand, demanded that prices for farm products be based on a fair exchange with industrial goods in order to insure farmers cost of production and a "two-price" system to dispose of the surplus commodities. Both the Farmers' Union and the Grange insisted that the federal program foster protection of the family-sized farm and that it keep soil conservation independent of the commodity programs. USDA officials also wanted to retain the production control features of the existing law but make it more effective, while Wallace talked about processing taxes to finance the programs, a two-price system that would enable the depressed third of the population to obtain farm products below the prevailing price levels, and lending rates on farm products that would not restrict movements into the export market.[30]

Spike Evans, Tolley's successor as head of the AAA, rose from the ranks and was proof that Wallace wanted to staff the agency with practical "down-to-earth" men who could speak to the farmers. A native of Cedar Rapids, Iowa and a graduate of Iowa State College in civil engineering, Evans was effective in communicating directly to farm folks and their representatives. He had an intimate knowledge of the programs and the inner workings of the USDA. He had been chairman of the first corn-hog committee organized under the original AAA, and chairman of the Iowa Agricultural Conservation Committee before coming to Washington, D.C. in the fall of 1936 as an assistant to Wallace. In this new capacity he devoted his full time to the various programs and agencies, kept his superior informed, and saw that letters addressed to the USDA by congressmen were answered.[31]

Final preparations for the referenda on cotton and tobacco were being made when Evans took office. The results that December were going to be looked upon as a test of sentiment in the South toward the crop control law. AAA officials believed that approval of the proposals would put the administration in a strong position to insist that Congress do little more with the existing farm legislation except to reenact the processing tax that would provide for benefit payments. But rejection of the marketing quotas a month after the heavy Democratic losses in the midwestern farm belt could force the administration to accept basic changes in the law.[32]

Wallace quickly interpreted the acceptance of the quotas by the cotton growers and the rejection of marketing controls by the flue-cured tobacco and rice growers to mean permanence for the farm program, because the decisive vote for cotton marketing quotas was more significant, in his opinion, than the vote on the other crops. On the one hand, the cotton farmers realized there was little prospect that the foreign and domestic market would absorb enough of their crops to bring the supply down to manageable proportions without a continuation of the existent control measures, while the rejection of the quotas by the tobacco and rice growers was based on the belief that their price and supply situations were not serious enough to warrant marketing restrictions for the following year. As far as Wallace was concerned, the referenda decisions were sufficient proof of economic democracy at work in the operation of a farm program.[33]

Critics, however, charged that the referenda were not democratic because the producers of cotton, tobacco, and rice were the only producers eligible to vote, and the consumers who had to pay the higher prices and outnumbered the producers did not vote. Furthermore, the cotton farmers simply voted on whether marketing quotas were going to be imposed, instead of on acreage restrictions.[34]

Meanwhile, a greatly distressed Tolley tried to put the unified program idea that Wallace had been talking about into practice by the establishment of the Division of State and Local Planning in the BAE. Each county was to have a land-use planning committee composed of representatives of the farmers, the FSA and the SCS if they were represented in the county, the FCA, and the county agent who was to become the secretary and manager of the county land-use planning committee. The county land-use planning committee, somewhat of a citizens' group, was to make suggestions on what the agricultural program of the county should be, and the changes desirable in the existing one. These suggestions were to be brought together at the state level through the state land-use planning committee that would be operating, and then at the national level through the Division of State and Local Planning headed by Bushrod W. Allin in the BAE.[35]

A technique also was devised to obtain directly from a representative group of farm people their thoughts on the state of agriculture, the programs, and the way they were being administered. The Division of Farm Surveys, headed by a social psychologist who brought together a small group of psychologists and statisticians who knew agriculture and farm life, assumed the nature of an opinion gathering agency. Carl F. Taeusch, formerly of the Harvard Business School, directed a program that encouraged local farm groups to discuss local and national problems.

During the first half of 1939 the state and county planning committees, the farm surveys, the discussion groups, and the BAE displayed a sense of mission and urgency. Even Wallace took part in the discussions. The personnel, recalled Tolley, believed they were doing the right thing in the right

way, and this new effort would bring about the desired results; but soon the
feeling developed that not much was happening in the other agencies, especially the AAA, which did not welcome the activities of the BAE. The AAA
had its own program and its own head who knew what the AAA wanted to
do and how, and made it plain that the agency did not need the help and advice of the BAE.

Evans as head of the AAA was a man of action, not a philosopher,
who liked to move quickly and get things done, and who probably had been
annoyed by Tolley's academic approach to things. Evans also had a forceful
expression and was an excellent salesman. "When I worked with him," said
John Hutson, "I felt that he could take two or three catch phrases and do as
much with them to influence a group as anyone with whom I had ever been
associated in administrative work."[36]

Tolley was convinced that the reorganization of the USDA had been
prompted by the desire to elevate Wallace to a higher political office; while
others in the USDA ignored, evaded, or discussed the issue privately among
their closest friends, Hutson came around to the Tolley point of view. Hutson, as an assistant adminstrator of the AAA, at first thought that the secretary's office wanted "more of a doer than a thinker" as head of the AAA,
but after working with Evans for a while he began to wonder whether the reorganization did not have a political significance to it. He said,

> There seemed to be more emphasis on the politics of the committee-
> men. Also, there seemed to be more political action—more interest on
> the part of committeemen in political work after the change was made.
> . . . I had noticed that there were certain offices being set up in the field
> that seemed to me to be more concerned with types of people that
> would become affiliated with the Democratic party or had been af-
> filiated, and were mending fences a little bit for the general Democratic
> organization. That was before the boom for Wallace had come to the
> fore.[37]

Talk about Wallace as a possible successor of FDR began as early as
1934. That spring the *Washington Post,* which had been purchased by
Eugene Meyer, Jr., the former governor of the Federal Reserve Board, set
forth various arguments in favor of Wallace. If he survived the political
wars he would be only fifty-two years old in 1940. Wallace as a person was
"modest, moral and magnetic" and "most of all he had a plan." He
tolerated inflation, regimentation, agricultural controls, curtailments, and
laws affecting supply and demand until he could get the tariff down all over
the world and foreign trade was restored. He could easily become the
prophet of his times and a presidential candidate. Such a commentary coming from a Republican newspaper would assume added significance, said
the *Des Moines Tribune,* if Wallace succeeded in leading the farmers out of

"the wilderness of mortgages and overproduction." With a score or more years of public service ahead of him, Wallace had enough time "to inscribe his name among the greats of the nation's history."[38]

After the overwhelming victory of 1936, people were talking about Wallace in terms of his availability in 1940 and Wallace was aware of it. His success in keeping the farm belt in the Roosevelt columns in 1936 gave him more confidence in his political abilities. In fact the groundwork for a liberal party had been built in the Middle West. Those closest to him—Paul Appleby, J. D. Le Cron, "Spike" Evans, and others—had become aware of his political potential, and talked more in terms of a Democratic nomination than a farmer-labor alignment. The questions that remained to be answered were whether Wallace had popular appeal, and would Roosevelt favor him as his successor.[39]

Developments after Evans became administrator of the AAA tended to confirm Wallace's desires to use the AAA as a political base. First there were the personnel changes. Rexford Tugwell, a political liability to the USDA, stepped down as under secretary of agriculture and as head of the RA. He was succeeded as under secretary of agriculture by M. L. Wilson, who was more acceptable to the farmers and the land grant colleges, and as head of the RA by Will Alexander, who had been his deputy. Wilson's successor as assistant secretary of agriculture was Harry L. Brown, who had experience farming and was former head of the Extension Service in Georgia and director of AAA activities in the state. The AAA under Tolley had maintained more of a scientific and nonpartisan stance, while under Evans its political potential became pronounced. Grover Hill, another farmer and former close associate of Marvin Jones, became assistant secretary of agriculture after Harry Brown resigned in late 1939 to accept a position with the TVA. Even more significant was the appointment of Claude Wickard, a director of the AAA, as under secretary of agriculture after Wilson became director of the Extension Service in early 1940. Wickard was a successful farmer from Indiana who was familiar with political maneuverings, and a person Evans believed could help the political aspirations of Wallace. Wickard came from a pivotal state and was very active in the political campaign of 1940.[40]

Also relevant to the political aspirations of Wallace was the elimination of the commodity sections of the AAA in March 1936 and the creation of five divisions that would help decentralize the program and bring the administration closer to the farmers themselves. The potential of such an arrangement was sensed by the more politically astute who were aware of the maneuverings of those close to Wallace. The efforts to aid the depressed farmers and protect others from crop losses and surpluses through crop insurance and the ever-normal granary also had its political appeal. The broadening of Wallace's public pronouncements, after Roosevelt was reelected, that transcended the field of agriculture had an unhappy meaning to the politically sensitive. The obvious lack of interest of the AAA in the research and planning efforts of the BAE under Tolley after the reorganization of the USDA would tend to confirm that the reorganization was designed not so much for the purpose of achieving better coordination between the land-use planning work of the USDA and the states and counties, as it was to aid the political ambitions of Wallace. The observations of John B. Hutson, Samuel B. Bledsoe, Rudolph M. Evans, and Tolley in general would support this view.

New Deal Farm Policy: An Appraisal

THE FEDERAL GOVERNMENT ATTEMPTED TO RESOLVE the almost unresolvable problems of the farm with greater vigor and optimism during the New Deal years than in any other period in our history. Decisions reached during these years more or less set the pace for policymaking in the post-World War II decades for Republicans and Democrats alike.

New Deal farm policy concerned itself with a series of complex and interrelated programs that aimed to elevate the long-range, as well as the short-range, social and economic position of the farmers, and involved more than the attainment of stated price objectives. The policy was as comprehensive and farsighted in character as political considerations permitted, seemingly contradictory and inconsistent, and the product of many minds and influences at work outside and inside the USDA before and after the Roosevelt administration took office. The USDA, which was among the—if not *the*—most prestigious of all federal government agencies of cabinet rank, played a crucial and dominant role in all this. But other federal agencies set up outside the USDA participated too; and since their actions had a definite bearing on the farmer, they and their programs must be considered a part of the general overall farm policy picture.

Agencies which liberal groups believed were more constructive and creative in their approach than the AAA included: the Federal Emergency Relief Administration (FERA), which during the course of its existence provided many rural communities with relief that previously had been without it; the Resettlement Administration (RA), which became an official part of the USDA only after Rexford Tugwell had stepped down as its director, and was eventually absorbed by the newly created Farm Security Administration (FSA); the Rural Electrification Administration (REA), which did extensive work before it became affiliated with the USDA in 1939 in preparing the groundwork for the electrification of many farms that had been without electricity; the Tennessee Valley Authority (TVA), whose influence on the agriculture of the South and many rural communities was incalculable; and the Farm Credit Administration (FCA), established as a private lending agency outside the government.[1]

An assessment of the New Deal in agriculture must begin with the AAA, which was the most publicized of the farm agencies. The philosophy behind the AAA was that farmers, who were in a highly competitive business, could improve their financial position by employing methods the prudent businessmen used: namely, adjusting their production to effective demand. The reduction or benefit payment, which was financed by the processing tax, enabled the farmer to secure his income in two different parts—first when the farmer sold his product, and second when he got his reduction payment.[2]

The general objectives of the much-heralded first AAA, which were also the objectives of the acts of 1936 and 1938, were to overcome the disparities between farm and nonfarm prices by granting benefit payments to producers of basic commodities cooperating with the federal government to balance production with demand, thereby bringing farmers a return more in line with their incomes for the years 1909–1914. Phase one of the AAA came to an end with the invalidation of the first AAA in 1936.[3]

Phase two began with the enactment of the Soil Conservation and Domestic Allotment Act (SCDAA) of 1936, which likewise placed emphasis on increasing the income of the farmers not through acreage controls and marketing agreements, as had been the case with the first AAA, but through the adoption of land use and farm practices that conserved and built up the fertility of the soil. Phase three began with the AAA of 1938 that sought "a middle course" between the programs of the AAA of 1933 and the SCDAA of 1936. This was deemed necessary because of a conviction that the adjustment value of the program begun in 1933 had been obscured by the droughts of 1934 and 1936, which had a greater effect on acreage and marketing adjustments than what had been planned under the program.

The lesson learned from the droughts of 1934 and 1936 was that a more permanent solution of the price imbalance was likely to be found in conservation rather than in acreage reduction or marketing agreements. This belief, which had been growing in 1935, was strongly reinforced by the rendering of the first AAA unconstitutional. But then the unusually favorable growing conditions of 1937 and the prospects of excellent crops in 1938 exposed the administration and the farmers to the inadequacy of the conservation approach in years of bumper crops, and emphasized the need for a broader program based on the control of a larger reserves storage, if the problems of the drought and surplus were going to be overcome. The

AAA responded to this challenge by establishing an ever-normal granary to provide for larger reserves as added protection against the drought, and to substitute surplus control—that is, through the control of marketing in interstate commerce—as a means of combating surpluses. The new AAA, or phase three, in addition provided for the beginnings of a federal crop insurance program for wheat.[4]

A reassessment of the three phases of the Agricultural Adjustment Administration calls for an evaluation of the price goals it sought, the effectiveness of acreage restrictions in controlling production, the accomplishments of the conservation program by 1939, the ever-normal granary, and the federal crop insurance program for wheat. An evaluation of New Deal agricultural policy is complicated by the fact that some of the programs were barely getting started when the New Deal came to an end, and were redirected after the outbreak of World War II.

Opinions naturally differed as to what the goals of the New Deal in agriculture were and how these goals were going to be achieved. Henry A. Wallace, M. L. Wilson, Howard R. Tolley, Mordecai Ezekiel, and members of the Wisconsin school of agricultural economics agreed that the primary objective of the AAA was to raise farm prices to parity levels, but also recognized that something more than the attainment of higher prices and incomes was needed to resolve the farmers' dilemma. This being the case, it can be said that the New Deal had achieved its objective only in part by the time it came to an end in 1939. The prices of most farm commodities in August 1939—the month before the Nazis invaded Poland—were low in comparison with parity or August 1929 price levels. Of the prices received for farm commodities, only one—for beef cattle—had attained parity by August 1939. On the other hand corn was 59 percent of parity; cotton 66 percent; wheat 50; butterfat 59; hogs 60; chickens 93; and eggs 49. The income of the farm population, which had some significant bearing on the purchase of farm products, after dropping to a low of $39 billion in 1933, had reached only $66 billion in 1939 and not the $79 billion of 1929.[5]

The farmers still complained about the cost of wages, which they blamed for the high cost of many of the articles they bought in the early 1940s. The average farm tax bill in 1940 was $450 or twice what it had been in 1910–1915. Middlemen, because of higher wages and rents, took a higher toll on the food products that passed through their hands, made them cost more to the consumer, and left less for the producer. The farmer in 1939 received only 41 percent of the average dollar spent by the consumer for food as compared with 52 percent in 1913–1915.[6]

The parity price formula did not create serious difficulties in the early New Deal years because it was employed as a broad, general directive to improve the economic status of agriculture, and also because Congress had given the USDA considerable latitude in applying the formula. But this period of grace came to an end. Beginning with the spring of 1941 Congress insisted on a more rigorous interpretation, as seen in the mandatory farm commodity loans of 85 percent of parity, the 90 percent loans, and the 110 percent ceilings that followed. The restriction in the range of administrative decision came at a time when the economic effects of the war were beginning to be felt, and made price relationships of the past unrealistic. The violent changes that the war brought in the value of goods and services produced exposed the weaknesses of parity prices.

Parity prices, in short, whether they took 1909–1914 or some other period as their base or whether they took the regional and quality differentials of a commodity into account—much as these refinements helped—were not suitable goals for a farm policy simply because the function of prices was to guide and direct economic activity. In the words of one farm economist, parity prices were "backward looking" and represented "the dead hand of the past." It was difficult if not impossible to force agriculture into a set of price relationships that existed years ago.[7]

The efforts to control production through the restriction of acreages and the adoption of conservation and adjustment practices can hardly be adjudged a success. The New Dealers had been inspired to some extent by American manufacturers and industrialists who had been able to slow down the volume of their production in periods of low consumer demand; but they soon discovered, if they had been unaware of it before, that restricting millions of agricultural producers was far more difficult than restricting comparatively few industrial producers.[8]

The farmer's instinct was to produce in order to feed, clothe, and otherwise provision the world; he hated to cut down his production deliberately. However expert he was in his work, there was little that he could do to control the quality and the quantity of his wheat, raw cotton, leaf tobacco, and other crops. Proper seeding, spraying, and care in the harvest could and did help the bounty and character of the crop; but a great deal of this could be undone, sometimes overnight, by heavy storms, floods, droughts, untimely frost, or the ravages of crop pests—all beyond, or largely beyond, the control of man. The droughts of 1934 and 1936 demonstrated that the forces of nature often were more significant in affecting the volume of the crop than was human planning.[9]

Before World War II a shrinking farm labor force was able to produce a surplus for a growing population of consumers because technical and mechanical advances steadily increased productivity. The census showed a gain of only 7 percent in the total population between 1935 and 1940, but a gain of 12 percent in agricultural production and 28 percent in the productivity of each farm worker. Clearly the New Dealers had been unable to retire land from cultivation fast enough to overcome the effects of mechanical and technical efficiency in increasing production. Ironically, one of the great contributions of the AAA, especially to the agriculture of the South, was that it helped increase the yields by encouraging planting on better land and cultivating with improved methods. The organized staple cotton growers of twelve counties in Mississippi, who were among the most prosperous cotton producers in the South, reduced their acreage from 1.7 million acres in 1930 to 1 million acres in 1939; but increased their yields 200 to 400 pounds per acre. About 581,000 bales of cotton were harvested in 1930 and again in 1933; by 1938 the yield had increased to 835,000 bales.[10]

One lesson learned from the AAA was that it was very difficult to contract production in a highly mechanized society such as the United States had become. Expansion came much more easily to the more developed countries that possessed improvement skills and techniques and the accessibility of capital than to the less-developed nations. Agricultural production under such circumstances was caught in the forward surge, and those who spoke for agriculture often were prone to ascribe the emerging surpluses to shortcomings in the market instead of to maladjustments in production.[11]

Soil conservation became a key objective during phase two of the AAA. Only the more concerned citizen was attracted to the concept of soil conservation. The interest of the general public, strange as it may sound, was not aroused until the problem of agricultural surpluses became acute. The reduction in the acreage of the basic crops under the AAA reduced the drain on soils, which was recognized as being in the public interest. This phase of the AAA had greater appeal to the nonfarm people, who were not especially favorable to plans to secure higher prices and income for the farmers. Conservation specialists cited the drought in the Great Plains states, and the resulting dust storms, as evidence of the pressing need for more effective measures. Support for research in conservation resulted in its rapid expansion, and the more comprehensive surveys made from year to year added to our knowledge of the problem.

The progress made in conservation by the time the New Deal came to an end was only encouraging, at best. According to the Soil Conservation Service (SCS), some 200 million acres of cropland in use in 1939 were subject to "moderate or severe erosion," but by that time farm conservation plans had been developed for only 39 million acres. Although there is no objective measure of the amount of erodible lands farmed in a manner aimed to maintain fertility of the soil in 1939, it probably was less than the 39 million acres for which plans had been developed. The SCS estimated that as a result of its program about 75,000 farm families were operating on fully protected land. The 75,000 farm families formed a small percentage of the total of 3.6 million familes on erodible land. It was apparent that although public awareness had been developed, erosion still was an unresolved problem when World War II broke out.[12]

Another development encouraged by the New Deal was the cultivation of soil-improving crops such as legumes, lespedeza, and soybeans. The range of these crops was extended northward, and the production of soybeans became a major item. The growing of flax likewise spread into a number of states, and experiments with other crops, particularly minor ones, were carried on over most of the United States. Hybrid corn was being used more extensively, and yields double the previous ones were reported in many areas. These changes and experiments were expected to have far-reaching effects on the economy.[13]

The controversial ever-normal granary, defined by its principal architect and exponent, Henry A. Wallace, as "a definite system whereby supplies following years of drought or other great calamity would be large enough to take care of the consumer, [and] under which the farmer would not be unduly penalized in years of favorable weather," also must figure in any evaluation of the New Deal. To avoid a repetition of the Farm Board experience of huge surpluses and sagging prices it became necessary, after the loan program had reached a certain point, "to keep the granary from running over by some practical program of production adjustment." Wallace considered storing grain in the soil instead of in the bin also a part of the ever-normal granary.[14]

Something akin to the ever-normal granary had been in operation from the beginning. During the drought of 1934 corn stored on farms under the first corn loan in 1933 helped provide food supplies for livestock. In 1939 a loan and storage program was in effect for wheat, the number one food crop, and for corn, the number one feed crop. Wheat reserves were held in the ever-normal granary through a federal crop insurance program under which the wheat growers put aside a portion of their crops as premiums to offset possible crop failures. By storing corn, a nonperishable potential supply of pork, beef, dairy products, eggs, and other products was being carried over.[15]

Administration leaders saw that the ever-normal granary system accommodated the defense requirements of the nation soon after the war began. For a time there was some "panicky buying," especially of sugar, which ended when the country realized that the prevailing program and the ever-normal granary provided for production as well as for reserves.

The reserve supply of agricultural products was exceptionally strong by 1940. The total crop production in 1939, although about 1 percent lower than that of the previous year, was nearly 4 percent above the average of the 1923–1932 period. By the end of the 1939–1940 crop season, the nation had reserves appreciably larger than those of the period 1935–1939, and this caused some to question the efficacy of the program. The adjustment of supply to demand was a continuing objective, and the first program of the AAA, was designed to reduce burdensome surpluses. The carry-over into

1940, however, of crops such as cotton and tobacco was in part a product of the recent catastrophic changes in the world market, the difficulties the country had in making exports, and the fact that the ever-normal granary deliberately provided for carry-overs that were larger than those of the past, particularly of wheat and corn. The means employed to achieve these larger carry-overs were a combination of acreage allotments, commodity loans, marketing quotas, special export programs, and storage in the ever-normal granary.

Wallace insisted that the planning for larger reserves was a product of the earlier years and not a response to the immediate war or national defense needs. He stated repeatedly that the droughts of 1934 and 1936, and the AAA policy of 1938, had prepared the groundwork. The supplies of wheat and corn in 1940, Wallace said, were at levels considered desirable by the AAA. The wheat reserve was about two, and the corn reserve about three, times the pre-AAA levels. Supplies of some types of tobacco were in excess of their goals, in part because the growers in 1939 chose not to use marketing quotas, and because of the war. The supply of cotton was excessive mainly because the war cut off most of the foreign market.[16]

Passage of the Federal Crop Insurance Act of 1938 marked the start of a new, voluntary program, purely experimental in character, to apply initially only to wheat. Proponents viewed the crop insurance program as being the agricultural counterpart of the Social Security Act which furnished unemployment insurance for nonagricultural workers. During the first year of the program, 1939, about 56,000 farmers received in excess of 10 million bushels of wheat or the cash equivalent in indemnities for crops destroyed by forces beyond their control. This provided them with income that otherwise would have been lost, and enabled many farmers to maintain their customary standard of living, provide for their families, pay taxes, and meet other expenses. About 94 percent of the losses paid on the insured crop in 1939 was paid in counties of the nation where wheat was the chief crop and in many cases the only source of income. By 1940 many requests were received for the extension of insurance protection to crops such as corn, cotton, tobacco, citrus fruits, and vegetables, which from an insurance standpoint posed difficulties not posed by wheat. By 1941 the insurance program was extended to include cotton, a major commodity.[17]

These early-year experiences brought to the surface the weaknesses of the first crop insurance program. Many growers took advantage of the voluntary features of the insurance program, especially when the prospects for crops were poor, and the result was a heavy participation in sections of the country where potential loss was great and light participation in areas where the prospects for crops were much better. Losses, as a consequence, were out of line with the actuarial picture. Plans naturally were contemplated for the future that required the grower to insure for a longer period of time, and to insure his total acreage instead of only those acres in which a loss was likely to occur.[18]

The criticism most frequently made of the AAA as well as other New Deal programs was that they catered primarily to the commercial, wealthier, and more substantial members of the middle classes; that they rendered little, if any, assistance to the tenants and sharecroppers; and that the AAA, in particular, if it did anything for the members of the low-income groups, reduced them from tenants and sharecroppers to farm laborers or pushed them off the land completely. These beliefs, said M. L. Wilson, were held especially by those who were not farmers, who did not live in farm communities, and who did not know much about farming. These misapprehensions, however, were not entertained by those who were better acquainted with farming and who based their thinking on the assumption that the AAA legislation was temporary, that prices were going to rise, that the depression was going to end, and that the emergency legislation was going to disappear.[19]

One can argue, if one chooses to, that these changes had been going on for years before the New Deal came into office and continued years after the New Deal ended. The difficulties of the small farmers, for the most part, came from the technological changes that increased the output per worker and substituted capital for human labor. Mechanization and the need for more capital had far more to do with consolidation of farms than the organization of the AAA. The AAA undoubtedly hastened the consolidation of small farms into larger ones, especially in the cotton industry and in farming that employed migratory labor; and it also focused attention on a situation which had already been there for some time and to which very little attention had been given.[20]

That the AAA did little for the tenants, sharecroppers, and farm laborers is beyond dispute, although an exception has to be made for those who came under the classification of managing farm tenants. Relief for farm laborers never was a part of the AAA policy; consequently little relief, if any, could have been expected. The failure of the AAA to come to the aid of the sharecroppers and tenants, the members of the disinherited classes, may be attributed to a way of thinking that prevailed in agricultural circles, including that of educators, farm lobbyists, farm journalists, congressional leaders, and other members of the so-called agricultural establishment.

The objective of the USDA and the land grant colleges all along had been to establish prosperous farm families through the application of the best that practical research and science could offer. The assumption had been that this assistance could be rendered most effectively to those farmers who were accustomed to the family-farm system and had incomes from their operations that were sufficient to attain a satisfactory standard of living. Agricultural thinking, research, teaching, and extension work through the years prior to the New Deal had been concentrated almost exclusively on the well-managed farm, and this approach strongly influenced the AAA.[21]

Strong attitudes also prevailed in the rural areas, as well as in the USDA, regarding poor farmers and what should be done for them. These attitudes were brought to bear on congressmen and senators through the farm organizations to which the more successful farmers belonged, and they influenced decisions on the kind of assistance provided to tenants and sharecroppers. The general feeling of many landlords and employers was that if the rural poor received too much assistance, they would become independent and difficult to deal with. "If they moved away, the labor market would be tightened. If they became owners they also became competitors. If something had to be done, the last of these alternatives was preferable." This probably would not affect many, and those who climbed the ladder to proprietorship soon would acquire the outlook of their fellow proprietors.[22]

As a consequence, persons associated with the agricultural colleges, agricultural experiment stations, and the USDA seldom bothered with the sharecroppers, tenants, and other low-income farmers, largely from the belief that such people would not be able to climb into "the good income group." Small wonder then that agricultural institutions of higher education and research were ill informed or uninformed about the nature and the extent of poverty in the rural areas, and unprepared to face the problem.[23] Had the USDA chosen to face this problem directly, which was unlikely, it would have encountered a hardened resistance not merely from the substantial and wealthier farmers, but from many others who believed that agriculture held a slim future for depressed farm groups.

The belief had been fixed firmly that too many farmers were attempting to scratch out an existence from the soil and that it would be to their personal best interests and the best interests of agriculture for them to go to the cities for a livelihood. The USDA and perhaps most of the agricultural establishment more or less subscribed to this position, although ground was given on it after the RA, FSA, and the Bankhead–Jones Act became the law. Still, those who believed that the nation suffered from a surplus of farmers, as well as from a surplus of crops, had influential forces at work for them. One was a bloc of congressmen and senators from the states of the South and Middle West who had the necessary votes and were in command of strategic committees. A second was the mechanization of cotton farming, especially the introduction of the cotton picker, which came into greater prominence in the very late 1930s and naturally lessened the demand for tenants and sharecroppers. And third was the ominous threat of war and the likelihood that the demands of the defense and civilian industries would absorb all available farm labor for their factories and assembly lines.[24]

A small, persistent, and less influential group opposed the view that the time had come to eliminate surplus farmers from the land. Even before the threat of war became imminent, this group argued that the cities had unemployment problems of their own, that the problems of rural poverty could not be resolved by shifting or dumping the surplus farmers onto the cities, and that a genuine attempt had to be made to keep these people on the land, not through making available to them small, subsistence farms, but through the establishment of agricultural or even of collective farms.

But expecting the federal government to subsidize collective farms and colonies was expecting far too much, considering the state of public opinion and the fact that the tenants and sharecroppers represented the least influential elements in the country; they further were handicapped by the lack of good leadership, funds with which to make contributions to the political parties, and the opposition of large blocs of voters in the poll-tax states. The only friend they had in Washington, outside the Southern Tenant Farmers' Union whose influence was minimal, was the National Farmers' Union. The Union's strength was concentrated in the northern Great Plains states and it had slender financial resources compared with those of its more affluent rivals—the American Farm Bureau Federation (AFBF) and the National Grange.[25]

Despite the limitations in the intentions and the accomplishments of the AAA in behalf of the tenants, sharecroppers, and small farmers, and the opposition of rural public opinion toward such a policy, it would be a mistake to assume that the New Deal did as little for these elements as is sometimes imagined. There is much evidence to the contrary, especially when one looks at the work of agencies other than the AAA. Between 1933 and 1935 when the Resettlement Administration came into existence, at least four governmental agencies had been formed to deal with various phases of rural poverty. Insofar as immediate relief was concerned, the most significant of these was the FERA, whose work was not confined exclusively to the farmers.

FERA became law on May 12, 1933, the same day the AAA was placed on the statute books, and it provided relief for many rural communities. By November of that year its relief load included 11 percent of all rural farm families. Besides giving work project jobs to rural people, the FERA late in 1933 announced the purchase of over 200 million pounds of meat obtained through the AAA to be distributed in areas where relief standards were low. Other commodities also were given as a means of providing reasonable standards of sustenance. Early in the spring of 1934 a new plan was submitted that stipulated on April 1 civil works and direct relief programs would be replaced in rural areas and towns of less than 5,000 people with a program of rural rehabilitation. The new objective was to help individual families to become self-supporting.[26]

After February 1935 when almost 1 million farm families—including farm laborers—were receiving relief grants or rehabilitation loans, they began to leave the general relief rolls rapidly, especially after the expansion of the rural rehabilitation program and the partial return of agricultural prosperity. Figures in June 1935 indicated that nearly three-fourths of the heads of families on relief in June 1935 were farmers and that slightly more than one-fourth were farm laborers. Tenants other than sharecroppers made up more than one-half of the farm operators on relief; farm owners accounted for another third, and sharecroppers for nearly one-eighth. In the cotton areas, the sharecroppers were represented more heavily on the relief rolls than either the owners or other kinds of tenants.

The Bankhead–Jones Act, passed in 1937 in response to the mounting pressure for tenancy reform, failed to meet the expectations of the more hopeful. From its inception in 1937 through the fiscal year 1947, the tenant-purchase program provided for by the act made available loans amounting to $293 million to only 47,104 farmers. This was a very modest beginning considering the fact that there were still 1.8 million tenants in the country in 1945. At the rate that tenant purchases were being made, it was going to take nearly 400 years to make them all owners. Yet the more optimistic viewed this as an encouraging demonstration of a program that was going to be expanded on "a scale commensurate with the magnitude of the problem [and] as rapidly as our experience and resources will permit." However, the coming of World War II and the inflation of land prices that followed postponed the expansion of the program.

The slow progress of the tenant-purchase program under the Bankhead–Jones Act cannot be blamed solely on the USDA. The loans were too small to make possible an efficient use of family labor or yield a "maximum-adequate" income. Public opinion and Congress would not tolerate significant improvement in the status of tenants, sharecroppers, and farm laborers "on the government." In five successive appropriations beginning with the act of 1941, Congress deliberately stipulated that no loan could be extended for the purchase of a farm of 30 acres or more in the county in which the farm was located. This was chiefly the work of Representative Malcolm C. Tarver of Georgia, chairman of the appropriations subcommittee, who believed that the loans, which averaged $3,900 in his state, were "twice too high." In the face of such a climate of opinion it became almost impossible to create adequate farm units. This unsympathetic attitude was held by others besides the large landowners and those who believed that the number of farmers on the land had to be diminished. In the South, public and congressional opinion objected to "setting up" a tenant-purchase borrower above his neighbor; hence, if the status of the borrower's neighbor was low, that of the borrower would have to remain low, too. The feeling also was widespread among FSA personnel in the South that "a very modest improvement in the position of the farmers was all that could be expected.''[27]

The belated efforts of the federal government to improve the status of the tenants and sharecroppers encouraged action at the state level as well. The Farm Landlord and Tenant Relationship Act passed by the Oklahoma legislature in 1937, but repealed in 1939, was a pioneer step in this direction. The governors of the states of Arkansas and South Carolina also requested appropriate agencies to study the farm tenancy situation and to report to the next sessions of the legislatures; and comparable action was taken in Louisiana and Texas.[28]

Much has been made of the unwillingness of the larger farmers and landlords under the AAA to share the benefit payments fairly with their tenants. That many tenants—the exact number has never been made known and probably never will be—were deprived of their just dues is beyond doubt. But even if these payments had been shared fairly, sharecroppers and tenants would not have experienced significant economic progress. These payments would have purchased a few more of the necessities of life, and little else. The payments listed in the public record represent the landlord's share on land operated by a number of tenants, who in theory earned proportionate shares. Individual payments to the tenants do not appear in this record. Of significance is the fact that fully 46 percent of the almost 5.25 million farmers receiving payments under the AAA in 1938 received $40 or less for the year. Fully 33 percent received sums ranging from $40 to $100 annually, and less than 2 percent got sums ranging from $1,000 to $10,000. The numbers receiving sums of over $3,000 averaged about 0.07 percent.[29]

The incentive payments were nothing more than their name suggests, designed primarily to introduce better farming methods to those who had a stake in the land and were going to stay on it. There was little in the program, fraud or no fraud on the part of the landlords, that would have encouraged poorer farmers to remain on the land if they had alternatives to farming.

The New Deal did show some response to the needs of the tenants and farmers receiving small payments and to those who had been defrauded under the AAA. An amendment to the SCDAA sought to render greater assistance to tenants and farmers receiving small payments. The amendment protected tenants against lease changes that would increase the share of the landlord's payments; and they were assured a division of payments between landlords and tenants in proportion to the shares in the crop. Payments that amounted to less than $200 annually were to be scaled upward, according to a specific schedule. And beginning in 1939 all individual payments were limited to $10,000.[30]

Some of the criticisms leveled against the AAA were unfair, the products more of hindsight than foresight. It was expecting far too much of the New Deal to undo within a few years a system of tenancy and sharecropping that had been years in the making. To accomplish the task, years of painstaking research and planning, a high degree of cooperation, a sympathetic Congress and generous financial outlays over a long period of time, endless patience and goodwill, and some good luck were needed. Unfortunately, these ingredients did not exist in sufficient quantity. Ridding the nation of sharecropping and tenancy required something more, considerably more, than favorable decisions at the administrative level.

There were other reasons, too, for the decline in the number of farms that cannot be attributed exclusively to New Deal farm programs and policy. One was the resumption of industrial occupations by those who had taken refuge on farms during the height of the depression. For some people it meant moving back to the cities and towns, and for others it meant dropping minor agricultural operations without a change in residence as soon as the factories opened. Another reason was the growing number of foreclosures during the 1930s. The defense program also had its effect. Recruiting for service in the armed forces, the building of cantonments, and the expansion of industry offered opportunities, especially for laborers from the farms of the South.[31]

The most striking decrease in the number of farms occurred in the drought area that extended from the Canadian line to the Texas Panhandle. Part of this was due to the droughts of 1934, 1936, and other unfavorable years. Many farmers who withstood the first drought were forced to abandon their operations. Changes from grain farming, ranching, or cultivated crops also occurred. In some areas there were increases in part-time farming caused by persons moving from the cities back to the land.

The FSA must rank as one of the most forward-looking as well as one of the most bitterly opposed agencies sponsored by the New Deal. Apart from the tenant-purchase program it administered under the Bankhead–Jones Act, the FSA including the work of the RA, its predecessor organization, helped work out debt reductions totaling (as of May 1, 1941) almost $100 million for 145,000 indebted farmers through the voluntary farm debt adjustment committees established in every farming county. This represented a reduction of nearly 23 percent on debts that originally amounted to more than $445 million.[32]

The FSA discovered that many of the farmers were in difficulties because of illness and could not do a good day's work; and in cooperation with state and local medical societies, the FSA worked out a special medical care program for borrowers. This proved so popular with both physicians and FSA clients that health associations were organized in 634 counties in 31 states during the very late 1930s and early 1940s. By May 1, 1941 about 80,000 families or 300,000 people were obtaining medical care through these associations. In many cases FSA included enough money in its rehabilitation loans to enable the borrower to make his first annual payment to the county health association. This resulted both in swifter progress toward rehabilitation and, as the health and ability of the family to support itself improved, in larger repayment on the loans.

The FSA further realized that small farmers could not compete with the commercial farmers and encouraged borrowers to pool their resources to buy tractors, lime-spreaders, purebred bulls, seed fertilizer, and other farm and household supplies in large quantities at lower prices. Small farmers also began to sell their pigs, chickens, and truck crops cooperatively. Often the FSA included enough money in a rehabilitation loan for a borrower to pay his share of the cost of a combine, feed mill, terrace, or other equipment he could use cooperatively with his neighbors. Originally the loan included a sum that enabled the borrower to join a long-established cooperative. More than 300,000 low-income farm families were taking part in about 16,000 small coops started with FSA help.

From 1935, when the rehabilitation program was initiated, until 1941, the FSA loaned more than $516 million to 870,000 farm families, many of whom, judged by normal standards, were among the worst possible credit risks. By May 1, 1941 they had paid $182 million into the federal treasury, and the expectations were that fully 80 percent of the money loaned would be repaid eventually with interest. The annual cost of the rehabilitation loans—including losses—amounted to less than $75 for each family assisted, according to FSA sources. This sum was considered quite low for relief of any kind; estimated costs of work relief ranged from $350 to $800 per year.

As a result of FSA assistance, many farm families made rapid gains in their net worth, standards of living, and abilities to support themselves. A survey made at the end of the crop year of 1939 to determine the progress of 360,000 regular rehabilitation borrowers on FSA rolls disclosed they had increased their net worth beyond and above all debts—including obligations to the government—by almost $83 million since they had obtained their first loan. This was an average increase of more than $230 per family, which meant a gain in new purchasing power in their communities.

Obviously the efforts of the FSA angered influential segments of the agricultural establishment, such as the leadership of the American Farm Bureau Federation and the Cooley Committee of the House of Representatives. The FSA, it was evident, was seeking to help those most in need to remain on the land. Its policy was contrary to the beliefs of those who held that the impoverished rural elements, and the farmers in general, would be better off if they left agriculture completely.[33]

In international trade some minor progress was made in unclogging the channels of commerce, especially in dealing with some of the nations of the

Western Hemisphere, but little headway was made in finding new outlets for cotton, which depended heavily on the overseas market. The causes for this failure to find new markets were beyond the power of any single nation to repair in a period of international crisis. The demand for cotton probably would have been considerably greater had it not been for the production and use of synthetic fibers in countries such as Germany, Italy, and Japan where the drive for self-sufficiency was great. Military preparations, rising trade barriers, and economic rivalries discouraged the sale of American cotton abroad. The total use of cotton in foreign lands had increased appreciably, but the demand for American cotton had diminished.[34]

Perhaps one of the greatest contributions the New Deal made to agriculture was expanding the use of electricity on the farms. This, of course, was tied in to a very great extent with the achievements of the TVA. Beginning in 1935 on a modest scale and outside the USDA, the REA expanded its activities in the years prior to the outbreak of World War II and especially after peace was restored. The federal government under the New Deal assumed a responsibility that the private utilities had been unwilling to assume and that they continued to resist until they saw the futility of their actions. And because of the spread of electricity in the rural areas under REA auspices, crop and livestock production improved; a wider use of farm machinery became possible; labor costs decreased; greater use was made of modern, efficient techniques of farming; much backbreaking toil and drudgery came to an end; the use of indoor plumbing and refrigeration spread; improved means of rural communication became possible; rural education benefited; and the morale of the farm wife was lifted.[35]

By 1940 progress also had been made toward better living conditions and more secure income for the commercial farm families of the South. Incomes from livestock and livestock products were larger, and the expenditures for food and feed were smaller as a result of a greater incentive to produce for home use. The rising production of livestock was accompanied by a substantial trend toward the production of feeds. It was expected that such self-sufficient practices would further broaden the net income base, reduce the cost of raising cash, and the dependence on it. Income from livestock, fruits, and vegetables in the cotton growing states of the South in 1939 was at about the same level as in 1929, but the income from cotton remained significantly below the 1929 level. North Carolina was a conspicuous example of the former, and Mississippi of the latter. Mississippi still was dependent primarily on cotton for an income that had been reduced to less than half of what it had been in 1929.[36]

Another significant contribution was the Shelterbelt Project that was launched after the drought and dust storms of 1934 for the purpose of lessening the effects of these disasters, protecting homes and livestock, and providing jobs for the residents of the stricken areas. Allowing for the hostility that the project encountered in the early years, and problems of a serious nature such as insects, disease, rodent pests, and replacement, the Shelterbelt Project turned out to be a far greater success than its critics had anticipated.[37]

Nor can one overlook the role of the New Deal in broadening the base of agricultural credit. The Farm Credit Administration created in 1933 extended loans totaling billions of dollars to farmers and their business cooperatives to finance production, market farm products, and purchase farm supplies. Its production credit activities—that is, loans to farmers to purchase livestock, machinery, and supplies—ranged from 230,000 to 250,000 in number annually and from $250 to $350 million in cash. The average amount advanced in 1940 was almost $1,500. District banks for cooperatives extended credit to farmers' cooperative associations that were marketing farm products, purchasing farm supplies, or furnishing farm business services to members. Loans by these banks reached a peak of slightly more than $100 million in 1940, as compared with an annual average of about $90 million during 1936–1939. Emergency crop and feed loans authorized by legislation in 1927 and later years helped farmers obtain assistance from other sources. Walter W. Wilcox estimated that by 1940 "if the land bank borrowers, production credit users, and emergency crop and feed loan borrowers had all been different people, about one million different farmers would have utilized credit made available by the FCA."[38]

Furthermore, the FCA improved the farm credit market for the farmer through the leadership and competition it provided. Credit was made available at the lowest possible rate consistent with good market practices. Credit was obtained by thousands of borrowers who otherwise would have lost their property through foreclosures. Federal land bank real estate loans reached a peak of almost $2.85 billion in 1936 and then declined to $2.5 billion in 1940. As Wilcox observed,

> Federal farm credit agencies pioneered in adopting a long-time amortized loan for real estate mortgages, in the use of long-time value as a basis for appraisal, and in the development of a budget plan for fitting the timing and the amount of the loan directly to the acquisition and liquidation of assets.[39]

Left-wing critics claim that the New Deal could have accomplished far more for the farmers than it actually did. They further assert that the mood of the American people was such that the USDA, Henry Wallace, and all surrounding him and his department could have brought about long overdue fundamental reforms for the low-income farmers had they wanted to.[40] Just what these reforms were to be is unclear, unless they were nationalization of the land and the establishment of cooperative or collective farms.

There is little evidence to support the claim that the American people were receptive to such proposals. The Farm Holiday movement which was at its peak in the initial stages of the New Deal did not advocate this kind of change. Even if the Farm Holiday was supposed to represent farmer or public indignation with the New Deal for its failure to provide greater assistance for farmers, it had very little support behind it. At best the Farm Holiday movement was a splinter group broken off the main branch of the Farmers' Union, the smallest of the general farmer organizations.

In attempting to summarize the effects of the New Deal on the American farmer one has to keep several things in mind. The New Deal happened in one of the most distressed periods of American history, one in which economies around the world were racked by comparable economic pains. The New Deal also sought to achieve relief, recovery, and reform in a set of economic conditions that had been years in the making, that could not possibly be undone in a short span of time under a system of government controlled by those who had faith in the capitalist system and political establishment and who depended on Congress, farmers, and the general public for continuation in office. Finally, the programs of the FSA, the Bankhead–Jones Act, rural electrification, crop insurance, and the ever-normal granary were just beginning to get off the ground when the New Deal came to an end.

Still, when all is said and done, the farmers who were able to remain in agriculture, especially those with capital and resources, had more to gain from the New Deal than those who lacked the capital and resources. The New Deal revived and maintained the morale of many farmers after it had fallen to the lowest depths in history. Farm prices failed to rise to the parity levels designated by the lawmakers, but they were lifted from the low levels of 1932–1933 and many of the gains can be attributed to the programs of the New Deal. Both farmers and the general public were made more aware of the need for conserving the soil; a laudable start was made in furnishing electricity for rural areas long neglected by private industry; the Shelterbelt Project helped make life on the Great Plains more bearable for more farmers; and statesmanlike measures, although unsuccessful in accomplishing their purposes, were adopted to improve international trade.

Whether Wallace had the future defense needs of the nation in mind when hostilities broke out may be a moot point. But beyond debate is the fact that "the peacetime programs of research, education, credit, rehabilitation, conservation, and adjustment carried on by the Land Grant Colleges and the Department of Agriculture were important factors contributing to agriculture's ability to respond to war needs."[41] With all its limitations and frustrations, the New Deal, by making operational the ideas and plans that had been long on the minds of agricultural researchers and thinkers, constituted the greatest innovative epoch in the history of American agriculture.

NOTES

CHAPTER ONE

1. *The Agricultural Problem in the United States* (New York: National Industrial Conference Board, 1926), 34, 49, and 67–68; Joseph S. Davis, *On Agricultural Policy, 1926–1938* (Stanford, 1939), 68–70; John D. Black, "Agriculture Now," *Journal of Farm Economics* 9 (April 1927): 151–52; Carl T. Schmidt, *American Farmers in the World Crisis* (New York: Oxford Univ. Press, 1941), 40–41; A. B. Genung, "The Purchasing Power of the Farmer's Dollar from 1913 to Date," *The Annals of the American Academy of Political Science* (hereafter *The Annals*) 117 (January 1925): 22; Louis Bean and Oscar C. Stine, "Income from Agricultural Production," *The Annals* 117 (January 1925): 28; Macy Campbell, *Rural Life at the Crossroads* (Boston: Ginn and Co., 1927), ch. 1; Benjamin H. Hibbard, "Discussion," *Journal of Farm Economics* 9 (January 1927): 43; George S. Wehrwein, "The Trend in Land Values and Land Utilization," *The Annals* 117 (January 1925): 47–48; Davis, *On Agricultural Policy,* 78. Compare Davis's views with those expressed in *The Agricultural Problem in the United States,* 28–32. See also J. M. Gillette, "Drift to the City," *American Journal of Sociology* 16 (March 1911): 645–67; Benjamin H. Hibbard, *Effects of the Great War Upon Agriculture in the United States and Great Britain* (New York: Carnegie Endowment For International Peace, 1919), 22–67; Edwin G. Nourse, *American Agriculture and the European Market* (New York: Institute of Economics, 1924), 44–61; *Report of the President's Committee On Social Trends:* (New York: McGraw-Hill, 1933), 498.

2. *Achieving a Balanced Agriculture,* a pamphlet (Washington, D.C.: USDA, 1940), 3.

3. Wehrwein, *"The Trend in Land Values,"* 49; Louis C. Gray, "A Domestic Market for American Farm Products," *The Annals* 117 (January 1925): 157; Schmidt, *American Farmers,* 13.

4. Florette Henri, *Black Migration: Movement North* (Garden City: Anchor Press/Doubleday, 1975), 49–80; Emmett G. Scott, *Negro Migration During the War* (New York: Arno/New York Times, 1969), 13–71; Theodore Saloutos, *Farmer Movements in the South, 1865–1933* (Berkeley and Los Angeles: Univ. of California Press, 1960), 250–51.

5. Arthur C. Bunce, *Economic Nationalism and the Farmer* (Ames: Iowa State Univ. Press, 1938), 15.

6. Sir George Paish, "The Rehabilitation of Europe Dependent Upon America," *The Annals* 102 (July 1922): 148; *The Condition of Agriculture in the United States and Measures for Its Improvement* (New York: Business Men's Commission on Agriculture, 1927), 94–95. See, also, Herbert Feis, *Europe the World's Banker 1876–1914* (New York: Norton, 1965); Austin A. Dowell and Oscar B. Jesness, *The American Farmer and the Export Market* (Minneapolis: Univ. of Minnesota Press, 1934), 211–12; Nourse, *American Agriculture and the European Market,* 65; Harold G. Moulton & Leo Pasvolsky, *War Debts and World Prosperity* (New York: Brookings Institution, 1932), 413–14; *Yearbook of Agriculture, 1920* (Washington, D.C., 1921), 501; Nourse, *American Agriculture and the European Market,* 65.

7. Nourse, *American Agriculture and the European Market,* 62–65.

8. James A. Shideler, *Farm Crisis, 1919–1923* (Berkeley and Los Angeles: Univ. of California Press, 1957: Theodore Saloutos and John D. Hicks, *Agricultural Discontent in the Middle West, 1900–1939* (Madison: Univ. of Wisconsin Press, 1951), 100–110; Davis, *On Agricultural Policy,* 75–76; George F. Warren, "The Agricultural Depression," *Quarterly Journal of Economics* 38 (February 1924): 183–213.

9. See especially George F. Warren, "Causes and Probable Duration of Agricultural Depression," *Proceedings of the Second International Conference of Agricultural Economists* (Menasha, Wis.: George Banta, 1930), 87–113; Davis, *On Agricultural Policy,* 24–26, 80–83, 91–95; *Yearbook of Agriculture, 1925* (Washington, D.C., 1926), *1926,* 1, *1928,* 1; Nourse, "The Outlook For Agriculture," *Journal of Farm Economics* 9 (January 1927): 21–32 and rejoinders, 33–52. See also Alfred C. True, *A History of Agricultural Experimentation and Research in the United States* (Washington, D.C.: USDA, 1937), Misc. Pub. 251, 236–37; Russell Lord, *The Agrarian Revival* (New York: American Association for Adult Education, 1939), 86–99.

10. Nourse, *"The Outlook For Agriculture,"* 21-26.

11. W. M. Hurst and Lillian M. Church, *Power and Machinery in Agriculture,* USDA, Misc. Pub. 157, 12-13.

12. Hurst and Church, *Power and Machinery in Agriculture,* 2.

13. Hurst and Church, *Power and Machinery in Agriculture,* 2-8.

14. Hurst and Church, *Power and Machinery in Agriculture,* 10.

15. O. C. Stine, "Discussion," *Journal of Farm Economics* 9 (January 1927): 46.

16. *Historical Statistics of the United States from Colonial Times to 1957* (Washington, D.C.: United States Department of Commerce, 1961), 415; A. E. Nielsen, *Production Credit for Southern Cotton Growers* (New York: King's Crown Press, 1946); I. W. Duggan, "Cotton, Land and People: A Statement of the Problem," *Journal of Farm Economics,* 22 (February 1940): 197.

17. O. E. Baker, "Changes in Production and Consumption of Our Farm Products and the Trend in Population," *The Annals* 142 (March 1929): 119-31.

18. Hazel K. Stiebling, "Food Habits, Old and New," *Yearbook of Agriculture, 1939* (Washington, D.C., 1939), 129.

19. Thomas N. Carver, "Rural Depopulation," *Journal of Farm Economics* 9 (January 1927): 1-3.

20. Richard O. Cummings, *The American and His Food* (Chicago: Univ. of Chicago Press, 1940), 139-42, 145-46.

21. Cummings, *The American and His Food,* 147-50, 153-154; R. H. Elsworth, *Cooperative Marketing and Purchasing 1920-1930* (Washington, D.C.: USDA, 1930), Cir. 121, 9; *Yearbook of Agriculture, 1914* (Washington, D. C., 1914), 25. By 1927-1928 some 2,479 cooperatives with a membership of 600,000 handled approximately $600,000,000 worth of dairy products; and 1,269 fruit and vegetable associations transacted about $300,000,000 worth of business.

22. O. E. Baker, "The Agricultural Significance of the Declining Birth Rate," *American Sociological Society* 24 (May 1930): 138-46; Warren S. Thompson and P. K. Whelpton, "The Population of the Nation," *Recent Social Trends* (New York: McGraw-Hill, 1932), 1, 2, 50.

23. *Historical Statistics from Colonial Times to 1957,* 56, 63; Thompson and Whelpton, *Recent Social Trends,* 37-38. Illustrative of the articles by O. E. Baker are: "Changes in Production and Consumption of Our Farm Products and the Trends in Population," *The Annals* 142 (March 1929): 97-146; and "Population, Food Supply and Agriculture," *Geographical Review* 18 (July 1928): 353-73.

24. Nourse, *American Agriculture and the European Market,* 61-65; Arthur P. Chew, "The Meaning of Foreign Trade for Agriculture," *Farmers in a Changing World* (Washington, D.C., 1940), 573; Moulton and Pasvolsky, *War Debts and World Prosperity,* 413-14.

25. Grover C. Huebner and Ronald Kramer, *Foreign Trade Principles and Practices,* rev. ed. (New York, 1942), 27-45; Moulton and Pasvolsky, *War Debts and World Prosperity,* 407-11.

26. Leo Pasvolsky, "International Relations and Financial Conditions in Foreign Countries Affecting the Demand for American Agricultural Products," *Journal of Farm Economics* 14 (1932): 258.

27. Pasvolsky, "International Relations and Financial Conditions," 257-60; *Historical Statistics from Colonial Times to 1957,* 555.

28. Pasvolsky, "International Relations and Financial Conditions," 260-62.

29. Pasvolsky, "International Relations and Financial Conditions," 262-63; Carl T. Schmidt, "The Italian 'Battle of Wheat'," *Journal of Farm Economics* 18 (1936): 645-46; N. W. Hazan, "The Agricultural Program of Fascist Italy," *Journal of Farm Economics* 15 (1933): 489-502.

30. Pasvolsky, "International Relations and Financial Conditions," 264-65.

31. Mordecai Ezekiel, "European Competition in Agricultural Production with Special Reference to Russia," *Journal of Farm Economics* 14 (1932): 271-73, 279.

32. Maurice Leven, Harold G. Moulton, and Clark Warburton, *America's Capacity to Consume* (New York: Brookings Institution, 1934), 21, 41; *Agricultural Statistics 1937,* 386; *Yearbook of Agriculture, 1933,* 93.

33. Leven, Moulton, and Warburton, *America's Capacity to Consume,* 41-43.

34. John H. Kolb and Edmund de S. Brunner, *A Study of Rural Society* (Boston: Houghton Mifflin, 1935), 335; *Historical Statistics of the United States from Colonial Times to 1957,* 286.

35. A. B. Genung, "The Recent Trend in the Purchasing Power of Farm Products," *The Annals* 142 (March 1929): 16–17; *Yearbook of Agriculture, 1930* (Washington, D.C., 1930), 12; *Yearbook of Agriculture, 1933* (Washington, D.C., 1933), 3–4.

36. For more details see Whitney Coombs, *Taxation of Farm Property* (Washington, D.C.: USDA, 1932), Tech. Bulletin 172.

37. Kolb and Brunner, *A Study of Rural Society,* 322–27.

38. Carl C. Taylor, "Our Rural Population Debacle," *American Economic Review,* Supplement, 16 (March 1926): 156–59, 162.

CHAPTER TWO

1. John D. Black, "Doctrines Relating to Agricultural Policy for the United States," *Proceedings of the Second International Conference of Agricultural Economists* (Menasha, Wis., 1930): 220; Chester C. Davis, "The Development of Agricultural Policy Since the End of the World War," *Farmers in a Changing World,* (Washington D.C., 1940), 297–316.

2. John D. Black, *Agricultural Reform in the United States* (New York: McGraw-Hill, 1929), 48–55; Benjamin H. Hibbard, "A Long Range View of National Agricultural Policy," *Journal of Farm Economics* 16 (January 1934): 14.

3. Charles M. Gardner, *The Grange—Friend of the Farmer* (Washington, D.C.: National Grange, 1950), 106; John H. Rich, *The Economic Position of Agriculture in the Northwestern Grain Raising Areas* (Washington, D.C.: Federal Reserve Board, 1923), 9; *Yearbook of Agriculture, 1920* (Washington, D.C., 1921), 9–10; *Mid-South Cotton News* (Memphis), May 1933.

4. *Proceedings of the Thirty-Fourth Annual Session of the Association of Land Grant Colleges and Universities, 1920,* 1–4, 21–28.

5. "Report of the Investigating Committee of the American Farm Economics Association," *Journal of Farm Economics* 2 (January 1920): 115–18.

6. William F. Gephart, "Provisions of the Food Act and Activities Which Should Be Made Permanent," *American Economic Review,* Supplement 9 (March 1919): 61–64, 65–70, 76–78; Wilfred Eldred, "The Grain Corporation and the Guaranteed Price for Wheat," *Quarterly Journal of Economics* 34 (August 1920): 698–719.

7. George F. Warren, "Some After-the-War Problems in Agriculture," *Journal of Farm Economics* 1 (June 1919): 12; *Yearbook of Agriculture, 1920,* 37–38; William S. Rossiter, *Increase of Population in the United States, 1910–1920* (Washington, D.C., 1922), 226–27; John D. Black, "National Agricultural Policy," *American Economic Review,* Supplement, 16 (1926): 134–36; Warren, "Some After-the-War Problems," 12.

8. Russell Lord, *The Wallaces of Iowa* (Boston, 1947), 214; *Yearbook of Agriculture, 1920,* 9–38.

9. Theodore Macklin, "Report of Committee on Farm Economic Investigational Work: The American Farm Economics Association," *Journal of Farm Economics* 3 (January 1921): 41–44; Henry C. Taylor, "The Adjustment of the Farm Business to Declining Price Levels," *Journal of Farm Economics* 3 (January 1921): 8–9.

10. Lord, *Wallaces of Iowa,* 215–17.

11. *Yearbook of Agriculture, 1921* (Washington, D.C., 1922), 15–17; Lord, *Wallaces of Iowa,* 218; Henry C. Taylor, "Courses in Marketing," *Journal of Farm Economics* 6 (January 1924): 26–27.

12. *Yearbook of Agriculture, 1921,* 17.

13. C. E. Ladd, "Report of the Committee on Resolutions," *Journal of Farm Economics* 4 (January 1922): 49.

14. Orville M. Kile, *The Farm Bureau Through Three Decades* (Baltimore, 1948), 114; Theodore Saloutos and John D. Hicks, *Agricultural Discontent in the Middle West, 1900–1939* (Madison: Univ. of Wisconsin Press, 1951), 273; William J. Block, *The Separation of the Farm Bureau and Extension Service* (Urbana: Univ. of Illinois Press, 1960), 10–11; Murray R. Benedict, *Farm Policies of the United States, 1790–1950* (New York: Twentieth Century Fund, 1953), 194–98.

15. Saloutos and Hicks, *Agricultural Discontent,* 274–75; Orville M. Kile, *The Farm Bureau Movement* (New York, 1921), 148–64.

16. *Journal of Proceedings,* National Grange, 54th an. sess., 1920, 159–61; 55th an. sess., 1921, 142; 56th an. sess., 1922, 175, 179–80, 194–95; 57th an. sess., 1923, 209–10; 58th an. sess., 1924, 235.

17. Commodore B. Fisher, *The Farmers' Union* (Lexington: Univ. of Kentucky Press, 1920), 33-51; Edward Wiest, *Agricultural Organization in the United States* (Lexington: Univ. of Kentucky Press, 1923), 499-502; Saloutos and Hicks, *Agricultural Discontent*, 219, 238 and 253.

18. Saloutos and Hicks, *Agricultural Discontent*, 322-32.

19. For a complete account of the McNary-Haugen battles see Gilbert C. Fite, *George N. Peek and The Fight for Farm Parity* (Norman: Univ. of Oklahoma Press, 1954); James A. Everitt, *The Third Power*, 4th ed. (Indianapolis, 1907), vii; *The Plan of the American Society of Equity*, a pamphlet (Indianapolis, n.d.), 1; Edwin G. Nourse, "The Place of Agriculture in Modern Industrial Society," *Journal of Political Economy* 27 (July 1921): 564-65.

20. *Yearbook of Agriculture, 1921*, 14-15; *Yearbook of Agriculture, 1922* (Washington, D.C., 1924), 2-3.

21. Kile, *The Farm Bureau Through Three Decades*, 107. For a convenient chronology of the AFBF campaign in behalf of farm relief from 1923 to 1929, see *AFBF Weekly News Letter* 8 (June 18, 1929): 2-4.

22. Lord, *Wallaces of Iowa*, 249-50.

23. *Yearbook of Agriculture, 1923*, 17; Henry C. Taylor and Anne Dewees Taylor, *The Story of Agricultural Economics in the United States, 1840-1932* (1951; reprint ed., Westport, Conn.: Greenwood Press, 1974), 648-52; James Shideler, *Farm Crisis, 1919-1923* (Berkeley and Los Angeles: Univ. of California Press, 1959), 258-59.

24. Taylor and Taylor, *The Story of Agricultural Economics*, 595-96.

25. *Yearbook of Agriculture, 1923* (Washington, D.C., 1923), 17-18.

26. "Can the Farm Be Bought Off?" *New Republic* 29 (February 15, 1922):323; "To Tide the Farmer Over an Emergency," *The World's Work* 48(May 1924): 10, 11.

27. Saloutos and Hicks, *Agricultural Discontent*, 380-82.

28. Claude Benner, *The Federal Intermediate Credit System* (New York, 1926), 103-4; *Yearbook of Agriculture, 1923*, 25; *Yearbook of Agriculture, 1924* (Washington, D.C.: 1924), 232-38; Black, *Agricultural Reform in the United States*, 70-71; Saloutos and Hicks, *Agricultural Discontent*, 383.

29. Lord, *Wallaces of Iowa*, 261-62; *The Outlook* 139 (February 25, 1925): 286; *Yearbook of Agriculture, 1925* (Washington, D.C., 1925), 1, 16-18. "Dr. Jardine's Farm Prescription," *Literary Digest* 90 (September 25, 1926), 12-13; *Yearbook of Agriculture, 1926* (Washington, D.C., 1926), 7.

30. Charles L. Stewart, "Historical Background of Farm Export Premiums," manuscript in possession of author; Joseph S. Davis, *The Farm Export Debenture Plan* (Stanford, 1929), 1-7; *Journal of Proceedings*, National Grange, 60th an. sess., 1926, 166; Charles L. Stewart, "Discussion," *Journal of Farm Economics* 10 (January 1928): 28-32; Davis, *The Farm Export Debenture Plan*, 1-11.

31. John Kenneth Galbraith, "John D. Black: A Portrait," in James P. Cavin, *Economics for Agriculture: Selected Writings of John D. Black* (Cambridge: Oxford Univ. Press, 1959), 1-19; "Reminiscences of Mordecai Ezekiel," Oral History Research Office, Columbia University, 11; John D. Black and Albert G. Black, *Production Organization* (New York, 1929).

32. John D. Black, "National Agricultural Policy," *American Economic Review*, Supplement 16 (March 1926): 146-55.

33. *The Agricultural Problem in the United States* (New York: National Industrial Conference, 1926), v-vi, 141-44, 149-50; Joseph Dorfman, *The Economic Mind in American Civilization*, 4 vols. (New York: Viking Press, 1949), 4:79-80, 197.

34. Black, "Agriculture Now," *Journal of Farm Economics* 9 (April 1927): 149; Joseph S. Davis, *On Agricultural Policy, 1926-1938* (Stanford, 1939), 63.

35. Davis, *On Agricultural Policy, 1926-1938*, 70-74.

36. Black, "Agriculture Now," 148, 151-52.

37. Joseph S. Davis, "Recent Books on the Agricultural Situation," *Quarterly Journal of Economics* 93 (May 1929): 538; *The Condition of Agriculture in The United States and Measures for Its Improvement* (New York: Business Men's Commission on Agriculture, 1927), 29-30, 31-33, 34-40; Davis, *"Recent Books,"* 540.

38. "Report of the Executive Committee as to the Agricultural Situation," in *Proceedings of the Forty-First Annual Convention of the Association of Land Grant Colleges and Universities, 1927*, 85, 86-87, 111-14.

39. *Yearbook of Agriculture, 1926*, 23-29.

40. Henry H. Bakken & Marvin Schaars, *The Economics of Cooperative Marketing* (New

York, 1938), 283-86; Saloutos and Hicks, *Agricultural Discontent,* 287-88; Black, *Agricultural Reform,* 337-48, 406-18.

41. Saloutos and Hicks, *Agricultural Discontent,* 395-96. Theodore Saloutos, *Farmer Movements in the South, 1865-1933* (Berkeley and Los Angeles: Univ. of California Press, 1960), 266-71.

42. Saloutos and Hicks, *Agricultural Discontent,* 396-402.

43. *Yearbook of Agriculture, 1928* (Washington, D.C., 1928), 28; Arthur P. Chew, "Nationalistic Trends in Agricultural Policy," *Journal of Farm Economics* 26 (February 1944): 66.

44. Saloutos, *Farmer Movements in the South,* 271. Ray L. Wilbur and Arthur M. Hyde, *The Hoover Policies* (New York, 1937), 149-50.

45. Walter W. Wilcox, and Willard W. Cochrane, *Economics of Agriculture,* 2d ed. (Englewood Cliffs, New Jersey: Prentice Hall, 1960), 468; E. S. Haskell, "Stabilization Operations and the Federal Farm Board," in W. L. Holland, ed., *Commodity Control in the Pacific Area* (Stanford, 1935), 90-91; *Yearbook of Agriculture, 1930* (Washington, D.C., 1930), 19-20.

46. Forrest Crissey, *Alexander Legge, 1866-1933* (Chicago, 1936), 181-83: *First Annual Report, Federal Farm Board* (Washington, D.C., 1930), 5-6.

47. Saloutos and Hicks, *Agricultural Discontent,* 409-11.

48. Wilcox and Cochrane, *Economics of Agriculture,* 492.

49. For more details on the politics of the Federal Farm Board, the external opposition, and other matters, see Saloutos and Hicks, *Agricultural Discontent,* 404-34; Rainer Schickele, *Agricultural Policy* (New York, 1954), 189.

50. "Reminiscences of Mordecai Ezekiel," 41-42; *Third Annual Report, Federal Farm Board* (Washington, D.C., 1933), 72-73. Haskell, "Stabilization Operations," 105-6.

51. Haskell, "Stabilization Operations," 106, 115-17; *Third Annual Report, Federal Farm Board,* 73.

52. Haskell, in Holland, *Commodity Control in the Pacific Area,* 117-18.

53. *Third Annual Report, Federal Farm Board,* 60-62.

54. *Government Control of Export and Import in Foreign Countries,* mimeographed (Washington, D.C.: USDA, BAE, 1926), Ag. Econ. Bibl. 12; *Price-Fixing By Government in Foreign Countries, 1926-1939,* mimeographed (Washington, D.C.: USDA, BAE, 1940) Ag. Econ. Bibl. 86; Black, *Agricultural Reform,* 80, 302-8; Charles L. Stewart, *The Debenture Plan and Countries to Which We Export,* a leaflet (n. p., 1930); C. L. Stewart to J. D. Black, February 2, 1928, J. D. Black Papers, Wisconsin Historical Society; Charles L. Stewart, "Farm Relief Measures in Europe," *Journal of Farm Economics* 12 (January 1930): 29-30.

55. John D. Black, "Planning, Control and Research in Agriculture After Recovery," *Journal of Farm Economics* 17 (February 1935): 20; L. C. Gray et al., "Utilization of Our Lands for Crops, Pasture and Forests," *Yearbook of Agriculture, 1923,* 500-506. For a good account of L. C. Gray see Richard S. Kirkendall, "L. C. Gray and the Supply of Agricultural Land," *Agricultural History* 37 (October 1963): 206-14; Victor Christgau, "Legislation Needed to Bring About Readjustments in Agriculture," *Proceedings of the Forty-Fourth Annual Convention of the Association of Land Grant Colleges and Universities* (Burlington, Vt., 1932), 128-29.

56. Lloyd P. Rice, "Attitudes of the Department of Agriculture Toward Land Policies and Land Utilization As Experienced in Their Published Reports 1926-1930," manuscript, J. D. Black Papers; B. Henderson, "Land Settlement Policies," *Yearbook of Agriculture, 1926,* 467-70; *Yearbook of Agriculture, 1930,* 36-49.

57. J. S. Davis to J. D. Black, April 30, 1931, Black Papers; Victor Christgau, "Legislation Needed," 108-14, 123-30, 143, 149; Edward A. Duddy, ed., *An Economic Policy for American Agriculture* (Chicago: Univ. of Chicago Press, 1932), ix, Minutes of the Meeting Held at Hotel La Salle, Chicago, Illinois, September 10, 1931, manuscript, 2 pages, Black Papers.

58. *Yearbook of Agriculture, 1932* (Washington, D.C., 1932), 38. "Final Report of the National Land-Use Planning Committee, Washington, 1933," General Records of the USDA, RG 16, National Archives.

59. Saloutos, *Farmer Movements in the South, 1866-1933,* 39, 97-99, 100-101, 152-54, 164, 195-98, 242, 278-81; Gilbert Fite, "Voluntary Attempts to Reduce Cotton Acreage in the South, 1914-1933," *Journal of Southern History* 14 (1948): 481-99.

60. Henry A. Wallace, "Controlling Agricultural Output," *Journal of Farm Economics* 5 (1923): 16.

61. J. D. Black, "Doctrines Relating to Agricultural Policy for the United States," *Pro-

ceedings of the International Conference of Agricultural Economists (Menasha, Wis., 1930), 16.

62. Saloutos, *Farmer Movements in the South,* 277–80; *First Annual Report, Federal Farm Board,* 41; Alexander Legge, "Federal Farm Board," *Proceedings of the Forty-Fourth Annual Convention of the Association of Land Grant Colleges and Universities,* 86–87; *Cotton Trade Journal* (New Orleans), January 18, February 8, and March 1, 1930; *Cotton Digest* (Houston) 2 (November 1, 1930): 1; *Cotton Trade Journal,* August 22, 29, September 12, 19, 26, October 10, 17, 1930.

CHAPTER THREE

1. The proposal of May 1, 1894, is reprinted in *Farmer and Farm, Stock and Home* 50 (October 1, 1932): 8.

2. *Farmstead, Stock and Home* 42 (February 1, 1926), 84–86; William J. Spillman, *Balancing the Farm Output* (New York, 1927), 84–104; John D. Black, *Agricultural Reform in the United States* (New York: McGraw-Hill, 1929), 271–74; Harry N. Owen to John D. Black, November 16, 1928, Black Papers, Wisconsin Historical Society. The fullest treatment of the relations between M. L. Wilson and W. J. Spillman is in William D. Rowley, *M. L. Wilson and the Compaign for Domestic Allotment* (Lincoln: Univ. of Nebraska Press, 1970), 33–39.

3. Black to Joseph S. Davis, April 1, 1929, Black Papers. For a discussion of the Black-Ruml version, see Black, *Agricultural Reform,* 271–301. For a fuller account of John D. Black see Bernard M. Klass, "John D. Black: Farm Economist and Policy Adviser, 1920–1942" (Ph.D. diss., Univ. of California, Los Angeles, 1969).

4. H. C. Taylor to Black, January 21 and 22, 1929; Mordecai Ezekiel to Black, March 18, 1929; O. C. Stine to Black, March 15 and April 9, 1929; Chester C. Davis to Black, February 20, 26, March 22, and April 8, 1929; Black to Taylor, March 19, 1929. For the appraisal of the Ruml-Black plan by Julius Barnes, see Barnes to Ruml, February 11, 1929; memorandum, Eric Englund to H. R. Tolley, April 5, 1929; Beardsley Ruml to J. D. Black, March 6, 1929, Black Papers.

5. Black to H. C. Taylor, March 19, 1929; H. C. Taylor to Black, January 21, 1929, Black Papers.

6. C. C. Davis to J. D. Black, March 22, 1929, Black Papers.

7. C. C. Davis to J. D. Black, April 8, 1929, Black Papers.

8. Wilson to Black, April 6, 1932, Black Papers; Wilson to James C. Stone, April 9, 1932, M. Ezekiel Correspondence, General Records of the USDA, RG 16, National Archives (hereafter NA).

9. Memorandum, Mordecai Ezekiel to James Stone, Chairman of the Federal Farm Board, on Mr. M. L. Wilson's Proposal, April 15, 1932; Wilson to Stone, April 9, 1932, Ezekiel Correspondence, RG 16, NA.

10. W. L. Stockton to the Group Meeting in Chciago to Frame Legislation Embodying the Principle of the Domestic Allotment Proposal, April 14, 1932, M. L. Wilson Papers, Montana State University; M. L. Wilson to James C. Stone, April 9, 1932, Ezekiel Correspondence, RG 16, NA.

11. "The Domestic Allotment Plan," U.S., Congress, Senate, *Congressional Record,* 72d Cong., 1st sess., 1932, vol. 75, pt. 10, p. 11144–45.

12. *The Voluntary Domestic Allotment Plan For Wheat* (Stanford: Food Research Institute, 1932), 27–28. Fulmer's bill was H.R. 12461 and Walsh's, S. 4859; the Rainey bill was H.R. 12649 and Kleberg's H.R. 12730. John K. Galbraith, "John D. Black: A Portrait," *Economic Essays in Agriculture, Selected Writings of John D. Black,* p. 14, edited by James Pierce Cavin (Cambridge, 1959). The Farmers' Union plan asked ". . . for allotments to individual producers of a pro-rata share of the total requirement for domestic consumption, without specifying the procedure by which individual allotments should be made; but in no other respect does it resemble the plans treated here," *The Voluntary Domestic Allotment Plan For Wheat,* 27.

13. M. L. Wilson to Mordecai Ezekiel, June 18, 1932, Ezekiel Correspondence, RG 16, NA.

14. Eugene Thwing, ed., *The Literary Digest Political Cyclopaedia* (New York: Literary Digest, 1932), 117–18. The Republican platform was adopted June 27, 1932.

15. Thwing, *The Literary Digest,* 131. The Democratic platform was adopted on July 22, 1932.

16. "Reminiscences of Rexford G. Tugwell," Oral History Research Office, Columbia University, 22–24.

17. Raymond Moley, *After Seven Years* (New York, 1939), 41–42.

18. Moley, *After Seven Years,* 44–45.

19. Thwing, *The Literary Digest,* 238; *The Voluntary Domestic Allotment Plan For Wheat,* 29; Samuel I. Rosenman, ed., *The Public Papers and Addresses of Franklin D. Roosevelt* (New York: Random House, 1938), I, 703–705.

20. M. L. Wilson to Lester Cole, September 21, 1932, Wilson to Mordecai Ezekiel, September 21, 1932, Wilson to Ezekiel, October 8, 1932, Wilson Papers.

21. Wilson to Black, October 7, 1932, Black Papers.

22. Moley, *After Seven Years,* 44–45.

23. Wilson to Black, October 7, 1932, Black Papers.

24. Wilson to Black, October 25, 1932, Black Papers; J. S. Davis, *Wheat and the AAA* (Washington, D.C., 1935), 34.

25. *New York Herald Tribune,* November 28, 1932; *Historical Statistics of the United States Colonial Times to 1957* (Washington, D.C.: USDA), 686–87; *New York Herald Tribune,* December 15, 1932.

26. *St. Paul Pioneer Press,* December 13, 1932; Theodore Saloutos and John D. Hicks, *Agricultural Discontent in the Middle West 1900–1939* (Madison: Univ. of Wisconsin Press, 1951), 460–61.

27. U.S. Congress, Senate, Committee on Agriculture and Forestry, *Hearing on: H.R. 13991,* 72d Cong., 2d sess., 13–14.

28. *St. Paul Pioneer Press,* December 15, 21, and 22, 1932.

29. *Congressional Digest* 12 (March 1933): 89–90; *Commercial and Financial Chronicle* 135 (December 31, 1932): 4457; Irvin M. May, *Marvin Jones: The Public Career of an Agrarian Advocate* (College Station: Texas A & M Press, 1980), 96–97.

30. Senate, *Hearing on: H.R. 13991,* 15–16, 22–28.

31. *Congressional Digest* 12 (March 1933): 89–90; May, *Marvin Jones,* 96.

32. *Des Moines Register,* February 27, 1933; Alfred Stedman to J. D. Le Cron, March 22, 1937, RG 16, National Archives (hereafter NA); Russell Lord, *The Wallaces of Iowa* (Boston, 1947), 323–24; Orville M. Kile, *The Farm Bureau through Three Decades* (Baltimore, 1948), 194; *Cotton Trade Journal,* January 21, 1933; *New York Times,* November 27, 1932; Roy V. Scott and J. G. Shoalmire, *The Public Career of Cully Cobb* (Jackson: University Press of Mississippi, 1973), 194–98. Tugwell says in his reminiscences it was clear that Morgenthau was unlikely to be named secretary of agriculture. He came from New York; he had few contacts with agriculture; and it would have been impolitic to appoint him. Besides, Roosevelt had other New Yorkers he wished to appoint to the cabinet, Frances Perkins for example. The "secretaryship of the Treasury was not settled and this might go to a New Yorker, too." Reminiscences of Rexford G. Tugwell," 33; Wilson to Tugwell, November 30, 1932, M. L. Wilson Papers.

33. Lord, *Wallaces of Iowa,* 324.

34. Lord, *Wallaces of Iowa,* 323; *Des Moines Register,* February 27, 1932.

35. *Des Moines Register,* February 27, 1932.

36. Ezekiel said that Wallace asked him what job he would like to do and what title he wanted. Ezekiel replied that he would like to be called "economic advisor to the Secretary," an idea he got from Herbert Feis, economic advisor to the secretary of state. The secretary of agriculture had never had an economic advisor before this. "Reminiscences of Mordecai Ezekiel," Oral History Research Office, Columbia University, 53; "Reminiscences of Rexford G. Tugwell," 44–45.

37. "Reminiscences of Rexford G. Tugwell," 43–45; "Reminiscences of Mordecai Ezekiel," 56. The processing tax was to be levied at the first step in the manufacturing process of the commodity subject to control and paid by the manufacturer, the proceeds or income to be used to provide benefit payments to the farmers participating in the program.

38. Mordecai Ezekiel to F. P. Lee, March 7, 1933; Ezekiel to Donald Murphy, March 7, 1933; Ezekiel to Edward A. O'Neal, March 7, 1933; Ezekiel to Clifford V. Gregory, March 7, 1933; Memorandum, Ezekiel to the Solicitor, March 7, 1933; Ezekiel to Commissioner of Internal Revenue, March 7, 1933, RG 16, NA.

39. Memorandum, H. A. Wallace to Nils Olsen, March 6, 1933, RG 16, NA.

40. Franklin Delano Roosevelt To The Congress of the United States, March 16, 1933, RG 16, NA.

41. Henry A. Wallace to Marvin Jones, March 20, 1933, RG 16, NA.

42. State of Kansas Concurrent Resolution No. 18, March 17, 1933; Concurrent Resolution passed by Iowa State Senate March 15, 1933 and House of Representatives March 21, 1933; Concurrent Resolution adopted by Michigan Senate April 11, 1933 and Michigan House of Representatives April 12, 1933. Copies of these resolutions and petitions, and others, filed with Senate Committee of Agriculture and Forestry, 73d Cong., 2d sess., 73A-Jl, 140. Governor Eugene Talmadge of Georgia asked that a general cotton holiday be called in 1934. H. A. Wallace to Eugene Talmadge, April 27, 1933, RG 16, NA.

43. Files of Senate Committee on Agriculture and Forestry, 73d Cong., 2d sess., 73A-Jl, 140.

44. Files of Senate Committee on Agriculture and Forestry, 73d Cong., 2d sess., 73A-Jl, 140.

45. Files of Senate Committee on Agriculture and Forestry, 73d Cong., 2d sess., 73A-Jl, 140.

46. C. W. Warburton to B. H. Crocheron, February 18, 1933, RG 16, NA.

47. C. W. Warburton to C. B. Martin, February 6, 1933, RG 16, NA.

48. Proposals for farm relief in March 1933 included bills with acreage reduction as a price-raising scheme, farm mortgages, farm credit and farm cooperatives, reforestation to utilize the unused lands, mandatory use of alcohol in gasoline sold to motorists, payment of taxes in commodities rather than money, and the government withholding the commodity from the market till the price became favorable. *New York Times,* March 26, 1933; E. G. Nourse, J. S. Davis, and J. D. Black, *Three Years of the AAA* (Washington, D.C., 1937), 15–16; *Wallace's Farmer and Iowa Homestead* 58 (April 29, 1933): 3.

49. *Agricultural Adjustment, A Report of the Administration of the AAA May 1933 to February 1934* (Washington, D.C.: USDA, 1934), 1–7.

50. Theodore W. Schultz and A. G. Black, "The Voluntary Domestic Allotment Plan," *The Agricultural Emergency in Iowa* (Ames: Iowa State Univ. Press, 1933), 104.

51. "Reminiscences of Milburn L. Wilson," Oral History Research Office, Columbia University, 1063; "Reminiscences of Mordecai Ezekiel," 67.

52. "Reminiscences of M. L. Wilson," 1060–61; "Reminiscences of Mordecai Ezekiel," 85–86.

CHAPTER FOUR

1. Russell Lord, *The Wallaces of Iowa* (Boston, 1947), 430–554; Richard Crabb, *The Hybrid-Corn Makers: Prophets of Plenty* (New Brunswick, 1947), 140–66.

2. Ray B. —— of Northwest Country Elevator Association, Minneapolis, to M. L. Wilson, March 20, 1933, M. L. Wilson Papers, Montana State University.

3. "Reminiscences of M. L. Wilson," Oral History Research Office, Columbia University, 1860, 1318. On the career of Warner W. Stockberger see Eldon L. Johnson, "The Administrative Career of Dr. W. W. Stockberger," *Public Administration Review,* 1 (Autumn 1940): 50. The career of William A. Jump is briefly outlined in A. W. Macmahon and J. D. Millett, *Federal Administrators* (New York: Columbia University Press, 1939), 47.

4. Paul W. Ward, "Wallace the Great Hesitator," *Nation* 140 (May 8, 1935): 535. See Lord's reaction in *Wallaces of Iowa,* 432–34.

5. Lord, *Wallaces of Iowa,* 434.

6. Lord, *Wallaces of Iowa,* 435–36.

7. "Reminiscences of H. R. Tolley," Oral History Research Office, Columbia University, 299; "Reminiscences of M. L. Wilson," 1034; John Franklin Carter, *The New Dealers* (New York, 1934), 96–99; "Frederic C. Howe," *Dictionary of American Biography,* Supplement 2 (New York, 1958), 326–28.

8. "Reminiscences of H. R. Tolley," 299, 393, 399; "Reminiscences of M. L. Wilson," 1463, 1469; "Reminiscences of Rexford G. Tugwell," Oral History Research Office, Columbia University, 69.

9. Bernard Baruch, *The Public Years* (New York, 1960), 250–51.

10. "Reminiscences of Mordecai Ezekiel," 52; "Reminiscences of Edward A. O'Neal," Oral History Research Office, Columbia University, 84–85.

11. George N. Peek and Samuel Crowther, *Why Quit Our Own* (New York, 1936), 99.

12. Peek and Crowther, *Why Quit Our Own,* 99.

13. Peek and Crowther, *Why Quit Our Own,* 13; "Reminiscences of Howard R. Tolley," 262.

14. "Reminiscences of H. R. Tolley," 100–101.

15. "Reminiscences of H. R. Tolley," 101-2.

16. Joseph G. Knapp, ed., *Great American Cooperators* (Washington, 1967), 84–87; "Charles J. Brand," *Agricultural History* 24 (January 1950): 62; Peek and Crowther, *Why Quit Our Own,* 104–5; Gilbert Fite, *George N. Peek and the Fight for Farm Parity* (Norman: Univ. of Oklahoma Press, 1954), 252; "Reminiscences of M. L. Wilson," 973–75, 999–1000; Donald L. Winters, *Henry Cantwell Wallace as Secretary of Agriculture* (Urbana: Univ. of Illinois Press, 1970), 210–12, 221, 267, 279.

17. Lord, *Wallaces of Iowa,* 323; John Franklin Carter, *The New Dealers* (New York: Simon and Schuster, 1934), 85–92.

18. "Reminiscences of M. L. Wilson," 1060–61; "Reminiscences of Mordecai Ezekiel," Oral History Research Office, Columbia University, 67.

19. Peek and Crowther, *Why Quit Our Own,* 104–5.

20. Peek and Crowther, *Why Quit Our Own,* 106.

21. *Kansas City Star,* December 12, 1933.

22. *Time,* December 12, 1933; Fite, *George N. Peek and the Fight for Farm Parity,* 84–85, 228–29; *Agricultural Adjustment, A Report of Administration of the AAA* (Washington, D.C.: USDA, 1934), 14–15.

23. "Reminiscences of M. L. Wilson," 1118, 1120–21.

24. "Reminiscences of M. L. Wilson," 1500, 1682–83, 1726–27.

25. Peek and Crowther, *Why Quit Our Own,* 106–7; Marquis and Bessie James, *Biography of a Bank* (New York, 1954), 401.

26. William I. Westervelt, "How the Agricultural Adjustment Act Will Function in the Marketing of Farm Commodities," *American Cooperation 1933* (Washington, D.C., 1934), 30.

27. Peek and Crowther, *Why Quit Our Own,* 13–14.

28. "Jerome Frank," *Current Biography 1941,* 301.

29. "Jerome Frank," 301–2; Jerome Frank, *A Man's Reach,* ed. by Barbara Frank Kristein (New York: Macmillan 1964), xiii.

30. "Jerome Frank," 302; "Reminiscences of Rexford G. Tugwell," 45; "Reminiscences of Gardner Jackson," Oral History Research Office, Columbia University, 561.

31. "Alger Hiss," *Current Biography 1947,* 308; William Jowitt, *The Strange Case of Alger Hiss* (Garden City, 1953), 61–62.

32. "Reminiscences of Gardner Jackson," 467, 473, 561.

33. Jowitt, *Strange Case of Alger Hiss,* 123; *New York Times,* November 21, 1969.

34. "Frederic C. Howe," 326–28, *Dictionary of American Biography:* Supplement 2. Entry by Landon Warner (New York: 1858).

35. *New York Times,* April 19, 1965; *New York Post,* April 19, 1965; Arthur M. Schlesinger, Jr., "Gardner Jackson 1897–1965," *New Republic,* May 1, 1965, 17; Sidney Baldwin, *Poverty and Politics: The Rise and Decline of the Farm Security Administration* (Chapel Hill: Univ. of North Carolina Press, 1968), 55.

36. "Reminiscences of Gardner Jackson," 491; "Reminiscences of Mordecai Ezekiel," 62.

37. "Reminiscences of H. R. Tolley," 234; "Reminiscences of M. L. Wilson," 1034; Russell Lord, *Wallaces of Iowa,* 354; Sidney Baldwin, *Poverty and Politics,* 55–56.

38. "Reminiscences of H. R. Tolley," 112–13.

39. Lord, *Wallaces of Iowa,* 193.

40. Peek and Crowther, *Why Quit Our Own,* 104–7, 117–22.

41. "Reminiscences of Rexford G. Tugwell," 45.

42. "Reminiscences of Gardner Jackson," 441, 561; "Reminiscences of M. L. Wilson," 1412.

43. "Reminiscences of M. L. Wilson," 1621.

44. "Reminiscences of M. L. Wilson," 1305.

45. "Reminiscences of M. L. Wilson," 1624–25.

CHAPTER FIVE

1. "Reminiscences of M. L. Wilson," Oral History Research Office, Columbia University, 1064; George Peek and Samuel Crowther, *Why Quit Our Own* (New York, 1936), 13–20; Cotton Leaflet No. 1, Commodity Information Series (Washington, D.C.: USDA, AAA, 1934), 1–2; National Emergency Council, *Report on Economic Conditions of the South* (Washington, D.C., 1938), 45.

2. *Who's Who in America, 1966-1967,* 405; Henry I. Richards, *Cotton and the AAA* (Washington, D.C., 1936), 72; "Reminiscences of M. L. Wilson," 998-99; "Reminiscences of Samuel B. Bledsoe," Oral History Research Office, Columbia University, 81, 107-8.

3. *Cotton Trade Journal* (New Orleans), January 7 and 21, 1933; Richards, *Cotton and the AAA,* 37-39; *Cotton Trade Journal,* January 21, 1933; *Des Moines Tribune,* May 19, 1933; John D. Black, *The Dairy Industry and the AAA* (Washington, D.C., 1935), 87-88.

4. Richards, *Cotton and the AAA,* 39-41.

5. *Agricultural Adjustment, A Report of Administration of the AAA, May 1933 to February 1934* (Washington, D.C.: USDA) 23-25; *Commercial and Financial Chronicle* 137 (August 12, 1933): 1141.

6. *Agricultural Adjustment,* 27.

7. *Agricultural Adjustment,* 28; *Yearbook of Agriculture, 1935,* 35; Calvin B. Hoover, "The Agricultural Adjustment Act," *Economic Journal* 44 (December 1934): 573.

8. *Agricultural Adjustment,* 28; Richards, *Cotton and the AAA,* 46-47, 213-14; *Commercial and Financial Chronicle* 137 (September 23, 1933): 2177-78; "Reminiscences of Samuel B. Bledsoe," 89.

9. Richards, *Cotton and the AAA,* 212-13.

10. Richards, *Cotton and the AAA,* 214-17; *Agricultural Adjustment,* 35-36.

11. "The Agricultural Adjustment Act," December 1933, typescript, 4 pages, General Records of the USDA, RG 16, National Archives (hereafter NA); "Farmers at the Crossroads," *Business Week,* November 11, 1933; Bruce Bliven, "The Corn Belt Cracks Down: The Blue Eagle in the Middle West," *New Republic* 77 (November 22, 1933): 36-38.

12. Henry A. Wallace to A. C. Willford, July 5, 1933, RG 16, NA; Guy C. Shepard to C. A. Young, July 18, 1933, RG 145, NA; U.S. Congress, Senate, *Economic Situation of Hog Producers,* 72d Cong., 2d sess., 1933, Sen. Doc. 184.

13. Dennis A. Fitz Gerald, *Livestock Under the AAA* (Washington, D.C.: The Brookings Institution, 1935), 55-56; *Wallace's Farmer and Iowa Homestead* 58 (June 24, 1933): 4, (August 5, 1933), 5; G. C. Shepard to Arthur E. Tuohy, July 11, 1933; Shepard to C. A. Young, July 18, 1933; Memorandum for C. C. Davis, and A. G. Black, August 12, 1933, RG 145, NA; George N. Peek to Hon. Henry Morgenthau, Jr., August 19, 1933, 2; Memorandum for C. C. Davis and A. G. Black, August 12, 1933, Records of the Agricultural Stabilization and Conservation Service, RG 145, NA; George T. Blakey, "Ham That Never Was: The 1933 Emergency Hog Slaughter," *Historian,* 30 (November, 1967).

14. Peek to Morgenthau, August 19, 1933, RG 145, NA; Fitz Gerald, *Livestock Under the AAA,* 63-65. The plan was adopted on July 20-21, 1933, announced by the secretary of agriculture on August 18, arrangements completed and purchases begun on August 23, additional arrangements completed at thirty-six other points, and 139 packing plants at 82 processing points were authorized to purchase, process, and handle pigs and sows for the secretary by September 7.

15. *Milwaukee Journal,* August 20, 1933; *Business Week* (September 2 and September 16, 1933); D. P. Trent to Henry A. Wallace, August 23, 1933; A. G. Black to Simon Newhoff, August 25, 1933; Newhoff to Franklin D. Roosevelt, August 14, 1933; George F. Henning to Black, September 11, 1933; G. N. Peek to A. G. Donovan, September 15, 1933; C. C. Davis to William Hirth, September 22, 1933; C. R. Hemenway to Wallace, August 18, 1933; Memorandum, Black to Victor Christgau, September 12, 1933, RG 145, NA.

16. Henry A. Wallace to Hugh S. Johnson, August 22, 1933, RG 145, NA.

17. A. G. Black to William Bracht, October 2, 1933, RG 145, NA.

18. Fitz Gerald, *Livestock Under the AAA,* 68-70.

19. These purchases were undertaken and financed directly by the AAA and the Federal Surplus Relief Corporation; *Yearbook of Agriculture, 1935,* 45-48; Fitz Gerald, *Livestock Under the AAA,* 71-78.

20. *Yearbook of Agriculture, 1935,* 45-48; Fitz Gerald, *Livestock Under the AAA,* 71-78; Dennis A. Fitz Gerald, *Corn and Hogs under the Agricultural Adjustment Act* (Washington, D.C., 1934), 64; *Agricultural Adjustment,* 119.

21. Cecil A. Johnson to R. Kunkel, June 12, 1934, RG 145, NA; *Agricultural Adjustment,* 119.

22. *Agricultural Adjustment,* 119-21.

23. Fitz Gerald, *Corn and Hogs,* 64-65.

24. Fitz Gerald, *Corn and Hogs,* 67. The program was announced on October 17, 1933; Henry A. Wallace, "Objectives of a Sound Corn-Hog Program," *Extension Service Review* 4 (October 1933): 81-82.

25. Fitz Gerald, *Corn and Hogs*, 68-70; *Agricultural Adjustment*, 126-31.

26. Fitz Gerald, *Livestock Under the AAA*, 97, 98; George E. Farrell, "The County Production Control Association," *Extension Service Review* 5 (February 1934): 23-24; Fitz Gerald, *Livestock Under the AAA*, 98-102.

27. Fitz Gerald, *Livestock Under the AAA*, 103-5.

28. Fitz Gerald, *Livestock Under the AAA*, 109-10, 121-24.

29. *Agricultural Adjustment*, 44; *New York Times*, May 5, 1933.

30. *Agricultural Adjustment*, 44, 66-67.

31. Joseph S. Davis, *Wheat and the AAA*, (Washington, D.C., 1935), 51. There was a serious surplus only in the Pacific Northwest.

32. Davis, *Wheat and the AAA*, 51; *Agricultural Adjustment*, 51.

33. Davis, *Wheat and the AAA*, 52-54.

34. *Agricultural Adjustment*, 52-53.

35. "Farm Troubles," *Business Week* (September 16, 1933): 16; "Farmers at the Crossroads," *Business Week* (November 11, 1933): 8-9; *Christian Century* 50 (November 1, 1933): 1, 355-56.

36. Theodore Saloutos and John D. Hicks, *Agricultural Discontent in the Middle West, 1900-1939* (Madison, 1951), 441-43, 482; John L. Shover, *Cornbelt Rebellion* (Urbana, 1965), 20-24; *Milwaukee Journal*, September 14, 1933; *Pioneer Press*, October 16, 17, 18, 1933; *St. Paul Dispatch*, October 16, 17, 18, 1933; John M. Holzworth, *The Fighting Governor* (Chicago, 1938), 39-40.

37. *Pioneer Press*, October 18, 1933; *St. Paul Dispatch*, October 19, 1933.

38. *Pioneer Press*, December 28, 1933.

39. Holzworth, *The Fighting Governor*, 41-42; *St. Paul Dispatch*, October 19, 1933.

40. *Pioneer Press*, December 28, 1933; *St. Paul Dispatch*, January 15, 1934; Holzworth, *The Fighting Governor*, 42-43.

41. John D. Black, *The Dairy Industry and the AAA* (Washington, D.C.: 1935), 84-86; Edwin G. Nourse, *Marketing Agreements Under the AAA* (Washington, 1935), 50-55, 206; *Milwaukee Journal*, May 15, 1933; Clyde King, "The Operation of the Agricultural Adjustment Act with Reference to Dairy Products," *American Cooperation, 1933* (Washington, 1934), 285-91.

42. Black, *The Dairy Industry and the AAA*, 90; Production Control Committee Report, June 27, 1933, Dairy Section, AAA, RG 145, NA.

43. *Agricultural Adjustment*, 159-61; *New York Times*, November 12, 1933; Black, *Dairy Industry and the AAA*, 93-102.

44. *Agricultural Adjustment*, 159-61.

45. *Agricultural Adjustment*, 158-59; *Yearbook of Agriculture, 1935*, 50; *Wallace's Farmer and Iowa Homestead* 58 (September 2, 1933): 4.

46. Black, *The Dairy Industry and the AAA*, 102-6, 115.

47. *Agricultural Adjustment*, 203-4; Black, *The Dairy Industry and the AAA*, 354-55, 375-77; *Business Week*, December 23, 1933, 18.

48. *Christian Science Monitor*, April 10, 1934.

49. Black, *The Dairy Industry and the AAA*, 377-79; Joseph P. Knapp, ed., *Great American Cooperators* (Washington, 1937), 227-32, 344-45; *Milwaukee Journal*, January 10, 1934.

50. *Agricultural Adjustment 1933 to 1935* (Washington, D.C., 1936), 183. For a detailed discussion of the tobacco situation in 1933, see Harold B. Rowe, *Tobacco Under the AAA* (Washington, D.C., Brookings Institution, 1935), 48-84.

51. John B. Hutson, "The Application of the Agricultural Adjustment Act to Tobacco Cooperation," *American Cooperation, 1933* (Washington, D.C.: American Institute of Cooperation, 1934), 477-79.

52. "Reminiscences of John B. Hutson," Oral History Research Office, Columbia University, 84, 94-106.

53. C. C. Davis to G. N. Peek and Charles Brand, June 16, 1933, RG 145, NA; Hutson, *American Cooperation, 1933*, 477; Theodore Saloutos, *Farmer Movements in the South, 1865-1933* (Berkeley, 1960), 66-67, 167-83.

54. J. B. Hutson to H. Eckles, July 21, 1933, RG 145, NA; Hutson, *American Cooperation, 1933*, 477; *Agricultural Adjustment*, 70-71; *Agricultural Adjustment 1933 to 1935*, 184.

55. J. B. Hutson to H. Eckles, July 21, 1933, RG 145, NA; Hutson, *American Cooperation, 1933*, 477-79; H. A. Wallace to Jonathan Daniels, August 23, 1933, RG 145; Harold B. Rowe, *Tobacco Under the AAA*, 98-103; J. B. Hutson to G. M. Pate, RG 145, NA.

56. *AAA in 1934* (Washington, D.C.: USDA, 1935), 137; *Agricultural Adjustment 1933 to 1935* (Washington, D.C., 1936), 184–85. *Agricultural Adjustment 1933 to 1935*, 185–86. See *Agricultural Adjustment 1933 to 1935* for data on the processing tax rates established effective October 1, 1933, the subsequent changes, and the rates existing at the end of 1935.

57. *Agricultural Adjustment 1933 to 1935*, 189–90.

58. *Agricultural Adjustment 1933 to 1935*, 190; E. G. Nourse, J. S. Davis, J. D. Black, *Three Years of the Agricultural Adjustment Act* (Washington, D.C., 1937), 40; *Yearbook of Agriculture, 1935*, 58; *AAA in 1934*, 138–41.

CHAPTER SIX

1. "Reminiscences of M. L. Wilson, Oral History Research Office, Columbia University, 1305, 1311, 1313, 1324, 1497.

2. "Reminiscences of H. R. Tolley," Oral History Research Office, Columbia University, 262; "Reminiscences of M. L. Wilson," 1298; George N. Peek and Samuel Crowther, *Why Quit Our Own* (New York, 1936), 75–91; *Kansas City Times,* May 20, 1933; "Reminiscences of M. L. Wilson," 1659, 1298.

3. Peek and Crowther, *Why Quit Our Own,* 151–55.

4. "Reminiscences of M. L. Wilson," 1305, 1324, 1497, 1617.

5. R. Carlyle Buley, *The Equitable Life Assurance Society of the United States 1859–1964,* 2 vols. (New York: Appleton-Century-Crofts, 1967), 2:1024; "Reminiscences of M. L. Wilson," 1305, 1324, 1497; "Reminiscences of H. R. Tolley," 178–79.

6. "Report on Relations Between the Bureau of Agricultural Economics and the Agricultural Adjustment Administration" addressed to Henry A. Wallace, June 1934, 2–4, John D. Black Papers, Wisconsin Historical Society.

7. "Report on Relations," 5, Black Papers.

8. "Reminiscences of Oscar C. Stine," Oral History Research Office, Columbia University, 292.

9. "Report on Relations," 5–6, Black Papers.

10. "Report on Relations," 7–8, Black Papers.

11. "Reminiscences of John B. Hutson," Oral History Research Office, Columbia University, 130.

12. Memorandum, Lee Pressman to Jerome Frank, July 19, 1933; Pressman to Frank, July 27, 1933, Records of the Agricultural Stabilization and Conservation Service, RG 145, National Archives (hereafter NA).

13. Memorandum, Jerome Frank to Charles Brand, August 1, 1933, RG 145, NA.

14. Memorandum, Lee Pressman to Jerome Frank, August 2, 1933, RG 145, NA.

15. Memorandum, Clyde King to Jerome Frank, August 9, 1933, RG 145; Memorandum, Adlai E. Stevenson to Frank, August 10, 1933, RG 145, NA.

16. Memorandum, Clyde King to Jerome Frank, August 16, 1933; Memorandum, Frank to King, August 16, 1933, RG 145, NA.

17. Memorandum, Howard Corcoran to Jerome Frank, August 26, 1933, RG 145, NA.

18. Memorandum, Thomas C. Blaisdell to Jerome Frank, August 28, 1933, RG 145, NA.

19. Memorandum, John Henry Lewin to Jerome Frank, September 6, 1933; Clyde King to Frank, September 9, 1933, RG 145, NA.

20. Memorandum, Lee Pressman to Jerome Frank, October 4, 1933, RG 145, NA.

21. Memorandum, L. B. Fuller to Jerome Frank, October 22, 1933, RG 145, NA.

22. Peek and Crowther, *Why Quit Our Own,* 140, 141–45.

23. Peek and Crowther, *Why Quit Our Own,* 147–49.

24. Memorandum, Jerome Frank to Paul Appleby, October 10, 1933, RG 145, NA.

25. For a copy of the "Marketing Agreement for Flue-Cured Tobacco," see Harold B. Rowe, *Tobacco Under the AAA* (Washington 1935), 263–72. Peek and Crowther, *Why Quit Our Own,* 149–50; "Reminiscences of Rexford G. Tugwell," Oral History Research Office, Columbia University, 67.

26. "Reminiscences of Chester C. Davis," Oral History Research Office, Columbia University, 125, 145–46; "Reminiscences of John B. Hutson," 163–64; "Reminiscences of H. R. Tolley," 272.

27. "Reminiscences of H. R. Tolley," 273–74.

CHAPTER SEVEN

1. "Reminiscences of Chester C. Davis," Oral History Research Office, Columbia University, 146.

2. "Reminiscences of Chester C. Davis," 151.

3. "Reminiscences of Chester C. Davis," 151–52.

4. "Reminiscences of Chester C. Davis," 152.

5. "Reminiscences of Chester C. Davis," 155–56.

6. Memorandum, D. P. Trent to C. C. Davis, February 15, 1934, Records of the Agricultural Stabilization and Conservation Service, RG 145, National Archives (hereafter NA).

7. Davis to Trent, February 15, 1934, RG 145, NA.

8. William R. Amberson to Cully Cobb, March 5, 1934, RG 145, NA.

9. *Memphis Commercial Appeal,* March 18, 1934; *Resolution* passed by the Incorporated Town of Tyronza, March 17, 1934, RG 145, NA.

10. Cully Cobb to Paul Appleby, March 28, 1934; D. P. Trent to Extension Directors in Southern States, April 12, 1934, RG 145, NA.

11. C. C. Davis to the chiefs of the commodities sections of the AAA, April 21, 1934; Memorandum, D. P. Trent to C. C. Davis, December 14, 1935; Trent to Davis, December 28, 1934, RG 145, NA. The men selected were: Judd Brooks, Tennessee; C. W. Davis, Louisiana; E. W. Gaither, North Carolina; W. J. Green, Oklahoma; J. G. Oliver, Georgia; C. C. Randall, Arkansas; C. C. Smith, Mississippi; and A. H. Howard, South Carolina. All of these men were district agents except Oliver, who was state leader of community demonstration work.

12. C. C. Davis to the chiefs of the commodities sections of the AAA, April 21, 1934, RG 145, NA.

13. Memorandum, D. P. Trent to Henry A. Wallace, June 12, 1934; D. P. Trent Memorandum, July 2, 1934, RG 16, NA.

14. Memorandum of Conference Held on Landlord-Tenant Questions, D. P. Trent's Office, July 3, 1934, RG 16, NA.

15. Report of Adjustment Committee on Investigation of Landlord-Tenant Complaints Under the Cotton and Tobacco Adjustment Contract, September 1, 1934, J. Phil Campbell, Chairman, 1–12, RG 145, NA.

16. "Reminiscences of H. R. Tolley," Oral History Research Office, Columbia University, 287–90.

17. Memorandum, Cully Cobb to Victor A. Christgau, September 8, 1934, RG 145, NA.

18. Memorandum, D. P. Trent to Jerome Frank, September 18, 1934, RG 145, NA.

19. Memorandum, R. K. McConnaughey to Jerome Frank, September 24, 1934, RG 145, NA.

20. "Reminiscences of Chester C. Davis," 152.

21. Memorandum, Cully Cobb to Jerome Frank, October 23, 1945, RG 145, NA.

22. William R. Amberson to Paul Appleby, November 21, 1934; Telegram, Appleby to Amberson, November 28, 1934; Amberson to Eva Sams, December 9, 1934, RG 145, NA.

23. Memorandum, D. P. Trent to C. C. Davis, December 14, 1934, RG 145, NA.

24. Memorandum, J. Phil Campbell to H. R. Tolley, December 21, 1934, RG 145, NA.

25. Memorandum, Paul Appleby to Cully Cobb, December 27, 1934, RG 145, NA.

26. Memorandum, D. P. Trent to C. C. Davis, December 28, 1934, RG 145, NA.

27. *New York Times,* June 2, 1969.

28. Frank Tannenbaum to Paul Appleby, December 29, 1934, RG 145, NA.

CHAPTER EIGHT

1. H. C. Malcolm to W. J. Green, January 2, 1935, RG 145, National Archives (hereafter NA). Diary Journal of Rexford G. Tugwell, 1935, Franklin Delano Roosevelt Presidential Library, Hyde Park, N.Y. (hereafter FDRL), 80. For a glimpse into the problems confronting the organizers of the Southern Tenant Farmers' Union see Harry L. Mitchell, *Mean Things Happening in This Land: The Life and Times of H. L. Mitchell, Cofounder of the Southern Tenant Farmers' Union* (Montclair, New Jersey: Allanheld, Osmun, 1979). Two other volumes that shed light on the struggles of the tenants and sharecroppers are by David E. Conrad, *The Forgotten Farmers: The Story of Sharecroppers and the New Deal* (Urbana, Univ. of Illinois Press, 1969) and Donald H. Grubbs, *Cry from the Cotton: The Southern*

Tenant Farmers and the New Deal (Chapel Hill: Univ. of North Carolina Press, 1971).

2. Memorandum, Mary Connor Myers to Jerome Frank, January 5, 1935, Records of the Agricultural Stabilization and Conservation Service, RG 145, NA.

3. Memorandum, William E. Byrd, Jr., to Jerome Frank, January 11, 1935, Jerome Frank Papers, Sterling Memorial Library, Yale University.

4. Memorandum, Jerome Frank to Victor Christgau, January 11, 1935, Frank Papers.

5. Memorandum, Jerome Frank to Victor Christgau, January 11, 1935; Memorandum, Frank to Henry A. Wallace, January 12, 1935, Frank Papers.

6. Memorandum, William E. Byrd to Cully Cobb, January 14, 1935; Memorandum, Jerome Frank to Francis Shea, January 14, 1935, Frank Papers.

7. Memorandum, Jerome Frank to William F. Byrd, January 14, 1935, Frank Papers.

8. Telegram, Mary Connor Myers to Jerome Frank, January 18, 1935; C. T. Carpenter to Jerome Frank, January 19, 1935, Frank Papers.

9. Telegram, Mary Connor Myers to Jerome Frank, January 21, 1935, Frank Papers.

10. Memorandum, La Fayette Patterson to Victor Christgau, January 22, 1935, Frank Papers.

11. Memorandum, Jerome Frank to Alfred D. Stedman, January 30, 1935, Frank Papers.

12. Lucille B. Milner to Paul Appleby, January 26, 1935, RG 145, NA.

13. Milner to Appleby, January 26, 1935, RG 145, NA.

14. Appleby to Milner, January 31, 1935, RG 145, NA.

15. Letter signed by ten agents to Chester Davis, January 26, 1935, RG 145, NA.

16. "Reminiscences of John B. Hutson," Oral History Research Office, Columbia University, 168–70; for an able presentation of the Appleby position see Gladys Baker, " 'And to Act for the Secretary,' Paul H. Appleby and the Department of Agriculture, 1933-1940," *Agricultural History* 45 (October 1971), 235–58.

17. "Reminiscences of H. R. Tolley," Oral History Research Office, Columbia University, 305–6.

18. "Reminiscences of Chester C. Davis," Oral History Research Office, Columbia University, 166.

19. "Reminiscences of Chester C. Davis," 167–68; "Reminiscences of H. R. Tolley," 307–9.

20. "Reminiscences of H. R. Tolley," 307–9.

21. "Reminiscences of John B. Hutson," 170–71; "Reminiscences of Gardner Jackson," Oral History Research Office, Columbia University, 490.

22. "Reminiscences of Gardner Jackson," 447.

23. "Reminiscences of Gardner Jackson," 586.

24. "Reminiscences of Gardner Jackson," 593–98.

25. "Reminiscenses of Gardner Jackson," 598. Address by Henry A. Wallace, "The Dairy Dilemma," Madison, Wisconsin, January 31, 1934, Gardner Jackson Papers, FDRL; *Dairy Record* 34 (February 7, 1934): 3, 5, 17. See also Memorandum, Gardner Jackson to Paul Appleby, March 17, 1934, Jackson Papers.

26. "Reminiscences of Gardner Jackson," 600–602.

27. "Reminiscences of Chester C. Davis," 173–75.

28. "Reminiscences of Chester C. Davis," 177–83.

29. Memorandum, Alfred D. Stedman to Chester C. Davis, February 6, 1935, Frank Papers.

30. "Reminiscences of Rexford G. Tugwell," Oral History Research Office, Columbia University, 64–65.

31. "Reminiscences of Gardner Jackson," 620–22.

32. "Reminiscences of Rexford G. Tugwell," 46–47; Telegram, R. G. Tugwell to Marguerite Le Hand, February 5, 1935, Franklin D. Roosevelt Papers, FDRL.

33. "Reminiscences of Rexford G. Tugwell," 64–65; Diary, Rexford G. Tugwell, 1935, 45, FDRL.

34. "Reminiscences of Rexford G. Tugwell," 68–69.

35. Drew Pearson and Robert S. Allen, *The Nine Old Men* (Garden City, N.Y.: Doubleday, 1936), 280.

36. "Reminiscences of H. R. Tolley," 349–50, 357–58.

37. "Reminiscences of Chester C. Davis," 188–89.

CHAPTER NINE

1. *Des Moines Tribune,* December 12, 1934.

2. *Buffalo News,* January 4, 1935; "Report of the Secretary of Agriculture to the President, December 10, 1935," *Yearbook of Agriculture, 1936* (Washington, D.C.), 2.

3. *Des Moines Register,* July 14, 1935.

4. "Reminiscences of H. R. Tolley," Oral History Research Office, Columbia University, 296-97; Robert J. Morgan, *Governing Soil Conservation* (Baltimore, 1966), 52-79.

5. "Reminiscences of H. R. Tolley," 296-97.

6. *Milwaukee Journal,* October 17, 1935.

7. *Des Moines Tribune,* May 15, 1934; Henry A. Wallace, "We Are More Than Economic Men," *Scribner's* 96 (1934): 323; *Des Moines Register,* May 9, 1935; H. A. Wallace to Frank Michl, March 17, 1936, General Records of the USDA, RG 16, National Archives (hereafter NA).

8. See editorial in *Chicago Journal of Commerce,* March 18, 1935; U.S., Congress, Senate, *Journal,* March 13, 1935, 74 Cong., 1st sess., p. 192. Secretary Wallace's Correspondence, Folder on Cotton, March-April 1935, RG 16, NA.

9. "Report of the Secretary of Agriculture to the President, December 10, 1935," *Yearbook of Agriculture, 1936,* 11-12.

10. Memorandum, Lawrence Myers to Chester C. Davis, December 3, 1934, Records of the Agricultural Stabilization and Conservation Service, RG 145, NA.

11. Memorandum, Mordecai Ezekiel to Victor Christgau, January 31, 1935, RG 16; Memorandum, Lawrence Myers to Chester Davis, February 19, 1935, RG 145, NA.

12. Rexford G. Tugwell to the Attorney General, March 15, 1935, RG 16, NA.

13. Charles L. Gifford to Henry Wallace, April 16, 1935, RG 16, NA. See also E. P. Learned, "The Cotton Textile Situation," *Harvard Business Review* 14 (Autumn 1935): 29-44; Henry A. Wallace to Ellison D. Smith, March 11, 1935, RG 16, NA.

14. Henry A. Wallace to Charles L. Gifford, April 13, 1935, RG 16, NA.

15. Charles L. Gifford to Henry A. Wallace, April 16, 1935, RG 16, NA.

16. Paul H. Appleby to F. C. Shackelford, April 29, 1935; Shackelford to Henry A. Wallace, April 29, 1935, RG 16, NA.

17. Henry A. Wallace to Charles Gifford, April 13, 1935; Gifford to Wallace, April 16, 1935; Howard Veit to Wallace, April 19, 1935; An Appeal To The North Carolina Legislature . . . and Senators and Representatives in Congress in Behalf of Maintaining the Processing Tax on Cotton, signed by Clarence Poe, B. W. Kilgore, and others; J. E. Edwards to John H. Bankhead, April 23, 1935; C. S. Love to Wallace, April 25, 1935; F. C. Shackelford to Wallace, April 25, 1935; RG 16, NA.

18. *Pioneer Press,* May 13, 1935; "Reminiscences of Chester C. Davis," Oral History Research Office, Columbia University, 191-92; Roy V. Scott and J. G. Shoalmire, *The Public Career of Cully A. Cobb* (Jackson: University and College Press of Mississippi, 1973), 232-35.

19. Henry A. Wallace to Daniel O. Hastings, May 24, 1935, RG 16, NA.

20. Henry A. Wallace to Daniel O. Hastings, May 24, 1935, RG 16, NA.

21. USDA, AAA, C. C. Davis, "A Report of Administration of the Agricultural Adjustment Act February 15, 1934 to December 31, 1934," *Agricultural Adjustment in 1934* (Washington, D.C., 1935), 255 and 261; Davis, "A Report of Administration of the Agricultural Adjustment Act May 12, 1933 to December 31, 1935," *Agricultural Adjustment 1933 to 1935* (Washington, D.C., 1936), 97; R. G. Tugwell to the Attorney General, March 15, 1935; Henry A. Wallace to Richard B. Russell, April 4, 1935, RG 16, NA.

22. For a summation of the amendments to the AAA in 1934 see *Agricultural Adjustment in 1934,* 249-53.

23. "Report of the Secretary of Agriculture," December 10, 1935," 12; *Des Moines Tribune,* December 12, 1934; *Minneapolis Journal,* June 29, July 3, 9, 14, August 25, and September 28, 1935; *New York Times,* November 30, December 1, 4, 5, 1935.

24. *Yearbook of Agriculture 1936,* 12-13; M. L. Wilson to Morris Sheppard, May 10, 1936, RG 16, NA.

25. *Yearbook of Agriculture 1936,* 13-14.

26. *New York Times,* August 4, 1935.

27. *Yearbook of Agriculture 1936,* 5.

28. *Yearbook of Agriculture 1936,* 5.

29. "Reminiscences of H. R. Tolley," 302.
30. *Yearbook of Agriculture 1936,* 6-7.
31. *Yearbook of Agriculture 1936,* 7-8.
32. An idea of the extent to which duplication of effort had taken place in land planning and administration was contained in a special memorandum that Phil Glick prepared when he served as an assistant to Jerome Frank. On November 21, 1934 he pointed out there were "a total of twenty-two agencies directly engaged in land administration, land planning or land acquisition, and a total of fourteen agencies whose functions are very closely related to the work of the land planning and administration agencies." Memorandum, November 21, 1934, RG 16, NA.
33. These conferences were held in Ames, Iowa; Salt Lake City, Utah; Birmingham, Alabama; and New York City. Representatives of the USDA attending these conferences included M. L. Wilson, assistant secretary of agriculture; H. R. Tolley, assistant administrator and director of the Division of Program Planning of the AAA; C. W. Warburton of the Extension Divison; and J. T. Jardine, chief, Office of Experiment Stations. H. A. Wallace to L. N. Duncan, February 20, 1935; Memorandum, Roy F. Hendrickson to F. A. Flood, March 22, 1935; and H. A. Wallace to Livingston Farrand, February 25, 1935, RG 16, NA.
34. *Yearbook of Agriculture 1936,* 9-10.
35. *Yearbook of Agriculture 1936,* 11.
36. Henry A. Wallace, "The A. A. A. Decision," *Vital Speeches* 2(February 1936): 29-31; *Des Moines Tribune,* January 7, 1936.
37. *New York Times,* January 12, 1970; C. L. Huxman to Clifford R. Hope, January 25, 1936; Hope to Huxman, January 28, 1936, Clifford R. Hope Papers, Kansas State Historical Society.

CHAPTER TEN

1. Henry A. Wallace, "Toward a Balanced Agriculture," December 12, 1935, *Yearbook of Agriculture, 1935,* 9-15; Henry J. Tasca, *The Reciprocal Trade Policy of the United States* (Philadelphia 1938), 18-28. "Reminiscences of M. L. Wilson," Oral History Research Office, Columbia University, 1471-72.
2. George N. Peek and Samuel Crowther, *Why Quit Our Own* (New York, 1936), 175-78.
3. Tasca, *Reciprocal Trade Policy,* 29.
4. Peek and Crowther, *Why Quit Our Own,* 180-83.
5. George N. Peek, "Are Trade Treaties Beneficial?" *Christian Science Monitor,* October 28, 1936, quoted in Tasca, Reciprocal Trade Policy, 90.
6. *Des Moines Register,* February 9, 1934; "Reminiscences of M. L. Wilson," 1490.
7. Henry A. Wallace, *America Must Choose* (New York 1934); Wallace, "America Must Choose," *Rural America* 12 (March 1934): 3-4. This same theme was presented in Wallace, "American Agriculture and World Markets," *Foreign Affairs* 12 (1934): 216-30.
8. Helen Howell Moorhead to Henry A. Wallace, February 26, 1934; M. L. Wilson to Raymond Leslie Buell, August 7, 1934, General Records of the USDA, RG 16, National Archives (hereafter NA).
9. *Des Moines Tribune,* June 20, 1935. See Wallace's address at Harvard, "Confusion, Choice and Unified Action," *Rural America* 13 (September 1935): 3-4. "Reminiscences of M. L. Wilson, "1490-92; *New York Times,* December 11, 12, 13, 1934; American Farm Bureau Federation, *Official News Letter* 13 (December 18, 1934): 1, 4.
10. "Report of the Secretary of Agriculture to the President," December 1935, *Yearbook of Agriculture 1936,* 14.
11. *Yearbook of Agriculture 1936* (Washington, D.C.), 5-15; *1935,* 9-15; USDA, AAA, *Agricultural Adjustment in 1934* (Washington, D. C., 1935), 287-88.
12. For a lengthy scholarly discussion of the general question of agricultural imports, see Don D. Humphrey, *American Imports* (New York 1955), 259-85.
13. *Yearbook of Agriculture, 1936,* 18-19.
14. *Yearbook of Agriculture, 1936,* 19-20.
15. *Operation of the Trade Agreement Program, 1934-1948,* pt. 2 (Washington, D. C.: Tariff Commission, 1934-1949); *History of the Trade Agreements Program* (Washington,

D.C., 1949), 6-7, 8-9, 17. See also "Governor Franklin D. Roosevelt, Democratic Nominee for President, Urges Reciprocal Tariffs to Restore Foreign Trade," *Commercial and Financial Chronicle* 135 (September 24, 1932): 2094-95; see also Tasca, *Reciprocal Trade Policy,* on "The Reciprocal Trade Act of 1934," 29-34, and on "The Problem of the Most-Favored Nation Treatment," 100-121; and Richard N. Kottman, "The Canadian-American Trade Agreement of 1935: The First Crack in the Wall," in *Reciprocity and the North American Triangle* (Ithaca: Cornell Univ. Press, 1968), 79-116.

16. *Kansas City Times,* September 21, 1934; *Kansas City Star,* November 23, 1934.

17. Henry A. Wallace to George N. Peek, November 27, 1934, RG 16, NA; Henry A. Wallace to Franklin D. Roosevelt, November 27, 1934, RG 16, NA.

18. Memorandum, Chester C. Davis to Henry A. Wallace, December 6, 1934, RG 16, NA.

19. Mordecai Ezekiel to Karl Mitchell, October 26, 1934, RG 16, NA.

20. Henry A. Wallace to Francis B. Sayre, February 8, 1935, RG 16, NA.

21. Wallace to Straus, March 21, 1935, RG 16, NA.

22. L. D. Le Cron to Rene A. Stiegler, April 22, 1935, RG 16, NA.

23. Henry A. Wallace to Arthur Capper, May 7, 1935, RG 16, NA.

24. Clifford V. Gregory to Henry A. Wallace, November 27, 1935, RG 16, NA.

25. *Proceedings of the 17th Annual Convention of the American Farm Bureau Federation,* December 9-11, 1935, 82.

26. *Proceedings of the 17th Annual Convention of the American Farm Bureau Federation,* 78-79, *American Farm Bureau Federation News Letter* 14 (December 10, 24, 1935): 3.

27. M. L. Wilson to J. Clyde Marquis, February 15, 1936; Ray Bowden to Wilson, January 20, 1936; Telegram, Frank Vandenheuwel to Rexford G. Tugwell, April 6, 1936; Henry A. Wallace to J. M. Hutson, May 16, 1936, RG 16, NA.

28. M. L. Wilson to Berkeley Spiller, February 6, 1936, RG 16, NA; *Proceedings of the 17th Annual Convention of the American Farm Bureau Federation,* December 9-11, 1935, 9; J. D. Le Cron to William Dietrich, February 24, 1936, RG 16, NA.

29. "Significance of Agricultural Imports, Xeroxed copy, June 17, 1935; Henry A. Wallace to Tom Berry, June 2, 1936; Wallace to John Flanagan, Jr., June 2, 1936; Rexford G. Tugwell to Louis Ludlow, June 9, 1936, RG 16, NA.

30. Chester C. Davis to Franklin D. Roosevelt, August 3, 1936, RG 16, NA; *Des Moines Register,* June 4 and 5, 1936.

31. Chester C. Davis to Franklin D. Roosevelt, August 3, 1936, RG 16, NA.

32. Tasca, *Reciprocal Trade Policy,* 90-91; M. L. Wilson to L. H. Goddard, July 1, 1936, RG 16, NA; see also the *New York Times,* July 3, August 16, 1936.

33. Tasca, *Reciprocal Trade Policy,* 96-97. See, for instance, Clifford V. Gregory to Henry A. Wallace, November 27, 1935, RG 16, NA.

34. *Des Moines Register,* May 5, 1936.

CHAPTER ELEVEN

1. "Reminiscences of H. R. Tolley," 397; "Reminiscences of M. L. Wilson," 1616, Oral History Research Office, Columbia University.

2. E. L. Morgan, "National Policy and Rural Public Welfare," *Rural Sociology* 1 (1936): 8-9. For a pioneer appraisal of rural charities and corrections see John M. Gillette, *Constructive Rural Sociology* (New York: Sturgis and Walton Co., 1916), 363-79.

3. Gillette, *Constructive Rural Sociology,* 10-14.

4. E. D. Tetrau to R. G. Tugwell, October 11, 1933, General Records of the USDA, RG 16, National Archives (hereafter NA).

5. Josephine C. Brown, "Rural Families on Relief," *Annals of the American Academy of Political and Social Science* 176 (November 1934): 90.

6. Harry Hopkins, *Spending to Save: The Complete Story of Relief* (New York, 1936), 139-41.

7. "Reminiscences of H. R. Tolley," 346.

8. "Reminiscences of H. R. Tolley," 346, 347.

9. "Reminiscences of M. L. Wilson," 1377-78.

10. U.S., Congress, Senate, *Resettlement Administration Program,* 74th Cong., 2d sess., S. Doc. 213, p. 1 (hereafter S. Doc. 213); Rebecca Farmhouse and Irene Link, *Effects of the*

Works Program on Rural Relief, WPA, Division of Social Research, Research Monograph 13 (Washington, D.C., 1938), xi.

11. Doris Carothers, *Chronology of the Federal Emergency Relief Administration, May 12, 1933 to December 31, 1935,* WPA, Division of Social Research, Research Monograph 6 (Washington, D.C., 1937), 1-3; A. R. Magnus, *Aspects of Rural Relief,* WPA, Division of Social Research, Research Monograph 14 (Washington, D.C. 1938), 14, 19.

12. Carothers, *Chronology of the Federal Farm Emergency Administration,* 16, 20, 25; Magnus, *Changing Aspects of Rural Relief,* 19-20.

13. Carothers, *Chronology of the Federal Emergency Relief Administration,* 16, 57, 60, 66, 70-71; Magnus, *Changing Aspects of Rural Relief,* 20.

14. Magnus, *Changing Aspects of Rural Relief,* 20.

15. Berta Asch and A. R. Magnus, *Farmers on Relief and Rehabilitation,* WPA, Research Monograph 8 (Washington, D.C., 1937), xiii.

16. Asch and Magnus, *Farmers on Relief,* xiv.

17. Asch and Magnus, *Farmers on Relief,* xix-xx.

18. "Reminiscences of M. L. Wilson," 1103-6; J. Blaine Gwin, "Subsistence Homesteads," *Social Forces* 12 (May 1934): 522-25; "Reminiscences of M. L. Wilson," 1069-78.

19. M. L. Wilson, "The Place of Subsistence Homesteads in Our National Economy," *Journal of Farm Economics* 14 (January 1934): 80-81.

20. Wilson, "The Place of Subsistence Homsteads," 75; "Reminiscences of M. L. Wilson," 1079-86; Sidney Baldwin, *Poverty and Politics: The Rise and Decline of the Farm Security Administration* (Chapel Hill 1968), 68-69.

21. Wilson, "The Place of Subsistence Homesteads," 80-81. See also M. L. Wilson to Stacy May, November 6, 1934, and Wilson to Robert J. Kohn, January 14, 1935, RG 16, NA.

22. Leonard A. Salter, Jr., "Research and Subsistence Homesteads," *Rural Sociology* 2 (June 1937): 206-10. See also B. L. Melvin, "Emergency and Permanent Legislation with Reference to the History of Subsistence Homesteads," *American Sociological Review* 1 (1936): 622-31; Phil M. Glick, "The Federal Subsistence Homesteads Program," *Yale Law Journal* 41 (June 1935): 1324-79; Noble Clark, "Social and Economic Implications of the National Land Program, Discussion," *Journal of Farm Economics* 18 (May 1936): 274-80; Henry A. Wallace to Claude E. Fox, April 30, 1934; Harold L. Ickes to Leo Kolcialkowski, March 15, 1934, RG 16, NA; "Reminiscences of M. L. Wilson," 1095-96. For an appraisal of the subsistence homestead idea and its alternatives, see Memorandum, L. C. Gray to M. L. Wilson, November 27, 1934, RG 16, NA.

23. "Reminiscences of M. L. Wilson," 1257-64.

24. "Reminiscences of M. L. Wilson," 1266-69, 1270-80.

25. Harold L. Ickes, *The Secret Diary of Harold L. Ickes,* 3 vols. (New York 1954), 1:152, 218-19, 272-73.

26. Carl C. Taylor, "Social and Economic Significance of the Subsistence Homesteads Program—From the Viewpoint of a Sociologist," *Journal of Farm Economics* 17 (November 1935): 720-22.

27. S. Doc. 213, p. 1; The Land Policy Section served as the planning agency for the FERA with responsibility for the selection, planning, and development of the agricultural projects of the program. "Report for Assistant Secretary of Agriculture M. L. Wilson on Progress of the Work by the Land Policy Section, Division of Program Planning, AAA," from L. C. Gray, August 29, 1934, RG 16, NA. "Reminiscences of M. L. Wilson," 1282, 1285; Rexford G. Tugwell, "The Resettlement Idea," *Agricultural History* 33 (1959): 159.

28. W. W. Alexander, "Overcrowded Farms," *Yearbook of Agriculture: Farmers in a Changing World* (Washington, D. C., USDA, 1940), 884-86.

29. S. Doc. 213, p. 2-4.

30. S. Doc. 213, p. 3-4.

31. S. Doc. 213, p. 6-7.

32. *New York Times,* December 11, 1935.

33. *Literary Digest,* May 30, 1936, 10; Ira S. Robbins, "Resettlement Administration, Only Partially Settled," *The American City,* June 1936, 5; *New York Times,* May 20, 1936.

34. Blair Bolles, "Resettling America," *American Mercury* 41 (November 1936): 337-38; *New York Times,* November 17, 1935; Clifford A. Hope to Mrs. Carl Plumb, January 31, 1936, Clifford R. Hope Papers, Kansas State Historical Society; *New York Times,* August 2, 1936.

35. *New York Times,* May 24 and Augugst 2, 1936.

36. *New York Times,* May 24, August 3 and 23, October 21, 23, 26, 1936.

37. Rexford G. Tugwell, "The Resettlement Idea," *Agricultural History* 33 (October 1949): 159–60.

38. Tugwell, "The Resettlement Idea," 161–63.

CHAPTER TWELVE

1. Lister Hill, Maury Maverick, et al. to James A. Farley, June 4, 1936, General Records of the USDA, RG 16, National Archives (hereafter NA); "Washington Notes: A Farm For Every Farmer," *New Republic* 87 (July 29, 1936): 352; Henry S. Commager, ed., *Documents of American History,* 5th ed. (New York, 1939), 535–36, 539–40.

2. Franklin D. Roosevelt to John H. Bankhead, September 17, 1936, RG 16, NA.

3. Paul Appleby to Carl C. Taylor, November 2, 1936, RG 16, NA.

4. Henry A. Wallace to Rexford G. Tugwell, November 5, 1936, RG 16, NA; *Report of the President's Committee on Farm Tenancy* (Washington, D.C.: National Resources Committee, 1937), 25; Clyde T. Ellis, *A Giant Step* (New York: Random House, 1966), 39.

5. Clarence Poe to Henry A. Wallace and L. C. Gray, December 22, 1936; Mack Roth to Claude Pepper, November [?], 1936; Pepper to Henry Wallace, December 2, 1936; William E. Zuech to M. L. Wilson, November 19, 1936, RG 16, NA.

6. Remarks of H. A. Wallace at the Opening Session of the President's Special Committee on Farm Tenancy, Washington, D.C., December 16, 1936, RG 16, NA.

7. Memorandum, L. C. Gray to members of the President's Special Committee on Farm Tenancy, December 22, 1936; H. A. Wallace to His Excellency The Governor of North Dakota, December 23, 1936, RG 16, NA.

8. M. L. Wilson to Howard Odum, January 14, 1937, RG 16, NA.

9. R. L. Burgess to M. L. Wilson, January 16, 1937, RG 16, NA.

10. Jonathan Garst to R. G. Tugwell, November 5, 1936, RG 16, NA.

11. Jonathan Garst to R. G. Tugwell, November 10, 1936, RG 16, NA.

12. National Committee on Rural Social Planning to Henry A. Wallace and Rexford G. Tugwell, November 12, 1936, RG 16, NA.

13. National Committee on Rural Social Planning to Henry A. Wallace and Rexford G. Tugwell, November 12, 1936, RG 16, NA.

14. J. R. Butler and H. L. Mitchell to Franklin D. Roosevelt, November 20, 1936, RG 83, NA.

15. Statement of Charles S. Johnson in Statement of Subcommittee of Southern Policy Association to Special Committee on Farm Tenancy, December 1936, 1–3, RG 16, NA.

16. Statement of H. Clarence Nixon, RG 16, NA.

17. Statement of Arthur Raper, RG 16, NA.

18. Statement of Rupert B. Vance, RG 16, NA.

19. C. E. Brehm to L. C. Gray, January 7, 1937, Records of the BAE, RG 83, NA.

20. C. E. Brehm to L. C. Gray, January 7, 1937, RG 83, NA.

21. Edward A. O'Neal to Henry A. Wallace, January 25, 1937, RG 16, NA.

22. Mary McLeod Bethune to L. C. Gray, January 23, 1937, RG 83, NA.

23. Katherine Bennett to L. C. Gray, January 23, 1937, RG 83, NA.

24. "Reminiscences of Will Alexander," Oral History Research Office, Columbia University, 396–97; Sidney Baldwin, *Poverty and Politics* (Chapel Hill, 1968), 119–21.

25. "Reminiscences of Will Alexander," 637. For a critical view of Will Alexander, see Donald Holley, *Uncle Sam's Farmers* (Urbana: Univ. of Illinois Press, 1975), 102–3.

26. "Reminiscences of Will Alexander," 640.

27. Paul Maris, *The Land Is Mine* (Washington, D.C., 1950), 2. For an authoritative and concise appraisal of the "agricultural ladder" thesis, see Richard T. Ely and George S. Wehrwein, *Land Economics* (Madison: Univ. of Wisconsin Press, 1940), 196–98. See also William J. Spillman, "The Agricultural Ladder," *American Economic Review,* Supplement 8 (March 1919): 170–79; B. H. Hibbard and Guy A. Petersen, *How Wisconsin Farmers Become Farm Owners,* Wisconsin Agricultural Experiment Station Bulletin No. 2 (Madison, 1928); David Rozman, "The Agricultural Ladder in Foreign Countries," *Journal of Land and Public Utility Economics* 2 (April 1926): 249–53; Carl F. Wehrwein, "The Pre-Ownership Steps on the Agricultural Ladder in a Low Tenancy Region," *Journal of Land and Public Utility Economics* 7 (February 1931): 65–66.

28. Maris, *The Land Is Mine,* 5.

29. Maris, *The Land Is Mine,* 8–9, 358.

30. Paul Appleby to Sherman Minton, August 7, 1937, RG 16, NA.

31. Rexford G. Tugwell, "The Resettlement Idea," *Agricultural History* 33 (1959): 160.

CHAPTER THIRTEEN

1. J. D. Le Cron to Louis R. Lautier, November 14, 1939, General Records of the USDA, RG 16, National Archives (hereafter NA). Address by Joseph H. B. Evans Before the Annual Meeting of the Joint Committee of National Recovery, Washington, D. C., November 23, 1935, Records of the Farm Home Administration, RG 96, NA.

2. Houston S. Schweich, "The Negro and the Farm," undated ms., 3–4; N. C. Bruce to Henry A. Wallace, June 28, 1933; Fred H. Hildebrandt to Wallace, June 30, 1933; Paul D. Scott et al. to Wallace, May 4, 1933; John P. Davis to Wallace, July 19, 1933; Travis B. Howard to Wallace, July 17, 1933, RG 16, NA.

3. N. C. Bruce to Henry A. Wallace, June 28, 1933; Fred H. Hildebrandt to Wallace, June 30, 1933; Benjamin F. Hubert to Wallace, September 17, 1933; R. G. Tugwell to Hildebrandt, August 4, 1933, RG 16, NA.

4. R. G. Tugwell to W. F. Reden, July 7, 1933; Tugwell to Fred H. Hildebrandt, August 4, 1933, RG 16, NA.

5. R. G. Tugwell to Fred H. Hildebrandt, August 4, 1933, RG 16, NA.

6. Henry A. Wallace to Fred H. Hildebrandt, July 19, 1933, RG 16, NA.

7. W. F. Reden to R. G. Tugwell, August 8, 1933; W. W. Stockberger to Henry A. Wallace, June 30, 1934, RG 16, NA.

8. Paul D. Scott et al. to H. A. Wallace, May 4, 1933; John P. Davis to H. A. Wallace, July 19, 1933; The Negro Industrial League to Henry A. Wallace, July 19, 1933 on "A Negro farm demonstration agent for Marion County, Texas"; H. A. Wallace to John P. Davis, July 25, 1933, RG 16, NA.

9. Memorandum, Cully Cobb to Chester C. Davis, October 31, 1933, RG 16, NA.

10. R. G. Tugwell to Travis B. Howard, July 25, 1933; Paul H. Appleby to Roland B. Kutsler, November 10, 1933, RG 16, NA.

11. Clark Foreman to Henry A. Wallace, January 2, 1934; C. W. Warburton to Paul H. Appleby, January 8, 1934; John P. Davis to Wallace, March 27, 1934; Appleby to Davis, April 3, 1934, RG 16, NA.

12. Bruce L. Melvin to R. R. Wright, April 6, 1934; Melvin to Wright, July 23, 1934; the general manager to R. R. Wright, November 10, 1934, RG 96, NA.

13. L. S. Moore to Henry A. Wallace, June 14, 1934; W. F. Reden to Chester C. Davis, June 16, 1934; A. L. Carr and W. H. Davis to Chester Davis, June 21, 1934; Lelia Flippin to Hugh S. Johnson, July 9, 1934, RG 145, NA; Roy Wilkins to Henry A. Wallace, May 28, 1934, Records of the Agricultural Stabilization and Conservation Service, RG 145, NA; Roy Wilkins to Cully Cobb, June 13, 1934, RG 145, NA.

14. Milo Perkins to William W. Sanders, November 11, 1935; Paul H. Appleby to Walter White, March 6, 1935, RG 16, NA.

15. "An Open Letter To The President," *Pittsburgh Courier,* March 9, 1935. *Pittsburgh Courier,* April 15, 1939. Dorothy Carothers, *Chronology of the Federal Emergency Relief Administration, May 12, 1933 to December 31, 1935,* WPA, Research Monograph 6 (Washington, D.C. 1937), 9 and 69.

16. H. R. Tolley to Robert J. Bulkley, January 5, 1938, RG 16, NA.

17. Charles S. Brown to Henry A. Wallace, November 4, 1937; Untitled ms. by Charles S. Brown, 1–3, November 9, 1937, RG 16, NA.

18. Brown, 3–5; C. W. Warburton to J. D. Le Cron, November 20, 1937; Warburton to Le Cron, December 1, 1937; C. B. Manifold to Le Cron, December 2, 1937; W. W. Alexander to Le Cron, December 10, 1937; Alfred D. Stedman to Le Cron, December 13, 1937; J. D. Le Cron to Charles S. Brown, December 16, 1937, RG 16, NA.

19. Henry A. Wallace to John W. Davis, January 28, 1938, RG 16, NA. For more details on the exchange of information between officials of the department on the points raised by Davis see James T. Jardine to Paul H. Appleby, December 30, 1937; W. W. Alexander to Appleby, January 5, 1938; H. R. Tolley to Robert J. Bulkley, January 5, 1938, RG 16, NA.

20. Mordecai Ezekiel to C. C. Randall, May 27, 1938, RG 16, NA.

21. Gladys Baker, *The County Agent* (Chicago: Univ. of Chicago Press, 1940), 205–6.

22. *The South's Landless Farmers* (Atlanta: Commission on Interracial Cooperation, 1937), pamphlet, p. 13; Rupert B. Vance, "The Negro Agricultural Worker," mimeographed (Committee on Negroes and Economic Reconstruction, 1934), 8.

23. Houston S. Schweich to Rexford G. Tugwell, January 31, 1934; Calvin B. Hoover to Schweich, February 8, 1934; W. P. Evans, "Negroes Would Farm," clipping dated February 1, 1935, RG 16, NA.

24. Schweich, "The Negro and the Farm," 1–2.

25. Schweich, "The Negro and the Farm," 3–5.

26. U.S. Special Comittee on Farm Tenancy: *Report* of the President's Committee, 1937, 99.

27. R. M. Evans to Edward A. Jones, May 2, 1938, RG 16, NA.

28. Address by Joseph H. B. Evans Before the Annual Meeting of the Joint Committee on National Recovery, Washington, D.C., November 23, 1935, 11–15, RG 96, NA.

29. W. Morse Salisbury to Anna A. Twonig, July 1, 1939, RG 161, NA. See also "The Negro Farm Owner Isn't Licked," *Opportunity* (June 1939).

30. Walter White to Henry A. Wallace, December 8, 1938, RG 16, NA.

CHAPTER FOURTEEN

1. See especially U.S., Congress, House, *The Future of the Great Plains,* 75th Cong., 1st sess., 1937, H. Doc. 144; *Northern Great Plains* (Washington, D.C.: United States National Resources Planning Board, 1940); R. S. Kifer and H. L. Stewart, *Farming Hazards in the Drought Area,* WPA Research Monograph 16 (Washington, D.C., 1938); Carl Kraenzel, *The Great Plains in Transition* (Norman, Okla., 1955); R. C. Smith, "Upsetting the Balance of Nature with Special Reference to Kansas and the Great Plains," *Science* 75 (June 24, 1932):649–54.

2. Lawrence Svobida, *An Empire of Dust* (Caldwell, Ida., 1940); George S. Reeves, *A Man from South Dakota* (New York, 1950); Mari Sandoz, *Old Jules* (Boston, 1935); Paul Sears, *Deserts on the March* (Norman, Okla., 1935); Dorothea Lange, *An American Exodus* (New York, 1939); "Drought and Insects Bring Havoc to Crops," *Newsweek* 3 (May 19, 1934): 5–6; Paul Sears, "The Black Blizzards," in Daniel Aaron, ed., *America in Crisis* (New York, 1947), 287–302; *Literary Digest* 117 (May 26, 1934): 12, (June 16, 1934): 4; "Unprecedented Heat Brings Death and Destruction to Half of the United States," *Newsweek* 4 (August 4, 1934): 6–7; M. Markey, "Nature and the Farmer in the Dakotas and Eastern Montana," *Saturday Evening Post* 207 (July 21, 1934): 5–7; *Literary Digest* 118 (August 18, 1934): 5; Margaret Bourke-White, "The Drought," *Fortune* 10 (October 1934): 76–83; "Drought Effects Deepen," *Business Week,* August 11, 1934, 5–6; *Milwaukee Journal,* May 7, 1934; *Pioneer Press,* July 19, 1934; *The Future of the Great Plains,* 1–6.

3. *The Future of the Great Plains, 5–6.*

4. First Annual Report, *Resettlement Administration* (Washington, 1936), 9.

5. *Yearbook of Agriculture, 1935* (Washington, D.C.: USDA, 1935), 18; D. A. Fitz Gerald, *Livestock Under the AAA* (Washington, D.C., 1935), 196–97.

6. Fitz Gerald, *Livestock Under the AAA,* 207–9.

7. *Participation Under AAA Programs, 1933–1935* (Washington, D.C.: USDA, 1938), 19.

8. *Participation Under AAA Programs, 1933–1935, 25.*

9. L. C. Gray, "Federal Purchase and Administration of Submarginal Lands in the Great Plains," *Journal of Farm Economics* 21 (February 1939): 123–31.

10. E. N. Munns and Joseph H. Stoeckler, "How Are the Great Plains Shelterbelts?" *Journal of Forestry* 44 (1946): 237.

11. Joseph H. Stoeckler and Ross A. Williams, "Windbreaks and Shelterbelts," *Yearbook of Agriculture, 1949* (Washington, D.C.: USDA, 1949), 191–92; Bryant Putney, "Reconstruction of the Dust Bowl," in Richard M. Boeckel, ed., *Editorial Research Reports* II (1936), f.n. 104.

12. "Shelterbelt Experience in Other Lands," in *Possibilities of Shelterbelt Planting in the Plains Region* (Washington, D.C.: United States Forest Service, Lake States Forest Experiment Station), 59–76; Munns and Stoeckler, "How Are the Great Plains Shelterbelts?" 237.

13. H. H. Chapman, "The Shelterbelt Tree Planting Project," *Journal of Forestry* 32 (November 1934): 801; H. H. Chapman, "Digest of Opinions Reviewed on the Shelterbelt Project," *Journal of Forestry* 32 (December 1934): 952-53.

14. Forest Service, Prairie States Forestry Project, "Forest For the Great Plains," mimeographed (Lincoln: USDA, June 30, 1937): 2-6.

15. E. L. Perry, "History of the Prairie States Forestry Project," typed manuscript, June 18, 1942, 60-62, Shelterbelt Laboratory, Bottineau, North Dakota.

16. Munns and Stoeckler, "How Are the Great Plains Shelterbelts?" 237-41, 257.

17. Robert J. Morgan, *Governing Soil Conservation* (Baltimore: Johns Hopkins Univ. Press, 1966), 1-6.

18. H. H. Bennett, "Soil Erosion and Its Prevention," in A. E. Parkins and J. R. Whitaker, *Our Natural Resources and Their Conservation* (New York: J. Wiley and Sons, Inc., 1939), 74; *Yearbook of Agriculture, 1936* (Washington, D.C.: USDA, 1936), 61.

19. "Surveying Wind Erosion Areas in Texas, Kansas, Colorado and Oklahoma," mimeographed (Washington, D.C.: SCS, USDA, Office of Information, January 6, 1936), General Records of the USDA, RG 16, NA.

20. This committee consisted of Lyman Carrier, L. C. Gray, and C. W. Warburton and was appointed by M. L. Wilson.

21. Memorandum, Land Policy Committee: Lyman Carrier, L. C. Gray, and C. W. Warburton to M. L. Wilson, April 9, 1935, RG 16, NA.

22. (Kansas) *Garden City Daily Telegram,* April 16, 17, 1935.

23. *Yearbook of Agriculture, 1935,* 20; see "References on Farm Storage of Grain and Other Food Products Taken From *Wallace's Farmer* 1912-1932," RG 16, NA; Buel W. Patch, "Farm Legislation and the Ever-Normal-Granary-Plan," *Editorial Research Report* 2 (1937), 244.

24. *Yearbook of Agriculture, 1935,* 23.

25. J. D. Le Cron to J. A. Waring, February 5, 1937; *National Grain Journal,* January [?], 1935, RG 16, NA.

26. Patch, "Farm Legislation and the Ever-Normal-Granary Plan," 246-47.

27. "Ever-Normal-Granary," March 9, 1937, Issued by SES, RG 16, NA.

28. U.S., Congress, House, President's Committee on Crop Insurance, 75th Cong., 1st sess., 1937, H. Doc. 150, p. 2, 15-16; "Events Leading Up To The Passage Of The Federal Crop Insurance Act in 1938," Xeroxed (Washington, D.C.: USDA, Federal Crop Insurance Corporation, September 1965), 2-6.

29. Gladys Baker, Wayne D. Rasmussen, Vivian Wiser, and Jane M. Porter, *Century of Service* (Washington, D.C.: USDA, 1963), 178-81, 298-99.

30. *The Future of the Great Plains,* 7-10.

31. *Northern Great Plains* (National Resources Planning Board, 1940), 5.

32. *Northern Great Plains,* 5-6.

33. *Land Tenure in the Great Plains,* mimeographed (Fargo, N.D.: Great Plains Resource Economic Committee, 1961), 10-12, 19-20.

CHAPTER FIFTEEN

1. *Fifteenth Census of the United States,* Agriculture, vol. 4 (1932), 12, 21, 508, 518, 533, 539; *Farmers in a Changing World* (Washington, D.C.: USDA, 1940), 790-809; *Progress in Rural and Farm Electrification, 1921-1931,* National Electric Light Association (NELA), Rural Electric Service Committee (August 1932), pub. no. 237; Morris L. Cooke, "National Plan for the Advancement of Rural Electrification" (1934), app. A, 16, typescript, Library of Congress.

2. *Fifteenth Census of the United States,* Agriculture, vol. 4, 518.

3. NELA, *Proceedings* (Chicago, 1923), 45-46; Harry Slattery, *Rural America Lights Up* (Washington, D.C., 1940), 15-16.

4. Marquis Childs, *The Farmer Takes a Hand* (New York, 1953), 39. O. E. Bradfute, president of the American Farm Bureau Federation, commented: "I believe that a great majority of the farmers who own and live on their farms believe in private ownership of public utilities rather than municipal, state, or Federal ownership." NELA, *Proceedings* (1923), 67.

5. *Progress in Rural and Farm Electrification, 1921-1931,* 5; "Electricity on the Farm and in Rural Communities," CREA *Bulletin,* no. 7 (November 1931); CREA, *Tenth Annual Report* (Chicago, 1933), 5; Slattery, *Rural America Lights Up,* 23-24; Childs, *Farmer Takes a Hand,* 42-43.

6. Mabel Honaker to Sam Rayburn, March 6, 1938; W. H. Hedges to Rayburn, November 9, 1936; E. B. Guthrie to Rayburn, March 23, 1938, Sam Rayburn Papers, Sam Rayburn Library, Bonham, Texas.

7. For a review of the activity of the University of North Carolina, see the files of the *UNC News Letter* in the North Carolina Room, University of North Carolina. *Progressive Farmer,* February 9, 1924, 156 (copies of editorials of the *Progressive Farmer* are in the Clarence Poe Papers, North Carolina Department of Archives and History, Raleigh); *Raleigh News and Observer,* July 29, 1925, June 10, 1945; *Greensboro Daily News,* October 7, 1932; Childs, *Farmer Takes a Hand,* 56; *North Carolina Rural Electrification Survey* (Raleigh: North Carolina Committee on Rural Electrification, 1934). *UNC News Letter* (May 1, 1935); J. C. B. Ehringhaus to Franklin D. Roosevelt, November 28, 1934, in *Addresses, Letters and Papers of John Christopher Blucher, Governor of North Carolina, 1933-1937,* ed. by David L. Corbitt (Raleigh, 1950), 389-92; Raleigh *News and Observer,* April 26, 1935.

8. *Report on the Electric Utility Situation in South Carolina* (Columbia: South Carolina Power Rate Investigating Committee, 1931), 43-44; State of South Carolina, *House Journal,* 80th General Assembly, 1st sess., 1932, pp. 408-9; South Carolina State Highway Department, *Application of the South Carolina Highway Department for a Loan of $5,912,800 from the Federal Emergency Administration of Public Works* (South Carolina State Highway Department, 1933); Albert N. Sanders, "State Regulation of Public Utilities by South Carolina, 1879-1935," (Ph.D. diss., University of North Carolina, 1956), 400-401; Allen J. Saville, "The Virginia Plan," *Public Utilities Fortnightly* 16 (September 12, 1935): 312-16; Saville and Associates, *Preliminary Survey of Rural Electrification in Virginia for State Corporation Commission* (March 1, 1935), typescript, National Archives Library; Federal Power Commission, Press Release, March 28, 1935 and W. E. Herring to Morris L. Cooke, December 6, 1934 in files of REA Administrator Morris L. Cooke, RG 221, National Archives (hereafter NA).

9. "List of Electric Cooperatives Prior to 1935," files of Information Services Division, 1935-1953, RG 221, NA; David Cushman Coyle, ed., *Electric Power on the Farm* (Washington, 1936), REA Special Pamphlet, 60-61; Kenneth E. Merrill, *Twenty Years with the REA* (Lawrence: Univ. of Kansas Press, 1960), 8-10.

10. Kenneth E. Trombley, *The Life and Times of a Happy Liberal, A Biography of Morris Llewellyn Cooke* (New York, 1954), 15-46, 106-7; *Giant Power: Report of the Giant Power Survey Board to the General Assembly* (Harrisburg: State Printing Office, 1925), 139-40; For a thorough explanation of Cooke's recommendation, see Morris Cooke, "A Note on Rates for Rural Electric Service," *Annals of the Academy of Political and Social Science,* 67 (March 1925): 52-59.

11. Morris L. Cooke, ed., *What Electricity Costs* (New York, 1933), 75-117.

12. David Lilienthal, *TVA, Democracy on the March* (New York: Harper Bros., 1944), 20; Lilienthal, "Future of Farm Electricity," November 18, 1939, Speeches of TVA Directors, TVA Library, Knoxville, Tennessee. Geoge Kable, "Rural Electrification in Alcorn County, Mississippi," paper presented before the American Society of Agricultural Engineers, Athens, Georgia, June 20, 1935, TVA Library.

13. Edward Falack, "Operations of Alcorn County Electric Cooperative," typescript (Beltsville, Maryland: National Agricultural Library), January 1935.

14. G. D. Munger, "Methods Employed for Financing Equipment and Appliance Purchases." Paper read at Third World Conference of the Electric Home and Farm Authority, Chicago, Illinois, September, 1936.

15. Munger, "Methods Employed for Financing Equipment and Appliance Purchases," 1-4; David Lilienthal, "Progress in the Electrification of the American Home and Farm," 6, Speech to Chattanooga Chamber of Commerce, September 19, 1934.

16. Falack, "Operations of Alcorn County Electric Cooperative," 4; Cooke, "The Early Days of the Rural Electrification Idea: 1914-1936," *American Political Science Review* 42 (June, 1948): 444.

17. *Report of the Mississippi Valley Committee of the Public Works Administration* (Washington: Mississippi Valley Committee, 1934), 51.

18. Cooke, "Early Days of the Rural Electrification Idea, 1914-1936," 445.

19. Cooke, "National Plan for the Advancement of Rural Electrification Under Federal Leadership and Control with State and Local Cooperation and as a Wholly Public Enterprise," 1934, 7, typescript, Library of Congress.

20. H. S. Person, "The Rural Electrification Administration in Perspective," *Agricultural History* 24 (April 1950): 73.

21. Person, "The Rural Electrification Administration," 73.

22. W. W. Freeman to Morris Cooke, July 24, 1935, Morris L. Cooke Papers, Franklin D. Roosevelt Presidential Library, Hyde Park, New York.

23. Morris Cooke to W. W. Freeman, July 31, 1935, Cooke Papers.

24. Lemont K. Richardson, *Wisconsin REA, The Struggle to Extend Electricity to Rural Wisconsin, 1935-1955* (Madison: University of Wisconsin, Experiment Station, College of Agriculture, 1961), 25-27.

25. Childs, *Farmer Takes a Hand,* 59; Frederick W. Muller, *Public Rural Electrification* (Washington, D.C.: Amer. Council of Public Affairs, 1944), 22-24; George W. Norris to Morris Cooke, August 1, 1935, George W. Norris Papers, Tray 71, Box 9, Library of Congress.

26. "Conference of Cooperative Representatives and Rural Electrification Administrators," June 6, 1935, Washington, D.C., typescript, National Agricultural Library, 21; Judson King, "Who Will Get the $100,000,000 for Farm Electrifications?" *National Popular Government League Bulletin* 171 (April 25, 1935), National Agricultural Library.

28. *Rural Electrification News* 1 (October 1935): 21.

29. Quoted in Person, "The Rural Electrification Administration," 74.

30. "Report of the Rural Electrification Administration to the National Emergency Council," October 14, 1935, typescript, National Agricultural Library.

31. U.S., Congress, House, Committee on Interstate and Foreign Commerce, *A Bill to Provide for Rural Electrification and for other Purposes,* 74th Cong., 2d sess., 1936; U.S., Congress, *Congressional Record,* 74th Cong., 2d sess., 1936, 80, pt. 3: 2819-33, pt. 5: 5287-5318; *New York Times,* March 5, 1936.

32. Norris, "Rural Electrification," in *Transcript of the First Meeting of the NRECA in Washington, D.C., 1944,* 144. Official Files of William Neal, 1938-1948, REA General Correspondence, RG 221, NA.

33. Morris Cooke to Sam Rayburn, May 6, 1936, Files of Administrator Cooke, RG 221, NA; *Moody's Public Utility Manual, 1955,* Special Features Section (New York, 1955), 4; Cooke to Roosevelt, May 7, 1936, Cooke Papers.

34. U.S., Cong., House, *Rural Electrification,* 74th Cong., 2d sess., conference report no. 2219. Congress gave the REA permanent status in 1944.

35. For an example of the rapid growth of cooperatives in their early stage of development, see Arkansas Valley Cooperative, Ozark, Arkansas, *Minutes of Board Meeting, November 13, 1947,* Management Division, RG 221, NA; Jilson McCullough to Sam Rayburn, July 19, 1937, and December 9, 1937, Rayburn Papers; Interview, James B. Richey, Manager, Fannin County (Texas) Cooperative, December 23, 1968, Oral History Collection, Sam Rayburn Library.

36. Joel E. Lennon to Sam Rayburn, July 16, 1937, Rayburn Papers.

37. In 1941 the administrator of the REA reported, "The number of power companies still actively engaged in obstruction tactics is small in comparison with the number which were actively hostile in the earlier stages of the REA program." *Report of the Administrator of the Rural Electrification Administration,* 1941 (Washington, D.C., 1941), 16.

38. "Rural Electric Service in Georgia," typescript, Atlanta, Georgia, Georgia Power Company, June 27, 1936, RG 221, NA.

39. *Report of the REA Administration, 1941,* 21-26.

40. Louisan Mamer, REA Home Economics Department, "Electricity Pays Its Way in the Rural Home," typescript, March 11, 1952, 10, National Agricultural Library; *Rural Lines: USA, The Story of Cooperative Rural Electrification* (Washington, D.C.: REA, March 1966), Misc. Pub. 811, 13.

41. Mamer, "Electricity Pays Its Way in the Rural Home," 10; Tennessee Agricultural Experiment Station, United States Bureau of Agricultural Economics, "Electricity on Farms and Rural Homes in East Tennessee Valley," Tennessee Agricultural Experiment Station Bulletin, no. 221 (April 1951): 7-8; 35; C. J. Hurd, "Farm and Community Refrigeration in the South," *Refrigerating Engineering* (November 1938): 1, copy in Mercer Green Johnston Papers, Container 78, Library of Congress; C. W. Hackson, "A Study of the Value of the Texas Farm and Home Radio Programs in Twenty Northeast Texas Counties," typescript (May, 1946); Edgar A. Schuler, Louisiana State University Extension Service, *Survey of Radio Listeners in Louisiana* (1943), a pamphlet. Both documents are in the National Agricultural Library.

42. Nora M. Kefauver, "Rural Electric Lighting in Areas of Newly Energized Lines, LaFollette Electric Department, LaFollette Tennessee, Extending into Campbell and Claiborne

Counties,'' typescript, Division of Electrical Development, TVA (March 30, 1942), TVA Library, Knoxville, Tennessee; REA, ''Rural Line USA.''

43. Thomas D. Clark, *The Emerging South* (New York, 1961), 86–91.

44. Slattery, *Rural America Lights Up,* 96–98. REA, Interbureau Coordinating Committee on Rural Elecrification, ''Effects of Use of Electricity on Agriculture and Rural Life'' (October 1941), typescript, Container 77, Mercer Green Johnston Papers, Library of Congress; Mamer, ''Electricity Pays Its Way in the Rural Home,'' 4.

CHAPTER SIXTEEN

1. M. L. Wilson to Louis S. Clarke, October 16, 1935; Wilson to Clarke, November 25, 1935, General Records of the USDA, RG 16, National Archives (hereafter NA).

2. Louis S. Clarke to M. L. Wilson, November 12, 1935; Wilson to Clarke, November 25, 1935, RG 16, NA.

3. ''Significance of Literary Digest Poll,'' Mordecai Ezekiel to Henry Wallace, January 27, 1936, RG 16, NA.

4. Drew Pearson to Paul Appleby, February 18, 1936, RG 16, NA.

5. William S. Maulsby to M. L. Wilson, June 4, 1936, RG 16, NA.

6. Memorandum, W. W. Stockberger to Chiefs and Offices, March 21, 1935, RG 16, NA.

7. Memorandum, Paul H. Appleby to Dr. R. G. Tugwell, May 6, 1935, RG 16, NA.

8. Henry A. Wallace to George McGill, March 13, 1936, RG 16, NA; Clifford R. Hope to Percy L. Cook, January 24, 1936, Clifford R. Hope Papers, Kansas State Historical Society (hereafter KSHS).

9. Clyde Tingley to Henry A. Wallace, May 7, 1936, RG 16, NA.

10. H. A. Wallace to Clyde Tingley, May 15, 1936, RG 16, NA.

11. E. J. MacMillan to Henry A. Wallace, April 29, 1936; Paul H. Appleby to E. J. Mac-Millan, n.d. [probably May 1936], RG 16, NA.

12. Paul H. Appleby to E. J. MacMillan, n.d., RG 16, NA.

13. Henry Steele Commager, *Documents of American History,* 7th ed., vol. 2 (New York: Appleton, 1963), 353–58, especially 355–56.

14. ''Landon's Job: To Win the West,'' *Business Week,* June 20, 1936, 27.

15. *New York Times,* June 24, 1936; Commager, *Documents of American History,* vol. 2, 358–61, especially 359–60.

16. *Memphis Commercial Appeal,* June 26, 1936.

17. The text of the letter is found in Henry A. Wallace, ''G. O. P. Platform Caters to Special Privilege,'' *The Prairie Farmer,* July 4, 1936, 5 and 17.

18. *Des Moines Register,* July 26, 1936.

19. Ray Yarnell to Alfred M. Landon, August 5, 1936, Alfred M. Landon Papers, KSHS.

20. Clifford R. Hope to J. A. Garber, August 6, 1936, Hope Papers, KSHS.

21. Clifford R. Hope to Paul E. Jorgensen, August 6, 1936; Charles W. Holman to Hope, August 24, 1936, Hope Papers; Frank Maher to Arthur Capper, September 3, 1936, Landon Papers, KSHS.

22. Alfred M. Landon, ''A Workable Farm Program,'' *Vital Speeches* 2 (October 1, 1936): 820–22.

23. Alfred M. Landon, ''Sold Down the River,'' *Vital Speeches* 3 (October 15, 1936): 23–26.

24. ''Who Sold Out? Secretary Hull Replies to Landon Charges,'' *Time* 28 (October 19, 1936): 16. See also Chapter 10 of this study for more details on the efforts to reopen the foreign market for farm products.

25. *Des Moines Register,* August 19, 1936.

26. E. R. MacIntyre to Henry A. Wallace, September 24, 1936, RG 16, NA.

27. Paul H. Appleby to Elmer A. Benson, September 25, 1936, RG 16, NA.

28. C. C. Talbott to Paul Appleby, September 3, 1936, RG 16, NA.

29. *Des Moines Tribune,* October 8, 1936.

30. ''Highlights on Farming With a Future,'' mimeographed (New York: Democratic National Campaign Headquarters, 1936): 1–3.

31. ''Highlights on Farming With a Future,'' 3–4.

32. ''Highlights on Farming With a Future,'' 4–7.

33. Clifford R. Hope to Bruce F. Hardy, November 7, 1936; Hope to W. P. Lambertson, November 7, 1936; Arthur M. Curtis to Hope, November 10, 1936, Hope Papers, KSHS.

34. "Reminiscences of M. L. Wilson," Oral History Research Office, Columbia University.

35. Svend Petersen, *A Statistical History of the American Presidential Elections* (New York, 1963), 181, 187, and 214. See also *California Cultivator* 83 (November 1936): 778.

CHAPTER SEVENTEEN

1. See story by Felix Belair, Jr., in *New York Times,* April 8, 1936, in which he comments upon a letter from Secretary Wallace to the Senate Agriculture Committee—Wallace placed the highest wheat benefit to a farmer under a single AAA contract at $78,634; *Des Moines Register,* April 29, 1936; Claude R. Wickard to Sam Rayburn, November 30, 1940, Sam Rayburn Papers, Sam Rayburn Library, Bonham, Texas. See also "Reminiscences of H. R. Tolley," Oral History Research Office, Columbia University, 392–93, 396–99. U.S., Congress, *Congressional Directory,* 75th Cong., 1st sess., March 1937, pp. 175 and 193, 75th Cong., 3d sess., May 1938, pp. 173 and 192, 76th Cong., 1st sess., April 1939, 177 and 197; *Des Moines Register,* November 15, 1936, February 20, 1938; "Reminiscences of Rexford G. Tugwell," Oral History Research Office, Columbia University, 69; "Reminiscences of H. R. Tolley," 392–93; *Report of the Secretary of Agriculture, 1936* (Washington, D.C.: USDA, 1936), 9–18, 44–47; U.S., Congress, House, *To Investigate the Activities of the Farm Security Administration Pursuant to House Res. 119,* 78th Cong., 1st sess., 1944, pt. 3, p. 962; "Reminiscences of Will Alexander," Oral History Research Office, Columbia University, 634–36; "Reminiscences of H. R. Tolley," 398–99; *Des Moines Register,* November 15, 1936.

2. "Reminiscences of H. R. Tolley," 349, 375–79, 381–87; "Acting Administrator Developed AAA Programs," "Tolley Succeeds Davis as AAA Administrator," (Washington, D.C.: USDA, AAA, March 11, 1936, June 5, 1936).

3. *Agricultural Conservation 1936* (Washington, D.C.: USDA, AAA, 1937), 14–15.

4. *Agricultural Conservation 1936,* 5, 14.

5. "Reminiscences of H. R. Tolley," 381–87; "AAA Establishes Five Regions for Soil Act Administration" (Washington, D.C.: USDA, AAA, March 17, 1936).

6. "Reminiscences of H. R. Tolley," 413–15; Memorandum, Bushrod R. Allin to D. C. Blaisdell, December 11, 1936, General Records of the USDA, RG 16, National Archives (hereafter NA).

7. Memorandum, Bushrod R. Allin to D. C. Blaisdell, December 11, 1936, 415–17, NA.

8. "Reminiscences of Samuel B. Bledsoe," 82–83, 105–6, Oral History Research Office, Columbia University.

9. "Reminiscences of H. R. Tolley," 396–97.

10. *Agricultural Adjustment 1937-1938* (Washington, D.C.: USDA, AAA, 1938), 17–18; *Des Moines Tribune,* December 12, 1934; Kansas City Times, December 27, 1934; *Des Moines Register,* April 21, 1935; H. A. Wallace to Otha D. Wearin, June 30, 1937, RG 16, NA; *St. Paul Pioneer Press,* May 22, 1937; "Farm Legislation and the Ever-Normal Granary," *Editorial Research Reports, 1937* 2 (Washington, D.C., 1938): 241–56. See also, U.S. Cong., Senate, Sub-committee of the Senate Committee on Agriculture and Forestry, *Hearings on Senate Res. 158,* 75th Cong., 2d sess., October 15–November 1, 1937, 20 pts.; and U.S. Congress, House, Committee on Agriculture, *Hearings on General Farm Legislation, H. R. 8505,* 75th Cong., 1st sess., May 17–21, 27–28, and June 8 and 10, 1937, ser. C, 135–55 and 157–83; "Reminiscences of H. R. Tolley," 429–32, 435; Derk Bodde, "Henry A. Wallace and the Ever-Normal Granary," *Far Eastern Quarterly* 5 (1946): 411–26.

11. "Reminiscences of H. R. Tolley," 429–32; J. S. Davis, "The Economics of the Ever-Normal Granary" with a discussion by Mordecai Ezekiel, *Journal of Farm Economics* 20 (February 1938): 8–23.

12. H. A. Wallace, "We Have a Full Pantry," *Talk* (October 1939): 19–22; *Report of the Secretary of Agriculture* (Washington, D.C., 1941), 114–15; Walter W. Wilcox, *The Farmer in the Second World War* (Ames: Iowa State Univ. Press, 1947), 374; Edward R. Stettinius, Jr., *Lend-Lease* (New York 1944), 286; *New York Times,* November 19, 1965.

13. "Reminiscences of Rudolph M. Evans," Oral History Research Office, Columbia University, 147–49.

14. *Report of the Secretary of Agriculture* (Washington, D.C., 1938), 48; John M. Gaus and Leon O. Wolcott, *Public Administration and the United States Department of Agriculture* (Chicago, 1940), 156–57.

15. Gaus and Wolcott, *Public Administration and the United States Department of Agriculture,* 157–58.

16. William J. Block, *The Separation of the Farm Bureau and the Extension Service* (Urbana: Univ. of Illinois Press, 1960), 22–23.

17. "Reminiscences of H. R. Tolley," 440–42.

18. *Milwaukee Journal,* October 11 and 19, 1938; "AAA Dilemma: Tobogganing Prices Spread Discontent in Wheat Bowl," *Newsweek* 12 (July 25, 1938): 33–35.

19. *Chicago Tribune,* April 19, 20, 1938, May 5, 7, 9, 15, 20, 1938; *Chicago Herald-Examiner,* April 29, 1938; *Wisconsin State Journal,* April 29, 1938; *Milwaukee Leader,* April 29, 1938; Milwaukee Sentinel, May 13 and July 28, 1938; *Milwaukee Journal,* October 11, 1938.

20. Memorandum, F. F. Elliott to Paul Appleby, July 12, 1938. This memo had attached to it the latest report on "Farmer Opinions on Best and World Parts of the New Deal," also dated July 12, 1938, RG 16, NA.

21. Joseph F. Guffey to Henry A. Wallace, November 17, 1936, RG 16, NA.

22. "Reminiscences of Samuel B. Bledsoe," 98–99, 109–10.

23. "Reminiscences of Rudolph M. Evans," 156–58.

24. "Reminiscences of Samuel B. Bledsoe," 98–99.

25. "Reminiscences of H. R. Tolley," 457–58.

26. "Department Unifies Its Work To Meet New Responsibilities," *Extension Service Review* 9 (November 1938): 168.

27. *Milwaukee Sentinel,* October 7, 1938; *Milwaukee Journal,* October 7, 1938.

28. *Chicago Tribune,* October 3 and 7, 1938.

29. *Christian Science Monitor,* November 12, 1938. For a breakdown of the vote, state by state, see U.S., Congress, *Congressional Directory,* 76th Cong., 1st sess., April, 1939, 250–57.

30. *New York Times,* December 4, 1938; See also, *Milwaukee Journal,* October 5, 1938, and *Milwaukee Sentinel,* November 6, 1938. *New York Times,* December 4 and 11, 1938.

31. "New AAA Administrator," *Extension Service Review* 11 (November 1938): 168; "Reminiscences of Rudolph M. Evans," 138–39.

32. *New York Times,* December 11, 1938.

33. *New York Times,* December 12, 1938.

34. *New York Times,* December 13, 1938; *Agricultural Adjustment, 1938–1939* (Washington, D.C.: USDA, AAA, 1939), 62, 63–66.

35. "Reminiscences of H. R. Tolley," 470–73.

36. "Reminiscences of John B. Hutson," Oral History Research Office, Columbia University, 237.

37. "Reminiscences of John B. Hutson," 239–40.

38. *Des Moines Tribune,* May 9, 1934.

39. *Des Moines Register,* November 16, 1936.

40. Russell Lord, *The Wallaces of Iowa* (Boston 1947), 458–60; "Biographical Sketch of Harry L. Brown," (Washington, D.C.: USDA, December 31, 1936); "Biographical Sketch of Grover Hill," (Washington, D.C.: USDA, December 21, 1938); M. L. Wilson to Harold G. Sears, January 21, 1940, RG 16, NA; "Reminiscences of Rudolph M. Evans," 204–5.

CHAPTER EIGHTEEN

1. Donald C. Blaisdell, *Government and Agriculture* (New York 1940), 149–59, 164–65, 179, 182, 184–85; Carle C. Zimmerman and Nathan L. Whetten, *Rural Families on Relief* (Washington, D.C.: WPA, Div. of Social Research, 1938), Research Monograph 17, pp. 8 and 110; A. R. Magnus, *Changing Aspects of Rural Relief* (Washington, D.C.: WPA, Div. of Social Research, 1938), Research Monograph 14, pp. 12–15; Edwin G. Nourse, *Government in Relation to Agriculture* (Washington, D.C.: The Brookings Institution, 1940), 904–37. See also Merle Fainsod and Lincoln Gordon, *Government and the American Economy* (New York, 1941), 328–30, 349–50; Robert T. Beall, "Rural Electrification," *Farmers in a Changing World* (Washington, D.C., 1940), 790–809; Norman I. Wengert, *Valley of Tomorrow: The TVA and Agriculture* (Knoxville: Bureau of Public Administration, University of Tennessee, 1952); Gordon R. Clapp, *The TVA: An Approach to the Development of a Region* (Chicago, 1955).

2. A. C. Black to H. T. Outwater, September 4, 1934, Records of the Agricultural Stabilization and Conservation Service, RG 145, National Archives (hereafter NA); *A Report of the Administration of the AAA May 1933 to February 1934* (Washington, D.C.: USDA,

AAA, 1934), 1-7 and *Agricultural Adjustment 1937-1938* (Washington, D.C.: USDA, AAA, 1939), 11-15.

3. *Agricultural Adjustment 1937-1938,* 15.

4. Walter W. Wilcox, *The Farmer in the Second World War* (Ames: Iowa State Univ. Press, 1947), 9; Bureau of the Census, *Historical Statistics of the United States . . . to 1957* (Washington, D.C.: 1961), 283.

5. John D. Black, *Parity, Parity, Parity* (Cambridge, Mass., 1942), 82-83.

6. Theodore Schultz, *Redirecting Farm Policy* (New York: Macmillan, 1943), 16-18, 33-36.

7. *Essays on Research in the Social Sciences* (Washington, D.C.: Brookings Institution, 1931), 82.

8. R. F. Breyer, *The Marketing Situation* (New York, 1934), 881.

9. *Yearbook of Agriculture, 1935* (Washington, D.C., 1935), 15-20; *Yearbook, 1937,* 33-47.

10. G. H. Aull, "Discussion," *Journal of Farm Economics* 23 (February 1941): 123; O. C. Stine, "Future of Cotton in the Economy of the South," *Journal of Farm Economics* 23 (February 1941): 119-20; Theodore Schultz, "Food, Agriculture, and Trade," *Proceedings Number, Journal of Farm Economics* 29 (February 1947): 5.

11. Wilcox, *The Farmer in the Second World War,* 14-16; Robert J. Morgan, *Governing Soil Conservation* (Baltimore: Johns Hopkins Univ. Press, 1966), 110-13.

12. Z. R. Pettit, "Highlights of the 1940 Census," *Proceedings Number, Journal of Farm Economics* 23 (February 1941): 269-70.

13. Geoffrey S. Shepherd, *Agricultural Price Policy* (Ames: Iowa State Univ. Press, 1947), 40.

14. *Agricultural Adjustment 1938-1939* (Washington, D.C.: USDA, AAA, 1939), 7.

15. *Report of the Secretary of Agriculture* (Washington, D.C., 1940), 27-29.

16. *Report of the Secretary of Agriculture* (Washington, D.C., 1938), 37.

17. *Report of the Secretary of Agriculture* (Washington, D.C., 1940), 58-61; *Report* (Washington, D.C., 1941), 128; *Report* (Washington, D.C., 1942), 149-50.

18. David Eugene Conrad, *The Forgotten Farmers* (Urbana: Univ. of Illinois Press, 1951), and Donald H. Grubbs, *Cry from the Cotton* (Chapel Hill: Univ. of North Carolina Press, 1971).

19. M. L. Wilson, "Problems of Poverty in Agriculture," *Proceedings Number, Journal of Farm Economics* 22 (February 1940): 10; Rexford G. Tugwell, "The Resettlement Idea," *Agricultural History* 33 (October 1959): 161-63.

20. Wilson, "Problems of Poverty in Agriculture," 10-11.

21. R. R. Renne, "On Agricultural Policy," *Journal of Farm Economics* 22 (May 1940): 488; Wilcox, *The Farmer in the Second World War,* 12, 13.

22. Wesley McCune, *The Farm Bloc* (Garden City: Doubleday, 1943), 36-57.

23. James A. Street, *The New Revolution in the Cotton Economy* (Chapel Hill: Univ. of North Carolina Press, 1957), 125-57, 175-91.

24. Street, *The New Revolution,* 176-78; Tugwell, "The Resettlement Idea," 161-63; U.S., Cong., Senate, *Resettlement Administration Program,* 74th Cong. 2d sess., 1936, Sen. Doc. 213, p. 1; Rebecca Farmhouse and Irene Link, *Effects of the Works Program on Rural Relief* (Washington, D.C.: WPA, Div. of Social Research, 1938), Research Monograph 13, p. xl; Magnus, *Changing Aspects of Rural Relief,* 14 and 19.

25. Doris Carothers, *Chronology of the Federal Emergency Relief Administration, May 12, 1933 to December 31, 1935* (Washington, D.C.: WPA, Div. of Social Research, 1937), Research Monograph 6, p. 16.

26. Berta Asch and A. R. Magnus, *Farmers on Relief and Rehabilitation* (Washington, D.C.: WPA, Div. of Social Research, 1937), Research Monograph 8, xiii, xviii-xix; Tugwell, "The Resettlement Idea," 159-60.

27. Edward C. Banfield, "Ten Years of the Farm Tenant Purchase Program, *Journal of Farm Economics* 31 (August 1949): 469-70, 474-75.

28. Joseph Ackerman, "Status and Appraisal of Research in Farm Tenancy," *Proceedings Number, Journal of Farm Economics* 23 (February 1941): 277-78.

29. Claude Wickard to Sam Rayburn, November 30, 1940, Sam Rayburn Papers, Sam Rayburn Library, Bonham, Texas.

30. *Agricultural Adjustment, 1937-1938,* B-19; *Agricultural Adjustment, 1938-1939,* 107-8.

31. Pettit, "Highlights of the 1940 Census," 269; Stine, "Future of Cotton in the Economy of the South," 119.

32. *Farm Security Administration* (Washington, D.C.: USDA, 1941), brochure, 12.

33. Statement by C. B. Baldwin, FSA Administrator, before House Committee Investigating FSA June 29, 1943 replying to charges by Ed O'Neal, President of the American Farm Bureau Federation before same committee on June 17, 1943, 15 pages, mimeographed, copy in UCLA Library. See also Grant McConnell, *The Decline of Agrarian Democracy* (New York: Atheneum, 1969), 128-77.

34. Bennett S. White, Jr., "Discussion," *Journal of Farm Economics* 23 (February 1941): 131-37.

35. D. Clayton Brown, "Rural Electrification," ms. provided basis for Chapter 15.

36. Stine, "Future of Cotton in the Economy of the South," 118-20.

37. Theodore Saloutos, "The New Deal and Farm Policy in the Great Plains," *Agricultural History* 43 (July 1969): 351; E. N. Munns and Joseph H. Stoeckler, "How Are the Great Plains Shelterbelts?" *Journal of Forestry* 44 (April 1946): 257.

38. E. C. Johnson, "Agricultural Credit," in *Farmers in a Changing World* (Washington, D.C., 1940), 745-49; Wilcox, *Farmer in the Second World War,* 23; W. I. Myers, *Cooperative Farm Mortgage Credit, 1916-1936* (Washington, D.C.: FCA, U.S. Farm Credit Administration, 1936), 12-13.

39. Wilcox, *Farmer in the Second World War,* 23.

40. Paul H. Conkin, *The New Deal* (New York: Crowell, 1967), 40-43, 59-61, 100-101; Howard Zinn, ed., *New Deal Thought* (Indianapolis: Bobbs-Merrill, 1966), xv-xxxvi; Alonzo L. Hamby, ed., *The New Deal* (New York: Longman, 1969), 232-40.

41. Wilcox, *Farmer in the Second World War,* 35-36.

A SELECTIVE
BIBLIOGRAPHY

THE PRINTED AND UNPRINTED SOURCES on agriculture and the New Deal are plentiful, complex, and intimidating. The inhouse biases of some government publications and the unsympathetic treatment that some members of the press gave the New Deal also pose problems. Cognizant of this, I have tried throughout to handle these sources judiciously. Whether I have succeeded may be a matter of opinion. The bibliography includes some sources not used for the text in the belief they might be useful to those wishing to pursue some phase of the subject further.

NATIONAL ARCHIVES

Record Group 16 (RG 16), consisting of the General Records of the USDA, is indispensable. Easily the best source on Henry A. Wallace while serving as secretary of agriculture, RG 16 also contains the papers of the under and assistant secretaries of agriculture, especially of M. L. Wilson who played a crucial role throughout the New Deal years, and the general correspondence of the Coordinator of Land Use Planning. Scattered throughout the correspondence of Wallace are letters to the Bureau of Agricultural Economics, the Extension Service, the Resettlement and Farm Security administrations, the Federal Crop Insurance Corporation, Land Use Coordination, Rural Electrification Administration, Soil Conservation Service, Surplus Commodities Corporation, and the under secretary of agriculture. Included, too, are letters and memos written to Mordecai Ezekiel in the initial stages of the AAA on landlords and tenants, the regional approach to planning and controlling production, the quest for foreign markets, the black farmers, subsistence homesteads, the Great Plains, and the election of 1936.

Record Group 145 (RG 145), the Records of the Agricultural Stabilization and Conservation Service, contains invaluable information on the launching of the various AAA programs; however, they should be supplemented with the useful studies of the Brookings Institution, which although contemporary in nature, contain information and insights unavailable elsewhere. The Brookings studies include those by Henry I. Richards, *Cotton and the AAA* (1936); Joseph S. Davis, *Wheat and the AAA* (1935); Harold B. Rowe, *Tobacco Under the AAA* (1935); John D. Black, *The Dairy Industry and the AAA* (1935); Edwin G. Nourse, *Marketing Agreements Under the AAA* (1935); D. A. Fitz Gerald, *Livestock Under the AAA* (1935); and E. G. Nourse, J. S. Davis, and J. D. Black, *Three Years of the Agricultural Adjustment Administration* (1937). RG 145 also contains memos, reports, and correspondence reflecting the dissension within the AAA, the status of the tenants and sharecroppers, the efforts made in their behalf outside the administration, and the difficulties the administration encountered in implementing its programs amidst the rising clamor to do something for the depressed elements.

Record Group 83 (RG 83), the Records of the Bureau of Agricultural Economics—the vigorous and at times controversial branch of the USDA—contains the files of the Division of Land Economics, Marketing and Transportation Research, Programs Analysis and Development, Program Surveys, State and Local Planning, Statistical and Historical Research, and materials on the campaign against rural poverty and the reactions of the agricultural establishment to these efforts.

Record Group 96 (RG 96), the Records of the Farm Home Administration, contains materials on subsistence homesteads, rural rehabilitation, farm ownership, and emergency crop and feed loans.

MANUSCRIPT COLLECTIONS

Those interested in the shaping of farm policy during the 1920s and 1930s will find the papers of John D. Black in the Wisconsin Historical Society, Madison (WHS), indispensable. Among Black's correspondents were Chester C. Davis, Joseph S. Davis, Mordecai Ezekiel, John Kenneth Galbraith, Beardsley Ruml, Oscar Stine, Henry C. Taylor, Howard R. Tolley, and Henry A. Wallace. Among his papers also are letters and statements from various farm economists in the mid-1920s expressing their views on farm policy and correspondence relating to his book *Agricultural Reform* and the reasons for writing it, the Federal Farm Board, proposals for land utilization reform in 1932, domestic allotment and other relief plans, tariffs and home markets, the work of the Social Science Reseach Council and the Committee on Government Statistics to improve Census reports and county planning in 1939–1940, and relations between the BAE and the AAA.

Copies of many M. L. Wilson letters from the M. L. Wilson Collection in the Montana State University Library, Bozeman (MSUL), shed much light on Wilson's role in making the domestic allotment plan a part of the law of the land. They were generously placed at my disposal by Professor Harry McDean. Letters between J. D. Black and Wilson dealing with the same subject also are found in the Black Papers.

The Jerome Frank Papers were uncatalogued at the time they were made available to me at the Sterling Memorial Library, Yale University, but a series of memos exchanged by Frank and members of the various government agencies dealing with the initial stages of the landlord-tenant controversy, other correspondence, and statements were located. The personal correspondence of Frank while general counsel of the AAA is in RG 145.

The American Country Life Papers (WHS) contain valuable information on the general field of agriculture rather than relating specifically to the New Deal.

The Franklin Delano Roosevelt letters on agriculture, on deposit at the Franklin Delano Roosevelt Library (FDRL), contain a few communications from Rexford G. Tugwell while he was administrator of the Resettlement Administration and under secretary of agriculture; a couple of letters from Henry A. Wallace bearing on the 1936 election; a memo on the Phil La Follette phenomenon in Wisconsin; a confidential statement on Wallace's anticipated hopes for the Democratic nomination in 1940; and a series of letters from Wallace to Roosevelt bearing on a wide variety of subjects, including agriculture, and letters on the election of 1940.

The Rexford G. Tugwell Papers (FDRL) are slender with respect to agriculture, but include communications from Ezekiel, Robert Lynd, Wolf Ladejinsky, Calvin B. Hoover, M. L. Wilson, and Edmund de S. Brunner. Rexford G. Tugwell's "Diary-Journal, 1932–1941" also contains his observations of various episodes in agencies he was identified with.

The papers of Alfred M. Landon and Clifford R. Hope in the Kansas Historical Society (KHS) contain material dealing with the farmers and the Republican candidates in the 1936 election. The George McGill Papers (KHS) are less helpful.

The transcriptions of tape recordings on deposit in the Oral History Research Office, Columbia University, especially of Will Alexander, Paul Appleby, Louis H. Bean, Samuel B. Bledsoe, Mordecai Ezekiel, John B. Hutson, Gardner Jackson, Oscar Stine, Howard R. Tolley, Rexford G. Tugwell, and Milburn L. Wilson were invaluable. Chester C. Davis placed a copy of the transcript of the interviews at the author's disposal.

UNITED STATES CONGRESSIONAL DOCUMENTS

72d Cong., 2d sess., 1932, Special Report of Federal Farm Board on Recommendations for Legislation, House Doc. 489.

72d Cong., 2d sess., 1933, Economic Situation of Hog Producers, Senate Doc. 184.

73d Cong., 2d sess., 1934, Committee on Agriculture of the House of Representatives, The Farmers' Tax Problem, House Doc. 406.

73d Cong., 2d sess., 1934, Encourage Sale of American Agricultural Surplus Products Abroad . . . , Senate Report 607.

74th Cong., 1st sess., 1935, Senate, United States Federal Emergency Relief Administration Expenditure of Funds.

74th Cong., 2d sess., 1936, The Western Range . . . , Senate Doc. 199.

74th Cong, 2d sess., 1936, Hearings Before the Senate Committee of Agriculture and Forestry to Investigate the Causes of the Decline of Cotton Prices, April 2, 3, and 6, 1936.

74th Cong., 2d sess., 1936, Interim Report of the Federal Trade Commission on Agricultural Income Inquiry, House Doc. 380.

75th Cong., 1st sess., 1937, President's Committee on Crop Insurance . . . , House Doc. 150.

75th Cong., 1st sess., 1937, Message from the President of the United States Transmitting the Report of the Special Committee on Farm Tenancy, House Doc. 149.

84th Cong., 2d sess., 1956, Program for the Great Plains . . . , House Doc. 289.

UNITED STATES GOVERNMENT AND AGRICULTURAL EXPERIMENT STATION PUBLICATIONS

Agricultural Yearbook, 1914 to 1940. Washington, D.C.: USDA.

Allred, B. W. *Range Conservation Practices for the Great Plains.* Washington, D. C.: USDA, 1940. Misc. Pub. 410.

Anderson, W. A. *Mobility of Rural Families.* Ithaca, New York: Cornell University Agricultural Experiment Station Bulletin 623, 1935.

Annual Report of the Secretary of the Interior. Washington, D.C.: Department of the Interior, 1934.

Annual Reports, 1933 to 1939. Washington, D.C.: USDA, AAA.

Annual Reports, 1936 and 1937. Washington, D.C.: Resettlement Administration.

Bates, C. G. *The Windbreak as a Farm Asset.* Washington, D.C.: USDA, 1944. Farmers' Bulletin 1405.

Carothers, Doris. *Chronology of the Federal Emergency Relief Administration, May 12, 1933 to December 31, 1935.* Washington, D.C.: WPA, Div. of Social Research, 1937, Monograph 6.

Cobb, Cully. "The Negro Farmer and the AAA." Mimeographed. Washington, D.C., 1936.

Coombs, Whitney. *Taxation of Farm Property*. Washington, D.C.: USDA, 1930. Techn. Bulletin, 172.

Cooper, Martin R., et al. *Progress of Farm Mechanization*. Washington, D.C.: USDA, 1947. Misc. Pub. 630.

Federal Farm Board. *First Annual Report*. Washington, D.C.: 1930.

_____. *Third Annual Report*. Washington, D.C.: 1932.

Final Statistical Report of the Federal Emergency Relief Administration. Washington, D.C.: Federal Emergency Relief Administration, 1942.

Future of the Great Plains, The. Washington, D.C.: Great Plains Committee, 1936.

Gates, Paul W. "Policies With Reference to Adjustments in Local Government and Finance." *Supplementary Report of the Land Planning Committee to the National Resources Board, Part VII*. Washington, D.C.: 1935, 56–85.

George, Ernest, J. *31-Year Results in Growing Shelterbelts on the Northern Great Plains*. Washington, D.C.: USDA, 1953. Cir. 924.

Gilbertson, H. W. "Extension-Farm Bureau Relationships." Mimeographed. Washington, D.C., 1947, 1948.

Glover, Lloyd. *Experience with Federal Land Purchase as a Means of Land Use Adjustment*. Brookings, S.D.: Agricultural Experiment Station, 1955. Agricultural Economics Pamphlet 65.

Gray, James R., and Chester Baker. *Cattle Ranching in the Northern Great Plains*. Bozeman, Mont.: Agricultural Experiment Station, 1953. Cir. 204.

Gray, Lewis C. "How the Resettlement Administration Is Functioning and Should Function . . . " Mimeographed. Washington, D.C.: 1936.

_____. "National Land Policy . . ." Address. Mimeographed. USDA, 1936.

"Housing under the Resettlement Administration." *Monthly Labor Review* 44 (June, 1937):1390–1400.

Hurst, William, and Lillian Church. *Power Machinery in Agriculture*. Washington, D.C.: USDA, 1933. Misc. Pub. 157.

"Increase in Farm Population During 1932."*Monthly Labor Review* 35 (December, 1932): 1304–5.

Interim Report of the Resettlement Administration. Washington, D.C.: Resettlement Administration, 1936.

Irrigation Agriculture in the West. Washington, D.C.: USDA, 1948. Misc. Pub. 670.

Joel, A. H. *Soil Conservation Reconnaissance Survey of the Southern Great Plains Wind Erosion Area*. Washington. D.C.: USDA, 1937. Techn. Bulletin 556.

Kinsman, D.C. *An Appraisal of Power Used on Farms in the United States*. Washington, D.C.: USDA, 1925. Dept. Bulletin 1348.

Landis, Paul, et al. *Rural Emergency Relief in Washington*. Pullman, Washington: Agricultural Experiment Station, 1936. Bulletin 334.

Lord, Russell, and Paul H. Johnstone. "A Place on Earth, A Critical Appraisal of Subsistence Homesteads." Washington D.C., 1942.

Lundy, Gabriel. *Farm Mortgage Experience in South Dakota, 1910–1940*. Brookings, S.D.: Agricultural Experiment Station, 1943. Bulletin 370.

"Migration to and from Farms in 1933." *Monthly Labor Review* 38 (May, 1934): 1078–79.

Negro Farmer in the United States. Washington, D.C.: Census of Agriculture. Census of the United States, 1930.

Nelson, Aaron, and Gerald Korzan, *Profits and Losses in Ranching, Western South Dakota, 1931–1940*. Brookings, S.D.: Agricultural Experiment Station, 1941. Bulletin 352.

Northern Great Plains. Washington, D.C.: National Resources Planning Board, 1940.

Operation of the Trade Agreement Program, 1934-1948. Washington, D.C.: Tariff Commission, 1934-1949.

Possibilities of Shelterbelt Planting in the Plains Region. Washington, D.C.: USDA, Forest, 1935.

Preliminary Report of the Research Subcommittee of the Northern Great Plains Agricultural Advisory Council. Mimeographed. Northern Great Plains Committee, 1940.

"Rehabilitation in the Northern Great Plains." Mimeographed. Washington, D.C.: Northern Great Plains Committee, 1938.

Report of Federal Surplus Commodities Corporation for the Fiscal Year 1939. Washington, D.C.: Federal Surplus Commodities Corporation, 1939.

Resettlement Administration. Washington, D.C.: Resettlement Administration, 1936.

Reynoldson, L. A., et al. *The Combined Harvester-Thresher in the Great Plains.* Washington, D.C.: USDA, 1928. Techn. Bulletin 70.

Richardson, Lemont K. *Wisconsin R. E. A.: The Struggle to Extend Electricity to Rural Wisconsin, 1935-1955.* Madison: University of Wisconsin Experiment Station, 1961.

Rowe, William H. "Events Leading Up to the Passage of the Federal Crop Insurance Act in 1938. Multigraph. Washington, D.C.: USDA, 1965. Federal Crop Insurance Corp.

Rule, Glenn K. *Crops Against the Wind in the Southern Great Plains.* Washington, D.C.: USDA, 1939. Farmers' Bulletin 1833.

_____. *Toward Soil Security in the Northern Great Plains.* Washington, D.C.: USDA, 1941. Farmers' Bulletin 1864.

Schultz, Theodore, and O. H. Brownlee. *Effects of Crop Acreage Control Features of AAA on Feed Production in 11 Midwest States.* Ames, Iowa: Agricultural Experiment Station, 1942. Bulletin 298.

Taylor, C. C.; Helen W. Wheeler; and E. L. Kirkpatrick. "Disdavantaged Classes in American Agriculture. Multigraphed. Washington, D.C.: USDA, 1938. Social Research Report 8.

Taylor, Paul S. "Power Farming and Labor Displacement in the Cotton Belt." *Monthly Labor Review* 46 (March, 1938): 595-607.

Tolley, H. R. "The Farmer, the College, the Department of Agriculture." Mimeographed. Washington, D.C.: USDA, AAA, 1936.

_____. "A Land Use Program for the Cotton Belt. Mimeographed. Washington, D.C.: USDA, AAA, 1935.

_____. "The Place of the Cooperative in the Adjustment Program." Mimeographed. Washington, D.C.: USDA, AAA, 1934.

_____. "The Soil Conservation Program with Special Reference to Farm Tenancy." Mimeographed. Washington, D.C.: USDA, AAA, 1937.

_____. "A Summary of Suggestions Made for Solving Problems of Disadvantaged Groups in Agriculture Presented before Senate Committee on Education and Labor." Typescript. Washington, D.C.: USDA, BAE, 1940.

Turner, Howard H. *A Graphic Summary of Farm Tenure.* Washington, D.C.: USDA, 1936. Misc. Pub. 261.

What the Resettlement Administration Has Done. Washington, D.C.: Resettlement Administration, 1936.

ARTICLES

"AAA Dilemma: Tobogganing Prices Spread Discontent in Wheat Bowl." *Newsweek* 12 (July 25, 1938): 33-35.

"AAA Hard-Pressed to Help Farmers." *Newsweek,* 12 (August 29, 1938): 34.

"AAA New Deal Instrument for Economic Planning." *Congressional Digest* 15 (March 1936): 73.

"Agriculture Price-Supporting Measures in Foreign Agriculture." *Congressional Digest* 12 (February 1933): 34–35.

Anderson, W. A. "Social Mobility among Farm Owner Operators." *Social Forces* 8 (March, 1930): 378–80.

_____. "Some Characteristics of Rural Families on Relief in New York State." *Rural Sociology* 1 (September 1936): 322–31.

Baker, O. E. "The Agricultural Significance of the Declining Birthrate." *American Sociological Society* 24 (May 1930): 138–46.

Banfield, Edward O. "Ten Years of the Farm Tenant Purchase Program." *Journal of Farm Economics* 31 (August 1949): 469–86.

Bean, Louis H. "Agriculture in the Post-War Decade." *Journal of American Statistical Association.* Supplement 25 (March 1930): 155–57.

_____, and P. H. Bollinger, "The Base Period for Parity Prices." *Journal of Farm Economics* 21 (February 1939): 253–57.

Bedelow, James B. "Depression and New Deal: Letters From the Plains." *Kansas Historical Quarterly* 43 (Summer 1977): 140–53.

Benedict, Murray R. "Economic Aspects of Remedial Measures Designed to Meet the Problems of Displaced Farm Tenants." *Rural Sociology* 5 (June 1940): 163–82.

Bennett, H. H. "Emergency and Permanent Control of Wind Erosion in the Great Plains." *Scientific Monthly* 47 (November 1938): 381–99.

"Big Payments Under the AAA." *New Republic* 86 (April 15, 1936): 265.

Black, Albert G. "Goal of Crop Insurance." *Nation's Business* 25 (June 1937): 120.

Black, John D. "National Agricultural Policy." *American Economic Review.* Supplement 16 (March 1926): 134–55.

Blackmer, F. M., "West, Water, and the Grazing Laws." *Survey Graphic* 26 (July 1937): 387.

Blackwell, Gordon W. "Rural Relief in the South: F.E.R.A.'s Problem in Eastern North Carolina." *Law and Contemporary Problems* 1 (June 1934): 390–97.

Blaisdell, T. C., Jr. "The Consumer's Place in the Organization of the New Deal." *Journal of the American Statistical Association* 30 (March 1935): 185–90.

Bodde, Derk. "Henry A. Wallace and the Ever-Normal Granary." *Far Eastern Quarterly* 5 (August 1946): 411–26.

Bowman, Isaiah. "The Land of Your Possession." *Science* 82 (September 27, 1935): 285–93.

Brandt, Karl. "The German Back-to-the-Land Movement." *Land Economics* 11 (May 1935): 123–32.

_____. "Germany's Bid for Agricultural Self-Sufficiency." *Journal of Farm Economics* 21 (May 1939): 435–61.

_____. "Recent Agrarian Policies in Germany, Great Britain and the United States." *Social Research* 3 (May 1936): 167–201.

Brown, Josephine C. "Rural Families on Relief." *Annals of the American Academy of Political and Social Science* 176 (November 1934): 90–94.

Bruton, Paul W. "Cotton Acreage Reduction and the Tenant Farmer." *Law and Contemporary Problems* 1 (June 1934): 275–91.

_____. "Relationships of Landlords to Farm Tenants. *Journal of Land and Public Utility Economics* 1 (July 1925): 336–42.

Bunn, Charles. "The AAA Decision and the Soil Conservation Act." *Journal of Land and Public Utility Economics* 12 (May 1936): 199–200.

Byers, M. R. "Distressful Dairymen." *North American* 237 (March 1934): 215–23.

Carey, James C. "The Farmers' Independence Council of America, 1935-1938." *Agricultural History* 35 (April 1961): 70–77.

Carpenter, C. T. "King Cotton's Slaves." *Scribner's Magazine* 98 (October 1935): 193–99.

Casement, D. D. "Hog Latin." *Saturday Evening Post* 207 (March 16, 1935): 27.

Clawson, Marion. "Resettlement Experience on Nine Selected Resettlement Projects." *Agricultural History* 52 (January 1978): 1–92.

Clayton, C. F. "The Land Utilization Program Begins Its Second Year." *Land Policy Review* 1 (September–October 1938): 11–13.

Connor, L. G. "European Competition in Agricultural Production." *Journal of Farm Economics* 14 (July 1932): 500–502.

Cotton, Albert H. "Regulation of Farm Landlord-Tenant Relationships." *Law and Contemporary Problems* 4 (October 1937): 508–38.

"Cotton Acreage Reduction Campaign in North Carolina. . . ." *Commercial and Financial Chronicle* 123 (November 20, 1926): 2602–3.

Cronin, F. D. "Displaced Families in the Land Utilization Program." *Southwestern Social Science Quarterly* 20 (June 1939): 43–57.

"Crop Insurance Marks New AAA." *Newsweek* 11 (February 21, 1938): 32.

Crosby, A. L. "Farmers Form a Union." *New Republic* 92 (September 8, 1937): 126–27.

Davis, Joseph S. "America's Agricultural Position and Policy." *Harvard Business Review* 6 (January 1928): 143–51.

_____. "Wheat, Wheat Policies, and the Depression." *Review of Economic Statistics* 16 (April 1934): 80–88.

"Disadvantaged Agricultural Classes." *Rural Sociology* 3 (1938): 325–27.

Dodds, Gordon B. "Conservation and Reclamation in the Trans Mississippi West: A Critical Bibliography." *Arizona and the West* 13 (Summer 1971): 143–71.

Dorn, Harold F. "Rural Health and Public Health Programs." Rural Sociology 8 (June 1942): 22–32.

Duggan, I. W. "Cotton, Land, and People: A Statement of the Problem." *Journal of Farm Economics* 22 (February 1940): 188–97.

Enfield, R. R. "The World's Wheat Situation." *Economic Journal* 41 (December 1931): 550–65.

Ezekiel, Mordecai. "Agriculture: Illustrating Limitations of Free Enterprise as a Remedy for Present Unemployment." *Journal of American Statistical Association* 27 (March 1933): 182–89.

_____. "The Broadening Field of Agricultural Economics." *Journal of Farm Economics* 19 (February 1937): 96–101.

_____. "European Competition in Agricultural Production with Special Reference to Russia." *Journal of Farm Economics* 14 (April 1932): 267–83.

_____. "Farm Aid, Fourth Stage." *Nation* 146 (February 26, 1938): 236–38.

_____. "Schisms in Agricultural Policy: The Shift in Agricultural Policy Toward Human Welfare." *Journal of Farm Economics* 24 (1942): 463–75.

_____, and J. S. Davis. "AAA as a Force in Recovery." *Journal of Farm Economics* 17 (February 1935): 1–14.

Fite, Gilbert. "Voluntary Attempts to Reduce Cotton Acreage in the South, 1914–1933." *Journal of Southern History* 14 (November 1948): 481–99.

Frey, Fred C., and T. Lynn Smith. "The Influence of the AAA Cotton Program Upon the Tenant, Cropper, and Laborer." *Rural Sociology* (December 1936): 483–505.

Garver, F. B., and Harry Trelogan. "The Agricultural Adjustment Act and the Reports of the Brookings Institution." *Quarterly Journal of Economics* 50 (August 1936): 594–621.

Gee, Wilson. "The Effects of Urbanization in the South." *Southern Economic Journal,* 2 (May 1935): 3–15.

Given, J. B. "Subsistence Homesteads." *Social Forces* 12 (May 1934): 522–25.

Glick, Philip M. "The Federal Subsistence Homesteads Program." *Yale Law Journal* 44 (June 1935): 1324–79.

_____. "The Soil and the Law." *Journal of Farm Economics* 20 (May 1938): 430–47.

_____. "The Soil and the Law." *Journal of Farm Economics* 20 (August 1938): 616–40.

Goodrich, Carter. "National Planning of Internal Improvements." *Political Science Quarterly* 63 (March 1948): 17–44.

Gray, Lewis C. "Disadvantaged Rural Classes." *Journal of Farm Economics* 20 (February 1938): 71–85.

_____. "Federal Purchase and Administration of Submarginal Lands in the Great Plains." *Journal of Farm Economics* 21 (February 1939): 123–31.

Hargreaves, Mary W. M. "Land-Use Planning in Response to Drought: The Experience of the Thirties." *Agricultural History* 50 (October 1976): 561–82.

Hazan, N. W. "The Agricultural Program of Fascist Italy." *Journal of Farm Economics* 15 (July 1933): 489–502.

Henderson, B. "State Policies in Agricultural Settlement." *Journal of Land and Public Utility Economics* 2 (July 1926): 284–96.

"Hired Men: Back to Farm Movement Brings Rural Wages to Lowest Point." *Business Week,* February 1, 1933, 12.

Hobbs, S. H. "Rural Housing Problems in the South." *Rural Sociology* 3 (September 1938): 279–95.

Hoffman, G. Wright. "The Outlook for Crop Insurance," *Annals of the American Academy of Political and Social Science,* 142 (March 1929): 302–11.

Hoffsommer, Harold. "The Disadvantaged Farm Family in Alabama." *Rural Sociology* 2 (September 1937): 382–92.

Holland, C. "Tenant Farmers Turn," *Survey Graphic* 24 (May 1935), 233–37.

Hoover, Calvin B. "Agrarian Reorganization in the South," *Journal of Farm Economics* 20 (May 1938): 474–81.

_____. "The Status of the Consumer During the Life of the Agricultural Adjustment Act." *Southern Economics Journal* 2 (April 1936): 12–19.

Hudgens, R. A. "The Plantation South Tries a New Way." *Land Policy Review* 3 (November 1940): 26–29.

Hunter, Robert F. "The AAA Between Neighbors: Virginia, North Carolina, and the New Deal Farm Programs." *Journal of Southern History* 44 (November 1978): 537–70.

Janeway, Eliot. "Problem of the Submarginal Farmer." *Nation* 148 (March 18, 1939): 314–17.

Johnson, Sherman E. "Irrigation Policies and Programs in the Northern Great Plains Region." *Journal of Farm Economics* 18 (August, 1936): 543–55.

Jorgenson, Lloyd P. "Agricultural Expansion into the Semiarid Lands of the West North Central States during the First World War." *Agricultural History* 23 (January 1949): 30–40.

"Judicial Review of Administrative Orders Under the N.R.A. and the A.A.A." *Yale Law Journal* 43 (1934): 599–610.

King, Joe J. "The Farm Security Administration and Its Attack on Rural Poverty." *Rural Sociology* 7 (June 1942): 155–61.

Koch, Lucian. "War in Arkansas." *New Republic* 82 (March 27, 1935): 182–84.

Kollmorgen, Walter. "Rainmakers on the Plains." *Scientific Monthly* 40 (February 1935): 146–52.

Lambert, C. Roger. "Texas Cattlemen and the AAA, 1933–1935," *Arizona and the West* 14 (Summer 1972): 137–54.

"The Land Grant College Report," *Journal of Farm Economics* 10 (January 1928): 84–105.

Larson, Olaf F. "Lessons from Rural Rehabilitation Experience." *Land Policy Review* 9 (February 1946): 13–18.

Learned, E. P. "The Cotton Textile Situation." *Harvard Business Review* 14 (Autumn 1935): 29–44.

Lindley, L. K. "War on the Brains Trust." *Scribner's Magazine* 94 (November 1933): 257–66.

Lord, Russell. "M. L. Wilson: Pioneer," *Survey Graphic* 30 (October 1941): 507–12.

Lowitt, Richard, ed. "Shelterbelts in Nebraska." *Nebraska History* 57 (Fall 1976): 405–22.

Lubell, Samuel, and Walter D. Everett. "As the Farmer Sees It," *Current History* 30 (December 1933): 290–94.

McCormick, Thomas C. "Rural Families on Relief," *Rural Sociology* 1 (June 1936): 430–40.

_____. "Cotton Acreage Laws and the Agrarian Movement." *Southwestern Social Science Quarterly* 12 (March 1932): 296–304.

McMillan, Robert T. "Some Observations on Oklahoma Population Movements." *Rural Sociology* 1 (September 1936): 332–43.

Maddox, James G. "The Bankhead–Jones Farm Tenant Act." *Law and Contemporary Problems* 4 (October 1937): 434–55.

_____. "Suggestions for a National Program of Rural Rehabilitation and Relief." *Journal of Farm Economics* 21 (November 1939): 881–96.

Mencken, H. L. "Dole for the Bogus Farmer." *American Mercury,* 39 (December 1936): 400–8.

Mitchell, H. L. "Organizing Southern Share-croppers." *New Republic* 80 (October 3, 1934): 217.

_____, and J. R. Butler. "Cropper Learns His Fate." *Nation* 141 (September 18, 1935), 328–29.

_____, and Howard Kester. "Share-croppers, Misery and Hope." *Nation* 142 (February 12, 1936): 184.

Munns, E. N., and Joseph H. Stoeckler. "How Are the Great Plains Shelterbelts?" *Journal of Forestry* 44 (April 1946): 237–57.

Myers, Howard B. "Relief in The Rural South," *Southern Economic Journal* 3 (January 1937): 281–91.

Nall, Garry L. "Dust Bowl Days: Panhandle Farming in the 1930's," *Panhandle-Plains Historical Review* 48(1975): 42–63.

Nelson, Lawrence J. "Oscar Johnston and The Cotton Subsidy Payments Controversy, 1936-1937." *Journal of Southern History* 40 (August 1974): 399–416.

Nelson, Lowry. "Action Programs for the Conservation of Rural Life and Culture." *Rural Sociology* 4 (December 1939): 414–32.

_____. "National Policies and Rural Social Organization." *Rural Sociology* 1 (March 1936): 73–89.

Nourse, E. G. "Can Agriculture Affect Prices by Controlling Production?" *Proceedings of the Academy of Political Science* 14 (1932): 523–33.

_____. "The Foreign Situation as Conditioning American Agricultural Policy." In *Conference on Economic Policy for American Agriculture,* edited by Edward A. Duddy, pp. 20–27. Chicago: Univ. of Chicago Press, 1931.

_____. "The Trend of Agricultural Exports." *Journal of Political Economy* 36 (1928): 330–52.

Noyes, Charles E. "Government Farm Loans." *Editorial Research Reports* 1 (1940): 391–407.

_____. "Shifting Markets for Farm Products," *Editorial Research Reports* 1 (1940): 1–20.

Oppenheimer, Monroe, "The Development of the Rural Rehabilitation Loan Program," *Law and Contemporary Problems,* 4 (October 1937): 473–88.

"Parting: Wallace and O'Neal." *Time* 30 (December 27, 1937): 9–10.

"Part-time and Small Enterprise Farming." *Rural Sociology* 3 (September 1938): 329.

Pasvolsky, Leo. "International Relations and Financial Conditions in Foreign Countries Affecting the Demand for American Agricultural Products." *Journal of Farm Economics* 14 (April 1932): 257–65.

Patch, Buel W. "Tariff Reciprocity and Trade Agreements," *Editorial Research Reports,* 1 (1940): 59–76.

Peck, H. W. "Economic Status of Agriculture." *Journal of Political Economy* 34 (October 1926): 624–41.

_____. The Influence of Agricultural Machinery and the Automobile on Farming Operations." *Quarterly Journal of Economics* 41 (August 1927): 534–44.

Penny, J. Russell, and Marion Clawson. "Administration of Grazing Districts," *Land Economics,* 29 (February 1953): 23–34.

Polenberg, Richard. "Conservation and Reorganization: The Forest Service Lobby, 1937–38." *Agricultural History* 39 (October 1965): 230–39.

_____. "The Great Conservation Contest." *Forest History* 10 (January 1967): 13–23.

Putney, Bryant. "Government Aid to Farm Tenants." *Editorial Research Reports* 2 (1936): 417–34.

_____. "Insurance of Growing Crops," *Editorial Research Reports,* 2 (1936): 257–70.

"Recent Developments in Tenancy Programs in North Carolina," *Journal of Land and Public Utility Economics* 14 (May 1938): 208–10.

Reid, T. R. "Public Assistance to Low Income Farmers in the South." *Journal of Farm Economics* 21 (February 1939): 188–94.

Renne, Roland R. "Rural Educational Institutions and Social Lag." *Rural Sociology* 1 (September 1936): 306–21.

"Resettling America." *Social Service Review* 9 (September 1935): 537–40.

Richardson, Rupert N. "The 'Summary Forward' of the Future of the Great Plains." *Mississippi Valley Historical Review* 30 (June, 1943): 49–68.

Rozman, David. "The 'Agricultural Ladder' in Foreign Countries." *Journal of Land and Public Utility Economics* 2 (April, 1926): 249–53.

"Rural Dependency." *Rural Sociology* 3 (September 1938): 331–32.

Russell, Ralph. "Membership of the American Farm Bureau Federation." *Rural Sociology* 2 (March 1937): 29–35.

Salamon, Lester M. "The Time Dimension in Policy Evaluation: The Case of the New Deal Land-Reform Experiments." *Public Policy* 27 (Spring 1979): 129–83.

Saloutos, Theodore. "The American Farm Bureau Federation and Farm Policy: 1933–1945." *Southwestern Social Science Quarterly* 28 (1948): 313–33.

_____. "Edward A. O'Neal: The Farm Bureau and the New Deal." *Current History* 27 (1955): 356–61.

_____. "Farmer Movements." *Encyclopedia of American Economic History.* Vol. 2. New York, 1980.

_____. "Land Policy and Its Relation to Agricultural Production, 1862 to 1933." *Journal of Economic History* 22 (1962): 445–60.

_____. "The New Deal and Farm Policy in the Great Plains." *Agricultural History* 43 (1969): 345–55.

_____. "William A. Hirth: Middle Western Agrarian." *Mississippi Valley Historical Review* 38 (1951): 215–32.

Sanderson, Dwight. "The Effect of the Depression on Tenancy in the Central States." *Rural Sociology* 2 (March 1937): 3–9.

Schell, Herbert S. "Adjustment Problems in South Dakota." *Agricultural History* 14 (April 1940): 65–74.

Schlebecker, John T. "Grasshoppers in American Agricultural History." *Agricultural History* 28 (July 1953): 85–93.

Schlesinger, Arthur, Jr. "Gardner Jackson 1897–1965." *New Republic* 152 (May 1, 1965): 17.

Schmidt, Carl T. "The Italian 'Battle of Wheat.' " *Journal of Farm Economics* 18 (November 1936): 645–56.

Schuyler, Michael W. "Federal Drought Relief Activities in Kansas, 1934." *Kansas Historical Quarterly* 42 (Winter 1976), 403–24.

Sharp, Paul F. "The Farm Tree Movement: Its Origin and Development." *Agricultural History* 23 (January 1949): 41–45.

Shepherd, Geoffrey S. "Stabilization Operations of the Commodity Credit Corporation." *Journal of Farm Economics* 24 (August 1942): 589–610.

Shideler, James H. "Herbert Hoover and the Federal Farm Board Project." *Mississippi Valley Historical Review* 42 (March 1956): 710–29.

Smick, A. A. "Recent Trends in Rural Social Work." *Sociology and Social Research* 22 (May–June 1939): 446–73.

_____. "Training for Rural Social Work." *Sociology and Social Research* 22 (July–August 1938): 538–44.

Smith, R. C. "Public Assistance to Low-Income Farmers in the North." *Journal of Farm Economics* 21 (February 1939): 178–87.

Snyder, Robert E. "The Cotton Holiday Movement in Mississippi, 1931." *Journal of Mississippi History* 40 (February 1978): 1–32.

"Some Farmers Roar: National Grange Expresses Viewpoint of Those Who Dislike Wallace's Program." *Business Week,* December 3, 1938.

Sorden, L. D. "The Northern Wisconsin Settler Relocation Project, 1934–1940." *Wisconsin Academy of Sciences, Arts, and Letters: Transactions* 53, Part A. Madison, 1964.

Sorenson, C. A. "Rural Electrification." *Nebraska History* 25 (October–December 1944): 257–71.

Soule, George. "Liberty League Liberty." *New Republic* 88 (September 2, 1936), 96.

Spillman, William J. "The Agricultural Ladder." *American Economic Review,* Supplement 8 (March 1919), 170–79.

Starch, Elmer. "A Better Life on the Plains." *Yearbook of Agriculture, 1979,* 197–204.

_____. "The Future of the Great Plains." *Journal of Farm Economics* 31 (November 1949): 917–27.

Stephens, Oren. "Revolt in the Delta: What Happened to the Sharecroppers' Union." *Harper's Magazine* 183 (November 1941): 656–64.

Stoeckler, J. H. "Narrow Shelterbelts for the Southern Great Plains." *Soil Conservation* 11 (July 1945): 16–20.

Stout, Joe A., Jr. "Cattlemen, Conservationists, and the Taylor Grazing Act." *New Mexico Historical Review* 45 (October 1970): 311–32.

Studensky, G. A. "The Agricultural Depression and the Technical Revolution in Farming." *Journal of Farm Economics* 12 (October 1930): 552–72.

Sullam, Victor B. "Some Limitations of 'Live-at-Home' Programs." *Rural Sociology* 8 (March 1943): 24–37.

Swain, Donald C. "The Bureau of Reclamation and the New Deal, 1933–1940." *Pacific Northwest Quarterly* 59 (July 1970): 137–46.

Swire, Florence M. "Housing in Rural America," *Rural Sociology* 4 (December 1939): 449–57.

Taueber, Conrad. "The Movement to Southern Farms," *Rural Sociology* 3 (March 1938): 69–78.

Taylor, Henry C. "L. C. Gray, Agricultural Historian and Land Economist." *Agricultural History* 26 (October 1952), 165.

_____, and Jacob Perlman. "The Share of Agriculture in the National Income." *Journal of Land and Public Utility Economics* 3 (May 1927): 145–62.

_____, and _____. "Revised Figures for 1925 and 1926," *Journal of Land and Public Utility Economics* 3 (November 1927): 432–33.

Taylor, Morton. "Middle West Answers the Court." *New Republic* 86 (February 26, 1936): 71–72.

Taylor, Paul S. "From the Ground Up: Demonstration Projects of the Resettlement Administration on the West Coast." *Survey Graphic* 25 (September 1936): 524–29.

Telser, Lester G. "The Support Program and the Stability of Cotton Prices (1933–1953)." *Journal of Farm Economics* 39 (May 1957): 398–408.

"Tenants on Strike." *Nation* 134 (October 19, 1932): 344.

Thomas, Norman. "Victims of Change." *Current History* 42 (April 1935): 36–41.

Thompson, H. M. "Plan of Forest Planting for the Great Plains of North America." *American Journal of Forestry* 1 (February 1883): 226–32.

Tontz, Robert L. "Legal Parity: Implementation of the Policy of Equality for Agriculture, 1929–1954." *Agricultural History* 29 (October 1955): 174–81.

_____. "Origin of the Base Period Concept of Parity—A Significant Value Judgement in Agricultural Policy." *Agricultural History* 32 (January 1958): 3–13.

Tugwell, Rexford G. "Cooperation and Resettlement." *Current History* 45 (1937): 71–76.

_____. "The Resettlement Idea." *Agricultural History* 33 (October 1959): 159–64.

_____. "The Sources of New Deal Reformism." *Ethics* 64 (1954): 249–76.

_____, and E. C. Banfield. "Grass Roots Democracy—Myth or Reality?" *Public Administration Review* 19 (1950): 47–55.

"United States Supreme Court Declares AAA Illegal." *Congressional Digest* 15 (March 1936): 74.

Vance, Rupert B. "Human Factors in the South's Agricultural Readjustment." *Law and Contemporary Problems* 1 (June 1934), 259–74.

Ventkataramani, M. S. "Norman Thomas, Arkansas Sharecroppers, and the Roosevelt Agricultural Policies, 1933–1937." *Mississippi Valley Historical Review* 47 (September 1960), 225–46.

Visher, S. S. "Climatic Effects of the Proposed Wooded Shelterbelt in the Great Plains." *Association of American Geographers Annual* 25(1935): 63–73.

Wallace, Henry A. "American Agriculture and World Markets." *Foreign Affairs* 12 (January 1934), 216–30.

_____. "Controlling Agricultural Output." *Journal of Farm Economics* 5 (January 1923), 16–27.

_____. "The South Faces Changing Demands." *Southern Economic Journal* 5 (1939): 423–41.

_____. "Wallace Answers His Critics." *Hoard's Dairyman* 78 (1933): 340.

_____. "We Are More Than Economic Men." *Scribner's Magazine* 96 (December 1934): 321–26.

_____. "World Cotton Drama." *Foreign Affairs* 13 (1935): 543–56.

Weaver, Robert C. "Economic Factors in Negro Migration—Past and Future." *Social Forces* 17 (October 1939): 90–101.

Wehrwein, Carl F. "The Agricultural Ladder in a High Tenancy Region." *Journal of Land and Public Utility Economics* 7 (February 1931): 67–77.

_____. "The Pre-Ownership Steps on the 'Agricultural Ladder' in a Low Tenancy Region." *Journal of Land and Public Utility Economics* 4 (November 1928): 417–25.

Wehrwein, George S. "An Appraisal of Resettlement," *Journal of Farm Economics,* 19 (February 1937): 191–202.

_____. "Changes in Farm and Farm Tenure, 1930-1935." *Journal of Land and Public Utility Economics* 12 (May 1936): 200-205.

Wells, Oris V. "Agricultural Planning and the Agricultural Economist." *Journal of Farm Economics* 20 (November 1938): 753-64.

_____. "How Many Farmers Do We Require?" *Land Policy Review* 3 (September 1940): 3-7.

Wengert, Norman. "Antecedents of TVA: The Legislative History of Muscle Shoals." *Agricultural History* 26 (October 1952): 141-47.

Westbrook, Lawrence. "The Program of Rural Rehabilitation of the F.E.R.A." *Journal of Farm Economics* 17 (February 1935): 89-100.

Wilcox, Walter W. "Social Scientists and Agricultural Policy (Since 1908)." *Journal of Farm Economics* 34 (May 1952), 173-83.

Wiley, Clarence A. "The Rust Mechanical Cotton Picker and Probable Land-Use Adjustments." *Journal of Land and Public Utility Economics* 15 (February 1939): 155-66.

_____. "Settlement and Unsettlement in the Resettlement Administration," *Law and Contemporary Problems* 4 (October 1937): 456-72.

Williams, Aubrey. "Rural Youth and the Government." *Rural Sociology* 3 (March 1938): 3-10.

Wilson, A. D. "Settler Relocation: A Description of the Minnesota Plan." *Journal of Land and Public Utility Economics* 14 (November 1938): 402-16.

Wilson, Milburn L. "Agricultural Conservation—An Aspect of Land Utilization." *Journal of Farm Economcs* 19 (1937): 3-12.

_____. "The Democratic Processes and the Formulation of Agricultural Policy." *Social Forces* 19 (1940): 1-12.

_____. "The Fairway Farms Project." *Journal of Land and Public Utility Economics* 2 (1926): 156-71.

_____. "A Land Use Program for the Federal Government." *Journal of Farm Economics* 15 (1933): 217-35.

_____. "Mechanization, Management and the Competitive Position of Agriculture." Agricultural Engineering 13 (1932): 3-5.

_____. "New Horizons in Agricultural Economics," *Journal of Farm Economics* 20 (1938): 1-7.

_____. "A New Land-Use Program: The Place of Subsistence Homesteads." *Journal of Land and Public Utility Economics* 10 (1934): 1-12.

Woofter, T. J., Jr. "Rural Relief and the Back-to-the-Farm Movement." *Social Forces* 14 (March 1936): 382-88.

Zapoleon, L. B. "Farm Relief, Agricultural Prices, and the Tariff." *Journal of Political Economy* 40 (February 1932), 73-100.

Zelomek, A. W., and Irving Mark. "Historical Perspectives for Post-War Agricultural Forecasts: 1870-1940." *Rural Sociology* 10 (March 1945): 48-70.

Zon, Raphael. "Shelterbelts—Futile Dream or Workable Plan." *Science,* n.s., 81 (April 26, 1935): 391-94.

BOOKS

Albertson, Dean. *Roosevelt's Farmer: Claude Wickard in the New Deal.* New York: Columbia Univ. Press. 1961.

Baker, Gladys. *The County Agent.* Chicago: Univ. of Chicago Press, 1940.

Baker, O. E., Ralph Borsodi, and M. L. Wilson. *Agriculture in Modern Life.* New York, 1939.

Baldwin, Sidney. *Poverty and Politics: The Rise and Decline of the Farm Security Administration.* Chapel Hill: Univ. of North Carolina Press, 1968.

Beckett, Grace L. *The Reciprocal Trade Agreement Program.* New York, 1941.

Black, John D. *Parity, Parity, Parity.* Cambridge: Harvard Univ. Press, 1942.

_____. *The Dairy Industry and the AAA*. Washington, D.C.: The Brookings Institution, 1935.

Blackorby, Edward C. *Prairie Rebel: The Public Life of William Lemke*. Lincoln: Univ. of Nebraska Press, 1963.

Block, William J. *The Separation of the Farm Bureau and the Extension Service: Political Issue in a Federal System*. Urbana: Univ. of Illinois Press, 1960.

Bonnifield, Paul. *The Dust Bowl: Men, Dirt and Depression*. Albuquerque: Univ. of New Mexico Press, 1979.

Brink, Wellington. *Big Hugh: The Father of Soil Conservation*. New York, 1951.

Brown, D. Clayton. *Electricity for Rural America; The Fight for the REA*. Westport: Greenwood, 1980.

Brunner, Edmund de S., and Irving Lorge. *Rural Trends in Depression Years*. New York, 1937.

Burnell, R., and Marion Clawson. *Soil Conservation in Perspective*. Baltimore: John Hopkins Univ. Press, 1965.

Campbell, Christina M. *The Farm Bureau and the New Deal: A Study of the Making of National Farm Policy, 1933–1940*. Urbana: Univ. of Illinois Press, 1962.

Cantor, Louis. *A Prologue to the Protest Movement*. Durham: Duke University Press, 1969.

Case, H. C. M., and D. B. Williams. *Fifty Years of Farm Management*. Urbana: Univ. of Illinois Press, 1957.

Cavin, James P., ed. *Economics for Agriculture: Selected Writings of John D. Black*. Cambridge: Harvard Univ. Press, 1959.

Charles, Searle F. *Minister of Relief: Harry Hopkins and the Depression*. Syracuse: Syracuse Univ. Press, 1963.

Clawson, Marion. *Man and Land in the United States*. Lincoln: Univ. of Nebraska Press, 1964.

Clements, Frederic E. *Environment and Life on the Great Plains*. Washington, D.C., 1936.

Cohn, David L. *God Shakes Creation*. New York, 1935.

Conkin, Paul K. *Tomorrow A New World: The New Deal Community Program*. Ithaca: Cornell Univ. Press, 1959.

_____. *The New Deal*. New York: T. Y. Crowell & Co., 1967.

Coyle, D. C. *Conservation: An American Story of Conflict and Accomplishment*. New Brunswick: Rutgers Univ. Press, 1957.

Crabb, Richard A. *The Hybrid-Corn Makers: Prophets of Plenty*. New Brunswick: Rutgers Univ. Press, 1947.

Crissey, Forrest. *Alexander Legge, 1866–1933*. Chicago, 1936.

Davis, Joseph S. *Wheat and the AAA*. Washington, D.C.: The Brookings Institution, 1935.

Droze, Wilmon. *Trees, Prairies, and People: Tree Planting in the Plains States*. Denton: Texas Woman's Univ. Press, 1977.

Duddy, Edward A. *Conference on Economic Policy for American Agriculture*. Chicago: Univ. of Chicago Press, 1932.

Ellis, Clyde T. *A Giant Step*. New York, 1966.

Everitt, James A. *The Third Power*, 4th Ed. Indianapolis, 1907.

Ezekiel, Mordecai, and Louis H. Bean. *The Economic Basis of the Agricultural Adjustment Act*. Washington, D.C., 1933.

Farnham, Rebecca T. *Effects of the Works Program on Rural Relief*. Washington, D.C., 1938.

Fisher, Commodore. *The Farmers' Union*. Lexington, 1920.

Fite, Gilbert C. *George N. Peek and the Fight for Farm Parity*. Norman: Univ. of Oklahoma Press, 1954.

Fitz Gerald, Dennis A. *Corn and Hogs Under the AAA to 1934*. Washington, D.C., 1934.

_____. *Livestock Under the AAA*. Washington: The Brookings Institution, 1935.

Foss, Philip O. *Politics and Grass: The Administration of the Public Domain*. Seattle: Univ. of Washington Press, 1960.

Fusfield, Daniel R. *The Economic Thought of Franklin D. Roosevelt and the Origins of the New Deal*. New York: Columbia University Press, 1956.

Gardner, Lloyd C. *Economic Aspects of New Deal Diplomacy*. Madison: Univ. of Wisconsin Press, 1964.

Gaus, John M., and Leon O. Wolcott. *Public Administration in the United States Department of Agriculture*. Chicago: University of Chicago Press, 1940.

Gold, Bela. *Wartime Economic Planning in Agriculture*. New York: Columbia Univ. Press, 1949.

Grant, H. Rogers, and L. Edward Purcell, eds. *Farm Diary of Elmer G. Powers, 1931–1936*. Ames: Iowa State University Press, 1976.

Green, James R. *Grass-Roots Socialism*. Baton Rouge: Louisiana State University Press, 1978.

Grubbs, Donald H. *Cry From the Cotton*. Chapel Hill: University of North Carolina Press, 1971.

Halcrow, Harold G. *Agricultural Policy of the United States*. New York, 1953.

Hardin, Charles M. *The Politics of Agriculture: Soil Conservation and the Struggle for Power in Rural America*. Glencoe, Ill.: The Free Press, 1952.

Hargreaves, Mary W. *Dry Farming in the Northern Great Plains, 1900–1925*. Cambridge: Harvard Univ. Press, 1957.

Hathaway, Dale E. *Government and Agriculture: Public Policy in A Democratic Society*. New York, 1963.

Higbee, Edward C. *The American Oasis: The Land and Its Use*. New York, 1957.

Holley, Donald. *Uncle Sam's Farmers: The New Deal Communities in Lower Mississippi*. Urbana: University of Illinois Press, 1975.

Hoover, Herbert C. *Memoirs, 1920–1933*. New York, 1952.

Hopkins, Harry L. *Spending To Save: The Complete Story of Relief*. New York: W. W. Norton, 1936.

Hullinger, Edwin W. *Plowing Through: The Story of the Negro in Agriculture*. New York, 1940.

Ickes, Harold L. *The Secret Diary of Harold L. Ickes*. 3 vols. New York: Simon and Schuster, 1953–1954.

Johnson, Charles S. *Growing Up in the Black Belt: Negro Youth in the Rural South*. Washington, D.C., 1941.

_____. *Shadow of the Plantation*. Chicago: Univ. of Chicago Press, 1934.

Kile, Orville M. *The Farm Bureau Through Three Decades*. Baltimore, 1948.

Kirkendall, Richard S. *Social Scientists and Farm Politics in the Age of Roosevelt*. Columbia: Univ. of Missouri Press, 1966.

Knapp, Joseph G. *Advance of American Cooperative Enterprise: 1920–1945*. Danville, Ill., 1973.

Kraenzel, Carl F. *The Great Plains in Transition*. Norman: Univ. of Oklahoma Press, 1955.

Kristein, Barbara F. *A Man's Reach: The Philosophy of Judge Jerome Frank*. New York, 1965.

Kyle, E. J., and A. R. Alexander. *Agriculture in the Southwest*. New York, 1940.

Lauber, Patricia. *Dust Bowl: The Story of Man on the Great Plains*. New York, 1958.

Letiche, John M. *Reciprocal Trade Agreements in the World Economy*. New York, 1948.

Leuchtenberg, William E. *Franklin D. Roosevelt and the New Deal*. New York: Harper & Row, 1963.

Lindley, Ernest K., and Jay Franklin. *The New Dealers*. New York, 1934.

Lord, Russell. *The Wallaces of Iowa*. Boston: Houghton Mifflin, 1947.

_____. *Agrarian Revival: A Study of Agricultural Extension*. New York, 1939.

_____. *Men of Earth*. London, 1931.

McConnell, Grant. *The Decline of Agrarian Democracy*. Berkeley: Univ. of California Press, 1953.

McCune, Wesley. *Who's Behind Our Farm Policy?* New York, 1956.

_____. *The Farm Bloc*. New York, 1943.

Meltzer, Milton. *Dorothea Lange: A Photographer's Life*. New York: Farrar, Strauss & Giroux, 1978.

Mertz, Paul E. *New Deal Policy and Southern Rural Poverty*. Baton Rouge: Louisiana State Univ. Press, 1978.

Mitchell, H. L. *Mean Things Happening in This Land: The Life & Times of H. L. Mitchell, Cofounder of the Southern Tenant Farmers' Union*. Montclair, N.J., 1979.

Moley, Raymond. *After Seven Years*. New York, 1943.

Morgan, Barton. *A History of the Extension Service of Iowa State*. Ames: Iowa State Univ. Press, 1934.

Morgan, Robert J. *Governing Soil Conservation*. Baltimore: Johns Hopkins Univ. Press, 1966.

The Negro in Southern Agriculture. New York: International Publishers, 1933.

Nixon, Edgar B., ed. *Franklin D. Roosevelt and Conservation*, 2 vols. General Services Administration, National Archives and Record Service, Franklin D. Roosevelt Library, 1957.

Norris, George W. *Fighting Liberal*. New York: Macmillan & Co., 1945.

Nourse, Edwin G. *Marketing Agreements Under the AAA*. Washington, D.C., 1935.

_____. *American Agriculture and the European Market*. New York, 1924.

_____, J. S. Davis, and J. D. Black. *Three Years of the Agricultural Adjustment Administration*. Washington, D.C., 1937.

Peek, George, and Samuel Crowther. *Why Quit Our Own*. New York, 1936.

Perkins, Van L. *Crisis in Agriculture: The Agricultural Adjustment Administration and the New Deal, 1933*. Berkeley and Los Angeles: Univ. of California Press, 1969.

Perlo, Victor. *The Negro in Southern Agriculture*. New York, 1953.

Raper, Arthur F. *Sharecroppers All*. Chapel Hill: Univ. of North Carolina Press, 1941.

_____. *Preface to Peasantry*. Chapel Hill: Univ. of North Carolina Press, 1936.

_____. *Tenants of the Almighty*. New York, 1943.

Rau, Allan. *Agricultural Policy and Trade Liberalization in the United States, 1934–1956*. Geneva, 1959.

Richards, Henry I. *Cotton and the AAA*. Washington, D.C.: The Brookings Institution, 1936.

Robinson, E. B. *History of North Dakota*. Lincoln: University of Nebraska Press, 1966.

Rochester, Anna. *Why Farmers Are Poor*. New York: International Publishers, 1940.

Rosenman, Samuel I., ed., *The Public Papers and Addresses of Franklin D. Roosevelt*. 13 vols. New York: Random House, Macmillan, and Harper, 1938–1950.

Saloutos, Theodore. *Farmer Movements in the South, 1865–1933*. Berkeley and Los Angeles: Univ. of California Press, 1960.

_____, and John D. Hicks. *Agricultural Discontent in the Middle West, 1900–1939*. Madison: Univ. of Wisconsin Press, 1951.

Salter, Leonard A., Jr. *A Critical Review of Research in Land Economics*. Minneapolis: Univ. of Minnesota Press, 1948.

Sanders, H. C., ed. *The Cooperative Extension Service*. Englewood, 1966.

Schapsmeier, E. L., and F. H. Shapsmeier. *Henry A. Wallace of Iowa: The Agrarian Years, 1910–1940.* Ames: Iowa State Univ. Press, 1968.

Schickele, Rainer. *Agricultural Policy: Farm Programs and National Welfare.* New York, 1954.

Schell, Herbert S. *History of South Dakota.* Lincoln: Univ. of Nebraska Press, 1961.

Schlebecker, John T. *Cattle Raising on the Plains, 1900–1961.* Lincoln: Univ. of Nebraska Press, 1963.

Schmidt, Carl T. *American Farmers and the World Crisis.* New York, 1940.

Schultz, Theodore W. *Vanishing Farm Markets and Our World Trade.* Boston, 1935.

Scott, Roy G., and J. G. Shoalmire. *The Public Career of Cully A. Cobb.* Jackson, Miss., 1973.

Sears, Paul B. *Deserts on the March.* Norman: Univ. of Oklahoma Press, 1935.

Shideler, James A. *Farm Crisis, 1919–1923.* Berkeley and Los Angeles: Univ. of California Press, 1957.

Shover, John L. *Cornbelt Rebellion.* Urbana: Univ. of Illinois Press, 1965.

Snow, Thad. *From Missouri.* Boston, 1954.

Soth, Lauren. *An Embarrassment of Plenty.* New York, 1965.

———. *Farm Trouble.* Princeton, 1957.

Stein, Walter. *California and the Dust Bowl Migration.* Westport: Greenwood Press, 1973.

Street, James H. *The New Revolution in the Cotton Economy: Mechanization and Its Consequences.* Chapel Hill: Univ. of North Carolina Press, 1957.

Swain, Donald. *Federal Conservation Policy 1921–1933.* Berkeley and Los Angeles: Univ. of California Press, 1963.

Tasca, Henry J. *The Reciprocal Trade Policy of the United States.* Philadelphia, 1938.

Taylor, Alonzo E. *The New Deal and Foreign Trade.* New York, 1935.

Taylor, Henry C., and Ann Dewees. *The Story of Agricultural Economics in the United States, 1840–1932.* Ames, 1952. Reprint ed., Westport: Greenwood Press, 1974.

Thomas, Norman. *Plight of the Sharecropper.* New York: League for Industrial Democracy, 1934.

Tolley, Howard R. *The Farmer Citizen at War.* New York, 1943.

Trombley, Kenneth E. *The Life and Times of a Happy Liberal: A Biography of Morris Llewellyn Cooke.* New York, 1954.

Tugwell, Rexford G. *The Democratic Roosevelt, A Biography of Franklin D. Roosevelt.* Garden City: Doubleday & Co., 1957.

Vance, Rupert B. *Rural Relief and Recovery.* Washington, D.C., 1939.

Wallace, Henry A. *New Frontiers.* New York, 1934.

Wengert, Norman I. *Valley of Tomorrow: The TVA and Agriculture.* Knoxville: Bureau of Public Administration, Univ. of Tennessee, 1952.

West, Edward. *Agricultural Organization in the United States.* Lexington, 1921.

Wilcox, Walter W. *The Farmer in the Second World War.* Ames: Iowa State Univ. Press, 1947.

Wilson, M. L. *Democracy Has Roots.* New York, 1939.

———. *Farm Relief and the Domestic Allotment Plan.* Minneapolis, 1933.

Winters, Donald L. *Henry Cantwell Wallace as Secretary of Agriculture, 1921–1924.* Urbana: Univ. of Illinois Press, 1970.

Worster, Donald. *Dust Bowl: The Southern Plains in the 1930s.* New York: Oxford Univ. Press, 1979.

Wolters, Raymond. *Negroes and the Great Depression.* Westport: Greenwood Press, 1970.

Woodson, Carter G. *The Rural Negro*. Washington, D.C., 1930.
Woofter, T. J., Jr., and Ellen Winston. *Seven Lean Years*. Chapel Hill: Univ. of North Carolina Press, 1939.

THESES AND DISSERTATIONS

Brown, D. Clayton. "Rural Electrification in the South, 1920-1955." Ph.D. diss. UCLA, 1970.
Eley, Lynn W. "The Agricultural Adjustment Administration and the Corn Program in Iowa, 1933-1940," Ph.D. diss. University of Iowa, 1952.
Everest, Allan S. "Morgenthau, the New Deal and Silver." Ph.D. diss. Columbia University, 1950.
Floyd, Fred. "A History of the Dust Bowl." Ph.D. diss. University of Oklahoma, 1951.
Ganger, David W. "The Impact of Mechanization and the New Deal's Acreage Reduction Programs on Cotton Farmers During the 1930s." Ph.D. diss. UCLA, 1973.
Heacock, Walter J. "William Brockman Bankhead, A Biography." Ph.D. diss. University of Wisconsin, 1952.
Helburn, Nicholas. "Land Use Adjustments in Blaine, Phillips, and Valley Counties, Montana, 1934 to 1940." Master's thesis. Montana State College, 1941.
Kifer, Allen F. "The Negro Under the New Deal, 1933-1941." Ph.D. diss. University of Wisconsin, 1961.
Kirkendall, Charles R. "New Deal Experiments in Production Control: The Livestock Industry, 1933-1935." Ph.D. diss., University of Oklahoma, 1962.
Klass, Bernard M. "John D. Black, Farm Economist and Political Adviser, 1920-1942," Ph.D. diss, UCLA, 1970.
Korgan, Julius. "Farmers Picket the Depression." Ph.D. diss. American University, 1961.
Lemmon, Sarah M. "The Public Career of Eugene Talmadge, 1926-1936," Ph.D. diss. University of North Carolina, 1952.
McCann, John. "New Deal Farm Production Controls, 1933-1936," Ph.D. diss., University of Illinois, 1950.
McDean, Harry C. "M. L. Wilson and Agricultural Reform in Twentieth Century America," Ph.D. diss., UCLA, 1969.
Maddox, James G. "The Farm Security Administration," Ph.D. diss., Harvard University, 1950.
Poland, Orville F. "Agricultural Pressure Groups and Problems of Reorganization of the United States Department of Agriculture, 1940-1950," Ph.D. diss., University of California, Berkeley, 1953.

PROCEEDINGS, ANNUAL REPORTS, PAMPHLETS, ETC.

The Agricultural Problem in the United States. New York: National Industrial Conference, 1926.
American Farm Bureau Federation, 1936. Chicago, 1936.
American Farm Bureau Federation, 1938. Chicago, 1938.
Annual Report of the American Farm Bureau Federation, 1937. Chicago, 1937.
The Condition of Agriculture in the United States and Measures for Its Improvement. New York: Business Men's Commission on Agriculture, 1927.
Journal of Proceedings. National Grange, 54th Annual Session, 1920.
Journal of Proceedings. National Grange, 55th Annual Session, 1921.

Journal of Proceedings. National Grange, 56th Annual Session, 1922.
Journal of Proceedings. National Grange, 57th Annual Session, 1923.
Journal of Proceedings. National Grange, 58th Annual Session, 1924.
Journal of Proceedings. National Grange, 60th Annual Session, 1926.
Proceedings of the American Federation of Labor 55th Annual Convention, 1935.
    Washington, D.C., 1935.
Proceedings of the Thirty-fourth Annual Convention of the Association of Land
    Grant Colleges, 1920.
Proceedings of the Thirty-Sixth Annual Convention of the Association of Land
    Grant Colleges, 1922.
Proceedings of the Forty-First Annual Convention of the Association of Land
    Grant Colleges, 1927.
Proceedings of the Second International Conference of Agricultural Economics.
    Menasha, Wisconsin, 1930.
Proceedings of the Forty-Fourth Annual Convention of the Association of Land
    Grant Colleges, 1932.
Proceedings of the Sixteenth American Country Life Association Conference, 1933.
Report of the American Farm Bureau Federation for the Fiscal Year, 1933.
    Chicago, 1933.
Proceedings of the Twenty-First American Country Life Association Conference,
    1938. Chicago, 1938.
Twenty Years with the American Farm Bureau Federation. Chicago, 1939.

NEWSPAPERS

Buffalo News
Capital Times (Madison, Wisconsin)
Chicago Herald-Examiner
Chicago Journal of Commerce
Chicago Tribune
Christian Science Monitor
Commercial Appeal (Memphis)
Cotton Trade Journal
Des Moines Register
Des Moines Tribune
Garden City Daily Telegram (Garden
    City, Kansas)
Kansas City Star
Kansas City Star Weekly
Kansas City Times
Memphis Press-Scimitar
Milwaukee Journal
Milwaukee News
Milwaukee Sentinel
Minneapolis Journal
Minneapolis Star
Minneapolis Tribune
New York Post
New York Times
Pittsburgh Courier
St. Louis Post-Dispatch
St. Paul Dispatch
St. Paul Pioneer Press

United States Daily News (Washington,
   D.C.)
Washington Post
Washington Star
Wisconsin State Journal (Madison,
   Wisconsin)

INTERVIEWS

Bushrod Allin
Louis H. Bean
Samuel Bledsoe
Cecil C. Clapp
Wayne Darrow
Chester C. Davis
Joseph S. Davis
Jonathan Garst
Phil Glick
Mrs. Morrie S. Hill
Mary Huss
Gardner Jackson
Hal Jenkins
Joseph G. Knapp
Alfred M. Landon
James E. McMahon
Don C. Murphy
Lauren Soth
Elmer Starch
Carl C. Taylor
Henry C. Taylor
Ernest Wiecking
M. L. Wilson

INDEX

AAA, xi, xiii; beginnings of, 34–49; staffing of, 50–65; cotton program, 66–70; commodity programs, 66–86; corn-hog program, 70–75; wheat program, 75–78; dairy program, 78–83; tobacco program, 84–86; dissension within, 87–97; and BAE, 86–92; and legal staff, 92–97; and sharecroppers and tenants, 98–118, 261, 263–66; political climate, 1935, 114; dairy section controversy, 116–17; purge of, 117–23; opposition to, 124–36; in 1935, 134–36; land policy section, 152; and blacks, 184; and landowners, 188–89; and Great Plains farmers, 195; and 1936 election, 233; from 1936 to 1939, 236–53; elimination of commodity programs, 252; philosophy and objectives of, 255; and prices, 256–57; and control of production, 257–58; and soil conservation, 258–59; and ever-normal granary, 259–60; and crop insurance, 260; criticism of, 261, 265–66
Abt, John, 59, 60
Adjustment Committee of AAA, 101–3, 110
Adjustment program, 242
Agricultural Adjustment Administration. *See* AAA
Agricultural credit, 269; Act of 1923, 20, 23
Agricultural Marketing Act of 1929, 19, 28, 38, 47
Agriculture: and World War I, 3–4; in 1920s, 5
Alcorn County, 211–13
Alexander, Will, 152, 175–76, 239, 252
Allen, Robert S., 122–23, 223
Allin, Bushrod W., 250
Alsop, Joseph, 245
Amberson, William R., 100, 105, 106, 110
American Agriculturalist, 42, 83
American Civil Liberties Union, 113
American Cotton Cooperative Association, 30–31, 33
American Council of Agriculture, 27
American Farm Bureau Federation, 16, 144, 215, 241, 263, 267; in 1920s, 18–19; and curtailment of production, 33
American Farm Economics Association, 16, 32
American Institute of Public Opinion, 223–24
American Society of Equity, 16
Amlie, Thomas R., 168
Appalachian-Ozark area, 153–54

Appleby, Paul, 62, 99, 106, 224; and landlord-tenant controversy, 110; and Davis, 114–15, 236; and purge, 119; and black farmers, 181, 182, 183; and 1936 election, 226, 231–32
Association of Land Grant Colleges and Universities, 16, 243; in 1920s, 24, 26

Baldwin, C. Benham, 62, 99, 119
Bankhead, John, 156, 164–65
Bankhead bill, 169
Bankhead Cotton Act, 126, 132
Bankhead-Jones Act, 171, 172, 176–77, 178, 240; and land acquisition, 196–97; and tenant-purchase program, 264
Barnes, Julius, 35, 36
Bartlett, Fred, 64
Baruch, Bernard, 53, 54, 63, 155
Bean, Louis H., 62
Belair, Felix, 58
Belgium, 142, 143, 147
Bennett, Hugh Hammond, 201
Bennett, M. Katherine, 174
Benson, Gov. Elmer, 232
Berle, Adolph A., Jr., 40, 64, 92
Bethune, Mary McLeod, 165, 174
Birthrate: in 1920s, 9–10
Black, Albert G., 33; and AAA, 58; and corn-hog program, 70; and 1936 election, 226
Black, John D., 24, 25, 33, 38; and farm policy, 15; and foreign countries' policies, 31; and domestic allotment, 35–36; and ever-normal granary, 204
Blacks: and AAA, 124; in South, 174; farmers, and New Deal, 179–91; as county agents, 181, 186–87; and subsistence homesteads, 182; and farm tenancy, 187; and RA, 190; and FSA, 190–91
Blaisdell, Donald, 61–62, 64, 94
Bledsoe, Samuel B., xii, 239, 247, 253
Bound Brook decision, 161
Boyle, Joseph, 204–5
Bradfute, Oscar E.: on cooperative marketing, 19
Brand, Charles J., 23, 63, 92; and AAA, 55–56; and Frank, 95
Brandeis, Louis, 116
Brandt plan, 82–83
Brazil, 143
Brehm, C. E., 173–74
Brown, Charles S., 184–85

DATE

2 4 '83